PREVIEW EDITION

Creating Mobile Apps with Xamarin.Forms

Cross-platform C# programming
for iOS, Android, and Windows Phone

Charles Petzold

PREVIEW EDITION

This excerpt provides early content from a book currently in development and is still in draft format. See additional notice below.

PUBLISHED BY

Microsoft Press
A Division of Microsoft Corporation
One Microsoft Way
Redmond, Washington 98052-6399

ISBN: 978-1-5093-0089-1

Microsoft Press books are available through booksellers and distributors worldwide. Please tell us what you think of this book at http://aka.ms/tellpress.

This document is provided for informational purposes only and Microsoft makes no warranties, either express or implied, in this document. Information in this document, including URL and other Internet website references, is subject to change without notice. The entire risk of the use or the results from the use of this document remains with the user.

This book expresses the author's views and opinions. The information contained in this book is provided without any express, statutory, or implied warranties. Neither the authors, Microsoft Corporation, nor its resellers, or distributors will be held liable for any damages caused or alleged to be caused either directly or indirectly by this book.

Microsoft and the trademarks listed at http://www.microsoft.com/about/legal/en/us/IntellectualProperty/ Trademarks/EN-US.aspx are trademarks of the Microsoft group of companies. All other marks are property of their respective owners.

The example companies, organizations, products, domain names, email addresses, logos, people, places, and events depicted herein are fictitious. No association with any real company, organization, product, domain name, email address, logo, person, place, or event is intended or should be inferred.

This book expresses the author's views and opinions. The information contained in this book is provided without any express, statutory, or implied warranties. Neither the authors, Microsoft Corporation, nor its resellers, or distributors will be held liable for any damages caused or alleged to be caused either directly or indirectly by this book.

Acquisitions and Project Editor: Devon Musgrave
Editorial production: John Pierce, Flying Squirrel Press
Cover illustration: Serena Zhang

Contents

Introduction

This is the second Preview Edition of a book about writing applications for Xamarin.Forms, the exciting new mobile development platform for iOS, Android, and Windows Phone unveiled by Xamarin in May 2014. Xamarin.Forms lets you write shared user-interface code in C# and XAML (the Extensible Application Markup Language) that maps to native controls on these three platforms.

This book is a Preview Edition because it's not complete. It has only 16 chapters and doesn't cover some important topics. The final edition of the book will probably be published in the summer of 2015.

All information about this book can be found on the book's home page at:

http://developer.xamarin.com/guides/cross-platform/xamarin-forms/creating-mobile-apps-xamarin-forms/

Who should read this book

This book is for C# programmers who want to write applications for the three most popular mobile platforms—iOS, Android, and Windows Phone—with a single code base. Xamarin.Forms also has applicability for those programmers who want eventually to use C# and the Xamarin.iOS and Xamarin.Android libraries to target the native application programming interfaces (APIs) of these platforms. Xamarin.Forms can be a big help in getting programmers started with these platforms or in constructing a prototype or proof-of-concept application.

This book assumes that you know C# and are familiar with the use of the .NET Framework. However, when I discuss some C# and .NET features that might be somewhat new to recent C# programmers, I adopt a somewhat slower pace.

Conventions and features in this book

This book has just a few typographical conventions:

- All programming elements referenced in the text—including classes, methods, properties, variable names, etc.—are shown in a monospaced font, such as the `StackLayout` class.

- Items that appear in the user interface of Visual Studio or Xamarin Studio, or the applications discussed in these chapters, appear in boldface, such as the **Add New Project** dialog.

- Application solutions and projects also appear in boldface, such as **MonkeyTap**.

The 1st and 2nd Preview Editions

This book is intended as a tutorial to learn Xamarin.Forms programming. It is not a replacement for the online API documentation, which can be found at the Xamarin.Forms Framework link on this page: http://api.xamarin.com/.

The first Preview Edition of this book was published in October 2014 to coincide with the Xamarin Evolve conference. It contained six chapters but no coverage of XAML.

This second Preview Edition was reconceived to contain shorter and more focused chapters. After the book establishes a solid foundation in code-only Xamarin.Forms programming, XAML is introduced in Chapter 7, and from that point on, XAML is used to define the user interface of most of the sample programs.

This Preview Edition unfortunately ends without covering some essential topics. The most obvious missing topics include the Grid, collection views such as ListView, page navigation, triggers, behaviors, and maps. However, it is our intention to publish chapters online just about as quickly as I can write them. New chapters will appear on the Xamarin webpage devoted to this book.

System requirements

This book assumes that you'll be using Xamarin.Forms to write applications that simultaneously target all three supported mobile platforms—iOS, Android, and Windows Phone. However, it's very likely that many readers will be targeting only one or two platforms in their Xamarin.Forms solutions. The platforms you target—and the Xamarin Platform package you purchase—govern your hardware and software requirements. For targeting iOS devices, you'll need a Mac installed with Apple Xcode as well as the Xamarin Platform, which includes Xamarin Studio. For targeting Windows Phone, you'll need Visual Studio 2012 or later (not an Express Edition) on a PC, and you'll need to have installed the Xamarin Platform.

However, you can also use Visual Studio on the PC to target iOS devices if the Mac with Xcode and the Xamarin Platform are accessible via WiFi. You can target Android devices from Visual Studio on the PC or from Xamarin Studio on either the PC or Mac.

Chapter 1 has more details on the various configurations you can use and resources for additional information and support. My setup for creating this book consisted of a Microsoft Surface Pro 2 (with external monitor, keyboard, and mouse) installed with Visual Studio 2013 and the Xamarin Platform, connected by WiFi with a MacBook Pro installed with Xcode and the Xamarin Platform.

All the screen shots in this book show an iPhone, an Android phone, and a Windows Phone in that order. The three devices shown in these screen shots reflect my setup and hardware:

- The iPhone 6 simulator on the MacBook Pro running iOS 8.2

- An LG Nexus 5 running Android 5.1.

- A Nokia Lumia 925 running Windows Phone 8.1

Some of the early screen shots in this book were from devices with somewhat earlier versions of the operating systems, for example Android 5.0 or 5.01 rather than 5.1.

The Xamarin.Forms programs in this book target the Xamarin.iOS Unified API and the Windows Phone 8.0 Silverlight API. (More about the Windows Phone API shortly.)

Downloads: Code samples

The sample programs shown in the pages of this book were compiled in late March 2015 with version 1.4.0 of Xamarin.Forms. The source code of these samples is hosted on a repository on GitHub: https://github.com/xamarin/xamarin-forms-book-preview-2/.

You can clone the directory structure to a local drive on your machine or download a big ZIP file. I'll try to keep the code updated with the latest release of Xamarin.Forms and to fix (and comment) any errors that might have sneaked through.

You can report problems, bugs, or other kinds of feedback about the book or source code by clicking the **Issues** button on this GitHub page. You can search through existing issues or file a new one. To file a new issue, you'll need to join GitHub (if you haven't already).

Use this GibHub page only for issues involving the book. For questions or discussions about Xamarin.Forms itself, use the Xamarin.Forms forum: http://forums.xamarin.com/categories/xamarin-forms.

Updating the code samples

The libraries that comprise Xamarin.Forms are distributed via the NuGet package manager. The Xamarin.Forms package consists of five dynamic-link libraries:

- Xamarin.Forms.Core.dll

- Xamarin.Forms.Xaml.dll

- Xamarin.Forms.Platform.iOS.dll

- Xamarin.Forms.Platform.Android.dll

- Xamarin.Forms.Platform.WP8.dll.

The Xamarin.Forms package also requires:

- Xamarin Support Library v4 (Xamarin.Android.Support.v4.dll)

- Windows Phone Toolkit (Microsoft.Phone.Controls.Toolkit.dll)

These should be automatically included.

When you create a new Xamarin.Forms solution using Visual Studio or Xamarin Studio, a version of the Xamarin.Forms package becomes part of that solution. However, that might not be the latest Xamarin.Forms package available from NuGet. Here's how to update to that package:

In Visual Studio, right-click the solution name in the **Solution Explorer** and select **Manage NuGet Packages for Solution**. Select **Installed packages** at the left of the dialog to see what's currently installed, and select **Updates** and **nuget.org** at the left to choose to update the package. If an update is available, clicking the **Update All** button is the easiest way to get it into the solution.

In Xamarin Studio, in the individual projects in the **Solution** list, under **Packages**, select the Xamarin.Forms package and select **Update** from the tool drop-down.

The source code for this book that is stored on GitHub does not include the actual NuGet packages. Xamarin Studio will automatically download them when you load the solution, but by default Visual Studio will not. After you first load the solution into Visual Studio, right-click the solution name in the **Solution Explorer** and select **Manage NuGet Packages for Solution**. You should be given the option to restore the packages with a **Restore** button at the top of the dialog. You can then update the package by selecting **Updates** and **nuget.org** at the left and (if an update exists) pressing the **Update All** button.

Big changes coming for Windows Phone

As this second Preview Edition is being finalized in late March 2015, a big change for Xamarin.Forms is just becoming available in a preview release: this is support for the Windows Runtime API supported by Windows Phone 8.1 and by Windows 8.0 Windows Store applications.

The contents of this book do not reflect that change! All the programs in this book target the Silverlight API of Windows Phone 8.0. Most of these programs should migrate easily to the Windows Runtime API. However, any program that relies upon Windows Phone 8.0 platform services—in particular, the programs in Chapter 9, "Platform-specific API calls"—will need some work.

By the time you see this book, some of the work converting the sample programs to the Windows Runtime platform should already have been completed. It is anticipated that the GitHub repository with the sample code for this book will have a branch named **windows-runtime** with the converted samples.

Acknowledgments

It's always seemed peculiar to me that authors of programming books are sometimes better known to programmers than the people who actually created the product that is the subject of the book! The real brains behind Xamarin.Forms are Jason Smith, Eric Maupin, Stephane Delcroix, Seth Rosetter, Rui Marinho, and Chris King. Congratulations, guys! We've been enjoying the fruits of your labor!

Over the months that the first and second Preview Editions were in progress, I have benefited from valuable feedback, corrections, and edits from several people. This book wouldn't exist without the collaboration of Bryan Costanich at Xamarin and Devon Musgrave at Microsoft Press. Both Bryan and Craig Dunn at Xamarin read some of my drafts of early chapters and managed to persuade me to take a somewhat different approach to the material. Later on, Craig kept me on track and reviewed the chapters in this second Preview Edition, and John Meade did the copyediting. For the first Preview Edition, Stephane Delcroix at Xamarin and Andy Wigley with Microsoft offered essential technical reads and persistently prodded me to make the book better. Microsoft's copyeditor for this second Preview Edition was John Pierce.

Almost nothing I do these days would be possible without the daily companionship and support of my wife, Deirdre Sinnott.

Charles Petzold
March 23, 2015

Free ebooks from Microsoft Press

From technical overviews to in-depth information on special topics, the free ebooks from Microsoft Press cover a wide range of topics. These ebooks are available in PDF, EPUB, and Mobi for Kindle formats, ready for you to download at http://aka.ms/mspressfree.

We want to hear from you

At Microsoft Press, your satisfaction is our top priority, and your feedback our most valuable asset. Please tell us what you think of this book at http://aka.ms/tellpress. Your feedback goes directly to the editors at Microsoft Press. (No personal information will be requested.) Thanks in advance for your input!

Chapter 1
How does Xamarin.Forms fit in?

There is much joy in programming. There is joy in analyzing a problem, breaking it down into pieces, formulating a solution, mapping out a strategy, approaching it from different directions, and crafting the code. There is very much joy in seeing the program run for the first time, and then more joy in eagerly diving back into the code to make it better and faster.

There is also often joy in hunting down bugs, in ensuring that the program runs smoothly and predictably. Few occasions are quite as joyful as finally identifying a particularly recalcitrant bug and definitively stamping it out.

There is even joy in realizing that the original approach you took is not quite the best. Many developers discover that they've learned a lot writing a program, including that there's a better way to structure the code. Sometimes, a partial or even a total rewrite can result in a much better application. The process is like standing on one's own shoulders, and there is much joy in attaining that perspective and knowledge.

However, not all aspects of programming are quite so joyful. One of the nastier programming jobs is taking a working program and rewriting it in an entirely different programming language or porting it to another operating system with an entirely different application programming interface (API).

A job like that can be a real grind. Yet, such a rewrite may very well be necessary: an application that's been so popular on the iPhone might be even more popular on Android devices, and there's only one way to find out.

But here's the problem: As you're going through the original source code and moving it to the new platform, do you maintain the same program structure so that the two versions exist in parallel? Or do you try to make improvements and enhancements?

The temptation, of course, is to entirely rethink the application and make the new version better. But the further the two versions drift apart, the harder they will be to maintain in the future.

For this reason, a sense of dread envelopes the forking of one application into two. With each line of code you write, you realize that all the future maintenance work, all the future revisions and enhancements, have become two jobs rather than one.

This is not a new problem. For over half a century, developers have craved the ability to write a single program that runs on multiple machines. This is one of the reasons that high-level languages were invented in the first place, and this is why the concept of "cross-platform development" continues to exert such a powerful attraction for programmers.

Cross-platform mobile development

The personal computer industry has experienced a massive shift in recent years. Desktop computers still exist, of course, and they remain vital for tasks that require keyboards and large screens: programming, writing, spread-sheeting, data tracking. But much of personal computing now occurs on smaller devices, particularly for quick information, media consumption, and social networking. Tablets and smartphones have a fundamentally different user-interaction paradigm based primarily on touch, with a keyboard that pops up only when necessary.

The mobile landscape

Although the mobile market has the potential for rapid change, currently two major phone and tablet platforms dominate:

- The Apple family of iPhones and iPads, all of which run the iOS operating system.

- The Android operating system, developed by Google based on the Linux kernel, which runs on a variety of phones and tablets.

How the world is divided between these two giants depends on how they are measured: there are more Android devices currently in use, but iPhone and iPad users are more devoted and spend more time with their devices.

There is also a third mobile development platform, which is not as popular as iOS and Android but involves a company with a strong history in the personal computer industry:

- Microsoft's Windows Phone.

In recent years, the Windows Phone has become a more compelling alternative as Microsoft has been merging the APIs of its platforms. A single API called the Windows Runtime (or WinRT) is now available for applications running on desktop machines, laptops, tablets, and phones.

For software developers, the optimum strategy is to target more than just one of these platforms. But that's not easy. There are four big obstacles:

Problem 1: Different user-interface paradigms

All three platforms incorporate similar ways of presenting the graphical user interface (GUI) and interaction with the device through multitouch, but there are many differences in detail. Each platform has different ways to navigate around applications and pages, different conventions for the presentation of data, different ways to invoke and display menus, and even different approaches to touch.

Users become accustomed to interacting with applications on a particular platform and expect to leverage that knowledge with future applications as well. Each platform acquires its own associated culture, and these cultural conventions then influence developers.

Problem 2: Different development environments

Programmers today are accustomed to working in a sophisticated integrated development environment (IDE). Such IDEs exist for all three platforms, but of course they are different:

- For iOS development, Xcode on the Mac.

- For Android development, Android Studio on a variety of platforms.

- For Windows Phone development, Visual Studio on the PC.

Problem 3: Different programming interfaces

All three of these platforms are based on different operating systems with different APIs. In many cases, the three platforms all implement similar types of user-interface objects but with different names.

For example, all three platforms have something that lets the user toggle a Boolean value:

- On the iPhone, it's a "view" called `UISwitch`.

- On Android devices, it's a "widget" called `Switch`.

- On Windows Phone, one possibility is a "control" called `ToggleSwitchButton` from the Windows Phone Toolkit NuGet package.

Of course, the differences go far beyond the names into the programming interfaces themselves.

Problem 4: Different programming languages

Developers have some flexibility in choosing a programming language for each of these three platforms, but, in general, each platform is very closely associated with a particular programming language:

- Objective-C for the iPhone

- Java for Android devices

- C# for Windows Phone

These three languages are cousins because they are all object-oriented descendants of C, but they have become rather distant cousins.

For these reasons, a company that wants to target multiple platforms might very well employ three different programmer teams, each team skilled and specialized in a particular language and API.

This language problem is particularly nasty, but it's the problem that is the most tempting to solve: If you could use the same programming language for these three platforms, you could at least share some code between the platforms. This shared code likely wouldn't be involved with the user interface because each platform has different APIs, but there might well be application code that doesn't touch the user interface at all.

A single language for these three platforms would certainly be convenient. But what language would that be?

The C# and .NET solution

A roomful of programmers would come up with a variety of answers to the question just posed, but a good argument can be made in favor of C#. Unveiled by Microsoft in the year 2000, C# is a fairly new programming language, at least when compared with Objective-C and Java. At first, C# seemed to be a rather straightforward, strongly typed, imperative object-oriented language, certainly influenced by C++ (and Java as well), but with a much cleaner syntax than C++ and none of the historical baggage. In addition, the first version of C# had language-level support for properties and events, which turn out to be member types that are particularly suited for programming graphical user interfaces.

But C# has continued to grow and get better over the years. The support of generics, lambda functions, LINQ, and asynchronous operations has successfully elevated C# to be classified as a multiparadigm programming language. C# code can be traditionally imperative or flavored with declarative or functional programming paradigms.

Also exciting is the future of C#: on April 3, 2014, C# creator Anders Hejlsberg stood on a stage at the Microsoft Build 2014 conference and clicked a button that published an open-source version of the C# compiler, called the .NET Compiler Platform (formerly known by its code name "Roslyn").

Since its inception, C# has been closely associated with the Microsoft .NET Framework. At the lowest level, .NET provides an infrastructure for the C# basic data types (`int`, `double`, `string`, and so forth). But the extensive .NET Framework class library provides support for many common chores encountered in many different types of programming. These include:

- Math

- Debugging

- Reflection

- Collections

- Globalization

- File I/O

- Networking

- Security

- Threading

- Web services

- Data handling

- XML and JSON reading and writing

Here's another big reason for C# and .NET to be regarded as a compelling cross-platform solution:

It's not just hypothetical. It's a reality.

Soon after Microsoft's announcement of .NET way back in June 2000, the company Ximian (founded by Miguel de Icaza and Nat Friedman) initiated an open-source project called Mono to create an alternative implementation of the C# compiler and the .NET Framework that could run on Linux.

A decade later, in 2011, the founders of Ximian (which had been acquired by Novell) founded Xamarin, which still contributes to the open-source version of Mono but which has also adapted Mono to form the basis of cross-platform mobile solutions.

Shortly after the open-source version of C# was published, Scott Guthrie of Microsoft announced the formation of the .NET Foundation, which serves as a steward for open-source .NET technologies, in which Xamarin plays a major part.

A single language for all platforms

For the first three years of its existence, Xamarin focused mainly on compiler technologies and three basic sets of .NET libraries:

- Xamarin.Mac, which has evolved from the MonoMac project.

- Xamarin.iOS, which evolved from MonoTouch.

- Xamarin.Android, which evolved from Mono for Android or (more informally) MonoDroid.

Collectively, these libraries are known as the Xamarin platform. The libraries consist of .NET versions of the native Mac, IOS, and Android APIs. Programmers using these libraries can write applications in C# to target the native APIs of these three platforms, but also (as a bonus) with access to the .NET Framework class library.

Xamarin also makes available Xamarin Studio, an integrated development environment that runs on both the Mac and PC and lets you develop iPhone and Android applications on the Mac and Android applications on the PC.

It is also possible to use Visual Studio with the Xamarin libraries to develop Mac, iPhone, and Android applications. (However, Mac and iPhone development also requires a Mac with Xcode and Xamarin Studio installed and connected through a local network with the PC.)

Of course, if you're using Visual Studio, you can also target Windows Phone and other Microsoft platforms.

Sharing code

The advantage of targeting multiple platforms with a single programming language comes from the ability to share code among the applications.

 Before code can be shared, an application must be structured for that purpose. Particularly since the widespread use of graphical user interfaces, programmers have understood the importance of separating application code into functional layers. Perhaps the most useful division is between user-interface code and the underlying data models and algorithms. The popular MVC (Model-View-Controller) application architecture formalizes this code separation into a Model (the underlying data), the View (the visual representation of the data), and the Controller (which handles input from the user).

 MVC originated in the 1980s. More recently, the MVVM (Model-View-ViewModel) architecture has effectively modernized MVC based on modern GUIs. MVVM separates code into the Model (the underlying data), the View (the user interface, including visuals and input), and the ViewModel (which manages data passing between the Model and the View).

 When a programmer develops an application that targets multiple mobile platforms, the MVVM architecture helps guide the developer into separating code into the platform-specific View—the code that requires interacting with the platform APIs—and the platform-independent Model and View-Model.

 Often this platform-independent code needs to access files or the network or use collections or threading. Normally these jobs would be considered part of an operating system API, but they are also jobs that can make use of the .NET Framework class library, and if the class library is available on each platform, it is effectively platform independent.

 The part of the application that is platform independent can then be isolated and—in the context of Visual Studio or Xamarin Studio—put into a separate project. This can be either a Shared Asset Project (SAP)—which simply consists of code and other asset files accessible from other projects—or a Portable Class Library (PCL), which encloses all the common code in a dynamic-link library (DLL) that can then be referenced from other projects.

 Whichever method is used, this common code has access to the .NET Framework class library, so it can perform file I/O, handle globalization, access web services, decompose XML, and so forth.

 This means that you can create a single Visual Studio solution that contains four C# projects to target the three major mobile platforms (all with access to a common SAP or PCL project), or you can use Xamarin Studio to target iPhone and Android devices.

 The following diagram illustrates the interrelationships between the Visual Studio or Xamarin Studio projects, the Xamarin libraries, and the platform APIs:

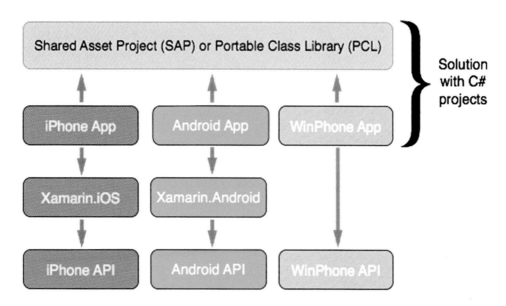

The boxes in the second row are the actual platform-specific applications. These apps make calls into the common project and also (with the iPhone and Android) the Xamarin libraries that implement the native platform APIs.

But the diagram is not quite complete: it doesn't show the SAP or PCL making calls to the .NET Framework class library. The PCL has access to its own version of .NET, while the SAP uses the version of .NET incorporated into each particular platform.

In this diagram, the Xamarin.iOS and Xamarin.Android libraries seem to be substantial, and while they are certainly important, they're mostly just language bindings and do not significantly add any overhead to API calls.

When the iPhone app is built, the Xamarin C# compiler generates C# Intermediate Language (IL) as usual, but it then makes use of the Apple compiler on the Mac to generate native iPhone machine code just like the Objective-C compiler. The calls from the app to the iPhone APIs are the same as though the application were written in Objective-C.

For the Android app, the Xamarin C# compiler generates IL, which runs on a version of Mono on the device alongside the Java engine, but the API calls from the app are pretty much the same as though   the app were written in Java.

For mobile applications that have very platform-specific needs, but also a potentially shareable chunk of platform-independent code, Xamarin.iOS and Xamarin.Android provide excellent solutions. You have access to the entire platform API, with all the power (and responsibility) that implies.

But for applications that might not need quite so much platform specificity, there is now an alternative that will simplify your life even more.

Introducing Xamarin.Forms

On May 28, 2014, Xamarin introduced Xamarin.Forms as part of a collection of enhancements to the Xamarin platform dubbed Xamarin 3. Xamarin.Forms allows you to write user-interface code that can be compiled for the iPhone, Android, and Windows Phone.

The Xamarin.Forms option

In the general case, a Xamarin.Forms application is three separate projects for the three mobile platforms, with a fourth project containing common code—very much like the diagram that appeared in the previous section. However, the three platform projects in a Xamarin.Forms application are typically quite small—often consisting of just stubs with a little boilerplate startup code. The Shared Asset Project, or the Portable Class Library project, contains the bulk of the application, including the user-interface code:

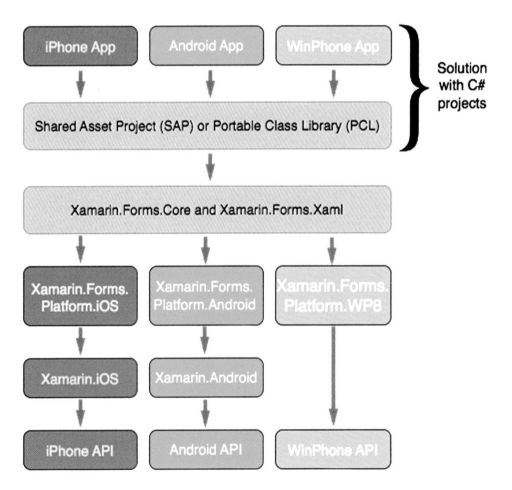

The Xamarin.Forms.Core and Xamarin.Forms.Xaml libraries implement the Xamarin.Forms API. Depending on the platform, Xamarin.Forms.Core then makes use of one of the Xamarin.Forms.Platform libraries. These libraries are mostly a collection of classes called *renderers* that transform the Xamarin.Forms user-interface objects into the platform-specific user interface.

The remainder of the diagram is the same as the one shown earlier.

For example, suppose you need the user-interface object discussed earlier that allows the user to toggle a Boolean value. When programming for Xamarin.Forms, this is called a `Switch`, and a class named `Switch` is implemented in the Xamarin.Forms.Core library. In the individual renderers for the three platforms, this `Switch` is mapped to a `UISwitch` on the iPhone, a `Switch` on Android, and a `ToggleSwitchButton` on Windows Phone.

Xamarin.Forms.Core also contains a class named `Slider` for displaying a horizontal bar that the user manipulates to choose a numeric value. In the renderers in the platform-specific libraries, this is mapped to a `UISlider` on the iPhone, a `SeekBar` on Android, and a `Slider` on Windows Phone.

This means that when you write a Xamarin.Forms program that has a `Switch` or a `Slider`, what's actually displayed is the corresponding object implemented in each platform.

Here's a little Xamarin.Forms program containing a `Label` reading "Hello, Xamarin.Forms!", a `Button` saying "Click Me!", a `Switch`, and a `Slider`. The program is running on (from left to right) the iPhone, Android, and Windows Phone:

You'll see triple screenshots like this one throughout this book. They're always in the same order—iPhone, Android, and Windows Phone—and they're always running the same program.

As you can see, the `Button`, `Switch`, and `Slider` all have different appearances on the three phones because they are all rendered with the object specific to each platform.

What's even more interesting is the inclusion in this program of six `ToolBarItem` objects, three identified as primary items with icons, and three as secondary items without icons. On the iPhone these are rendered with `UIBarButtonItem` objects as the three icons and three buttons at the top of the page. On the Android, the first three are rendered as items on an `ActionBar`, also at the top of the page. On Windows Phone, they're realized as items on the `ApplicationBar` at the page's bottom.

The Android `ActionBar` has a vertical ellipsis and the Windows Phone `ApplicationBar` has a horizontal ellipsis. Tapping this ellipsis causes the secondary items to be displayed in a manner appropriate to these two platforms:

In one sense, Xamarin.Forms is an API that virtualizes the user-interface paradigms on each platform.

XAML support

Xamarin.Forms also supports XAML (pronounced "zammel" to rhyme with "camel"), the XML-based Extensible Application Markup Language developed at Microsoft as a general-purpose markup language for instantiating and initializing objects. XAML isn't limited to defining initial layouts of user interfaces, but historically, that's how it's been used the most, and that's what it's used for in Xamarin.Forms.

Here's the XAML file for the program whose screenshots you've just seen:

```
<ContentPage xmlns="http://xamarin.com/schemas/2014/forms"
             xmlns:x="http://schemas.microsoft.com/winfx/2009/xaml"
             x:Class="PlatformVisuals.PlatformVisualsPage"
```

```
                    Title="Visuals">

    <StackLayout Padding="10,0">
        <Label Text="Hello, Xamarin.Forms!"
                VerticalOptions="CenterAndExpand"
                HorizontalOptions="Center" />

        <Button Text = "Click Me!"
                VerticalOptions="CenterAndExpand"
                HorizontalOptions="Center" />

        <Switch VerticalOptions="CenterAndExpand"
                HorizontalOptions="Center" />

        <Slider VerticalOptions="CenterAndExpand" />
    </StackLayout>

    <ContentPage.ToolbarItems>
        <ToolbarItem Text="edit" Order="Primary">
            <ToolbarItem.Icon>
                <OnPlatform x:TypeArguments="FileImageSource"
                            iOS="edit.png"
                            Android="ic_action_edit.png"
                            WinPhone="Images/edit.png" />
            </ToolbarItem.Icon>
        </ToolbarItem>

        <ToolbarItem Text="search" Order="Primary">
            <ToolbarItem.Icon>
                <OnPlatform x:TypeArguments="FileImageSource"
                            iOS="search.png"
                            Android="ic_action_search.png"
                            WinPhone="Images/feature.search.png" />
            </ToolbarItem.Icon>
        </ToolbarItem>

        <ToolbarItem Text="refresh" Order="Primary">
            <ToolbarItem.Icon>
                <OnPlatform x:TypeArguments="FileImageSource"
                            iOS="reload.png"
                            Android="ic_action_refresh.png"
                            WinPhone="Images/refresh.png" />
            </ToolbarItem.Icon>
        </ToolbarItem>

        <ToolbarItem Text="explore" Order="Secondary" />
        <ToolbarItem Text="discover" Order="Secondary" />
        <ToolbarItem Text="evolve" Order="Secondary" />
    </ContentPage.ToolbarItems>
</ContentPage>
```

Unless you have experience with XAML, some syntax details might be a little obscure. (Don't worry; you'll learn all about them later on in this book.) But even so, you can see the `Label`, `Button`, `Switch`, and `Slider` tags. In a real program, the `Button`, `Switch`, and `Slider` would probably have event

handlers attached that would be implemented in a C# code file. Here they do not. The `VerticalOp-`
`tions` and `HorizontalOptions` attributes assist in layout; they are discussed in the next chapter.

Platform specificity

In the section of that XAML file involving the `ToolbarItem`, you can also see a tag named `OnPlat-`
`form`. This is one of several techniques in Xamarin.Forms that allow introducing some platform specificity in otherwise platform-independent code or markup. It's used here because each of the separate
platforms has somewhat different image format and size requirements associated with these icons.

A similar facility exists in code with the `Device` class. It's possible to determine what platform the
code is running on and to choose values or objects based on the platform. For example, you can specify different font sizes for each platform or run different blocks of code based on the platform. You
might want to let the user manipulate a `Slider` to select a value in one platform but pick a number
from a set of explicit values in another platform.

In some applications, deeper platform specificities might be desired. For example, suppose your application requires the GPS coordinates of the user's phone. This is not something that the initial version
of Xamarin.Forms provides, so you'd need to write your own code specific to each platform to obtain
this information.

The `DependencyService` class provides a way to do this in a structured manner. You define an interface with the methods you need (for example, `IGetCurrentLocation`) and then implement that
interface with a class in each of the platform projects. You can then call the methods in that interface
from the Xamarin.Forms project almost as easily as if it were part of the API.

As discussed earlier, each of the standard Xamarin.Forms visual objects—such as `Label`, `Button`,
`Switch`, and `Slider`—are supported by a renderer class in the three Xamarin.Forms.Platform libraries.
Each renderer class implements the platform-specific object that maps to the Xamarin.Forms object.

You can create your own custom visual objects with your own custom renderers. The custom visual
object goes in the common code project, and the custom renderers go in the individual platform projects. To make it a bit easier, generally you'll want to derive from an existing class. Within the individual
Xamarin.Forms platform libraries, all the corresponding renderers are public classes, and you can derive
from them as well.

Xamarin.Forms allows you to be as platform independent or as platform specific as you need to be.
Xamarin.Forms doesn't replace Xamarin.iOS and Xamarin.Android; rather, it integrates with them.

A cross-platform panacea?

For the most part, Xamarin.Forms defines its abstractions with a focus on areas of the mobile user interface that are common to iOS, Android, and Windows Phone. These Xamarin.Forms visual objects are
mapped to platform-specific objects, but Xamarin.Forms has tended to avoid implementing anything
that is unique to a particular platform.

For this reason, despite the enormous help that Xamarin.Forms can offer in creating platform-independent applications, it is not a complete replacement for native API programming. If your application relies heavily on native API features such as particular types of controls or widgets, then you might want to stick with Xamarin.iOS, Xamarin.Android, and the native Windows Phone API.

You'll probably also want to stick with the native APIs for applications that require vector graphics or complex touch interaction. The current version of Xamarin.Forms is not quite ready for these scenarios.

On the other hand, Xamarin.Forms is great for prototyping or making a quick proof-of-concept application. And after you've done that, you might just find that you can continue using Xamarin.Forms features to build the entire application. Xamarin.Forms is ideal for line-of-business applications.

Even if you begin building an application with Xamarin.Forms and then implement major parts of it with platform APIs, you're doing so within a framework that allows you to share code and that offers structured ways to make platform-specific visuals.

Your development environment

How you set up your hardware and software depends on what mobile platforms you're targeting and what computing environments are most comfortable for you.

The requirements for Xamarin.Forms are no different from the requirements for using Xamarin.iOS or Xamarin.Android or for programming for Windows Phone.

This means that nothing in this section (and the remainder of this chapter) is specific to Xamarin.Forms. There exists much documentation on the Xamarin website on setting up machines and software for Xamarin.iOS and Xamarin.Android programming, and on the Microsoft website about Windows Phone.

Machines and IDEs

If you want to target the iPhone, you're going to need a Mac. Apple requires that a Mac be used for building iPhone and other iOS applications. You'll need to install Xcode on this machine and, of course, the Xamarin platform that includes the necessary libraries and Xamarin Studio. You can then use Xamarin Studio and Xamarin.Forms on the Mac for your iPhone development.

Once you have a Mac with Xcode and the Xamarin platform installed, you can also install the Xamarin platform on a PC and program for the iPhone by using Visual Studio. The PC and Mac must be connected via a network (such as Wi-Fi). You run the Xamarin.iOS Build Host on the Mac for this interconnection, and Visual Studio uses that to build and deploy the executable on the Mac.

Although you can run Xamarin Studio on the PC, you cannot use Xamarin Studio on the PC to do iPhone programming.

If you want to target Android phones, you have lots of flexibility. You can do so by using Xamarin Studio on the Mac, Xamarin Studio on the PC, or Visual Studio on the PC.

If you want to target Windows Phone, you'll need to use Visual Studio 2012 or 2013, but not an Express edition.

This means that if you want to target all three platforms in a single IDE, you can do so with Visual Studio running on a PC connected to the Mac via a network. Another option is to run Visual Studio in a virtual machine on the Mac.

Devices and emulators

You can test your programs on real phones connected to the machine via a USB cable, or you can test your programs with onscreen emulators.

There are advantages and disadvantages to each approach. A real phone is essential for testing complex touch interaction or when getting a feel for startup or response time. However, emulators allow you to see how your application adapts to a variety of sizes and form factors.

Perhaps the smoothest running emulator is that for the iPhone. However, because Mac desktop machines don't have touch screens, you'll need to use the mouse or trackpad to simulate touch. The touch gestures on the Mac touchpad do not translate to the emulator. You can also connect a real iPhone to the Mac, but you'll need to provision it as a developer device.

The Windows Phone emulator is capable of several different screen resolutions and also tends to run fairly smoothly, albeit consuming lots of memory. If you run the Windows Phone emulator on a touch screen, you can use touch on the emulator screen. Connecting a real Windows Phone to the PC requires unlocking the phone. If you want to unlock more than one phone, you'll need a developer account.

Android emulators are the most problematic. They tend to be slow and cranky, although they are often extremely versatile in emulating a vast array of actual Android devices. On the up side, it's very easy to connect a real Android phone to either a Mac or PC for testing. All you really need do is enable USB Debugging on the device.

If you like the idea of testing on real devices but want to test on more real devices than you can possibly manage yourself, look into the Xamarin Test Cloud.

Installation

Before writing applications for Xamarin.Forms, you'll need to install the Xamarin platform on your Mac, PC, or both (if you're using that setup). See the articles on the Xamarin website at:

http://developer.xamarin.com/guides/cross-platform/getting_started/installation/

You're probably eager to create your first Xamarin.Forms application, but before you do, you'll want to try creating normal Xamarin projects for the iPhone and Android and a normal Windows Phone project.

This is important: if you're experiencing a problem using Xamarin.iOS or Xamarin.Android, that's not a problem with Xamarin.Forms, and you'll need to solve that problem before using Xamarin.Forms.

Creating an iOS app

If you're interested in using Xamarin.Forms to target the iPhone, first become familiar with the appropriate Getting Started documents on the Xamarin website:

   http://developer.xamarin.com/guides/ios/getting_started/

This will give you guidance on using the Xamarin.iOS library to develop an iPhone application in C#. All you really need to do is get to the point where you can build and deploy a simple iPhone application on either a real iPhone or the iPhone simulator.

If you're using Visual Studio, and if everything is installed correctly, you should be able to select **File > New > Project** from the menu, and in the **New Project** dialog, from the left select **Visual C#** and **iOS** and then **Universal**, and from the template list in the center select **Blank App (iOS)**.

If you're using Xamarin Studio, you should be able to select **File > New > Solution** from the menu, and in the **New Solution** dialog, from the left select **C#** and **iOS** and then **Unified API** and **Universal**, and from the template list in the center select **Empty Project**.

In either case, select a location and name for the solution. Build and deploy the skeleton application created in the project. If you're having a problem with this, it's not a Xamarin.Forms issue. You might want to check the Xamarin.iOS forums to see if anybody else has a similar problem:

   http://forums.xamarin.com/categories/ios/

Creating an Android app

If you're interested in using Xamarin.Forms to target Android devices, first become familiar with the Getting Started documents on the Xamarin website:

   http://developer.xamarin.com/guides/android/getting_started/

If you're using Visual Studio, and if everything is installed correctly, you should be able to select **File > New > Project** from the menu, and in the **New Project** dialog, from the left select **Visual C#** and then **Android**, and from the template list in the center select **Blank App (Android)**.

If you're using Xamarin Studio, you should be able to select **File > New > Solution** from the menu, and in the **New Solution** dialog, from the left select **C#** and **Android**, and in the template list in the center select **Android Application**.

Give it a location and a name; build and deploy. If you can't get this process to work, it's not a Xamarin.Forms issue, and you might want to check the Xamarin.Android forums for a similar problem:

http://forums.xamarin.com/categories/android/

Creating a Windows Phone app

If you're interested in using Xamarin.Forms to target Windows Phone, you'll need to become familiar with at least the rudiments of using Visual Studio to develop Windows Phone applications:

http://dev.windows.com/

In Visual Studio 2013, if everything is installed correctly, you should be able select **File > New > Project** from the menu, and in the **New Project** dialog, at the left select **Visual C#**, then **Store Apps**, and **Windows Phone Apps**. In the center area, select the **Blank App (Windows Phone Silverlight)** template. In the dialog that follows, select **Windows Phone 8**.

You should be able to build and deploy the skeleton application to a real phone or an emulator. If not, search the Microsoft website or online forums such as Stack Overflow.

All ready?

If you can build Xamarin.iOS, Xamarin.Android, and Windows Phone applications (or some subset of those), then you're ready to create your first Xamarin.Forms application. It's time to say "Hello, Xamarin.Forms" to a new era in cross-platform mobile development.

Chapter 2
Anatomy of an app

The modern user interface is constructed from visual objects of various sorts. Depending on the operating system, these visual objects might go by different names—controls, elements, views, widgets—but they are all devoted to the jobs of presentation or interaction.

In Xamarin.Forms, the objects that appear on the screen are collectively called *visual elements*. They come in three main categories:

- page
- layout
- view

These are not abstract concepts! The Xamarin.Forms application programming interface (API) defines classes named `VisualElement`, `Page`, `Layout`, and `View`. These classes and their descendants form the backbone of the Xamarin.Forms user interface. `VisualElement` is an exceptionally important class in Xamarin.Forms. A `VisualElement` object is anything that occupies space on the screen.

A Xamarin.Forms application consists of one or more pages. A page usually occupies all (or at least a large area) of the screen. Some applications consist of only a single page, while others allow navigating between multiple pages. In many of the early chapters in this book, you'll see just one type of page, called a `ContentPage`.

On each page, the visual elements are organized in a parent-child hierarchy. The child of a `ContentPage` is generally a layout of some sort to organize the visuals. Some layouts have a single child, but many layouts have multiple children that the layout arranges within itself. These children can be other layouts or views. Different types of layouts arrange children in a stack, in a two-dimensional grid, or in a more freeform manner. In this chapter, however, our pages will contain just a single child.

The term *view* in Xamarin.Forms denotes familiar types of presentation and interactive objects: text, bitmaps, buttons, text-entry fields, sliders, switches, progress bars, date and time pickers, and others of your own devising. These are often called controls or widgets in other programming environments. This book refers to them as views or elements. In this chapter, you'll encounter the `Label` view for displaying text.

Say hello

Using either Microsoft Visual Studio or Xamarin Studio, let's create a new Xamarin.Forms application by using a standard template. This process creates a solution that contains up to four projects: three plat-form projects—for iOS, Android, and Windows Phone—and a common project for the greater part of your application code.

In Visual Studio, select the menu option **File > New > Project**. At the left of the **New Project** dia-log, select **Visual C#** and then **Mobile Apps**.

In Xamarin Studio, select **File > New > Solution** from the menu, and at the left of the **New Solu-tion** dialog, select **C#** and then **Mobile Apps**.

In either case, the center section of the dialog lists three available solution templates:

- **Blank App (Xamarin.Forms Portable)**

- **Blank App (Xamarin.Forms Shared)**

- **Class Library (Xamarin.Forms Portable)**

Now what? We definitely want to create a **Blank App** solution, but what kind?

The term "Portable" in this context refers to a Portable Class Library (PCL). All the common applica-tion code becomes a dynamic-link library (DLL) that is referenced by all the individual platform pro-jects.

The term "Shared" in this context means a Shared Asset Project (SAP) containing loose code files (and perhaps other files) that are shared among the platform projects, essentially becoming part of each platform project.

For now, pick the first one: **Blank App (Xamarin.Forms Portable)**. Select a disk location for the so-lution, and give it a name—for example, **Hello**.

If you're running Visual Studio, four projects are created: one common project (the PCL project) and three application projects. For a solution named **Hello**, these are:

- A Portable Class Library project named **Hello** that is referenced by the three application pro-jects;

- An application project for Android, named **Hello.Droid**;

- An application project for iOS, named **Hello.iOS**; and

- An application project for Windows Phone, named **Hello.WinPhone**.

If you're running Xamarin Studio on the Mac, the Windows Phone project isn't created, and if you're running Xamarin Studio on the PC, neither the iOS nor the Windows Phone program is created.

Before continuing, check to be sure that the project configurations are okay. In Visual Studio, select the **Build > Configuration Manager** menu item. In the **Configuration Manager** dialog, you'll see the PCL project and the three application projects. Make sure the **Build** box is checked for all the projects and the **Deploy** box is checked for all the application projects (unless the box is grayed out). Take note of the **Platform** column: If the **Hello** project is listed, it should be flagged as **Any CPU**. The **Hello.Droid** project should also be flagged as **Any CPU**. (For those two project types, **Any CPU** is the only option.) For the **Hello.iOS** project, choose either **iPhone** or **iPhoneSimulator** depending on how you'll be testing the program. For the **Hello.WinPhone** project, you can select **x86** if you'll be using an on-screen emulator, **ARM** if you'll be deploying to a real phone, or **Any CPU** for deploying to either. Regardless of your choice, Visual Studio generates the same code.

If a project doesn't seem to be compiling or deploying in Visual Studio, recheck the settings in the **Configuration Manager** dialog. Sometimes a different configuration becomes active and might not include the PCL project.

In Xamarin Studio on the Mac, you can switch between deploying to the iPhone and iPhone simulator through the **Project > Active Configuration** menu item.

In Visual Studio, you'll probably want to display the iOS and Android toolbars. These toolbars let you choose among emulators and devices and allow you to manage the emulators. From the main menu, make sure the **View > Toolbars > iOS** and **View > Toolbars > Android** items are checked.

Because the solution contains anywhere from two to four projects, you must designate which program starts up when you elect to run or debug an application.

In the **Solution Explorer** of Visual Studio, right-click any of the three application projects and select the **Set As StartUp Project** item from the menu. You can then select to deploy to either an emulator or a real device. To build and run the program, select the menu item **Debug > Start Debugging**.

In the **Solution** list in Xamarin Studio, click the little tool icon that appears to the right of a selected project and select **Set as Startup Project** from the menu. You can then pick **Run > Start Debugging** from the main menu.

If all goes well, the skeleton application created by the template will run and you'll see a short message:

As you can see, these platforms have different color schemes. By default, the Windows Phone color scheme is like the Android color scheme in that it displays light text on a dark background—but on Windows Phone this color scheme is changeable by the user. Even on a Windows Phone emulator, you can change the color scheme in the **Themes** section of the **Settings** application and then rerun the program.

The app is not only run on the device or emulator but deployed. It appears with the other apps on the phone or emulator and can be run from there. If you don't like the application icon or how the app name displays, you can change that in the individual platform projects.

Inside the files

Clearly, the program created by the Xamarin.Forms template is very simple, so this is an excellent opportunity to examine the generated code files and figure out their interrelationships and how they work.

Let's begin with the code that's responsible for defining the text that you see on the screen. This is the `App` class in the **Hello** project. In a project created by Visual Studio, the `App` class is defined in the App.cs file, but in Xamarin Studio, the file is Hello.cs. If the project template hasn't changed too much since this chapter was written, it probably looks something like this:

```
using System;
using System.Collections.Generic;
using System.Linq;
using System.Text;
```

```
using Xamarin.Forms;

namespace Hello
{
    public class App : Application
    {
        public App()
        {
            // The root page of your application
            MainPage = new ContentPage
            {
                Content = new StackLayout
                {
                    VerticalOptions = LayoutOptions.Center,
                    Children = {
                        new Label {
                            XAlign = TextAlignment.Center,
                            Text = "Welcome to Xamarin Forms!"
                        }
                    }
                }
            };
        }

        protected override void OnStart()
        {
            // Handle when your app starts
        }

        protected override void OnSleep()
        {
            // Handle when your app sleeps
        }

        protected override void OnResume()
        {
            // Handle when your app resumes
        }
    }
}
```

Notice that the namespace is the same as the project name. This `App` class is defined as public and derives from the Xamarin.Forms `Application` class. The constructor really has just one responsibility: to set the `MainPage` property of the `Application` class to an object of type `Page`.

The code that the Xamarin.Forms template has generated here shows one very simple approach to defining this constructor: The `ContentPage` class derives from `Page` and is very common in single-page Xamarin.Forms applications. (You'll see a lot of `ContentPage` throughout this book.) It occupies most of the phone's screen with the exception of the status bar at the top of the Android screen, the buttons on the bottom of the Android screen, and the status bar at the top of the Windows Phone screen. (As you'll discover, the iOS status bar is actually part of the `ContentPage`.)

The `ContentPage` class defines a property named `Content` that you set to the content of the page. Generally this content is a layout that in turn contains a bunch of views, and in this case it's set to a `StackLayout`, which arranges its children in a stack.

This `StackLayout` has only one child, which is a `Label`. The `Label` class derives from `View` and is used in Xamarin.Forms applications to display up to a paragraph of text. The `VerticalOptions` and `XAlign` properties are discussed in more detail later in this chapter.

For your own single-page Xamarin.Forms applications, you'll generally be defining your own class that derives from `ContentPage`. The constructor of the `App` class then sets an instance of the class that you define to its `MainPage` property. You'll see how this works shortly.

In the **Hello** solution, you'll also see an AssemblyInfo.cs file for creating the PCL and a packages.config file that contains the NuGet packages required by the program. In the **References** section under **Hello** in the solution list, you'll see the three libraries this PCL requires:

- .NET (displayed as .NET Portable Subset in Xamarin Studio)

- Xamarin.Forms.Core

- Xamarin.Forms.Xaml

It is this PCL project that will receive the bulk of your attention as you're writing a Xamarin.Forms application. In some circumstances the code in this project might require some tailoring for the three different platforms, and you'll see shortly how to do that. You can also include platform-specific code in the three application projects.

The three application projects have their own assets in the form of icons and metadata, and you must pay particular attention to these assets if you intend to bring the application to market. But during the time that you're learning how to develop applications using Xamarin.Forms, these assets can generally be ignored. You'll probably want to keep these application projects collapsed in the solution list because you don't need to bother much with their contents.

But you really should know what's in these application projects, so let's take a closer look.

In the **References** section of each application project, you'll see references to the common PCL project (**Hello** in this case), as well as various .NET assemblies, the Xamarin.Forms assembles listed above, and additional Xamarin.Forms assemblies applicable to each platform:

- Xamarin.Forms.Platform.Android

- Xamarin.Forms.Platform.iOS

- Xamarin.Forms.Platform.WP8

Each of these three libraries defines a static `Forms.Init` method in the `Xamarin.Forms` namespace that initializes the Xamarin.Forms system for that particular platform. The startup code in each platform must make a call to this method.

You've also just seen that the PCL project derives a public class named `App` that derives from `Application`. The startup code in each platform must also instantiate this `App` class.

If you're familiar with iOS, Android, or Windows Phone development, you might be curious to see how the platform startup code handles these jobs.

The iOS Project

An iOS project typically contains a class that derives from `UIApplicationDelegate`. However, the Xamarin.Forms.Platform.iOS library defines an alternative base class named `FormsApplicationDelegate`. In the **Hello.iOS** project, you'll see this AppDelegate.cs file, here stripped of all extraneous `using` directives and comments:

```
using Foundation;
using UIKit;

namespace Hello.iOS
{
    [Register("AppDelegate")]
    public partial class AppDelegate :
                            global::Xamarin.Forms.Platform.iOS.FormsApplicationDelegate
    {
        public override bool FinishedLaunching(UIApplication app, NSDictionary options)
        {
            global::Xamarin.Forms.Forms.Init();
            LoadApplication(new App());

            return base.FinishedLaunching(app, options);
        }
    }
}
```

The `FinishedLaunching` override begins by calling the `Forms.Init` method defined in the **Xamarin.Forms.Platform.iOS** assembly. It then calls a `LoadApplication` method (defined by the `FormsApplicationDelegate`), passing to it a new instance of the `App` class defined in the shared PCL. The page object set to the `MainPage` property of this `App` object can then be used to create an object of type `UIViewController`, which is responsible for rendering the page's contents.

The Android project

In the Android application, the typical `MainActivity` class must be derived from a Xamarin.Forms class named `FormsApplicationActivity` defined in the **Xamarin.Forms.Platform.Android** assembly, and the `Forms.Init` call requires some additional information:

```
using Android.App;
using Android.Content.PM;
using Android.OS;

namespace Hello.Droid
```

```
{
    [Activity(Label = "Hello", Icon = "@drawable/icon", MainLauncher = true,
        ConfigurationChanges = ConfigChanges.ScreenSize | ConfigChanges.Orientation)]
    public class MainActivity : global::Xamarin.Forms.Platform.Android.FormsApplicationActivity
    {
        protected override void OnCreate(Bundle bundle)
        {
            base.OnCreate(bundle);

            global::Xamarin.Forms.Forms.Init(this, bundle);
            LoadApplication(new App());
        }
    }
}
```

The new instance of the `App` class is then passed to a `LoadApplication` method defined by `FormsApplicationActivity`. The attribute set on the `MainActivity` class indicates that the activity is *not* re-created when the phone changes orientation (from portrait to landscape or back) or the screen changes size.

The Windows Phone project

In the Windows Phone project, look at the MainPage.xaml.cs file tucked underneath the Main-Page.xaml file in the project file list. This file defines the customary `MainPage` class, but notice that it derives from a Xamarin.Forms class named `FormsApplicationPage`. The newly instantiated `App` class is passed to the `LoadApplication` method defined by this base class:

```
using Microsoft.Phone.Controls;

namespace Hello.WinPhone
{
    public partial class MainPage : global::Xamarin.Forms.Platform.WinPhone.FormsApplicationPage
    {
        public MainPage()
        {
            InitializeComponent();
            SupportedOrientations = SupportedPageOrientation.PortraitOrLandscape;

            global::Xamarin.Forms.Forms.Init();
            LoadApplication(new Hello.App());
        }
    }
}
```

The setting of the `SupportedOrientations` property allows the phone to respond to orientation changes between portrait and landscape. The iOS and Android projects are enabled for orientation changes by default as well, so you should be able to turn the phone or simulator side to side and see the text realigned in the center of the screen.

Nothing special!

If you've created a Xamarin.Forms solution under Visual Studio and don't want to target one or more platforms, simply delete those projects.

If you later change your mind about those projects—or you originally created the solution in Xamarin Studio and want to move it to Visual Studio to target Windows Phone—you can add new platform projects to the Xamarin.Forms solution. In the Add New Project dialog, you can create a Unified API (not Classic API) Xamarin.iOS project by selecting the iOS project **Universal** type and **Blank App** template. Create a Xamarin.Android project with the Android **Blank App** template, or a Windows Phone 8.1 Silverlight project by selecting **Store Apps**, then **Windows Phone Apps**, then **Blank App (Windows Phone Silverlight) template**.

For these new projects, you can get the correct references and boilerplate code by consulting the projects generated by the standard Xamarin.Forms template.

To summarize: there's really nothing all that special in a Xamarin.Forms app compared with normal Xamarin or Windows Phone projects—except the Xamarin.Forms libraries.

PCL or SAP?

When you first created the **Hello** solution, you had a choice of two application templates:

- **Blank App (Xamarin.Forms Portable)**

- **Blank App (Xamarin.Forms Shared)**

The first creates a Portable Class Library (PCL), whereas the second creates a Shared Asset Project (SAP) consisting only of shared code files. The original **Hello** solution used the PCL template. Now let's create a second solution named **HelloSap** with the SAP template.

As you'll see, everything looks pretty much the same, except that the **HelloSap** project itself contains only one item: the App.cs file.

With both the PCL and SAP approaches, code is shared among the three applications, but in decidedly different ways: With the PCL approach, all the common code is bundled into a dynamic-link library that each application project references and binds to at run time. With the SAP approach, the common code files are effectively included with the three application projects at build time. By default, the SAP has only a single file named App.cs, but effectively it's as if this **HelloSap** project did not exist and instead there were three different copies of this file in the three application projects.

Some subtle (and not-so-subtle) problems can manifest themselves with the **Blank App (Xamarin.Forms Shared)** template:

The iOS and Android projects have access to pretty much the same version of .NET, but it is not the same version of .NET that a Windows Phone project uses. This means that any .NET classes accessed by the shared code might be somewhat different depending on the platform. As you'll discover later in this book, this is the case for some file I/O classes in the `System.IO` namespace.

You can compensate for these differences by using C# preprocessor directives, particularly `#if` and `#elif`. In the projects generated by the Xamarin.Forms template, the Windows Phone and iPhone projects define symbols that you can use with these directives.

What are these symbols?

In Visual Studio, right-click the project name in the **Solution Explorer** and select **Properties**. At the left of the properties screen, select **Build**, and look for the **Conditional compilation symbols** field.

In Xamarin Studio, select an application project in the **Solution** list, invoke the drop-down tools menu, and select **Options**. In the left of the **Project Options** dialog, select **Build > Compiler**, and look for the **Define Symbols** field.

You discover that the symbol `__IOS__` is defined for the iOS project (that's two underscores before and after) and `WINDOWS_PHONE` is defined for the Windows Phone project. You won't see anything for Android, but the identifier `__ANDROID__` is defined anyway, as well as multiple `__ANDROID_nn__` identifiers, where `nn` is each Android API level supported. Your shared code file can include blocks like this:

```
#if __IOS__
            // iOS specific code
#elif __ANDROID__
            // Android specific code
#elif WINDOWS_PHONE
            // Windows Phone specific code
#endif
```

This allows your shared code files to run platform-specific code or access platform-specific classes, including classes in the individual platform projects. You can also define your own conditional compilation symbols if you'd like.

These preprocessor directives make no sense in a Portable Class Library project. The PCL is entirely independent of the three platforms, and these identifiers in the platform projects are ignored when the PCL is compiled.

The concept of the PCL originally arose because every platform that uses .NET actually uses a somewhat different subset of .NET. If you want to create a library that can be used among multiple .NET platforms, you need to use only the common parts of those .NET subsets.

The PCL is intended to help by containing code that is usable on multiple (but specific) .NET platforms. Consequently, any particular PCL contains some embedded flags that indicate what platforms it supports. A PCL used in a Xamarin.Forms application must support the following platforms:

- .NET Framework 4.5

- Windows 8

- Windows Phone Silverlight 8

- Xamarin.Android

- Xamarin.iOS

- Xamarin.iOS (Classic)

If you need platform-specific behavior in the PCL, you can't use the C# preprocessor directives because those work only at build time. You need something that works at run time, such as the Xamarin.Forms `Device` class. You'll see an example shortly.

The Xamarin.Forms PCL can access other PCLs supporting the same platforms, but it cannot directly access classes defined in the individual application projects. However, if that's something you need to do—and you'll see an example in Chapter 9—Xamarin.Forms provides a class named `Dependency-Service` that allows you to access platform-specific code from the PCL in a methodical manner.

Most of the programs in this book use the PCL approach. This is the recommended approach for Xamarin.Forms and is preferred by many programmers who have been working with Xamarin.Forms for a while. However, the SAP approach is also supported and definitely has its advocates as well. Programs within these pages that demonstrate the SAP approach contain the letters **Sap** at the end of their names, such as the **HelloSap** program.

But why choose? You can have both in the same solution. If you've created a Xamarin.Forms solution with a Shared Asset Project, you can add a new PCL project to the solution by selecting the Class Library (Xamarin.Forms Portable) template. The application projects can access both the SAP and PCL, and the SAP can access the PCL as well.

Labels for text

Let's create a new Xamarin.Forms PCL solution, named **Greetings**, using the same process described above for creating the **Hello** solution. This new solution will be structured more like a typical Xamarin.Forms program, which means that it will define a new class that derives from `ContentPage`. Most of the time in this book, every class and structure defined by a program will get its own file. This means that a new file must be added to the **Greetings** project:

In Visual Studio, you can right-click the **Greetings** project in the **Solution Explorer** and select **Add > New Item** from the menu. At the left of the **Add New Item** dialog, select **Visual C#** and **Code**, and in the center area, select **Forms ContentPage**. (Watch out: There's also a **Forms ContentView** option. Don't pick that one!)

In Xamarin Studio, from the tool icon on the **Greetings** project, select **Add > New File** from the menu. In the left of the **New File** dialog, select **Forms**, and in the central area, select **Forms**

ContentPage. (Watch out: There are also **Forms ContentView** and **Forms ContentPage Xaml** options. Don't pick those!)

In either case, give the new file a name of GreetingsPage.cs.

The GreetingsPage.cs file will be initialized with some skeleton code for a class named `Greetings-`
`Page` that derives from `ContentPage`. Because `ContentPage` is in the `Xamarin.Forms` namespace,
a `using` directive includes that namespace. The class is defined as `public`, but it need not be because
it won't be directly accessed from outside the `Greetings` project.

Let's delete all of the code in the `GreetingsPage` constructor and most of the `using` directives, so
the file looks something like this:

```
using System;
using Xamarin.Forms;

namespace Greetings
{
    class GreetingsPage : ContentPage
    {
        public GreetingsPage()
        {

        }
    }
}
```

In the constructor of the `GreetingsPage` class, instantiate a `Label` view, set its `Text` property, and
set that `Label` instance to the `Content` property that `GreetingsPage` inherits from `ContentPage`:

```
using System;
using Xamarin.Forms;

namespace Greetings
{
    class GreetingsPage : ContentPage
    {
        public GreetingsPage()
        {
            Label label = new Label();
            label.Text = "Greetings, Xamarin.Forms!";
            this.Content = label;
        }
    }
}
```

Now change the `App` class in App.cs to set the `MainPage` property to an instance of this `Greeting-`
`sPage` class:

```
using System;
using Xamarin.Forms;
```

```
namespace Greetings
{
    public class App : Application
    {
        public App()
        {
            MainPage = new GreetingsPage();
        }

        protected override void OnStart()
        {
            // Handle when your app starts
        }

        protected override void OnSleep()
        {
            // Handle when your app sleeps
        }

        protected override void OnResume()
        {
            // Handle when your app resumes
        }
    }
}
```

It's easy to forget this step, and you'll be puzzled that your program seems to completely ignore your page class and still says "Welcome to Xamarin Forms!"

It is in the `GreetingsPage` class (and others like it) where you'll be spending most of your time in early Xamarin.Forms programming. For some single-page, UI-intensive programs, this class might contain the only application code that you'll need to write. Of course, you can add additional classes to the project if you need them.

In many of the single-page sample programs in this book, the class that derives from `ContentPage` will have a name that is the same as the application but with `Page` appended. That naming convention should help you identify the code listings in this book from just the class or constructor name without seeing the entire file. In most cases, the code snippets in the pages of this book won't include the `using` directives or the `namespace` definition.

Many Xamarin.Forms programmers prefer to use the C# 3.0 style of object creation and property initialization in their page constructors. Following the `Label` constructor, a pair of curly braces enclose one or more property settings separated by commas. Here's an alternative (but functionally equivalent) `GreetingsPage` definition:

```
class GreetingsPage : ContentPage
{
    public GreetingsPage()
    {
        Label label = new Label
        {
```

```
              Text = "Greetings, Xamarin.Forms!"
        };
        this.Content = label;
    }
}
```

This style allows the `Label` instance to be set to the `Content` property directly, so the `Label` doesn't require a name, like so:

```
class GreetingsPage : ContentPage
{
    public GreetingsPage()
    {
        Content = new Label
        {
            Text = "Greetings, Xamarin.Forms!"
        };
    }
}
```

For more complex page layouts, this style of instantiation and initialization provides a better visual analogue of the organization of layouts and views on the page. However, it's not always as simple as this example might indicate if you need to call methods on these objects or set event handlers.

Whichever way you do it, if you can successfully compile and run the program on the three platforms on either an emulator or a device, here's what you'll see:

The most disappointing version of this **Greetings** program is definitely the iPhone: Beginning in iOS 7, a single-page application shares the screen with the status bar at the top. Anything the application displays at the top of its page will occupy the same space as the status bar unless the application compensates for it.

This problem disappears in multipage-navigation applications discussed later in this book, but until that time, here are four ways (or five ways if you're using an SAP) to solve this problem right away.

1. Include padding on the page

The `Page` class defines a property named `Padding` that marks an area around the interior perimeter of the page into which content cannot intrude. The `Padding` property is of type `Thickness`, a structure that defines four properties named `Left`, `Top`, `Right`, `Bottom`. (You might want to memorize that order because that's the order you'll define the properties in the `Thickness` constructor as well as in XAML.) The `Thickness` structure also defines constructors for setting the same amount of padding on all four sides or for setting the same amount on the left and right and on the top and bottom.

A little research in your favorite search engine will reveal that the iOS status bar has a height of 20. (Twenty what? you might ask. Twenty pixels? Actually, no. For now, just think of them as 20 "units." For most Xamarin.Forms programming you shouldn't need to bother with numeric sizes, but Chapter 5, "Dealing with sizes," will provide some guidance when you need to get down to the pixel level.)

You can accommodate the status bar like so:

```
namespace GreetingsSap
{
    public class GreetingsSapPage : ContentPage
    {
        public GreetingsSapPage ()
        {
            Content = new Label
            {
                Text = "Greetings, Xamarin.Forms!"
            };

            Padding = new Thickness(0, 20, 0, 0);
        }
    }
}
```

Now the greeting appears 20 units from the top of the page:

Setting the `Padding` property on the `ContentPage` solves the problem of the text overwriting the iOS status bar, but it also sets the same padding on the Android and Windows Phone, where it's not required. Is there a way to set this padding only on the iPhone?

2. Include padding just for iOS (Shared Asset Project only)

One of the advantages of the Shared Asset Project (SAP) approach is that the classes in the project are extensions of the application projects, so you can use conditional compilation directives.

Let's try this out. We'll need a new solution named **GreetingsSap** based on the SAP template, and a new page class in the **GreetingsSap** project named `GreetingsSapPage`. That class looks like this:

```
namespace GreetingsSap
{
    public class GreetingsSapPage : ContentPage
    {
        public GreetingsSapPage ()
        {
            Content = new Label
            {
                Text = "Greetings, Xamarin.Forms!"
            };

#if __IOS__

            Padding = new Thickness(0, 20, 0, 0);

#endif
        }
    }
```

```
}
```

The `#if` directive references the conditional compilation symbol `__IOS__`, so the `Padding` property is set only for the iOS project. The results look like this:

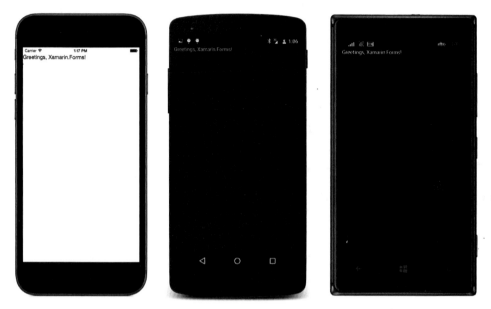

However, these conditional compilation symbols affect only the compilation of the program, so they have no effect in a PCL. Is there a way for a PCL project to include different `Padding` for the three platforms?

3. Include padding just for iOS (PCL or SAP)

Yes! The static `Device` class includes several properties and methods that allow your code to deal with device differences at run time in a very simple and straightforward manner:

- The `Device.OS` property returns a member of the `TargetPlatform` enumeration: `iOS`, `Android`, `WinPhone`, or `Other`.

- The `Device.Idiom` property returns a member of the `TargetIdiom` enumeration: `Phone`, `Tablet`, `Desktop`, or `Unsupported`. (Although Xamarin.Forms is mostly intended for phones, you can certainly experiment with deploying to tablets.)

You can use these two properties in `if` and `else` statements to execute code specific to a particular platform.

Two methods named `OnPlatform` provide even more elegant solutions:

- The static generic method `OnPlatform<T>` takes three arguments of type `T`—the first for iOS, the second for Android, and the third for Windows Phone—and returns the argument for the running platform.

- The static method `OnPlatform` has four arguments of type `Action` (the .NET function delegate that has no arguments and returns void), also in the order iOS, Android, and Windows Phone, with a fourth for a default, and executes the argument for the running platform.

The `Device` class has some other purposes as well: It defines a static method to start running a timer and another to run some code on the main thread. This latter method comes in handy when you're working with asynchronous methods and supplemental threads because code that manipulates the user interface can generally be run only on the main user-interface thread.

Rather than setting the same `Padding` property on all three platforms, you can restrict the `Padding` to just the iPhone by using the `Device.OnPlatform` generic method:

```
Padding = Device.OnPlatform<Thickness>(new Thickness(0, 20, 0, 0),
                                       new Thickness(0),
                                       new Thickness(0));
```

The first `Thickness` argument is for iOS, the second is for Android, and the third is for Windows Phone. Explicitly specifying the type of the `Device.OnPlatform` arguments within the angle brackets isn't required if the compiler can figure it out from the arguments, so this works as well:

```
Padding = Device.OnPlatform(new Thickness(0, 20, 0, 0),
                            new Thickness(0),
                            new Thickness(0));
```

Or, you can have just one `Thickness` constructor and use `Device.OnPlatform` for the second argument:

```
Padding = new Thickness(0, Device.OnPlatform(20, 0, 0), 0, 0);
```

This is how the `Padding` will usually be set in the programs that follow when it's required. Of course, you can substitute some other numbers for the 0s if you want some additional padding on the page. Sometimes a little padding on the sides makes for a more attractive display.

However, if you just need to set `Padding` for iOS, you can use the version of `Device.OnPlatform` with `Action` arguments. These arguments are `null` by default, so you can just set the first for an action to be performed on iOS:

```
class GreetingsPage : ContentPage
{
    public GreetingsPage()
    {
        Content = new Label
        {
            Text = "Greetings, Xamarin.Forms!"
        };

        Device.OnPlatform(() =>
            {
                Padding = new Thickness(0, 20, 0, 0);
```

```
        });
    }
}
```

Now the statement to set the padding is executed only when the program is running on iOS. Of course, with just that one argument to `Device.OnPlatform`, it could be a little obscure to people who need to read your code, so you might want to include the parameter name preceding the argument to make it explicit that this statement executes just for iOS:

```
Device.OnPlatform(iOS: () =>
    {
        Padding = new Thickness(0, 20, 0, 0);
    });
```

Naming the argument like that is a feature introduced in C# 4.0.

The `Device.OnPlatform` method is very handy and has the advantage of working in both PCL and SAP projects. However, it can't access APIs within the individual platforms. For that you'll need `DependencyService`, which is discussed in Chapter 9.

4. Center the label within the page

The problem with the text overlapping the iOS status bar occurs only because the text, by default, is displayed at the upper-left corner. Is it possible to center the text on the page?

Xamarin.Forms supports a number of facilities to ease layout without requiring the program to perform calculations involving sizes and coordinates. The `View` class defines two properties, named `HorizontalOptions` and `VerticalOptions`, that specify how a view is to be positioned relative to its parent (in this case the `ContentPage`). These two properties are of type `LayoutOptions`, a structure with eight public static read-only fields that return `LayoutOptions` values:

- `Start`

- `Center`

- `End`

- `Fill`

- `StartAndExpand`

- `CenterAndExpand`

- `EndAndExpand`

- `FillAndExpand`

The `LayoutOptions` structure also defines two instance properties that let you formulate these same combinations:

- An `Alignment` property of type `LayoutAlignment`, an enumeration with four members: `Start`, `Center`, `End`, and `Fill`.

- An `Expands` property of type `bool`.

A fuller explanation of how these work awaits you in Chapter 4, "Scrolling the stack," but for now you can set the `HorizontalOptions` and `VerticalOptions` properties of the `Label` to one of the static fields defined by `LayoutOptions` values. For `HorizontalOptions`, the word `Start` means left and `End` means right; for `VerticalOptions`, `Start` means top and `End` means bottom.

Mastering the use of the `HorizontalOptions` and `VerticalOptions` properties is a major part of acquiring skill in the Xamarin.Forms layout system, but here's a simple example that positions the `Label` in the center of the page:

```
class GreetingsPage : ContentPage
{
    public GreetingsPage()
    {
        Content = new Label
        {
            Text = "Greetings, Xamarin.Forms!",
            HorizontalOptions = LayoutOptions.Center,
            VerticalOptions = LayoutOptions.Center
        };
    }
}
```

Here's how it looks:

This is the version of the **Greetings** program that is included in the sample code for this chapter. You can use various combinations of `HorizontalOptions` and `VerticalOptions` to position the text in any of nine places relative to the page.

5. Center the text within the label

The `Label` is intended to display text up to a paragraph in length. It is often desirable to control how the lines of text are horizontally aligned: left justified, right justified, or centered.

The `Label` view defines an `XAlign` property for that purpose and also a `YAlign` property for positioning text vertically. Both properties are set to a member of the `TextAlignment` enumeration, which has members named `Start`, `Center`, and `End` to be versatile enough for text that runs from right to left or from top to bottom. For English and other European languages, `Start` means left or top and `End` means right or bottom.

For this final solution to the iOS status bar problem, set `XAlign` and `YAlign` to `TextAlignment.Center`:

```
class GreetingsPage : ContentPage
{
    public GreetingsPage()
    {
        Content = new Label
        {
            Text = "Greetings, Xamarin.Forms!",
            XAlign = TextAlignment.Center,
            YAlign = TextAlignment.Center
        };
    }
}
```

Visually, the result with this single line of text is the same as setting `HorizontalOptions` and `VerticalOptions` to `Center`, and you can also use various combinations of these properties to position the text in one of nine different locations around the page.

However, these two techniques to center the text are actually quite different, as you'll see in the next chapter.

Chapter 3
Deeper into text

Despite how graphical user interfaces have become, text remains the backbone of most applications. Yet text is potentially one of the most complex visual objects because it carries baggage of hundreds of years of typography. The primary consideration is that text must be readable. This requires that text not be too small, yet text mustn't be so large that it hogs a lot of space on the screen.

For these reasons, the subject of text is continued in several subsequent chapters, most notably Chapter 5, "Dealing with sizes." Very often, Xamarin.Forms programmers define font characteristics in styles, which are the subject of Chapter 12.

Wrapping paragraphs

Displaying a paragraph of text is as easy as displaying a single line of text. Just make the text long enough to wrap into multiple lines:

```
public class BaskervillesPage : ContentPage
{
    public BaskervillesPage()
    {
        Content = new Label
        {
            VerticalOptions = LayoutOptions.Center,
            Text =
                "Mr. Sherlock Holmes, who was usually very late in " +
                "the mornings, save upon those not infrequent " +
                "occasions when he was up all night, was seated at " +
                "the breakfast table. I stood upon the hearth-rug " +
                "and picked up the stick which our visitor had left " +
                "behind him the night before. It was a fine, thick " +
                "piece of wood, bulbous-headed, of the sort which " +
                "is known as a \u201CPenang lawyer.\u201D Just " +
                "under the head was a broad silver band, nearly an " +
                "inch across, \u201CTo James Mortimer, M.R.C.S., " +
                "from his friends of the C.C.H.,\u201D was engraved " +
                "upon it, with the date \u201C1884.\u201D It was " +
                "just such a stick as the old-fashioned family " +
                "practitioner used to carry\u2014dignified, solid, " +
                "and reassuring."
        };

        Padding = new Thickness(5, Device.OnPlatform(20, 5, 5), 5, 5);
    }
}
```

Notice the use of embedded Unicode codes for opened and closed "smart quotes" (\u201C and \u201D) and the em dash (\u2014). `Padding` has been set for 5 units around the page to avoid the text butting up against the edges of the screen, but the `VerticalOptions` property has been used as well to vertically center the entire paragraph on the page:

For this paragraph of text, setting `HorizontalOptions` will shift the entire paragraph horizontally slightly to the left, center, or right. The shifting is only slight because the width of the paragraph is the width of the longest line of text. Since word wrapping is governed by the page width (minus the padding), the paragraph likely occupies just slightly less width than the width available for it on the page.

But setting `XAlign` has a much more profound effect: Setting this property affects the alignment of the individual lines. A setting of `TextAlignment.Center` will center all the lines of the paragraph, and `TextAlignment.Right` aligns them all at the right. You can use `HorizontalOptions` in addition to `XAlign` to shift the entire paragraph slightly to the center or the right.

However, after you've set `VerticalOptions` to `Start`, `Center`, or `End`, any setting of `YAlign` has no effect.

`Label` defines a `LineBreakMode` property that you can set to a member of the `LineBreakMode` enumeration if you don't want the text to wrap, or to select truncation options.

There is no property to specify a first-line indent for the paragraph, but you can add one of your own with space characters of various types, such as the em space (Unicode \u2003).

You can display multiple paragraphs with a single `Label` view by ending each paragraph with one or more line feed characters (\n). However, it makes more sense to use a separate `Label` view for each paragraph, as will be demonstrated in Chapter 4, "Scrolling the stack."

The `Label` class has lots of formatting flexibility. As you'll see shortly, properties defined by `Label` allow you to specify a font size or bold or italic text, and you can also specify different text formatting within a single paragraph.

`Label` also allows specifying color, and a little experimentation with color will demonstrate the profound difference between `HorizontalOptions` and `VerticalOptions` and `XAlign` and `YAlign`.

Text and background colors

As you've seen, the `Label` view displays text in a color appropriate for the device. You can override that behavior by setting two properties, named `TextColor` and `BackgroundColor`. `Label` itself defines `TextColor`, but it inherits `BackgroundColor` from `VisualElement`, which means that `Page` and `Layout` also have a `BackgroundColor` property.

You set `TextColor` and `BackgroundColor` to a value of type `Color`, which is a structure that defines 17 static fields for obtaining common colors. You can experiment with these properties with the **Greetings** program from the previous chapter. Here are two of them used in conjunction with `XAlign` and `YAlign` to center the text:

```
class GreetingsPage : ContentPage
{
    public GreetingsPage()
    {
        Content = new Label
        {
            Text = "Greetings, Xamarin.Forms!",
            XAlign = TextAlignment.Center,
            YAlign = TextAlignment.Center,
            BackgroundColor = Color.Yellow,
            TextColor = Color.Blue
        };
    }
}
```

The result might surprise you. As these screenshots illustrate, the `Label` actually occupies the entire area of the page (including underneath the iOS status bar), and the `XAlign` and `YAlign` properties position the text within that area:

Here's some code that colors the text the same but instead centers the text using the HorizontalOptions and VerticalOptions properties:

```
class GreetingsPage : ContentPage
{
    public GreetingsPage()
    {
        Content = new Label
        {
            Text = "Greetings, Xamarin.Forms!",
            HorizontalOptions = LayoutOptions.Center,
            VerticalOptions = LayoutOptions.Center,
            BackgroundColor = Color.Yellow,
            TextColor = Color.Blue
        };
    }
}
```

Now the Label occupies only as much space as required for the text, and that's what's positioned in the center of the page:

The default value of `HorizontalOptions` and `VerticalOptions` is not `LayoutOptions.Start`, as the default appearance of the text might suggest. The default value is instead `LayoutOp-tions.Fill`. This is the setting that causes the `Label` to fill the page. The default `XAlign` and `YAlign` value of `TextAlignment.Start` is what caused the text to be positioned at the upper-left in the first version of the **Greetings** program in the previous chapter.

You might wonder: what are the default values of the `TextColor` and `BackgroundColor` proper-ties, because the default values result in different colors for the different platforms?

The default value of `TextColor` and `BackgroundColor` is actually a special color value named `Color.Default`, which does not represent a real color but instead is used to reference the text and background colors appropriate for the particular platform.

Let's explore color in more detail.

The Color structure

Internally, the `Color` structure stores colors in two different ways:

- As red, green, and blue (RGB) values of type `double` that range from 0 to 1. Read-only proper-ties named `R`, `G`, and `B` expose these values.

- As hue, saturation, and luminosity values of type `double`, which also range from 0 to 1. These values are exposed with read-only properties named `Hue`, `Saturation`, and `Luminosity`.

The `Color` structure also supports an alpha channel for indicating degrees of opacity. A read-only property named `A` exposes this value, which ranges from 0 for transparent to 1 for opaque. All these properties are read-only. Once created, a `Color` value is immutable.

You can create a `Color` value in one of several ways. The three constructors are the easiest:

- `new Color(double grayShade)`

- `new Color(double r, double g, double b)`

- `new Color(double r, double g, double b, double a)`

Arguments can range from 0 to 1. `Color` also defines several static creation methods, including:

- `Color.FromRgb(double r, double g, double b)`

- `Color.FromRgb(int r, int g, int b)`

- `Color.FromRgba(double r, double g, double b, double a)`

- `Color.FromRgba(int r, int g, int b, int a)`

- `Color.FromHsla(double h, double s, double l, double a)`

The two static methods with integer arguments assume that the values range from 0 to 255, which is the customary representation of RGB colors. Internally, the constructor simply divides the integer values by 255.0 to convert to `double`.

Watch out! You might think that you're creating a red color with this call:

```
Color.FromRgb(1, 0, 0)
```

However, the C# compiler will assume that these arguments are integers. The integer method will be invoked, and the first argument will be divided by 255.0, with a result that is nearly zero. If you want the method that has `double` arguments, be explicit:

```
Color.FromRgb(1.0, 0, 0)
```

`Color` also defines static creation methods for a packed `uint` format and a hexadecimal format in a string, but these are used less frequently.

The `Color` structure also defines 17 public static read-only fields of type `Color`. In the table below, the integer RGB values that the `Color` structure uses internally to define these fields are shown together with the corresponding `Hue`, `Saturation`, and `Luminosity` values, somewhat rounded for purposes of clarity:

Color Fields	Color	Red	Green	Blue	Hue	Saturation	Luminosity
White		255	255	255	0	0	1.00
Silver		192	192	192	0	0	0.75
Gray		128	128	128	0	0	0.50
Black		0	0	0	0	0	0
Red		255	0	0	1.00	1	0.50
Maroon		128	0	0	1.00	1	0.25
Yellow		255	255	0	0.17	1	0.50
Olive		128	128	0	0.17	1	0.25
Lime		0	255	0	0.33	1	0.50
Green		0	128	0	0.33	1	0.25
Aqua		0	255	255	0.50	1	0.50
Teal		0	128	128	0.50	1	0.25
Blue		0	0	255	0.67	1	0.50
Navy		0	0	128	0.67	1	0.25
Pink		255	102	255	0.83	1	0.70
Fuchsia		255	0	255	0.83	1	0.50
Purple		128	0	128	0.83	1	0.25

With the exception of Pink, you might recognize these as the color names supported in HTML. An 18th public static read-only field is named Transparent, which has R, G, B, and A properties all set to zero.

When people are given an opportunity to interactively formulate a color, the HSL color model is often more intuitive than RGB. The Hue cycles through the colors of the visible spectrum (and the rainbow) beginning with red at 0, green at 0.33, blue at 0.67, and back to red at 1.

The Saturation indicates the degree of the hue in the color, ranging from 0, which is no hue at all and results in a gray shade, to 1 for full saturation.

The Luminosity is a measure of lightness, ranging from 0 for black to 1 for white.

Color-selection programs in Chapter 15, "The interactive interface," let you explore the RGB and HSL models more interactively.

The Color structure includes several interesting instance methods that allow creating new colors that are modifications of existing colors:

- AddLuminosity(double delta)

- MultiplyAlpha(double alpha)

- WithHue(double newHue)

- WithLuminosity(double newLuminosity)

- WithSaturation(double newSaturation)

Finally, Color defines two special static read-only properties of type Color:

- `Color.Default`

- `Color.Accent`

The `Color.Default` property is used extensively with Xamarin.Forms to define the default color of views. The `VisualElement` class initializes its `BackgroundColor` property to `Color.Default`, and the `Label` class initializes its `TextColor` property as `Color.Default`.

However, `Color.Default` is a `Color` value with its `R`, `G`, `B`, and `A` properties all set to −1, which means that it's a special "mock" value that means nothing in itself but indicates that the actual value is platform specific.

For `Label` and `ContentPage` (and most classes that derive from `VisualElement`), the `BackgroundColor` setting of `Color.Default` means transparent.

On the `Label`, the `TextColor` value of `Color.Default` means black on an iOS device, white on an Android device, and either white or black on Windows Phone, depending on the color theme selected by the user.

Without you writing code that digs into platform-specific user-interface objects, your Xamarin.Forms program cannot determine whether the underlying color scheme is white-on-black or black-on-white. This can be a little frustrating if you want to create colors that are compatible with the color scheme—for example, a dark-blue text color if the default background is white or light-yellow text if the default background is dark.

You have a couple of strategies for working with color: You can choose to do your Xamarin.Forms programming in a very platform-independent manner and avoid making any assumptions about the default color scheme of any phone. Or, you can use your knowledge about the color schemes of the various platforms and use `Device.OnPlatform` to specify platform-specific colors.

But don't try to just ignore all the platform defaults and explicitly set all the colors in your application to your own color scheme. This probably won't work as well as you hope because many views use other colors that relate to the color theme of the operating system but that are not exposed through Xamarin.Forms properties.

One straightforward option is to use the `Color.Accent` property for an alternative text color. On the iPhone and Android platforms, it's a color that is visible against the default background, but it's not the default text color. On Windows Phone, it's a color selected by the user as part of the color theme.

You can make text semitransparent by setting `TextColor` to a `Color` value with an `A` property less than 1. However, if you want a semitransparent version of the default text color, use the `Opacity` property of the `Label` instead. This property is defined by the `VisualElement` class and has a default value of 1. Set it to values less than 1 for various degrees of transparency.

Font sizes and attributes

The `Label` uses a default (or system) font defined by each platform, but `Label` also defines several properties that you can use to change this font. `Label` is one of only two classes with these font-related properties; `Button` is the other.

The properties that let you change this font are:

- `FontFamily` of type `string`

- `FontSize` of type `double`

- `FontAttributes` of type `FontAttributes`, an enumeration with three members: `None`, `Bold`, and `Italic`.

There is also a `Font` property and corresponding `Font` structure, but this is deprecated and should not be used.

The hardest of these to use is `FontFamily`. In theory you can set it to a font family name such as "Times Roman," but it will work only if that particular font family is supported on the particular platform. For this reason, you'll probably use `FontFamily` in connection with `Device.OnPlatform`, and you'll need to know each platform's supported font family names. For this reason, a demonstration of `FontFamily` must await a future chapter.

The `FontSize` property is a little awkward as well. You need a number that roughly indicates the height of the font, but what numbers should you use? This is a thorny issue, and for that reason, it's relegated to Chapter 5, "Dealing with sizes," when the tools to pick a good font size will become available.

Until then, however, the `Device` class helps out with a static method called `GetNamedSize`. This method requires a member of the `NamedSize` enumeration:

- `Default`

- `Micro`

- `Small`

- `Medium`

- `Large`

`GetNamedSize` also requires the type of the class you're sizing with this font size, and that argument will be either `typeof(Label)` or `typeof(Button)`. You can also use an instance of `Label` or `Button` itself rather than the `Type`, but this is often inconvenient.

A warning: specifying `NamedSize.Medium` does not necessarily return the same size as `NamedSize.Default`.

`FontAttributes` is the least complicated of the three font-related properties to use. You can specify `Bold` or `Italic` or both, as this little snippet of code (adapted from the **Greetings** program from the previous chapter) demonstrates:

```
class GreetingsPage : ContentPage
{
    public GreetingsPage()
    {
        Content = new Label
        {
            Text = "Greetings, Xamarin.Forms!",
            HorizontalOptions = LayoutOptions.Center,
            VerticalOptions = LayoutOptions.Center,
            FontSize = Device.GetNamedSize(NamedSize.Large, typeof(Label)),
            FontAttributes = FontAttributes.Bold | FontAttributes.Italic
        };
    }
}
```

Here it is on the three platforms:

Formatted text

As you've seen, `Label` has a `Text` property that you can set to a string. But `Label` also has an alternative `FormattedText` property that constructs a paragraph with nonuniform formatting.

The `FormattedText` property is of type `FormattedString`, which has a `Spans` property of type

`IList<Span>`, a collection of `Span` objects. Each `Span` object is a uniformly formatted chunk of text that is governed by six properties:

- `Text`

- `FontFamily`

- `FontSize`

- `FontAttributes`

- `ForegroundColor`

- `BackgroundColor`

Here's one way to instantiate a `FormattedString` object and then add `Span` instances to its `Spans` collection property:

```
public class VariableFormattedTextPage : ContentPage
{
    public VariableFormattedTextPage()
    {
        FormattedString formattedString = new FormattedString();

        formattedString.Spans.Add(new Span
        {
            Text = "I "
        });

        formattedString.Spans.Add(new Span
        {
            Text = "love",
            FontSize = Device.GetNamedSize(NamedSize.Large, typeof(Label)),
            FontAttributes = FontAttributes.Bold
        });

        formattedString.Spans.Add(new Span
        {
            Text = " Xamarin.Forms!"
        });

        Content = new Label
        {
            FormattedText = formattedString,
            HorizontalOptions = LayoutOptions.Center,
            VerticalOptions = LayoutOptions.Center,
            FontSize = Device.GetNamedSize(NamedSize.Large, typeof(Label))
        };
    }
}
```

As each `Span` is created, it is directly passed to the `Add` method of the `Spans` collection. Notice that the Label is given a FontSize of NamedSize.Large, and the Span with the Bold setting is also explicitly given that same size. When a Span is given a FontAttributes setting, it does not currently inherit the FontSize setting of the Label.

Alternatively, it's possible to initialize the contents of the Spans collection by following it with a pair of curly braces. Within these curly braces, the Span objects are instantiated. Because no method calls are required, the entire FormattedString initialization can occur within the Label initialization:

```
public class VariableFormattedTextPage : ContentPage
{
    public VariableFormattedTextPage()
    {
        Content = new Label
        {
            FormattedText = new FormattedString
            {
                Spans =
                {
                    new Span
                    {
                        Text = "I "
                    },
                    new Span
                    {
                        Text = "love",
                        FontSize = Device.GetNamedSize(NamedSize.Large, typeof(Label)),
                        FontAttributes = FontAttributes.Bold
                    },
                    new Span
                    {
                        Text = " Xamarin.Forms!"
                    }
                }
            },

            HorizontalOptions = LayoutOptions.Center,
            VerticalOptions = LayoutOptions.Center,
            FontSize = Device.GetNamedSize(NamedSize.Large, typeof(Label))
        };
    }
}
```

This is the version of the program that you'll see in the collection of sample code for this chapter. Regardless of which approach you use, here's what it looks like:

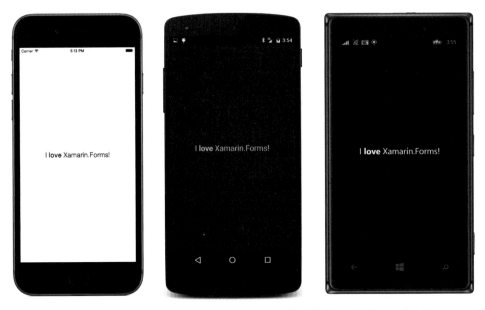

You can also use the `FormattedText` property to embed italic or bold words within an entire paragraph, as the **VariableFormattedParagraph** program demonstrates:

```
public class VariableFormattedParagraphPage : ContentPage
{
    public VariableFormattedParagraphPage()
    {
        Content = new Label
        {
            FormattedText = new FormattedString
            {
                Spans =
                {
                    new Span
                    {
                        Text = "\u2003There was nothing so "
                    },
                    new Span
                    {
                        Text = "very",
                        FontAttributes = FontAttributes.Italic
                    },
                    new Span
                    {
                        Text = " remarkable in that; nor did Alice " +
                                "think it so "
                    },
                    new Span
                    {
                        Text = "very",
                        FontAttributes = FontAttributes.Italic
```

```
                },
                new Span
                {
                    Text = " much out of the way to hear the " +
                           "Rabbit say to itself \u2018Oh " +
                           "dear! Oh dear! I shall be too late!" +
                           "\u2019 (when she thought it over " +
                           "afterwards, it occurred to her that " +
                           "she ought to have wondered at this, " +
                           "but at the time it all seemed quite " +
                           "natural); but, when the Rabbit actually "
                },
                new Span
                {
                    Text = "took a watch out of its waistcoat-pocket",
                    FontAttributes = FontAttributes.Italic
                },
                new Span
                {
                    Text = ", and looked at it, and then hurried on, " +
                           "Alice started to her feet, for it flashed " +
                           "across her mind that she had never before " +
                           "seen a rabbit with either a waistcoat-" +
                           "pocket, or a watch to take out of it, " +
                           "and, burning with curiosity, she ran " +
                           "across the field after it, and was just " +
                           "in time to see it pop down a large " +
                           "rabbit-hold under the hedge."
                }
            }
        },

        HorizontalOptions = LayoutOptions.Center,
        VerticalOptions = LayoutOptions.Center
    };
  }
}
```

The paragraph begins with an em space (Unicode \u2003) and contains so-called smart quotes (\u201C and \u201D), and several words are italicized:

You can persuade a single `Label` to display multiple lines or paragraphs with the insertion of line-feed characters (\n). This is demonstrated in the **NamedFontSizes** program. Multiple `Span` objects are added to a `FormattedString` object in a `foreach` loop. Each `Span` object uses a different `NamedFont` value and also displays the actual size returned from `Device.GetNamedSize`:

```csharp
public class NamedFontSizesPage : ContentPage
{
    public NamedFontSizesPage()
    {
        FormattedString formattedString = new FormattedString();
        NamedSize[] namedSizes =
        {
            NamedSize.Default, NamedSize.Micro, NamedSize.Small,
            NamedSize.Medium, NamedSize.Large
        };

        foreach (NamedSize namedSize in namedSizes)
        {
            double fontSize = Device.GetNamedSize(namedSize, typeof(Label));

            formattedString.Spans.Add(new Span
                {
                    Text = String.Format("Named Size = {0} ({1:F2})",
                                         namedSize, fontSize),
                    FontSize = fontSize
                });

            if (namedSize != namedSizes.Last())
            {
                formattedString.Spans.Add(new Span
                    {
```

```
                    Text = "\n\n"
                });
            }
        }

        Content = new Label
        {
            FormattedText = formattedString,
            HorizontalOptions = LayoutOptions.Center,
            VerticalOptions = LayoutOptions.Center
        };
    }
}
```

Notice that a separate `Span` contains the two line-feed characters to space the individual lines. This ensures that the line spacing is based on the default font size rather than the font size just displayed:

These are not pixel sizes! As with the height of the iOS status bar, it's best to refer to these sizes only vaguely as some kind of "units." Some additional clarity is coming in Chapter 5.

Of course, the use of multiple `Span` objects in a single `Label` is not a good way to render multiple paragraphs of text. Moreover, text often has so many paragraphs that it must be scrolled. This is the job for the next chapter and its exploration of `StackLayout` and `ScrollView`.

Chapter 4
Scrolling the stack

If you're like most programmers, as soon as you saw that list of static `Color` properties in the previous chapter, you wanted to write a program to display them all, perhaps using the `Text` property of `Label` to identify the color, and the `TextColor` property to show the actual color.

Although you could do this with a single `Label` using a `FormattedString` object, it's much easier with multiple `Label` objects. Because multiple `Label` objects are involved, this job also requires some way to display all the `Label` objects on the screen.

The `ContentPage` class defines a `Content` property of type `View` that you can set to an object— but only one object. Displaying multiple views requires setting `Content` to an instance of a class that can have multiple children of type `View`. Such a class is `Layout<T>`, which defines a `Children` property of type `IList<T>`.

The `Layout<T>` class is abstract, but four classes derive from `Layout<View>`, a class that can have multiple children of type `View`. In alphabetical order, these four classes are:

- `AbsoluteLayout`

- `Grid`

- `RelativeLayout`

- `StackLayout`

Each of them arranges its children in a characteristic manner. This chapter focuses on `StackLayout`.

Stacks of views

The `StackLayout` class arranges its children in a stack. It defines only two properties on its own:

- `Orientation` of type `StackOrientation`, an enumeration with two members: `Vertical` (the default) and `Horizontal`.

- `Spacing` of type `double`, initialized to 6.

`StackLayout` seems ideal for the job of listing colors. You can use the `Add` method defined by `IList<T>` to add children to the `Children` collection of a `StackLayout` instance. Here's some code that creates multiple `Label` objects from two arrays and then adds each `Label` to the `Children` collection of a `StackLayout`:

```
Color[] colors =
```

```
{
    Color.White, Color.Silver, Color.Gray, Color.Black, Color.Red,
    Color.Maroon, Color.Yellow, Color.Olive, Color.Lime, Color.Green,
    Color.Aqua, Color.Teal, Color.Blue, Color.Navy, Color.Pink,
    Color.Fuchsia, Color.Purple
};

string[] colorNames =
{
    "White", "Silver", "Gray", "Black", "Red",
    "Maroon", "Yellow", "Olive", "Lime", "Green",
    "Aqua", "Teal", "Blue", "Navy", "Pink",
    "Fuchsia", "Purple"
};

StackLayout stackLayout = new StackLayout();

for (int i = 0; i < colors.Length; i++)
{
    Label label = new Label
    {
        Text = colorNames[i],
        TextColor = colors[i],
        FontSize = Device.GetNamedSize(NamedSize.Large, typeof(Label))
    };
    stackLayout.Children.Add(label);
}
```

The `StackLayout` object can then be set to the `Content` property of the page.

But the technique of using parallel arrays is rather perilous. What if they're out of sync or have a different number of elements? A better approach is to keep the color and name together, perhaps in a tiny structure with `Color` and `Name` fields, or as an array of `Tuple<Color, string>` values, or as an anonymous type, as demonstrated in the **ColorLoop** program:

```
class ColorLoopPage : ContentPage
{
    public ColorLoopPage()
    {
        var colors = new[]
        {
            new { value = Color.White, name = "White" },
            new { value = Color.Silver, name = "Silver" },
            new { value = Color.Gray, name = "Gray" },
            new { value = Color.Black, name = "Black" },
            new { value = Color.Red, name = "Red" },
            new { value = Color.Maroon, name = "Maroon" },
            new { value = Color.Yellow, name = "Yellow" },
            new { value = Color.Olive, name = "Olive" },
            new { value = Color.Lime, name = "Lime" },
            new { value = Color.Green, name = "Green" },
            new { value = Color.Aqua, name = "Aqua" },
            new { value = Color.Teal, name = "Teal" },
```

```
                    new { value = Color.Blue, name = "Blue" },
                    new { value = Color.Navy, name = "Navy" },
                    new { value = Color.Pink, name = "Pink" },
                    new { value = Color.Fuchsia, name = "Fuchsia" },
                    new { value = Color.Purple, name = "Purple" }
            };

            StackLayout stackLayout = new StackLayout();

            foreach (var color in colors)
            {
                stackLayout.Children.Add(
                    new Label
                    {
                        Text = color.name,
                        TextColor = color.value,
                        FontSize = Device.GetNamedSize(NamedSize.Large, typeof(Label))
                    });
            }

            Padding = new Thickness(5, Device.OnPlatform(20, 5, 5), 5, 5);
            Content = stackLayout;
        }
    }
```

Or you can initialize the `Children` property of `StackLayout` with an explicit collection of views (similar to the way the `Spans` collection of a `FormattedString` object was initialized in the previous chapter). The **ColorList** program sets the `Content` property of the page to a `StackLayout` object, which then has its `Children` property initialized with 17 `Label` views:

```
class ColorListPage : ContentPage
{
    public ColorListPage()
    {
        Padding = new Thickness (5, Device.OnPlatform (20, 5, 5), 5, 5);
        double fontSize = Device.GetNamedSize(NamedSize.Large, typeof(Label));
        Content = new StackLayout
        {
            Children =
            {
                new Label
                {
                    Text = "White",
                    TextColor = Color.White,
                    FontSize = fontSize
                },
                new Label
                {
                    Text = "Silver",
                    TextColor = Color.Silver,
                    FontSize = fontSize
                },
```

```
            ...
            new Label
            {
                Text = "Fuchsia",
                TextColor = Color.Fuchsia,
                FontSize = fontSize
            },
            new Label
            {
                Text = "Purple",
                TextColor = Color.Purple,
                FontSize = fontSize
            }
        }
    };
}
}
```

You don't need to see the code for all 17 children to get the idea! Regardless of how you fill the `Children` collection, here's the result:

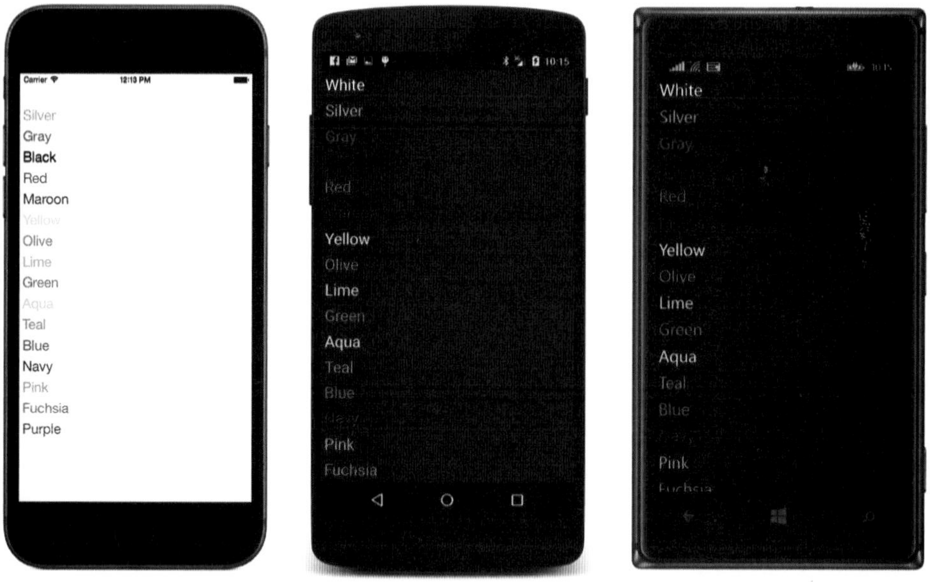

Obviously, this isn't optimum. Some colors aren't visible at all, and some of them are too faint to read well. Moreover, the list overflows the page on two platforms, and there's no way to scroll it up.

One solution is to reduce the text size. Instead of using `NamedSize.Large`, try one of the smaller values.

Another solution is in `StackLayout` itself: `StackLayout` defines a `Spacing` property of type `double` that indicates how much space to leave between the children. By default, it's 6.0, but you can set it to something smaller (for example, zero) to help ensure that all the items will fit:

```
Content = new StackLayout
{
    Spacing = 0,
    Children =
    {
        new Label
        {
            Text = "White",
            TextColor = Color.White,
            FontSize = fontSize
        },
        ...
```

Now all the `Label` views occupy only as much vertical space as required for the text. You can even set `Spacing` to negative values to make the items overlap!

Scrolling isn't automatic and must be added with a `ScrollView`. But there's another issue with these programs: they need to either explicitly create an array of colors and names or explicitly create `Label` views for each color. This is somewhat tedious, and hence somewhat repulsive, to programmers. Might it be automated?

Scrolling content

Keep in mind that a Xamarin.Forms program has access to the .NET base class libraries and can use .NET reflection to obtain information about all the classes and structures defined in an assembly, such as Xamarin.Forms.Core. This suggests that obtaining the static fields and properties of the `Color` structure can be automated.

Most .NET reflection begins with a `Type` object. You can obtain a `Type` object for any class or structure by using the C# `typeof` operator. For example, the expression `typeof(Color)` returns a `Type` object for the `Color` structure.

In the version of .NET available in the PCL, an extension method for the `Type` class, named `GetTypeInfo`, returns a `TypeInfo` object from which additional information can be obtained. But that's not required in this program. Instead, other extension methods are defined for the `Type` class, named `GetRuntimeFields` and `GetRuntimeProperties`, that return the fields and properties of the type. These are in the form of collections of `FieldInfo` and `PropertyInfo` objects. From these, the names as well as the values of the properties can be obtained.

This is demonstrated by the **ReflectedColors** program. The ReflectedColorsPage.cs file requires a `using` directive for `System.Reflection`.

In two separate `foreach` statements, the `ReflectedColorsPage` class loops through all the fields and properties of the `Color` structure. For all the public static members that return `Color` values, the two loops call `CreateColorLabel` to create a `Label` with the `Color` value and name and then add that `Label` to the `StackLayout`.

By including all the public static fields and properties, the program lists `Color.Transparent`, `Color.Default`, and `Color.Accent` along with the 17 static fields displayed in the earlier program.

```
public class ReflectedColorsPage : ContentPage
{
    public ReflectedColorsPage()
    {
        StackLayout stackLayout = new StackLayout();

        // Loop through the Color structure fields.
        foreach (FieldInfo info in typeof(Color).GetRuntimeFields())
        {
            // Skip the obsolete (i.e. misspelled) colors.
            if (info.GetCustomAttribute<ObsoleteAttribute>() != null)
                continue;

            if (info.IsPublic &&
                info.IsStatic &&
                info.FieldType == typeof(Color))
            {
                stackLayout.Children.Add(
                    CreateColorLabel((Color)info.GetValue(null), info.Name));
            }
        }

        // Loop through the Color structure properties.
        foreach (PropertyInfo info in typeof(Color).GetRuntimeProperties())
        {
            MethodInfo methodInfo = info.GetMethod;

            if (methodInfo.IsPublic &&
                methodInfo.IsStatic &&
                methodInfo.ReturnType == typeof(Color))
            {
                stackLayout.Children.Add(
                    CreateColorLabel((Color)info.GetValue(null), info.Name));
            }
        }

        Padding = new Thickness(5, Device.OnPlatform(20, 5, 5), 5, 5);

        // Put the StackLayout in a ScrollView.
        Content = new ScrollView
        {
            Content = stackLayout
        };
    }

    Label CreateColorLabel(Color color, string name)
    {
        Color backgroundColor = Color.Default;
```

```
        if (color != Color.Default)
        {
            // Standard luminance calculation.
            double luminance = 0.30 * color.R +
                               0.59 * color.G +
                               0.11 * color.B;

            backgroundColor = luminance > 0.5 ? Color.Black : Color.White;
        }

        // Create the Label.
        return new Label
        {
            Text = name,
            TextColor = color,
            FontSize = Device.GetNamedSize(NamedSize.Large, typeof(Label)),
            BackgroundColor = backgroundColor
        };
    }
}
```

Toward the end of the constructor, the StackLayout is set to the Content property of a ScrollView, which is then set to the Content property of the page.

When using code to add children to a StackLayout, it's usually a good idea for the StackLayout to be disconnected from the page that will eventually display it. Every new child added to StackLayout causes the size of the StackLayout to change, and if the StackLayout is connected to the page, a lot of layout goes on that isn't really required.

The CreateColorLabel method in the class attempts to make each color visible by setting a contrasting background. The method calculates a luminance value based on a standard weighted average of the red, green, and blue components and then selects a background of either white or black.

This technique won't work for Transparent, so that item can't be displayed at all, and the method treats Color.Default as a special case and displays that color (whatever it may be) against a Color.Default background.

Here are the results, which are still quite short of being aesthetically satisfying:

But you can scroll the display because the `StackLayout` is the child of a `ScrollView`. You'll recall that the `Layout<T>` class defines the `Children` property that `StackLayout` inherits. The generic `Layout<T>` class derives from the nongeneric `Layout` class, and `ScrollView` also derives from this nongeneric `Layout`. Theoretically, `ScrollView` is a type of layout object—even though it has only one child.

As you can see from the screen shot, the background color of the `Label` extends to the full width of the `StackLayout`, which means that each `Label` is as wide as the `StackLayout`.

Let's experiment a bit to get a better understanding of Xamarin.Forms layout. For these experiments, you might want to temporarily give the `StackLayout` and the `ScrollView` distinct background colors:

```
public ReflectedColorsPage()
{
    StackLayout stackLayout = new StackLayout
    {
        BackgroundColor = Color.Blue
    };
    ...
    Content = new ScrollView
    {
        BackgroundColor = Color.Red,
        Content = stackLayout
    };
}
```

Layout objects usually have transparent backgrounds by default. Although they occupy an area on the screen, they are not directly visible. Giving layout objects temporary colors is a great way to see exactly where they are on the screen. It's a good debugging technique for complex layouts.

You will discover that the blue `StackLayout` peeks out in the space between the individual `Label` views—this is a result of the default `Spacing` property of `StackLayout`—and also through the `Label` for `Color.Default`, which has a transparent background.

Try setting the `HorizontalOptions` property of all the `Label` views to `LayoutOptions.Start`:

```
return new Label
{
    Text = name,
    TextColor = color,
    FontSize = Device.GetNamedSize(NamedSize.Large, typeof(Label)),
    BackgroundColor = backgroundColor,
    HorizontalOptions = LayoutOptions.Start
};
```

Now the blue background of the `StackLayout` is even more prominent because all the `Label` views occupy only as much horizontal space as the text requires, and they are all pushed over to the left side. Because each `Label` view is a different width, this display looks even uglier than the first version!

Now remove the `HorizontalOptions` setting from the `Label`, and instead set a `HorizontalOptions` on the `StackLayout`:

```
StackLayout stackLayout = new StackLayout
{
    BackgroundColor = Color.Blue,
    HorizontalOptions = LayoutOptions.Start
};
```

Now the `StackLayout` becomes only as wide as the widest `Label`. The `StackLayout` hugs the labels within the `ScrollView`—at the left on iPhone and Android, and in the center (oddly enough) on Windows Phone—with the red background of the `ScrollView` now clearly in view.

As you begin constructing a tree of visual objects, these objects acquire a parent-child relationship. A parent object is sometimes referred to as the *container* of its child or children because the child's location and size is contained within its parent.

By default, `HorizontalOptions` and `VerticalOptions` are set to `LayoutOptions.Fill`, which means that child views attempt to fill the parent container. (At least with the containers encountered so far. As you'll see, other layout classes have somewhat different behavior.) Even a `Label` fills its parent container by default, although without a background color, the `Label` appears to occupy only as much space as it requires.

Setting a view's `HorizontalOptions` or `VerticalOptions` property to `LayoutOptions.Start`, `Center`, or `End` effectively forces the view to shrink down—either horizontally, vertically, or both—to only the size the view requires.

A StackLayout has this same effect on its child's vertical size: every child in a StackLayout occupies only as much height as it requires. Setting the VerticalOptions property on a child of a Stack-Layout to Start, Center, or End has no effect! However, the child views still expand to fill the width of the StackLayout, except when the children are given a HorizontalOptions property other than LayoutOptions.Fill.

If a StackLayout is set to the Content property of a ContentPage, you can set HorizontalOptions or VerticalOptions on the StackLayout. These properties have two effects: first, they shrink the StackLayout width or height (or both) to the size of its children, and second, they govern where the StackLayout is positioned relative to the page.

If a StackLayout is in a ScrollView, the ScrollView causes the StackLayout to be only as tall as the sum of the heights of its children. This is how the ScrollView can determine how to vertically scroll the StackLayout. You can continue to set HorizontalOptions on the StackLayout to control the width and horizontal placement.

However, what you do not want to do is set VerticalOptions on the ScrollView to LayoutOptions.Start, Center, or End. The ScrollView must be able to scroll its child content, and the only way ScrollView can do that is by forcing its child (usually a StackLayout) to assume a height that reflects only what the child needs and then to use the height of this child and its own height to calculate how much to scroll that content.

If you set VerticalOptions on the ScrollView to LayoutOptions.Start, Center, or End, you are effectively telling the ScrollView to be only as tall as it needs to be. But what is that? Because ScrollView can scroll its contents, it doesn't need to be any particular height, so it will shrink down to nothing.

Although putting a StackLayout in a ScrollView is normal, putting a ScrollView in a Stack-Layout is dangerous. The StackLayout will force the ScrollView to have a height of only what it requires, and that required height is basically zero.

However, there is a way to put a ScrollView in a StackLayout successfully, and that will be demonstrated shortly.

The preceding discussion applies to a vertically oriented StackLayout and ScrollView. Stack-Layout has a property named Orientation that you can set to a member of the StackOrientation enumeration—Vertical (the default) or Horizontal. Similarly, ScrollView has a Scroll-Orientation property that you set to a member of the ScrollOrientation enumeration. Try this:

```
public ReflectedColorsPage()
{
    StackLayout stackLayout = new StackLayout
    {
        Orientation = StackOrientation.Horizontal
    };
    ...
    Content = new ScrollView
```

```
    {
        Orientation = ScrollOrientation.Horizontal,
        Content = stackLayout
    };
}
```

Now the `Label` views are stacked horizontally, and the `ScrollView` fills the page vertically but allows horizontal scrolling of the `StackLayout`, which vertically fills the `ScrollView`:

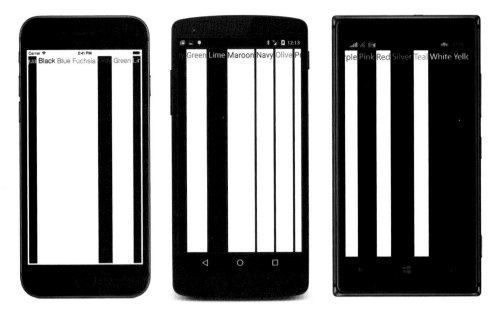

It looks pretty weird with the default vertical layout options, but those could be fixed to make it look a little better.

The Expands option

You probably noticed that the `HorizontalOptions` and `VerticalOptions` properties are plurals, as if there's more than one option. These properties are generally set to a static field of the `LayoutOptions` structure—another plural.

The discussions so far have focused on the following static read-only `LayoutOptions` fields that returned predefined values of `LayoutOptions`:

- `LayoutOptions.Start`

- `LayoutOptions.Center`

- `LayoutOptions.End`

- `LayoutOptions.Fill`

The default—established by the `View` class—is `LayoutOptions.Fill`, which means that the view fills its container.

As you've seen, a `VerticalOptions` setting on a `Label` doesn't make a difference when the `Label` is a child of a vertical `StackLayout`. The `StackLayout` itself constrains the height of its children to only the height they require, so the child has no freedom to move vertically within that slot.

Be prepared for this rule to be slightly amended!

The `LayoutOptions` structure has four additional static read-only fields not discussed yet:

- `LayoutOptions.StartAndExpand`

- `LayoutOptions.CenterAndExpand`

- `LayoutOptions.EndAndExpand`

- `LayoutOptions.FillAndExpand`

`LayoutOptions` also defines two instance properties named `Alignment` and `Expands`. The four instances of `LayoutOptions` returned by the static fields ending with `AndExpand` all have the `Expands` property set to `true`. This `Expands` property can be very useful for managing the layout of the page, but it can be confusing on first encounter. Here are the requirements for `Expands` to play a role in a vertical `StackLayout`:

- The vertical `StackLayout` must have a height that is less than the height of its container. In other words, some extra unused vertical space must exist in the `StackLayout`.

- That first requirement implies that the vertical `StackLayout` cannot have its own `VerticalOptions` property set to `Start`, `Center`, or `End` because that would cause the `StackLayout` to have a height equal to the aggregate height of its children and it would have no extra space.

- At least one child of the `StackLayout` must have a `VerticalOptions` setting with the `Expands` property set to `true`.

If these conditions are satisfied, the `StackLayout` allocates the extra vertical space equally among all the children that have a `VerticalOptions` setting with `Expands` equal to `true`. Each of these children gets a larger slot in the `StackLayout` than normal. How the child occupies that slot depends on the `Alignment` setting: `Start`, `Center`, `End`, or `Fill`.

Here's a program, named **VerticalOptionsDemo,** that uses reflection to create `Label` objects with all the possible `VerticalOptions` settings in a vertical `StackLayout`. The background and foreground colors are alternated so that you can see exactly how much space each `Label` occupies. The program uses Language Integrated Query (LINQ) to sort the fields of the `LayoutOptions` structure in a visually more illuminating manner:

```
public class VerticalOptionsDemoPage : ContentPage
```

```
{
    public VerticalOptionsDemoPage()
    {
        Color[] colors = { Color.Yellow, Color.Blue };
        int flipFlopper = 0;

        // Create Labels sorted by LayoutAlignment property.
        IEnumerable<Label> labels =
            from field in typeof(LayoutOptions).GetRuntimeFields()
            where field.IsPublic && field.IsStatic
            orderby ((LayoutOptions)field.GetValue(null)).Alignment
            select new Label
            {
                Text = "VerticalOptions = " + field.Name,
                VerticalOptions = (LayoutOptions)field.GetValue(null),
                XAlign = TextAlignment.Center,
                FontSize = Device.GetNamedSize(NamedSize.Medium, typeof(Label)),
                TextColor = colors[flipFlopper],
                BackgroundColor = colors[flipFlopper = 1 - flipFlopper]
            };

        // Transfer to StackLayout.
        StackLayout stackLayout = new StackLayout();

        foreach (Label label in labels)
        {
            stackLayout.Children.Add(label);
        }

        Padding = new Thickness(0, Device.OnPlatform(20, 0, 0), 0, 0);
        Content = stackLayout;
    }
}
```

You might want to study the results a little:

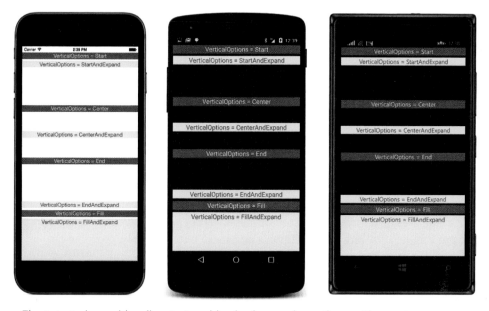

The `Label` views with yellow text on blue backgrounds are those with `VerticalOptions` properties set to `LayoutOptions` values without the `Expands` flag set. If the `Expands` flag is not set on the `LayoutOptions` value of an item in a vertical `StackLayout`, the `VerticalOptions` setting is ignored. As you can see, the `Label` occupies only as much vertical space as it needs in the vertical `StackLayout`.

The total height of the children in this `StackLayout` is less than the height of the `StackLayout`, so the `StackLayout` has extra space. It contains four children with their `VerticalOptions` properties set to `LayoutOptions` values with the `Expands` flag set, so this extra space is allocated equally among those four children.

In these four cases—the `Label` views with blue text on yellow backgrounds—the `Alignment` property of the `LayoutOptions` value indicates how the child is aligned within the area that includes the extra space. The first one—with the `VerticalOptions` property set to `LayoutOptions.StartAndExpand`—is above this extra space. The second (`CenterAndExpand`) is in the middle of the extra space. The third (`EndAndExpand`) is below the extra space. However, in all these three cases, the `Label` is getting only as much vertical space as it needs, as indicated by the background color. The rest of the space belongs to the `StackLayout`, which shows the background color of the page.

The last `Label` has its `VerticalOptions` property set to `LayoutOptions.FillAndExpand`. In this case, the `Label` occupies the entire slot including the extra space, as the large area of yellow background indicates. The text is at the top of this area; that's because the default setting of `YAlign` is `TextAlignment.Start`. Set it to something else to position the text vertically within the area.

The `Expands` property of `LayoutOptions` plays a role only when the view is a child of a `StackLayout`. In other contexts, it's superfluous.

Frame and BoxView

Two simple rectangular views are often useful for presentation purposes:

The `BoxView` is a filled rectangle. It derives from `View` and defines a `Color` property that's transparent by default.

The `Frame` displays a rectangular border surrounding some content. `Frame` derives from `Layout` by way of `ContentView`, from which it inherits a `Content` property. The content of a `Frame` can be a single view or a layout containing a bunch of views. From `VisualElement`, `Frame` inherits a `BackgroundColor` property that's white on the iPhone but transparent on Android and Windows Phone. From `Layout`, `Frame` inherits a `Padding` property that it initializes to 20 units on all sides to give the content a little breathing room. `Frame` itself defines an `OutlineColor` property that is transparent by default and a `HasShadow` property that is `true` by default, but the shadow shows up only on the iPhone.

Both the `Frame` outline and the `BoxView` are transparent by default, so you might be a little uncertain how to color them: White won't show up against the default background of the iPhone, and black won't show up against the default background of the Android and Windows Phone. One good choice is `Color.Accent`, which is guaranteed to show up regardless. Or, you can take control over coloring the background as well as the `Frame` outline and `BoxView`.

If the `BoxView` or `Frame` is not constrained in size in any way—that is, if it's not in a `StackLayout` and has its `HorizontalOptions` and `VerticalOptions` set to default values of `LayoutOptions.Fill`—these views expand to fill their containers.

For example, here's a program that has a centered `Label` set to the `Content` property of a `Frame`:

```
public class FramedTextPage : ContentPage
{
    public FramedTextPage()
    {
        Padding = new Thickness(20);
        Content = new Frame
        {
            OutlineColor = Color.Accent,
            Content = new Label
            {
                Text = "I've been framed!",
                FontSize = Device.GetNamedSize(NamedSize.Large, typeof(Label)),
                HorizontalOptions = LayoutOptions.Center,
                VerticalOptions = LayoutOptions.Center
            }
        };
    }
}
```

The `Label` is centered in the `Frame`, but the `Frame` fills the whole page, and you might not even be able to see the Frame clearly if the page had not been given a Padding of 20 on all sides:

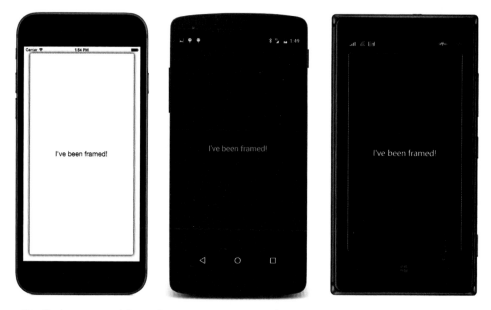

To display centered framed text, you want to set the HorizontalOptions and VerticalOptions properties on the Frame (rather than the Label) to LayoutOptions.Center:

```
public class FramedTextPage : ContentPage
{
    public FramedTextPage()
    {
        Padding = new Thickness(20);
        Content = new Frame
        {
            OutlineColor = Color.Accent,
            HorizontalOptions = LayoutOptions.Center,
            VerticalOptions = LayoutOptions.Center,
            Content = new Label
            {
                Text = "I've been framed!",
                FontSize = Device.GetNamedSize(NamedSize.Large, typeof(Label))
            }
        };
    }
}
```

Now the Frame hugs the text (but with a 20-unit default padding) in the center of the page:

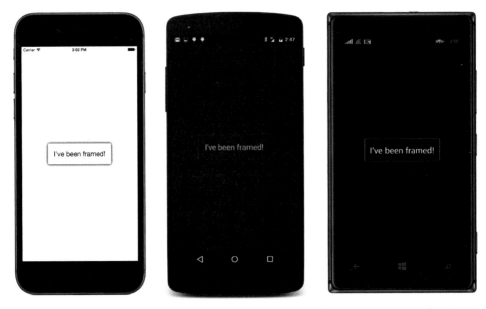

The version of **FramedText** included with the sample code for this chapter exercises the freedom to give everything a custom color:

```
public class FramedTextPage : ContentPage
{
    public FramedTextPage()
    {
        BackgroundColor = Color.Aqua;

        Content = new Frame
        {
            OutlineColor = Color.Black,
            BackgroundColor = Color.Yellow,
            HorizontalOptions = LayoutOptions.Center,
            VerticalOptions = LayoutOptions.Center,

            Content = new Label
            {
                Text = "I've been framed!",
                FontSize = Device.GetNamedSize(NamedSize.Large, typeof(Label)),
                FontAttributes = FontAttributes.Italic,
                TextColor = Color.Blue
            }
        };
    }
}
```

The result looks roughly the same on all three platforms:

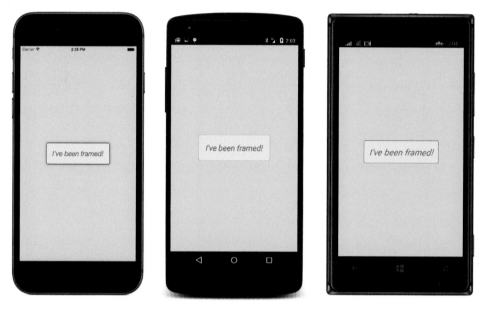

Try setting a `BoxView` to the `Content` property of a `ContentPage`, like so:

```
public class SizedBoxViewPage : ContentPage
{
    public SizedBoxViewPage()
    {
        Content = new BoxView
        {
            Color = Color.Accent
        };
    }
}
```

Be sure to set the `Color` property so you can see it. The `BoxView` fills the whole area of its container, just as `Label` does with its default `HorizontalOptions` or `VerticalOptions` settings:

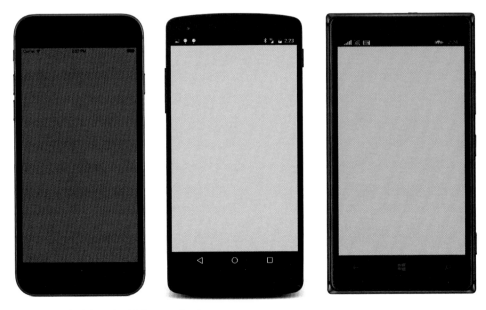

It's even underlying the iOS status bar!

Now try setting the HorizontalOptions and VerticalOptions properties of the BoxView to something other than Fill, as in this code sample:

```
public class SizedBoxViewPage : ContentPage
{
    public SizedBoxViewPage()
    {
        Content = new BoxView
        {
            Color = Color.Accent,
            HorizontalOptions = LayoutOptions.Center,
            VerticalOptions = LayoutOptions.Center
        };
    }
}
```

In this case, the BoxView will assume its default dimensions of 40 units square:

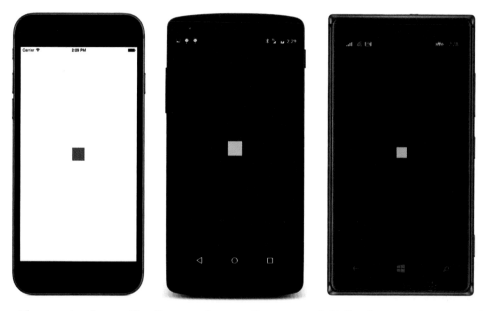

The BoxView is now 40 units square because the BoxView initializes its WidthRequest and HeightRequest properties to 40. These two properties require a little explanation:

VisualElement defines Width and Height properties, but these properties are read-only. VisualElement also defines WidthRequest and HeightRequest properties that are both settable and gettable. Normally, all these properties are initialized to –1 (which effectively means they are un-defined), but some View derivatives, such as BoxView, set the WidthRequest and HeightRequest properties to specific values.

Following the layout of a page, the Width and Height properties indicate actual dimensions of the view—the area that the view occupies on the screen. Because Width and Height are read-only, they are for informational purposes only. (Chapter 5, "Dealing with sizes," describes how to work with these values.)

If you want a view to be a specific size, you can set the WidthRequest and HeightRequest prop-erties. But these properties indicate (as their names suggest) a *requested* size or a *preferred* size. If the view is allowed to fill its container, these properties will be ignored.

BoxView sets its own WidthRequest and HeightRequest properties to 40. You can think of these settings as a size that BoxView would like to be if nobody else has any opinions in the matter. You've already seen that WidthRequest and HeightRequest are ignored when the BoxView is allowed to fill the page. The WidthRequest kicks in if the HorizontalOptions is set to LayoutOptions.Left, Center, or Right, or if the BoxView is a child of a horizontal StackLayout. The HeightRequest be-haves similarly.

Here's the version of the **SizedBoxView** program included with the code for this chapter:

```
public class SizedBoxViewPage : ContentPage
{
    public SizedBoxViewPage()
    {
        BackgroundColor = Color.Pink;

        Content = new BoxView
        {
            Color = Color.Navy,
            HorizontalOptions = LayoutOptions.Center,
            VerticalOptions = LayoutOptions.Center,
            WidthRequest = 200,
            HeightRequest = 100
        };
    }
}
```

Now we get a `BoxView` with that specific size and the colors explicitly set:

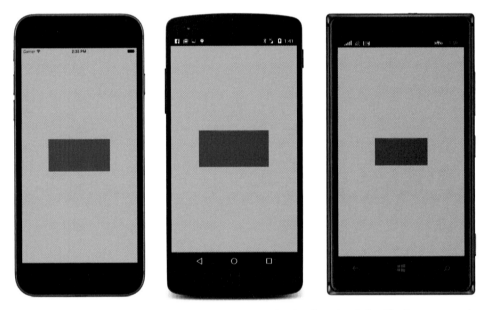

Let's use both `Frame` and `BoxView` in an enhanced color list. The **ColorBlocks** program has a page constructor that is virtually identical to the one in **ReflectedColors**, except that it calls a method named `CreateColorView` rather than `CreateColorLabel`. Here's that method:

```
class ColorBlocksPage : ContentPage
{
    ...

    View CreateColorView(Color color, string name)
    {
        return new Frame
        {
```

```
            OutlineColor = Color.Accent,
            Padding = new Thickness(5),
            Content = new StackLayout
            {
                Orientation = StackOrientation.Horizontal,
                Spacing = 15,
                Children =
                {
                    new BoxView
                    {
                        Color = color
                    },
                    new Label
                    {
                        Text = name,
                        FontSize = Device.GetNamedSize(NamedSize.Large, typeof(Label)),
                        FontAttributes = FontAttributes.Bold,
                        VerticalOptions = LayoutOptions.Center,
                        HorizontalOptions = LayoutOptions.StartAndExpand
                    },
                    new StackLayout
                    {
                        Children =
                        {
                            new Label
                            {
                                Text = String.Format("{0:X2}-{1:X2}-{2:X2}",
                                                (int)(255 * color.R),
                                                (int)(255 * color.G),
                                                (int)(255 * color.B)),
                                VerticalOptions = LayoutOptions.CenterAndExpand,
                                IsVisible = color != Color.Default
                            },
                            new Label
                            {
                                Text = String.Format("{0:F2}, {1:F2}, {2:F2}",
                                                color.Hue,
                                                color.Saturation,
                                                color.Luminosity),
                                VerticalOptions = LayoutOptions.CenterAndExpand,
                                IsVisible = color != Color.Default
                            }
                        },
                        HorizontalOptions = LayoutOptions.End
                    }
                }
            }
        };
    }
}
```

The `CreateColorView` method returns a `Frame` containing a horizontal `StackLayout` with a `Box-View` indicating the color, a `Label` for the name of the color, and another `StackLayout` with two more `Label` views for the RGB composition and the `Hue`, `Saturation`, and `Luminosity` values. The RGB and HSL displays are meaningless for the `Color.Default` value, so that inner `StackLayout` has its `IsVisible` property set to `false` in that case. The `StackLayout` still exists, but it's ignored when the page is rendered.

The program doesn't know which element will determine the height of each color item—the `Box-View`, the `Label` with the color name, or the two `Label` views with the RGB and HSL values—so it centers all the `Label` views. As you can see, the `BoxView` expands in height to accommodate the height of the text:

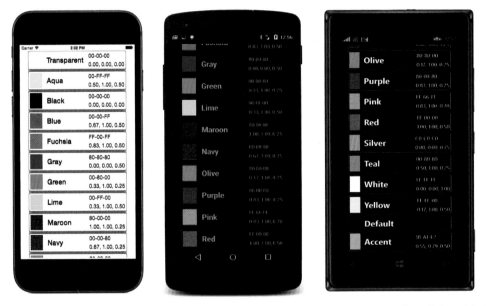

Now this is a scrollable color list that's beginning to be something we can take a little pride in.

A ScrollView in a StackLayout?

It's common to put a `StackLayout` in a `ScrollView`, but can you put a `ScrollView` in a `StackLay-out`? And why would you even want to?

It's a general rule in layout systems like the one in Xamarin.Forms that you can't put a scroll in a stack. A `ScrollView` needs to have a specific height to compute the difference between the height of its content and its own height. That difference is the amount that the `ScrollView` can scroll its contents. If the `ScrollView` is in a `StackLayout`, it doesn't get that specific height. The `StackLayout` wants the `ScrollView` to be as short as possible, and that's either the height of the `ScrollView` contents or zero, and neither solution works.

So why would you want a `ScrollView` in a `StackLayout` anyway?

Sometimes it's precisely what you need. Consider a primitive e-book reader that implements scrolling. You might want a `Label` at the top of the page always displaying the book's title, followed by a `ScrollView` containing a `StackLayout` with the content of the book itself. It would be convenient for that `Label` and the `ScrollView` to be children of a `StackLayout` that fills the page.

With Xamarin.Forms, such a thing is possible. If you give the `ScrollView` a `VerticalOptions` setting of `LayoutOptions.FillAndExpand`, it can indeed be a child of a `StackLayout`. The `StackLayout` will give the `ScrollView` all the extra space not required by the other children, and the `ScrollView` will then have a specific height.

The **BlackCat** project displays the text of Edgar Allan Poe's short story "The Black Cat," which is stored in a text file named TheBlackCat.txt in a one-line-per-paragraph format.

How does the **BlackCat** program access the file with this short story? It is sometimes convenient to embed files that an application requires right in the program executable or—in the case of a Xamarin.Forms application—right in the Portable Class Library DLL. These files are known as *embedded resources*, and that's what TheBlackCat.txt file is in this program.

To make an embedded resource in either Visual Studio or Xamarin Studio, you'll probably first want to create a folder in the project by selecting the **Add > New Folder** option from the project menu. A folder for text files might be called **Texts**, for example. The folder is optional, but it helps organize program assets. Then, to that folder, you can select the **Add > Existing Item** in Visual Studio or **Add > Add Files** in Xamarin Studio. Navigate to the file, select it, and click **Add** in Visual Studio or **Open** in Xamarin Studio.

Now here's the important part: Once the file is part of the project, bring up the **Properties** dialog from the menu associated with the file. Specify that the **Build Action** for the file is **EmbeddedResource**. This is an easy step to forget, but it is essential.

This was done for the **BlackCat** project, and consequently the TheBlackCat.txt file becomes embedded in the BlackCat.dll file.

In code, the file can be retrieved by calling the `GetManifestResourceStream` method defined by the `Assembly` class in the `System.Reflection` namespace. To get the assembly of the PCL, all you need to do is get the `Type` of any class defined in the assembly. You can use `typeof` with the page type you've derived from `ContentPage` or `GetType` on the instance of that class. Then call `GetTypeInfo` on this `Type` object. `Assembly` is a property of the resultant `TypeInfo` object:

```
Assembly assembly = GetType().GetTypeInfo().Assembly;
```

In the `GetManifestResourceStream` method of `Assembly`, you'll need to specify the name of the resource. For embedded resources, that name is not the filename of the resource but the *resource ID*. It's easy to confuse these because that ID might look vaguely like a fully qualified filename.

The resource ID begins with the default namespace of the assembly. This is not the .NET namespace! To get the default namespace of the assembly in Visual Studio, select **Properties** from the project menu, and in the properties dialog, select **Library** at the left and look for the **Default namespace** field. In Xamarin Studio, select **Options** from the project menu, and in the **Project Options** dialog, select **Main Settings** at the left, and look for a field labeled **Default Namespace**.

For the **BlackCat** project, that default namespace is the same as the assembly: "BlackCat". However, you can actually set that default namespace to whatever you want.

The resource ID begins with that default namespace, followed by a period, followed by the folder name you might have used, followed by another period and the filename. For this example, the resource ID is "BlackCat.Texts.TheBlackCat.txt"—and that's what you'll see passed to the `GetMani-festResourceStream` method in the code. The method returns a .NET `Stream` object, and from that a `StreamReader` can be created to read the lines of text.

It's a good idea to use `using` statements with the `Stream` object returned from `GetManifestRe-sourceStream` and the `StreamReader` object because that will properly dispose of the objects when they're no longer needed or if they raise exceptions.

For layout purposes, the `BlackCatPage` constructor creates two `StackLayout` objects: `mainStack` and `textStack`. The first line from the file (containing the story's title and author) becomes a bolded and centered Label in `mainStack`; all the subsequent lines go in `textStack`. The `mainStack` instance also contains a `ScrollView` with `textStack`.

```
class BlackCatPage : ContentPage
{
    public BlackCatPage()
    {
        StackLayout mainStack = new StackLayout();
        StackLayout textStack = new StackLayout
        {
            Padding = new Thickness(5),
            Spacing = 10
        };

        // Get access to the text resource.
        Assembly assembly = GetType().GetTypeInfo().Assembly;
        string resource = "BlackCat.Texts.TheBlackCat.txt";

        using (Stream stream = assembly.GetManifestResourceStream (resource))
        {
            using (StreamReader reader = new StreamReader (stream))
            {
                bool gotTitle = false;
                string line;

                // Read in a line (which is actually a paragraph).
                while (null != (line = reader.ReadLine()))
                {
                    Label label = new Label
                    {
                        Text = line,
```

```
                    // Black text for ebooks!
                    TextColor = Color.Black
                };

                if (!gotTitle)
                {
                    // Add first label (the title) to mainStack.
                    label.HorizontalOptions = LayoutOptions.Center;
                    label.FontSize = Device.GetNamedSize(NamedSize.Medium, label);
                    label.FontAttributes = FontAttributes.Bold;
                    mainStack.Children.Add(label);
                    gotTitle = true;
                }
                else
                {
                    // Add subsequent labels to textStack.
                    textStack.Children.Add(label);
                }
            }
        }
    }

    // Put the textStack in a ScrollView with FillAndExpand.
    ScrollView scrollView = new ScrollView
    {
        Content = textStack,
        VerticalOptions = LayoutOptions.FillAndExpand,
        Padding = new Thickness(5, 0),
    };

    // Add the ScrollView as a second child of mainStack.
    mainStack.Children.Add(scrollView);

    // Set page content to mainStack.
    Content = mainStack;

    // White background for ebooks!
    BackgroundColor = Color.White;

    // Add some iOS padding for the page.
    Padding = new Thickness (0, Device.OnPlatform (20, 0, 0), 0, 0);
    }
}
```

Notice that the ScrollView has its VerticalOptions property set to LayoutOptions.FillAndExpand. Without that, this program won't work. With it, the text is scrollable while the title stays in place.

Because this is basically an e-book reader, and humans have been reading black text on white paper for hundreds of years, the BackgroundColor of the page is set to white and the TextColor of each Label is set to black:

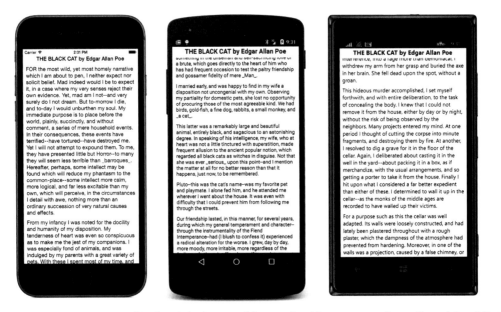

BlackCat is a PCL application. It is also possible to write this program using a Shared Asset Project rather than a PCL, and included with the code for this chapter is **BlackCatSap**. However, if you put an embedded resource into an SAP, the folder name is not part of the resource ID. It's basically ignored. Also, because the resource actually becomes part of the application project, you'll need the default namespace for the application, and that's different for each platform. The code to set the resource variable looks like this:

```
#if __IOS__
        string resource = "BlackCatSap.iOS.TheBlackCat.txt";
#elif __ANDROID__
        string resource = "BlackCatSap.Droid.TheBlackCat.txt";
#elif WINDOWS_PHONE
        string resource = "BlackCatSap.WinPhone.TheBlackCat.txt";
#endif
```

If you're having problems referencing an embedded resource, you might be using an incorrect name. Try calling `GetManifestResourceNames` on the `Assembly` object to get a list of the resource IDs of all embedded resources.

Chapter 5
Dealing with sizes

Already you've seen some references to sizes in connection with various visual elements:

- The iOS status bar has a height of 20, which you can adjust for with a `Padding` setting on the page.

- The `BoxView` sets its default requested width and height to 40.

- The default `Padding` within a `Frame` is 20.

- The default `Spacing` property on the `StackLayout` is 6.

And then there's `Device.GetNamedSize`, which for various members of the `NamedSize` enumeration returns a platform-dependent number appropriate for `FontSize` values for a `Label` or `Button`.

What are these numbers? What are their units? And how do we intelligently set properties requiring sizes to other values?

Good questions. Sizes also affect the display of text. As you've seen, the three platforms display a different quantity of text on the screen. Is that quantity of text something that a Xamarin.Forms application can anticipate or control? And even if it's possible, is it a proper programming practice? Should an application adjust font sizes to achieve a desired text density on the screen?

In general, when programming a Xamarin.Forms application, it's best not to get too close to the actual numeric dimensions of visual objects. It's preferable to trust Xamarin.Forms and the three platforms to make the best default choices.

However, there are times when a programmer needs to know something about the size of particular visual objects, and the size of the screen on which they appear.

As you know, video displays consist of a rectangular array of pixels. Any object displayed on the screen also has a pixel size. In the early days of personal computers, programmers sized and positioned visual objects in units of pixels. But as a greater variety of screen sizes and pixel densities became available, working with pixels became undesirable for programmers attempting to write applications that look roughly the same on many devices. Another solution was required.

Pixels, points, dps, DIPs, and DIUs

Solutions to the problem of working with pixels began with operating systems for desktop computers, and these solutions were then adapted for mobile devices. For this reason, it's illuminating to begin this exploration with the desktop.

Desktop video displays have a wide range of pixel dimensions, from the nearly obsolete 640 × 480 on up into the thousands. The aspect ratio of 4:3 was once standard for computer displays—and for movies and television as well—but the high-definition aspect ratio of 16:9 (or the similar 16:10) is now more common.

Desktop video displays also have a physical dimension usually measured along the diagonal of the screen in inches or centimeters. The pixel dimension combined with the physical dimension allows you to calculate the video display's resolution or pixel density in dots per inch (DPI), sometimes also referred to as pixels per inch (PPI). The display resolution can also be measured as a dot pitch, which is the distance between adjacent pixel centers, usually measured in millimeters.

For example, you can use the Pythagorean theorem to calculate that an ancient 800 × 600 display has a diagonal length that would accommodate 1,000 pixels horizontally or vertically. If this monitor has a 13-inch diagonal, that's a pixel density of 77 DPI, or a dot pitch of 0.33 millimeters. However, the 13-inch screen on a modern laptop might have pixel dimensions of 2560 × 1600, which is a pixel density of about 230 DPI, or a dot pitch of about 0.11 millimeters. A 100-pixel square object on this screen is one-third the size of the same object on the older screen.

Programmers should have a fighting chance when attempting to size visual elements correctly. For this reason, both Apple and Microsoft devised systems for desktop computing that allow programmers to work with the video display in some form of device-independent units instead of pixels. Most of the dimensions that a programmer encounters and specifies are in these device-independent units. It is the responsibility of the operating system to convert back and forth between these units and pixels.

In the Apple world, desktop video displays were traditionally assumed to have a resolution of 72 units to the inch. This number comes from typography, where many measurements are in units of *points*. In classical typography, there are approximately 72 points to the inch, but in digital typography the point has been standardized to exactly one seventy-second of an inch. By working with points rather than pixels, a programmer has an intuitive sense of the relationship between numeric sizes and the area that visual objects occupy on the screen.

In the Windows world, a similar technique was developed, called *device-independent pixels* (DIPs) or *device-independent units* (DIUs). To a Windows programmer, desktop video displays are assumed to have a resolution of 96 DIUs, which is exactly one-third higher than 72 DPI, although it can be adjusted by the user.

Mobile devices, however, have somewhat different rules: The pixel densities achieved on modern phones are typically much higher than desktop displays. This higher pixel density allows text and other visual objects to shrink much more in size before becoming illegible.

Phones are also typically held much closer to the user's face than is a desktop or laptop screen. This difference also implies that visual objects on the phone can be smaller than comparable objects on desktop or laptop screens. Because the physical dimensions of the phone are much smaller than desktop displays, shrinking down visual objects is very desirable because it allows much more to fit on the screen.

Apple continues to refer to the device-independent units on the iPhone as *points*. Until recently, all of Apple's high-density displays—which Apple refers to by the brand name Retina—have a conversion of two pixels to the point. This was true for the MacBook Pro, iPad, and iPhone. The recent exception is the iPhone 6 Plus, which has three pixels to the point.

For example, the 640 × 960 pixel dimension of the 3.5-inch screen of the iPhone 4 has an actual pixel density of about 320 DPI. There are two pixels to the point, so to an application program running on the iPhone 4, the screen appears to have a dimension of 320 × 480 points. The iPhone 3 actually did have a pixel dimension of 320 × 480, and points equaled pixels, so to a program, the displays of the iPhone 3 and iPhone 4 appear to be the same size. Despite the same perceived sizes, graphical objects and text are displayed in greater resolution on the iPhone 4 than the iPhone 3.

For the iPhone 3 and iPhone 4, the relationship between the screen size and point dimensions implies a conversion factor of 160 points to the inch rather than the desktop standard of 72.

The iPhone 5 has a 4-inch screen, but the pixel dimension is 640 × 1136. The pixel density is about the same as the iPhone 4. To a program, this screen has a size of 320 × 768 points.

The iPhone 6 has a 4.7-inch screen and a pixel dimension of 750 × 1334. The pixel density is also about 320 DPI. There are two pixels to the point, so to a program, the screen appears to have a point size of 375 × 667.

However, the iPhone 6 Plus has a 5.5-inch screen and a pixel dimension of 1080 × 1920, which is a pixel density of 400 DPI. This higher pixel density implies more pixels to the point, and for the iPhone 6 Plus, Apple has set the point equal to three pixels. That would normally imply a perceived screen size of 360 × 640 points, but to a program, the iPhone 6 Plus screen has a point size of 414 × 736, so the perceived resolution is about 150 points to the inch.

This information is summarized in the following table:

Model	iPhone 2, 3	iPhone 4	iPhone 5	iPhone 6	iPhone 6 Plus*
Pixel size	320 × 480	640 × 960	640 × 1136	750 × 1334	1080 × 1920
Screen diagonal	3.5 in.	3.5 in.	4 in.	4.7 in.	5.5 in.
Pixel density	165 DPI	330 DPI	326 DPI	326 DPI	401 DPI
Pixels per point	1	2	2	2	3
Point size	320 × 480	320 × 480	320 × 568	375 × 667	414 × 736
Points per inch	165	165	163	163	154

* Includes 115 percent downsampling.

Android does something quite similar: Android devices have a wide variety of sizes and pixel dimensions, but an Android programmer generally works in units of density-independent pixels (dps). The relationship between pixels and dps is set assuming 160 dps to the inch, which means that Apple and Android device-independent units are very similar.

Microsoft took a different approach with the Windows Phone, however. Windows Phone 7 devices have a uniform pixel dimension of either 320 × 480—but devices using this screen size were very rare and can be ignored for this discussion—or 480 × 800, which is often referred to as WVGA (Wide Video Graphics Array). Windows Phone 7 programs work with this display in units of pixels. If you assume an average screen size of 4 inches for a 480 × 800 Windows Phone 7 device, this means that the Windows Phone is implicitly assuming a pixel density of about 240 DPI. That's 1.5 times the assumed pixel density of iPhone and Android devices.

With Windows Phone 8, several larger screen sizes are allowed: 768 × 1280 (WXGA or Wide Extended Graphics Array), 720 × 1280 (referred to using high-definition television lingo as 720p), and 1080 × 1920 (called 1080p).

For these additional display sizes, programmers work in device-independent units. An internal scaling factor translates between pixels and device-independent units so that the width of the screen in portrait mode always appears to be 480 pixels. The scaling factors are 1.6 (for WXGA), 1.5 (720p), and 2.25 (1080p). This is summarized in the following table:

Screen type	WVGA	WXGA	720p	1080p
Pixel size	480 × 800	768 × 1280	720 × 1280	1080 × 1920
Scaling factor	1	1.6	1.5	2.25
Size in DIUs	480 × 800	480 × 800	480 × 853	480 × 853

Xamarin.Forms has a philosophy of using the conventions of the underlying platforms as much as possible. In accordance with this philosophy, a Xamarin.Forms programmer works with sizes defined by each particular platform. All sizes that the programmer encounters through the Xamarin.Forms API are in these platform-specific, device-independent units.

Xamarin.Forms programmers can generally treat the phone display in a device-independent manner, but a little differently for each of the three platforms:

- iOS: assume 160 units to the inch

- Android: assume 160 units to the inch

- Windows Phone: assume 240 units to the inch

If it's desirable to size visual objects so that they appear about the same physical size on all three platforms, dimensions on the Windows Phone should be about 150 percent larger than dimensions on the iPhone and Android. If you compare the iOS value of 160 with the Apple desktop value of 72 units to the inch, and the Windows Phone value of 240 with the Windows desktop value of 96, you'll discover an implicit assumption that phones are held a little closer than half the distance from the eyes than is a desktop display.

The VisualElement class defines two properties, named Width and Height, that provide the rendered dimensions of views, layouts, and pages in these device-independent units. However, the initial settings of Width and Height are "mock" values of –1. The values of these properties become valid only when the layout system has positioned and sized everything on the page. Also, keep in mind that the default `Fill` setting for `HorizontalOptions` or `VerticalOptions` often causes a view to occupy more space than it would otherwise. The `Width` and `Height` values reflect this extra space. The `Width` and `Height` values also include any `Padding` that may be set and are consistent with the area colored by the view's `BackgroundColor` property.

`VisualElement` defines an event named `SizeChanged` that is fired whenever the `Width` or `Height` property of the visual element changes. This event is part of several notifications that occur when a page is laid out, a process that involves the various elements of the page being sized and positioned. This layout process occurs following the first definition of a page (generally in the page constructor), and a new layout pass takes place in response to any change that might affect layout—for example, when views are added to a `ContentPage` or a `StackLayout`, removed from these objects, or when properties are set on visual elements that might result in their sizes changing.

A new layout is also triggered when the screen size changes. This happens mostly when the phone is swiveled between portrait and landscape modes.

A full familiarity with the Xamarin.Forms layout system often accompanies the job of writing your own `Layout<View>` derivatives. This task awaits us in a future chapter. Until then, simply knowing when `Width` and `Height` properties change is helpful for working with sizes of visual objects. You can attach a `SizeChanged` handler to any visual object on the page, including the page itself. The **WhatSize** program demonstrates how to obtain the page's size and display it:

```
public class WhatSizePage : ContentPage
{
    Label label;

    public WhatSizePage()
    {
        label = new Label
        {
            FontSize = Device.GetNamedSize(NamedSize.Large, typeof(Label)),
            HorizontalOptions = LayoutOptions.Center,
            VerticalOptions = LayoutOptions.Center
        };

        Content = label;

        SizeChanged += OnPageSizeChanged;
    }

    void OnPageSizeChanged(object sender, EventArgs args)
    {
        label.Text = String.Format("{0} \u00D7 {1}", Width, Height);
    }
}
```

This is the first example of event handling in this book, and you can see that events are handled in the normal C# and .NET manner. The code at the end of the constructor attaches the `OnPageSizeCh-anged` event handler to the `SizeChanged` event of the page. The first argument to the event handler (customarily named `sender`) is the object firing the event, in this case the instance of `WhatSizePage`, but the event handler doesn't use that. Nor does the event handler use the second argument—the so-called *event arguments*—which sometimes provides more information about the event.

Instead, the event handler accesses the `Label` element (conveniently saved as a field) to display the `Width` and `Height` properties of the page. The Unicode character in the `String.Format` call is a times (×) symbol.

The `SizeChanged` event is not the only opportunity to obtain an element's size. `VisualElement` also defines a protected virtual method named `OnSizeAllocated` that indicates when the visual element is assigned a size. You can override this method in your `ContentPage` derivative rather than handling the `SizeChanged` event, but `OnSizeAllocated` is sometimes called when the size isn't actually changing.

Here's the program running on the three platforms:

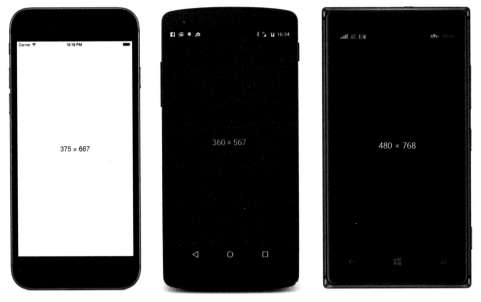

For the record, these are the sources of the screens in these three images:

- The iPhone 6 simulator, with pixel dimensions of 750 × 1334.

- An LG Nexus 5 with a screen size of 1080 × 1920 pixels.

- A Nokia Lumia 925 with a screen size of 768 × 1280 pixels.

Notice that the vertical size perceived by the program on the Android does not include the area occupied by the status bar or bottom buttons; the vertical size on the Windows Phone does not include the area occupied by the status bar.

By default, all three platforms respond to device orientation changes. If you turn the phones (or em-ulators) 90 degrees counterclockwise, the phones display the following sizes:

The screen shots for this book are designed only for portrait mode, so you'll need to turn this book sideways to see what the program looks like in landscape. The 598-pixel width on the Android excludes the area for the buttons; the 335-pixel height excludes the status bar, which always appears above the page. On the Windows Phone, the 728-pixel width excludes the area for the status bar, which appears in the same place but with rotated icons to reflect the new orientation.

The **WhatSize** program creates a single `Label` in its constructor and sets the `Text` property in the event handler. That's not the only way to write such a program. The program could use the `SizeCh-anged` handler to create a whole new `Label` with the new text and set that new `Label` as the content of the page, in which case the previous `Label` would become unreferenced and hence eligible for gar-bage collection. But creating new visual elements is unnecessary and wasteful in this program. It's best for the program to create only one `Label` view and just set the `Text` property to indicate the page's new size.

Monitoring size changes is the only way a Xamarin.Forms application can detect orientation changes without obtaining platform-specific information. Is the width greater than the height? That's landscape. Otherwise, it's portrait.

By default, the Visual Studio and Xamarin Studio templates for Xamarin.Forms solutions enable de-vice orientation changes for all three platforms. If you want to disable orientation changes—for exam-ple, if you have an application that just doesn't work well in portrait or landscape mode—you can do so.

For iOS, first display the contents of Info.plist in Visual Studio or Xamarin Studio. In the **iPhone Deployment Info** section, use the **Supported Device Orientations** area to specify which orientations are allowed.

For Android, in the `Activity` attribute on the `MainActivity` class, add:

```
ScreenOrientation = ScreenOrientation.Landscape
```

or

```
ScreenOrientation = ScreenOrientation.Portrait
```

The `Activity` attribute generated by the solution template contains a `ConfigurationChanges` argument that also refers to screen orientation, but the purpose of `ConfigurationChanges` is to inhibit a restart of the activity when the phone's orientation or screen size changes.

For Windows Phone, in the MainPage.xaml.cs file, change the `SupportedPageOrientation` enumeration member to `Portrait` or `Landscape`.

Metrical sizes

Here again are the underlying assumed relationships between device-independent units and inches on the three platforms:

- iOS: 160 units to the inch

- Android: 160 units to the inch

- Windows Phone: 240 units to the inch

If the metric system is more comfortable to you, here are the same values for centimeters (rounded to easily memorable and easily divisible numbers):

- iOS: 64 units to the centimeter

- Android: assume 64 units to the centimeter

- Windows Phone: 96 units to the centimeter

This means that Xamarin.Forms applications can size a visual object in terms of metrical dimension—that is, in familiar units of inches and centimeters. Here's a program called **MetricalBoxView** that displays a `BoxView` with a width of approximately one centimeter and a height of approximately one inch:

```
public class MetricalBoxViewPage : ContentPage
{
    public MetricalBoxViewPage()
```

```
    {
        Content = new BoxView
        {
            Color = Color.Accent,
            WidthRequest = Device.OnPlatform(64, 64, 96),
            HeightRequest = Device.OnPlatform(160, 160, 240),
            HorizontalOptions = LayoutOptions.Center,
            VerticalOptions = LayoutOptions.Center
        };
    }
}
```

If you actually take a ruler to the object on your phone's screen, you'll find that it's not exactly the desired size but certainly close to it, as these screen shots also confirm:

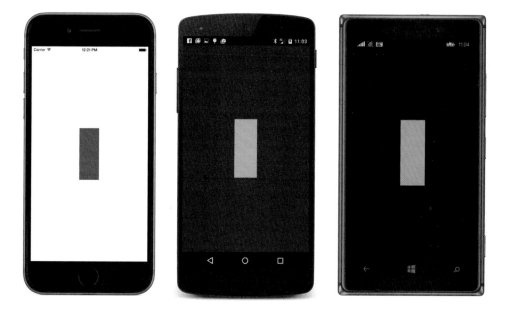

Estimated font sizes

The `FontSize` property on `Label` and `Button` is of type `double`. `FontSize` indicates the approximate height of font characters from the bottom of descenders to the top of ascenders, often (depending on the font) including diacritical marks as well. In most cases you'll want to set this property to a value returned by the `Device.GetNamedSize` method. This allows you to specify a member of the `NamedSize` enumeration: `Default`, `Micro`, `Small`, `Medium`, or `Large`.

You can work with actual numeric font sizes, but there's a little problem involved (to be discussed in detail shortly). For the most part, font sizes are expressed in the same device-independent units used through Xamarin.Forms, which means that you can calculate device-independent font sizes based on the platform resolution.

For example, suppose you want to use a 12-point font in your program. The first thing you should know is that while a 12-point font might be a comfortable size for printed material or a desktop screen, on a phone it's quite large. But let's continue.

There are 72 points to the inch, so a 12-point font is one-sixth of an inch. Multiply by the DPI resolution. That's about 27 device-independent units on iOS and Android and 40 device-independent units on Windows Phone.

Let's write a little program called **FontSizes**, which begins with a display similar to the **NamedFont-Sizes** program in Chapter 3 but then displays some text with numeric point sizes, converted to device-independent units using the device resolution:

```
public class FontSizesPage : ContentPage
{
    public FontSizesPage()
    {
        BackgroundColor = Color.White;
        StackLayout stackLayout = new StackLayout
        {
            HorizontalOptions = LayoutOptions.Center,
            VerticalOptions = LayoutOptions.Center
        };

        // Do the NamedSize values.
        NamedSize[] namedSizes =
        {
            NamedSize.Default, NamedSize.Micro, NamedSize.Small,
            NamedSize.Medium, NamedSize.Large
        };

        foreach (NamedSize namedSize in namedSizes)
        {
            double fontSize = Device.GetNamedSize(namedSize, typeof(Label));

            stackLayout.Children.Add(new Label
                {
                    Text = String.Format("Named Size = {0} ({1:F2})",
                                        namedSize, fontSize),
                    FontSize = fontSize,
                    TextColor = Color.Black
                });
        }

        // Resolution in device-independent units per inch.
        double resolution = Device.OnPlatform(160, 160, 240);

        // Draw horizontal separator line.
        stackLayout.Children.Add(
            new BoxView
            {
```

```
                Color = Color.Accent,
                HeightRequest = resolution / 80
            });

    // Do some numeric point sizes.
    int[] ptSizes = { 4, 6, 8, 10, 12 };

    foreach (double ptSize in ptSizes)
    {
        double fontSize = resolution * ptSize / 72;

        stackLayout.Children.Add(new Label
            {
                Text = String.Format("Point Size = {0} ({1:F2})",
                                      ptSize, fontSize),
                FontSize = fontSize,
                TextColor = Color.Black
            });
    }

    Content = stackLayout;
    }
}
```

To facilitate comparisons among the three screens, the backgrounds have been uniformly set to white and the labels to black. Notice the BoxView inserted into the StackLayout between the two foreach blocks: the HeightRequest setting gives it a device-independent height of approximately one-eightieth of an inch, and it resembles a horizontal rule.

The resultant visual sizes are fairly consistent between the three platforms and provide a rough idea of what you can expect. The numbers in parentheses are the numeric FontSize values in platform-specific device-independent units:

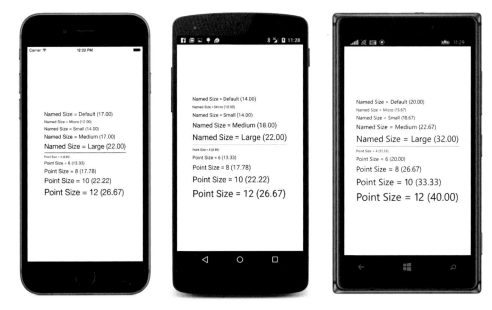

There is a problem, however. It involves Android. Run the Android **Settings** app. Go to the **Display** page, and select the **Font size** item. You'll see that you can select a size of **Small**, **Normal** (the default), **Large**, or **Huge**. This facility is for the benefit of people who can't comfortably read text because it's too small, or who have no problem reading tiny text and actually prefer apps to display a bit more text on the screen.

Select something other than **Normal**. When you run the **FontSizes** program again, you'll see that all the text displayed by the program is a different size—either smaller or larger depending on what setting you selected. As you'll be able to note from the numbers in parentheses on the top half of the list, the `Device.GetNamedSize` method returns different values based on this setting. For `NamedSize.Default`, the method returns 14 when the setting is **Normal** (as the screen shot above demonstrates), but returns 12 for a setting of **Small**, 16 for **Large**, and 18 1/3 for **Huge.**

Apart from the value returned from `Device.GetNamedSize`, the underlying text-rendering logic also affects the size of the text. The program continues to calculate the same values for the various point sizes, but the text in the bottom half of the display also changes size. This is a result of the Android renderer for `Label` using the enumeration value `ComplexUnitType.Sp` (which translates to the Android `COMPLEX_UNIT_SP` constant) to calculate the font size. The `SP` part stands for *scaled pixel*, an additional scaling just for text beyond the use of device-independent pixels.

Fitting text to available size

You might need to fit a block of text to a particular rectangular area. It's possible to calculate a value for the `FontSize` property of `Label` based on the number of text characters, the size of the rectangular area, and just two numbers. (However, this technique will not work on Android unless the **Font size** setting is **Normal**.)

The first number is line spacing. This is the vertical height of a `Label` view per line of text. For the default fonts associated with the three platforms, it is roughly related to the `FontSize` property as follows:

- iOS: `lineSpacing` = 1.2 * `label.FontSize`

- Android: `lineSpacing` = 1.2 * `label.FontSize`

- Windows Phone: `lineSpacing` = 1.3 * `label.FontSize`

The second helpful number is average character width. For a normal mix of uppercase and lowercase letters for the default fonts, this average character width is about half of the font size, regardless of the platform:

- `averageCharacterWidth` = 0.5 * `label.FontSize`

For example, suppose you want to fit a text string containing 80 characters in a width of 320 units, and you'd like the font size to be as large as possible. Divide the width (320) by half the number of characters (40), and you get a font size of 8, which you can set to the `FontSize` property of `Label`. For text that's somewhat indeterminate and can't be tested beforehand, you might want to make this calculation a little more conservative to avoid surprises.

The following program uses both line spacing and average character width to fit a paragraph of text on the page—or rather, on the page minus the area at the top of the iPhone occupied by the status bar. To make the exclusion of the iOS status bar a bit easier in this program, the program uses a `ContentView`.

`ContentView` derives from `Layout` but adds a `Content` property only to what it inherits from `Layout`. `ContentView` is the base class to `Frame` but doesn't really add much functionality of its own. Yet it can be useful for parenting a group of views to define a new custom view and to simulate a margin.

As you might have noticed, Xamarin.Forms has no concept of a margin, which traditionally is similar to padding except that padding is inside a view and a part of the view, while a margin is outside the view and actually part of the parent's view. A `ContentView` lets us simulate this. If you find a need to set a margin on a view, put the view in a `ContentView` and set the `Padding` property on the `ContentView`. `ContentView` inherits a `Padding` property from `Layout`.

The **EstimatedFontSize** program uses `ContentView` in a slightly different manner: It sets the customary padding on the page to avoid the iOS status bar, but then sets a `ContentView` as the content of that page. Hence, this `ContentView` is the same size as the page, but excluding the iOS status bar. It is on this `ContentView` that the `SizeChanged` event is attached, and it is the size of this `ContentView` that is used to calculate the text font size.

The `SizeChanged` handler uses the first argument to obtain the object firing the event (in this case the `ContentView`), which is the object in which the `Label` must fit. The calculation is described in comments:

```csharp
public class EstimatedFontSizePage : ContentPage
{
    Label label;

    public EstimatedFontSizePage()
    {
        label = new Label();
        Padding = new Thickness(0, Device.OnPlatform(20, 0, 0), 0, 0);
        ContentView contentView = new ContentView
        {
            Content = label
        };
        contentView.SizeChanged += OnContentViewSizeChanged;
        Content = contentView;
    }

    void OnContentViewSizeChanged(object sender, EventArgs args)
    {
        string text =
            "A default system font with a font size of S " +
            "has a line height of about ({0:F1} * S) and an " +
            "average character width of about ({1:F1} * S). " +
            "On this page, which has a width of {2:F0} and a " +
            "height of {3:F0}, a font size of ?1 should " +
            "comfortably render the ??2 characters in this " +
            "paragraph with ?3 lines and about ?4 characters " +
            "per line. Does it work?";

        // Get View whose size is changing.
        View view = (View)sender;

        // Two values as multiples of font size
        double lineHeight = Device.OnPlatform(1.2, 1.2, 1.3);
        double charWidth = 0.5;

        // Format the text and get its length
        text = String.Format(text, lineHeight, charWidth, view.Width, view.Height);
        int charCount = text.Length;

        // Because:
        //    lineCount = view.Height / (lineHeight * fontSize)
        //    charsPerLine = view.Width / (charWidth * fontSize)
        //    charCount = lineCount * charsPerLine
        // Hence, solving for fontSize:
        int fontSize = (int)Math.Sqrt(view.Width * view.Height /
                       (charCount * lineHeight * charWidth));

        // Now these values can be calculated.
        int lineCount = (int)(view.Height / (lineHeight * fontSize));
        int charsPerLine = (int)(view.Width / (charWidth * fontSize));
```

```
        // Replace the placeholders with the values.
        text = text.Replace("?1", fontSize.ToString());
        text = text.Replace("??2", charCount.ToString());
        text = text.Replace("?3", lineCount.ToString());
        text = text.Replace("?4", charsPerLine.ToString());

        // Set the Label properties.
        label.Text = text;
        label.FontSize = fontSize;
    }
}
```

The text placeholders named "?1", "??2", "?3", and "?4" were chosen to be unique but also to be the same number of characters as the numbers that replace them.

If the goal is to make the text as large as possible without the text spilling off the page, the results validate the approach:

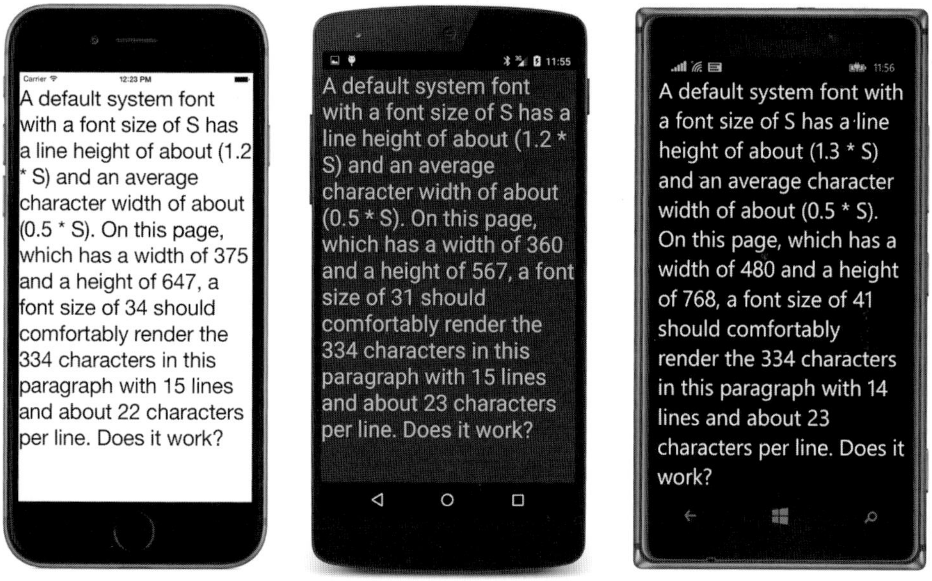

Not bad. Not bad at all. The text actually displays on the iPhone and Android in 14 lines, but the technique seems sound. It's not necessary for the same FontSize to be calculated for landscape mode, but it happens sometimes:

A fit-to-size clock

The `Device` class includes a static `StartTimer` method that lets you set a timer that fires a periodic event. The availability of a timer event means that a clock application is possible, even if it displays the time only in text.

The first argument to `Device.StartTimer` is an interval expressed as a `TimeSpan` value. The timer fires an event periodically based on that interval. (You can go down as low as 15 or 16 milliseconds, which is about the period of the frame rate of 60 frames per second common on video displays.) The event handler has no arguments but must return `true` to keep the timer going.

The **FitToSizeClock** program creates a `Label` for displaying the time and then sets two events: the `SizeChanged` event on the page for changing the font size, and the `Device.StartTimer` event for one-second intervals to change the `Text` property. Both event handlers simply change a property of the `Label`, and they are both expressed as lambda functions so that they can access the `Label` without it being stored as a field:

```
public class FitToSizeClockPage : ContentPage
{
    public FitToSizeClockPage()
    {
        Label clockLabel = new Label
        {
            HorizontalOptions = LayoutOptions.Center,
            VerticalOptions = LayoutOptions.Center
        };
```

```
            Content = clockLabel;

            // Handle the SizeChanged event for the page.
            SizeChanged += (object sender, EventArgs args) =>
                {
                    // Scale the font size to the page width
                    //       (based on 11 characters in the displayed string).
                    if (this.Width > 0)
                        clockLabel.FontSize = this.Width / 6;
                };

            // Start the timer going.
            Device.StartTimer(TimeSpan.FromSeconds(1), () =>
                {
                    // Set the Text property of the Label.
                    clockLabel.Text = DateTime.Now.ToString("h:mm:ss tt");
                    return true;
                });
    }
}
```

The `StartTimer` handler specifies a custom formatting string for `DateTime` that results in 10 or 11 characters, but two of those are capital letters, and those are wider than average characters. The `SizeChanged` handler implicitly assumes that 12 characters are displayed by setting the font size to one-sixth of the page width:

Of course, the text is much larger in landscape mode:

Again, this technique works on Android only if **Font size** in system settings is set to **Normal**.

This one-second timer doesn't tick exactly at the beginning of every second, so the displayed time might not precisely agree with other time displays on the same device. You can make it more accurate by setting a more frequent timer tick. Performance won't be impacted much because the display still changes only once per second and won't require a new layout cycle until then.

Empirically fitting text

Another approach to fitting text within a rectangle of a particular size involves empirically determining the size of the rendered text based on a particular font size and then adjusting that font size up or down. This approach has the advantage of working on Android devices regardless of how the user has set the **Font size** setting.

But the process can be tricky: The first problem is that there is not a clean linear relationship between the font size and the height of the rendered text. As text gets larger relative to the width of its container, the lines break more frequently between words, and more wasted space results. A calculation to find the optimum font size often involves a loop that narrows in on the value.

A second problem involves the actual mechanism of obtaining the size of a `Label` rendered with a particular font size. You can set a `SizeChanged` handler on the `Label`, but within that handler you don't want to make any changes (such as setting a new `FontSize` property) that will cause recursive calls to that handler.

A better approach is calling the `GetSizeRequest` method defined by `VisualElement` and inherited by `Label` and all other views. `GetSizeRequest` requires two arguments—a width constraint and a height constraint. These values indicate the size of the rectangle in which you want to fit the element, and one or the other can be infinity. When using `GetSizeRequest` with a `Label`, generally you set the width constraint argument to the width of the container and set the height request to `Double.PositiveInfinity`.

The `GetSizeRequest` method returns a value of type `SizeRequest`, a structure with two properties named `Minimum` and `Request`, both of type `Size`. The `Request` property indicates the size of the rendered text. (More information on this and related methods appear in forthcoming chapters on custom views and layouts.)

The **EmpiricalFontSize** project demonstrates this technique. For convenience, it defines a small structure named `FontCalc` that makes the call to `GetSizeRequest` for a particular `Label` (already initialized with text), a font size, and a text width:

```
struct FontCalc
{
    public FontCalc(Label label, double fontSize, double containerWidth)
        : this()
    {
        // Save the font size.
        FontSize = fontSize;

        // Recalculate the Label height.
        label.FontSize = fontSize;
        SizeRequest sizeRequest =
            label.GetSizeRequest(containerWidth, Double.PositiveInfinity);

        // Save that height.
        TextHeight = sizeRequest.Request.Height;
    }

    public double FontSize { private set; get; }

    public double TextHeight { private set; get; }
}
```

The resultant height of the rendered `Label` is saved in the `TextHeight` property.

When you make a call to `GetSizeRequest` on a page or a layout, the page or layout needs to obtain the sizes of all of its children down through the visual tree. This has a performance penalty, of course, so you should avoid making calls like that unless necessary. But a `Label` has no children, so calling `GetSizeRequest` on a `Label` is not nearly as bad. However, you should still try to optimize the calls. Avoid looping through a sequential series of font size values to determine the maximum value that doesn't result in text exceeding the container height. A process that algorithmically narrows in on an optimum value is better.

`GetSizeRequest` requires that the element be part of a visual tree and that the layout process has at least partially begun. Don't call `GetSizeRequest` in the constructor of your page class. You won't get information from it. The first reasonable opportunity is in an override of the page's `OnAppearing` method. Of course, you might not have sufficient information at this time to pass arguments to the `GetSizeRequest` method.

The `EmpiricalFontSizePage` class instantiates `FontCalc` values in the `SizeChanged` handler of the `ContentView` that hosts the `Label`. (This is the same event handler used in the **EstimatedFont-Size** program.) The constructor of each `FontCalc` value makes `GetSizeRequest` calls on the `Label` and saves the resultant `TextHeight`. The `SizeChanged` handler begins with trial font sizes of 10 and 100 under the assumption that the optimum value is somewhere between these two and that these represent lower and upper bounds. Hence the variable names `lowerFontCalc` and `upperFontCalc`:

```
public class EmpiricalFontSizePage : ContentPage
{
    Label label;

    public EmpiricalFontSizePage()
    {
        label = new Label();

        Padding = new Thickness(0, Device.OnPlatform(20, 0, 0), 0, 0);
        ContentView contentView = new ContentView
        {
            Content = label
        };
        contentView.SizeChanged += OnContentViewSizeChanged;
        Content = contentView;
    }

    void OnContentViewSizeChanged(object sender, EventArgs args)
    {
        // Get View whose size is changing.
        View view = (View)sender;

        if (view.Width <= 0 || view.Height <= 0)
            return;

        label.Text =
            "This is a paragraph of text displayed with " +
            "a FontSize value of ?? that is empirically " +
            "calculated in a loop within the SizeChanged " +
            "handler of the Label's container. This technique " +
            "can be tricky: You don't want to get into " +
            "an infinite loop by triggering a layout pass " +
            "with every calculation. Does it work?";

        // Calculate the height of the rendered text.
        FontCalc lowerFontCalc = new FontCalc(label, 10, view.Width);
        FontCalc upperFontCalc = new FontCalc(label, 100, view.Width);

        while (upperFontCalc.FontSize - lowerFontCalc.FontSize > 1)
        {
```

```
        // Get the average font size of the upper and lower bounds.
        double fontSize = (lowerFontCalc.FontSize + upperFontCalc.FontSize) / 2;

        // Check the new text height against the container height.
        FontCalc newFontCalc = new FontCalc(label, fontSize, view.Width);

        if (newFontCalc.TextHeight > view.Height)
        {
            upperFontCalc = newFontCalc;
        }
        else
        {
            lowerFontCalc = newFontCalc;
        }
    }

    // Set the final font size and the text with the embedded value.
    label.FontSize = lowerFontCalc.FontSize;
    label.Text = label.Text.Replace("??", label.FontSize.ToString("F0"));
    }
}
```

In each iteration of the `while` loop, the `FontSize` properties of those two `FontCalc` values are averaged and a new `FontCalc` is obtained. This becomes the new `lowerFontCalc` or `upperFontCalc` value depending on the height of the rendered text. The loop ends when the calculated font size is within one unit of the optimum value.

About seven iterations of the loop are sufficient to get a value that is clearly better than the estimated value calculated in the earlier program:

Turning the phone sideways triggers another recalculation that results in a similar (though not necessarily the same) font size:

It might seem that the algorithm could be improved beyond simply averaging the `FontSize` properties from the lower and upper `FontCalc` values. But the relationship between the font size and rendered text height is rather complex, and sometimes the easiest approach is just as good.

Chapter 6
Button clicks

The components of a graphical user interface can be divided roughly into views that are used for presentation (displaying information *to* the user) and interaction (obtaining input *from* the user). While the Label is the most basic presentation view, the Button is probably the archetypal interactive view. The Button signals a command. It's the user's way of telling the program to initiate some action—to do something.

A Xamarin.Forms button displays text, with or without an accompanying image. (Only text buttons are described in this chapter; adding an image button is covered in Chapter 13, "Bitmaps.") When a finger presses on the button, the button changes its appearance somewhat to provide feedback to the user. When the finger is released, the button fires a Clicked event. The two arguments of the Clicked handler are typical of Xamarin.Forms event handlers:

- The first argument is the object firing the event. For the Clicked handler, this is the particular Button object that's been tapped.

- The second argument sometimes provides more information about the event. For the Clicked event, the second argument is simply an EventArgs object that provides no additional information.

Once a user begins interacting with an application, some special needs arise: The application should make an effort to save the results of that interaction if the program happens to be terminated before the user has finished working with it. For that reason, this chapter also discusses how an application can save transient data, particularly in the context of application lifecycle events.

Processing the click

Here's a program named **ButtonLogger** with a Button that shares a StackLayout with a ScrollView containing another StackLayout. Every time the Button is clicked, the program adds a new Label to the scrollable StackLayout, in effect logging all the button clicks:

```
public class ButtonLoggerPage : ContentPage
{
    StackLayout loggerLayout = new StackLayout();

    public ButtonLoggerPage()
    {
        // Create the Button and attach Clicked handler.
        Button button = new Button
        {
            Text = "Log the Click Time"
```

```
        };
        button.Clicked += OnButtonClicked;

        this.Padding = new Thickness(5, Device.OnPlatform(20, 0, 0), 5, 0);

        // Assemble the page.
        this.Content = new StackLayout
        {
            Children =
            {
                button,
                new ScrollView
                {
                    VerticalOptions = LayoutOptions.FillAndExpand,
                    Content = loggerLayout
                }
            }
        };
    }

    void OnButtonClicked(object sender, EventArgs args)
    {
        // Add Label to scrollable StackLayout.
        loggerLayout.Children.Add(new Label
        {
            Text = "Button clicked at " + DateTime.Now.ToString("T")
        });
    }
}
```

In the programs in this book, event handlers are given names beginning with the word `On`, followed by some kind of identification of the view firing the event (sometimes just the view type), followed by the event name. The resultant name in this case is `OnButtonClicked`.

The constructor attaches the `Clicked` handler to the `Button` right after the `Button` is created. The page is then assembled with a `StackLayout` containing the `Button` and a `ScrollView` with another `StackLayout`, named `loggerLayout`. Notice that the `ScrollView` has its `VerticalOptions` set to `FillAndExpand` so that it can share the `StackLayout` with the `Button` and still be visible and scrollable.

Here's the display after several `Button` clicks:

As you can see, the `Button` looks a little different on the three screens. That's because the button is rendered natively on the individual platforms: on the iPhone it's a `UIButton`, on Android it's an Android `Button`, and on Windows Phone it's a Windows Phone `Button`. By default the button always fills the area available for it and centers the text inside.

`Button` defines several properties that let you customize its appearance:

- `FontFamily`

- `FontSize`

- `FontAttributes`

- `TextColor`

- `BorderColor`

- `BorderWidth`

- `BorderRadius`

- `Image` (to be discussed in Chapter 13)

`Button` also inherits the `BackgroundColor` property (and a bunch of other properties) from `VisualElement` and inherits `HorizontalOptions` and `VerticalOptions` from `View`.

Some `Button` properties might not work on all platforms. On the iPhone you need to set `Border-Width` to a positive value for a border to be displayed, but that's normal for an iPhone button. The Android button won't display a border unless `BackgroundColor` is set, and then it requires a nondefault setting of `BorderColor` and a positive `BorderWidth`. The `BorderRadius` property is intended to round off the sharp corners of the border, but it doesn't work on Windows Phone.

Suppose you wrote a program similar to **ButtonLogger** but did not save the `loggerLayout` object as a field. Could you get access to that `StackLayout` object in the `Clicked` event handler?

Yes! It's possible to obtain parent and child visual elements by the technique of walking the visual tree. The `sender` argument to the `OnButtonClicked` handler is the object firing the event, in this case the `Button`, so you can begin the `Clicked` handler by casting that argument:

```
Button button = (Button)sender;
```

You know that the `Button` is a child of a `StackLayout`, so that object is accessible from the `ParentView` property. Again, some casting is required:

```
StackLayout outerLayout = (StackLayout)button.ParentView;
```

The second child of this `StackLayout` is the `ScrollView`, so the `Children` property can be indexed to obtain that:

```
ScrollView scrollView = (ScrollView)outerLayout.Children[1];
```

The `Content` property of this `ScrollView` is exactly the `StackLayout` you were looking for:

```
StackLayout loggerLayout = (StackLayout)scrollView.Content;
```

Of course, the danger in doing something like this is that you might change the layout someday and forget to change your tree-walking code similarly. But the technique comes in handy if the code that assembles your page is separate from the code handling events from views on that page.

Sharing button clicks

If a program contains multiple `Button` views, each `Button` can have its own `Clicked` handler. But in some cases it might be more convenient for multiple `Button` views to share a common `Clicked` handler.

Consider a calculator program. Each of the buttons labeled 0 through 9 basically does the same thing, and having 10 separate `Clicked` handlers for these 10 buttons—even if they share some common code—simply wouldn't make much sense.

You've seen how the first argument to the `Clicked` handler can be cast to an object of type `Button`. But how do you know which `Button` it is?

One approach is to store all the `Button` objects as fields and then compare the `Button` object firing the event with these fields.

The **TwoButtons** program demonstrates this technique. This program is similar to the previous program but with two buttons—one to add `Label` objects to the `StackLayout`, and the other to remove them. The two `Button` objects are stored as fields so that the `Clicked` handler can determine which one fired the event:

```
public class TwoButtonsPage : ContentPage
{
    Button addButton, removeButton;
    StackLayout loggerLayout = new StackLayout();

    public TwoButtonsPage()
    {
        // Create the Button views and attach Clicked handlers.
        addButton = new Button
        {
            Text = "Add",
            HorizontalOptions = LayoutOptions.CenterAndExpand
        };
        addButton.Clicked += OnButtonClicked;

        removeButton = new Button
        {
            Text = "Remove",
            HorizontalOptions = LayoutOptions.CenterAndExpand,
            IsEnabled = false
        };
        removeButton.Clicked += OnButtonClicked;

        this.Padding = new Thickness(5, Device.OnPlatform(20, 0, 0), 5, 0);

        // Assemble the page.
        this.Content = new StackLayout
        {
            Children =
            {
                new StackLayout
                {
                    Orientation = StackOrientation.Horizontal,
                    Children =
                    {
                        addButton,
                        removeButton
                    }
                },

                new ScrollView
                {
                    VerticalOptions = LayoutOptions.FillAndExpand,
                    Content = loggerLayout
                }
            }
        };
    }

    void OnButtonClicked(object sender, EventArgs args)
    {
```

```
        Button button = (Button)sender;

        if (button == addButton)
        {
            // Add Label to scrollable StackLayout.
            loggerLayout.Children.Add(new Label
            {
                Text = "Button clicked at " + DateTime.Now.ToString("T")
            });
        }
        else
        {
            // Remove topmost Label from StackLayout.
            loggerLayout.Children.RemoveAt(0);
        }

        // Enable "Remove" button only if children are present.
        removeButton.IsEnabled = loggerLayout.Children.Count > 0;
    }
}
```

Both buttons are given a `HorizontalOptions` value of `CenterAndExpand` so that they can be displayed side by side at the top of the screen by using a horizontal `StackLayout`:

Notice that when the `Clicked` handler detects `removeButton`, it simply calls the `RemoveAt` method on the `Children` property:

```
loggerLayout.Children.RemoveAt(0);
```

But what happens if there are no children? Won't `RemoveAt` raise an exception?

It can't happen! When the **TwoButtons** program begins, the `IsEnabled` property of the remove-
`Button` is initialized to `false`. When a button is disabled in this way, a dim appearance causes it to
appear to be nonfunctional, and it actually is nonfunctional. It does not provide feedback to the user
and it does not fire `Clicked` events. Toward the end of the `Clicked` handler, the `IsEnabled` property
on `removeButton` is set to `true` only if the `loggerLayout` has at least one child.

This illustrates a good general rule: if your code needs to determine whether a button `Clicked`
event is valid, it's probably better to prevent invalid button clicks by disabling the button.

Anonymous event handlers

Many C# programmers these days like to define small event handlers as anonymous lambda functions.
This allows the event-handling code to be very close to the instantiation and initialization of the object
firing the event instead of somewhere else in the file. It also allows referencing objects within the event
handler without storing those objects as fields.

Here's a program named **ButtonLambdas** that has a `Label` displaying a number and two buttons.
One button doubles the number, and the other halves the number. Normally the number and `Label`
variables would be saved as fields. But because the anonymous event handlers are defined right in the
constructor after these variables are defined, the event handlers have access to them:

```
public class ButtonLambdasPage : ContentPage
{
    public ButtonLambdasPage()
    {
        // Number to manipulate.
        double number = 1;

        // Create the Label for display.
        Label label = new Label
        {
            Text = number.ToString(),
            FontSize = Device.GetNamedSize(NamedSize.Large, typeof(Label)),
            HorizontalOptions = LayoutOptions.Center,
            VerticalOptions = LayoutOptions.CenterAndExpand
        };

        // Create the first Button and attach Clicked handler.
        Button timesButton = new Button
        {
            Text = "Double",
            FontSize = Device.GetNamedSize(NamedSize.Large, typeof(Button)),
            HorizontalOptions = LayoutOptions.CenterAndExpand
        };
        timesButton.Clicked += (sender, args) =>
        {
            number *= 2;
            label.Text = number.ToString();
```

```
        };

        // Create the second Button and attach Clicked handler.
        Button divideButton = new Button
        {
            Text = "Half",
            FontSize = Device.GetNamedSize(NamedSize.Large, typeof(Button)),
            HorizontalOptions = LayoutOptions.CenterAndExpand
        };
        divideButton.Clicked += (sender, args) =>
        {
            number /= 2;
            label.Text = number.ToString();
        };

        // Assemble the page.
        this.Content = new StackLayout
        {
            Children =
            {
                label,
                new StackLayout
                {
                    Orientation = StackOrientation.Horizontal,
                    VerticalOptions = LayoutOptions.CenterAndExpand,
                    Children =
                    {
                        timesButton,
                        divideButton
                    }
                }
            }
        };
    }
}
```

Notice the use of `Device.GetNamedSize` to get large text for both the `Label` and the `Button`. The second argument of `GetNamedSize` is different for these two view types to obtain an appropriate size for the particular view.

Like the previous program, the two buttons share a horizontal `StackLayout`:

The disadvantage of defining event handlers as anonymous lambda functions is that they can't be shared among multiple views. (Actually they can, but some messy reflection code is involved.)

Distinguishing views with IDs

In the **TwoButtons** program, you saw a technique for sharing an event handler that distinguishes views by comparing objects. This works fine when there aren't very many views to distinguish, but it would be a terrible approach for a calculator program.

The `Element` class defines a `StyleId` property of type `string` specifically for the purpose of identifying views. Set it to whatever is convenient for the application. You can test the values by using `if` and `else` statements or in a `switch` and `case`, or you can use a `Parse` method to convert the strings into numbers or enumeration members.

The following program isn't a calculator, but it is a numeric keypad, which is certainly part of a calculator. The program is called **SimplestKeypad** and uses a `StackLayout` for organizing the rows and columns of keys. (One of the intents of this program is to demonstrate that `StackLayout` is not quite the right tool for this job!)

The program creates a total of five `StackLayout` instances. The `mainStack` is vertically oriented, and four horizontal `StackLayout` objects arrange the 10 digit buttons. To keep things simple, the keypad is arranged with telephone ordering rather than calculator ordering:

```
public class SimplestKeypadPage : ContentPage
{
    Label displayLabel;
```

```
Button backspaceButton;

public SimplestKeypadPage()
{
    // Create a vertical stack for the entire keypad.
    StackLayout mainStack = new StackLayout
    {
        VerticalOptions = LayoutOptions.Center,
        HorizontalOptions = LayoutOptions.Center
    };

    // First row is the Label.
    displayLabel = new Label
    {
        FontSize = Device.GetNamedSize(NamedSize.Large, typeof(Label)),
        VerticalOptions = LayoutOptions.Center,
        XAlign = TextAlignment.End
    };
    mainStack.Children.Add(displayLabel);

    // Second row is the backspace Button.
    backspaceButton = new Button
    {
        Text = "\u21E6",
        FontSize = Device.GetNamedSize(NamedSize.Large, typeof(Button)),
        IsEnabled = false
    };
    backspaceButton.Clicked += OnBackspaceButtonClicked;
    mainStack.Children.Add(backspaceButton);

    // Now do the 10 number keys.
    StackLayout rowStack = null;

    for (int num = 1; num <= 10; num++)
    {
        if ((num - 1) % 3 == 0)
        {
            rowStack = new StackLayout
            {
                Orientation = StackOrientation.Horizontal
            };
            mainStack.Children.Add(rowStack);
        }

        Button digitButton = new Button
        {
            Text = (num % 10).ToString(),
            FontSize = Device.GetNamedSize(NamedSize.Large, typeof(Button)),
            StyleId = (num % 10).ToString()
        };
        digitButton.Clicked += OnDigitButtonClicked;

        // For the zero button, expand to fill horizontally.
        if (num == 10)
```

```
            {
                digitButton.HorizontalOptions = LayoutOptions.FillAndExpand;
            }
            rowStack.Children.Add(digitButton);
        }

        this.Content = mainStack;
    }

    void OnDigitButtonClicked(object sender, EventArgs args)
    {
        Button button = (Button)sender;
        displayLabel.Text += (string)button.StyleId;
        backspaceButton.IsEnabled = true;
    }

    void OnBackspaceButtonClicked(object sender, EventArgs args)
    {
        string text = displayLabel.Text;
        displayLabel.Text = text.Substring(0, text.Length - 1);
        backspaceButton.IsEnabled = displayLabel.Text.Length > 0;
    }
}
```

The 10 number keys share a single `Clicked` handler. The `StyleId` property indicates the number associated with the key, so the program can simply append that number to the string displayed by the `Label`. The `StyleId` happens to be identical to the `Text` property of the `Button`, and the `Text` property could be used instead, but in the general case, things aren't quite that convenient.

The backspace `Button` is sufficiently different in function to warrant its own `Clicked` handler, although it would surely be possible to combine the two methods into one to take advantage of any code they might have in common.

To give the keypad a slightly larger size, all the text is given a `FontSize` using `NamedSize.Large`. Here are the three renderings of the **SimplestKeypad** program:

Of course, you'll want to press the keys repeatedly until you see how the program responds to a really large string of digits, and you'll discover that it doesn't adequately anticipate such a thing. When the `Label` gets too wide, it begins to govern the overall width of the vertical `StackLayout`, and the buttons start shifting as well.

But even before that, you might notice a little irregularity in the `Button` widths, particularly on the Windows Phone. The widths of the individual `Button` objects are based on their content, and in many fonts the widths of the decimal digits are not the same.

Can you fix this problem with the `Expands` flag on the `HorizontalOptions` property? No. The `Expands` flag causes extra space to be distributed equally among the views in the `StackLayout`. Each view will increase additively by the same amount, so they still won't be the same width. For example, take a look at the two buttons in the **TwoButtons** or **ButtonLambdas** program. They have their `HorizontalOptions` properties set to `FillAndExpand`, but they are different widths because the width of the `Button` content is different.

A better solution for these programs is the layout known as the `Grid`, coming up in Chapter 18.

Saving transient data

Suppose you're entering an important number in the **SimplestKeypad** program and you're interrupted—perhaps with a phone call. Later on, you shut off the phone, effectively terminating the program.

What should happen the next time you run **SimplestKeypad**? Should the long string of numbers you entered earlier be discarded? Or should it seem as though the program resumed from the state you last left it? Of course, it doesn't matter for a simple demo program like **SimplestKeypad**, but in the general case, users expect mobile applications to remember exactly what they were doing the last time they interacted with the program.

For this reason, the `Application` class supports two facilities that help the program save and restore data:

- The `Properties` property of `Application` is a dictionary with `string` keys and `object` items. The contents of this dictionary are automatically saved prior to the application being terminated, and the saved contents become available the next time the application runs.

- The `Application` class defines three protected virtual methods named `OnStart`, `OnSleep`, and `OnResume`, and the `App` class generated by the Xamarin.Forms template overrides these methods. These methods help an application deal with what are known as *application lifecycle* events.

To use these facilities, you need to identify what information your application needs to save so that it can restore its state after being terminated and restarted. In general, this is a combination of *application settings*—such as colors and font sizes that the user might be given an opportunity to set—and *transient data*, such as half-entered entry fields. Application settings usually apply to the entire application, while transient data is unique to each page in the application. If each item of this data is an entry in the `Properties` dictionary, each item needs a dictionary key. However, if a program needs to save a large file such as a word-processing document, it shouldn't use the `Properties` dictionary, but instead should access the platform's file system directly. (That's a job for a later chapter.)

The **SimplestKeypad** program needs to save only a single item of transient data, and the dictionary key "displayLabelText" seems reasonable.

Sometimes a program can use the `Properties` dictionary to save and retrieve data without getting involved with application lifecycle events. For example, the **SimplestKeypad** program knows exactly when the `Text` property of `displayLabel` changes. It happens only in the two `Clicked` event handlers for the number keys and the delete key. Those two event handlers could simply store the new value in the `Properties` dictionary.

But wait: `Properties` is a property of the `Application` class. Do we need to save the instance of the `App` class so that code in the `SimplestKeypadPage` can get access to the dictionary? No, it's not necessary. `Application` defines a static property named `Current` that returns the current application's instance of the `Application` class.

To store the `Text` property of the `Label` in the dictionary, simply add the following line at the bottom of the two `Clicked` event handlers in **SimplestKeypad**:

```
Application.Current.Properties["displayLabelText"] = displayLabel.Text;
```

Don't worry if the `displayLabelText` key does not yet exist in the dictionary: The `Properties` dictionary implements the generic `IDictionary` interface, which explicitly defines the indexer to replace the previous item if the key already exists or to add a new item to the dictionary if the key does not exist. That behavior is exactly what you want here.

The `SimplestKeypadPage` constructor can then conclude by initializing the `Text` property of the `Label` with the following code, which retrieves the item from the dictionary:

```
IDictionary<string, object> properties = Application.Current.Properties;

if (properties.ContainsKey("displayLabelText"))
{
    displayLabel.Text = properties["displayLabelText"] as string;
    backspaceButton.IsEnabled = displayLabel.Text.Length > 0;
}
```

This is all your application needs to do: just save information in the `Properties` dictionary and retrieve it. Xamarin.Forms itself is responsible for the job of saving and loading the contents of the dictionary in platform-specific application storage.

In general, however, it's better for an application to interact with the `Properties` dictionary in a more structured manner, and here's where the application lifecycle events come into play. These are the three methods that appear in the `App` class generated by the Xamarin.Forms template:

```
public class App : Application
{
    public App()
    {
        …
    }

    protected override void OnStart()
    {
        // Handle when your app starts
    }

    protected override void OnSleep()
    {
        // Handle when your app sleeps
    }

    protected override void OnResume()
    {
        // Handle when your app resumes
    }
}
```

The most important is the `OnSleep` call. In general, an application goes into the sleep mode when it no longer commands the screen and has become inactive (apart from some background jobs it might have initiated). From this sleep mode, an application can be resumed (signaled by an `OnResume` call) or terminated. But this is important: After the `OnSleep` call, there is no further notification that an application is being terminated. The `OnSleep` call is as close as you get to a termination notification, and it always precedes a termination. For example, if your application is running and the user turns off the phone, the application gets an `OnSleep` call as the phone is shutting down.

Actually, there are some exceptions to the rule that a call to `OnSleep` always precedes program termination: a program that crashes does not get an `OnSleep` call first, but you probably expect that. But here's a case that you might not anticipate: When you are debugging a Xamarin.Forms application, and use Visual Studio or Xamarin Studio to stop debugging, the program is terminated without a preceding `OnSleep` call. This means that when you are debugging code that uses these application lifecycle events, you should get into the habit of using the phone itself to put your program to sleep, to resume the program, and to terminate it.

When your Xamarin.Forms application is running, the easiest way to trigger an `OnSleep` call on a phone or simulator is by pressing the phone's **Home** button. You can then bring the program back to the foreground and trigger an `OnResume` call by selecting the application from the home menu (on iOS devices or Android devices) or by pressing the **Back** button (on Android and Windows Phone devices).

If your Xamarin.Forms program is running and you invoke the phone's application switcher—by pressing the **Home** button twice on iOS devices, by pressing the **Multitask** button on Android devices (or by holding down the **Home** button on older Android devices), or by holding down the **Back** button on a Windows Phone—the application gets an `OnSleep` call. If you then select that program, the application gets an `OnResume` call as it resumes execution. If you instead terminate the application—by swiping the application's image upward on iOS devices or by tapping the X on the upper-right corner of the application's image on Android and Windows Phone devices—the program stops executing with no further notification.

So here's the basic rule: whenever your application gets a call to `OnSleep`, you should ensure that the `Properties` dictionary contains all the information about the application you want to save.

If you're using lifecycle events solely for saving and restoring program data, you don't need to handle the `OnResume` method. When your program gets an `OnResume` call, the operating system has already automatically restored the program contents and state. If you want to, you can use `OnResume` as an opportunity to clear out the `Properties` dictionary because you are assured of getting another `OnSleep` call before your program terminates. However, if your program has established a connection with a web service—or is in the process of establishing such a connection—you might want to use `OnResume` to restore that connection. Perhaps the connection has timed out in the interval that the program was inactive. Or perhaps some fresh data is available.

You have some flexibility when you restore the data from the `Properties` dictionary to your application as your program starts running. When a Xamarin.Forms program starts up, the first opportunity you have to execute some code in the Portable Class Library is the constructor of the `App` class. At that time, the `Properties` dictionary has already been filled with the saved data from platform-specific storage. The next code that executes is generally the constructor of the first page in your application instantiated from the App constructor. The OnStart call in Application (and App) follows that, and then an overridable method called OnAppearing is called in the page class. You can retrieve the data at any time during this startup process.

The data that an application needs to save is usually in a page class, but the OnSleep override is in the App class. So somehow the page class and App class must communicate. One approach is to define an OnSleep method in the page class that saves the data to the Properties dictionary and then call the page's OnSleep method from the OnSleep method in App. This approach works fine for a single-page application—indeed, the Application class has a static property named MainPage that is set in the App constructor and which the OnSleep method can use to get access to that page—but it doesn't work nearly as well for multipage applications.

Here's a somewhat different approach: define all the data you need to save as public properties in the App class, for example:

```
public class App : Application
{
    public App()
    {
        ...
    }

    public string DisplayLabelText { set; get; }
    ...

}
```

The page class (or classes) can then set and retrieve those properties when convenient. The App class can restore any such properties from the Properties dictionary in its constructor prior to instantiating the page and can store the properties in the Properties dictionary in its OnSleep override.

That's the approach taken by the **PersistentKeypad** project. This program is identical to **Simplest-Keypad** except that it includes code to save and restore the contents of the keypad. Here's the App class that maintains a public DisplayLabelText property that is saved in the OnSleep override and loaded in the App constructor:

```
namespace PersistentKeypad
{
    public class App : Application
    {
        const string displayLabelText = "displayLabelText";

        public App()
        {
            if (Properties.ContainsKey(displayLabelText))
            {
                DisplayLabelText = (string)Properties[displayLabelText];
            }
```

```
            MainPage = new PersistentKeypadPage();
        }

        public string DisplayLabelText { set; get; }

        protected override void OnStart()
        {
            // Handle when your app starts
        }

        protected override void OnSleep()
        {
            // Handle when your app sleeps
            Properties[displayLabelText] = DisplayLabelText;
        }

        protected override void OnResume()
        {
            // Handle when your app resumes
        }
    }
}
```

To avoid spelling errors, the App class defines the string dictionary key as a constant. It's the same as the property name except that it begins with a lowercase letter. Notice that the DisplayLabelText property is set prior to instantiating PersistentKeypadPage so that it's available in the PersistentKeypadPage constructor.

An application with a lot more items might want to consolidate them in a class named AppSettings (for example), serialize that class to an XML or a JSON string, and then save the string in the dictionary.

The PersistentKeypadPage class accesses that DisplayLabelText property in its constructor and sets the property in its two event handlers:

```
public class PersistentKeypadPage : ContentPage
{
    Label displayLabel;
    Button backspaceButton;

    public PersistentKeypadPage()
    {

        ...


        // New code for loading previous keypad text.
        App app = Application.Current as App;
        displayLabel.Text = app.DisplayLabelText;
        backspaceButton.IsEnabled = displayLabel.Text != null &&
                                    displayLabel.Text.Length > 0;

    }
```

```
void OnDigitButtonClicked(object sender, EventArgs args)
{
    Button button = (Button)sender;
    displayLabel.Text += (string)button.StyleId;
    backspaceButton.IsEnabled = true;

    // Save keypad text.
    App app = Application.Current as App;
    app.DisplayLabelText = displayLabel.Text;
}

void OnBackspaceButtonClicked(object sender, EventArgs args)
{
    string text = displayLabel.Text;
    displayLabel.Text = text.Substring(0, text.Length - 1);
    backspaceButton.IsEnabled = displayLabel.Text.Length > 0;

    // Save keypad text.
    App app = Application.Current as App;
    app.DisplayLabelText = displayLabel.Text;
}
}
```

When testing programs that use the `Properties` dictionary and application lifecycle events, you'll want to occasionally uninstall the program from the phone or simulator. Uninstalling a program from a device also deletes any stored data, so the next time the program is deployed from Visual Studio or Xamarin Studio, the program encounters an empty dictionary, as though it were being run for the very first time.

Chapter 7
XAML vs. code

C# is undoubtedly one of the greatest programming languages the world has ever seen. You can write entire Xamarin.Forms applications in C#, and it's conceivable that you've found C# to be so ideally suited for Xamarin.Forms that you haven't even considered using anything else.

But keep an open mind. Xamarin.Forms provides an alternative to C# that has some distinct advantages for certain aspects of program development. This alternative is XAML (pronounced "zammel"), which stands for the Extensible Application Markup Language. Like C#, XAML was developed at Microsoft Corporation, and it is only a few years younger than C#.

As its name suggests, XAML adheres to the syntax of XML, the Extensible Markup Language. This book assumes that you have familiarity with the basic concepts and syntax of XML.

In the most general sense, XAML is a declarative markup language used for instantiating and initializing objects. That definition might seem excessively general, and XAML is indeed quite flexible. But most real-world XAML has been used for defining tree-structured visual user interfaces characteristic of graphical programming environments. The history of XAML-based user interfaces begins with the Windows Presentation Foundation (WPF) and continues with Silverlight, Windows Phone 7 and 8, and Windows 8 and 10. Each of these XAML implementations supports a somewhat different set of visual elements defined by the particular platform. Likewise, the XAML implementation in Xamarin.Forms supports the visual elements defined by Xamarin.Forms, such as `Label`, `BoxView`, `Frame`, `Button`, `StackLayout`, and `ContentPage`.

As you've seen, a Xamarin.Forms application written entirely in code generally defines the initial appearance of its user interface in the constructor of a class that derives from `ContentPage`. If you choose to use XAML, the markup generally replaces this constructor code. You will find that XAML provides a more succinct and elegant definition of the user interface and has a visual structure that better mimics the tree organization of the visual elements on the page.

XAML is also generally easier to maintain and modify than equivalent code. Because XAML is XML, it is also potentially toolable: XAML can more easily be parsed and edited by software tools than the equivalent C# code. Indeed, an early impetus behind XAML was to facilitate a collaboration between programmers and designers: Designers can use design tools that generate XAML, while programmers focus on the code that interacts with the markup. While this vision has perhaps only rarely been fulfilled to perfection, it certainly suggests how applications can be structured to accommodate XAML. You use XAML for the visuals and code for the underlying logic.

Yet, XAML goes beyond that simple division of labor. As you'll see in a future chapter, it's possible to define bindings right in the XAML that link user-interface objects with underlying data.

When creating XAML for Microsoft platforms, some developers use interactive design tools such as Microsoft Blend, but many others prefer to handwrite XAML. No design tools are available for Xamarin.Forms, so handwriting is the only option. Obviously, all the XAML examples in this book are handwritten. But even when design tools are available, the ability to handwrite XAML is an important skill.

The prospect of handwriting XAML might cause some consternation among developers for another reason: XML is notoriously verbose. Yet, you'll see almost immediately that XAML is often more concise than the equivalent C# code. The real power of XAML becomes evident only incrementally, however, and won't be fully apparent until Chapter 19 when you use XAML for constructing templates for multiple items displayed in a `ListView`.

It is natural for programmers who prefer strongly typed languages such as C# to be skeptical of a markup language where everything is a text string. But you'll see shortly how XAML is a very strict analog of programming code. Much of what's allowed in your XAML files is defined by the classes and properties that make up the Xamarin.Forms application programming interface. For this reason, you might even begin to think of XAML as a "strongly typed" markup language. The XAML parser does its job in a very mechanical manner based on the underlying API infrastructure. One of the objectives of this chapter and the next is to demystify XAML and illuminate what happens when the XAML is parsed.

Yet, code and markup are very different: Code defines a process while markup defines a state. XAML has several deficiencies that are intrinsic to markup languages: XAML has no loops, no flow control, no algebraic calculation syntax, and no event handlers. However, XAML defines several features that help compensate for some of these deficiencies. You'll see many of these features in future chapters.

If you do not want to use XAML, you don't need to. Anything that can be done in XAML can be done in C#. But watch out: Sometimes developers get a little taste of XAML and get carried away and try to do everything in XAML! As usual, the best rule is "moderation in all things." Many of the best techniques involve combining code and XAML in interactive ways.

Let's begin this exploration with a few snippets of code and the equivalent XAML, and then see how XAML and code fit together in a Xamarin.Forms application.

Properties and attributes

Here is a Xamarin.Forms `Label` instantiated and initialized in code, much as it might appear in the constructor of a page class:

```
new Label
{
    Text = "Hello from Code!",
    IsVisible = true,
    Opacity = 0.75,
    XAlign = TextAlignment.Center,
    VerticalOptions = LayoutOptions.CenterAndExpand,
    TextColor = Color.Blue,
```

```
    BackgroundColor = Color.FromRgb(255, 128, 128),
    FontSize = Device.GetNamedSize(NamedSize.Large, typeof(Label)),
    FontAttributes = FontAttributes.Bold | FontAttributes.Italic
};
```

Here is a very similar `Label` instantiated and initialized in XAML, which you can see immediately is more concise than the equivalent code:

```
<Label Text="Hello from XAML!"
       IsVisible="True"
       Opacity="0.75"
       XAlign="Center"
       VerticalOptions="CenterAndExpand"
       TextColor="Blue"
       BackgroundColor="#FF8080"
       FontSize="Large"
       FontAttributes="Bold,Italic" />
```

Xamarin.Forms classes such as `Label` become XML elements in XAML. Properties such as `Text`, `IsVisible`, and the rest become XML attributes in XAML.

To be instantiated in XAML, a class such as `Label` must have a public parameterless constructor. (In the next chapter, you'll see that there is a technique to pass arguments to a constructor in XAML, but it's generally used for special purposes.) The properties set in XAML must have public `set` accessors. By convention, spaces surround an equal sign in code but not in XML (or XAML), but you can use as much white space as you want.

The concision of the XAML results mostly from the brevity of the attribute values—for example, the use of the word "Large" rather than a call to the `Device.GetNamedSize` method. These abbreviations are not built into the XAML parser. The XAML parser is instead assisted by various converter classes defined specifically for this purpose.

When the XAML parser encounters the `Label` element, it can use reflection to determine whether Xamarin.Forms has a class named `Label`, and if so, it can instantiate that class. Now it is ready to initialize that object. The `Text` property is of type `string`, and the attribute value is simply assigned to that property.

Because XAML is XML, you can include Unicode characters in the text by using the standard XML syntax. Precede the decimal Unicode value with `&#` (or the hexadecimal Unicode value with `&#x`) and follow it with a semicolon:

```
Text="Cost &#x2014; &#x20AC;123.45"
```

Those are the Unicode values for the em dash and euro symbol. To force a line break, use the line-feed character `&#x000A`, or (because leading zeros aren't required) `&#xA`, or with the decimal code, `&#10`.

Angle brackets, ampersands, and quotation marks have a special meaning in XML, so to include those characters in a text string, use one of the standard predefined entities:

- `&lt;` for <

- `&gt;` for >

- `&amp;` for &

- `&apos;` for '

- `&quot;` for "

The HTML predefined entities such as ` ` are not supported. For a nonbreaking space use ` ` instead.

In addition, curly braces ({ and }) have a special meaning in XAML. If you need to begin an attribute value with a left curly brace, begin it with a pair of curly braces ({}) and then the left curly brace.

The `IsVisible` and `Opacity` properties of `Label` are of type `bool` and `double`, respectively, and these are as simple as you might expect. The XAML parser uses the `Boolean.Parse` and `Double.Parse` methods to convert the attribute values. The `Boolean.Parse` method is case insensitive, but generally Boolean values are capitalized as "True" and "False" in XAML. The `Double.Parse` method is passed a `CultureInfo.InvariantCulture` argument, so the conversion doesn't depend on the local culture of the programmer or user.

The `XAlign` property of `Label` is of type `TextAlignment`, which is an enumeration. For any property that is an enumeration type, the XAML parser uses the `Enum.Parse` method to convert from the string to the value.

The `VerticalOptions` property is of type `LayoutOptions`, a structure. When the XAML parser references the `LayoutOptions` structure using reflection, it discovers that the structure has a C# attribute defined:

```
[TypeConverter (typeof(LayoutOptionsConverter))]
public struct LayoutOptions
{
    …
}
```

(Watch out! This discussion involves two types of attributes: XML attributes such as `XAlign` and C# attributes such as this `TypeConverter`.)

The `TypeConverter` attribute is supported by a class named `TypeConverterAttribute`. This `TypeConverter` attribute on `LayoutOptions` references a class named `LayoutOptionsConverter`. This is a class private to Xamarin.Forms, but it derives from a public abstract class named `TypeConverter` that defines methods named `CanConvertFrom` and `ConvertFrom`. When the XAML parser encounters this `TypeConverter` attribute, it instantiates the `LayoutOptionsConverter`. The `VerticalOptions` attribute in the XAML is assigned the string "Center", so the XAML parser passes that "Center" string to the `ConvertFrom` method of `LayoutOptionsConverter`, and out pops a `LayoutOptions` value. This is assigned to the `VerticalOptions` property of the `Label` object.

Similarly, when the XAML parser encounters the `TextColor` and `BackgroundColor` properties, it uses reflection to determine that those properties are of type `Color`. The `Color` structure is also adorned with a `TypeConverter` attribute:

```
[TypeConverter (typeof(ColorTypeConverter))]
public struct Color
{
    …
}
```

`ColorTypeConverter` is a public class, so you can experiment with it if you'd like. It accepts color definitions in several formats: It can convert a string like "Blue" to the `Color.Blue` value, and the "Default" and "Accent" strings to the `Color.Default` and `Color.Accent` values. `ColorTypeConverter` can also parse strings that encode red-green-blue values, such as "#FF8080", which is a red value of 0xFF, a green value of 0x80, and a blue value also of 0x80.

All numeric RGB values begin with a number sign prefix, but that prefix can be followed with eight, six, four, or three hexadecimal digits for specifying color values with or without an alpha channel. Here's the most extensive syntax:

```
BackgroundColor="#aarrggbb"
```

Each of the letters represents a hexadecimal digit, in the order alpha (opacity), red, green, and blue. For the alpha channel, keep in mind that 0xFF is fully opaque and 0x00 is fully transparent. Here's the syntax without an alpha channel:

```
BackgroundColor="#rrggbb"
```

In this case the alpha value is set to 0xFF for full opacity.

Two other formats allow you to specify only a single hexadecimal digit for each channel:

```
BackgroundColor="#argb"
BackgroundColor="#rgb"
```

In these cases, the digit is repeated to form the value. For example, #CF3 is the RGB color 0xCC-0xFF-0x33. These short formats are rarely used.

The `FontSize` property is of type `double`. This is a little different from properties of type `LayoutOptions` and `Color`. The `LayoutOptions` and `Color` structures are part of Xamarin.Forms, so they can be flagged with the C# `TypeConverter` attribute, but it's not possible to flag the .NET `Double` structure with a `TypeConverter` attribute just for font sizes!

Instead, the `FontSize` property within the `Label` class has the `TypeConverter` attribute:

```
public class Label : View, IFontElement
{
    …
    [TypeConverter (typeof (FontSizeConverter))]
    public double FontSize
    {
        …
```

```
    }
    …
}
```

The `FontSizeConverter` determines whether the string passed to it is one of the members of the `NamedSize` enumeration. If not, `FontSizeConverter` assumes the value is a `double`.

The last attribute set in the example is `FontAttributes`. The `FontAttributes` property is an enumeration named `FontAttributes`, and you already know that the XAML parser handles enumeration types automatically. However, the `FontAttributes` enumeration has a C# `Flags` attribute set like so:

```
[Flags]
public enum FontAttributes
{
    None = 0,
    Bold = 1,
    Italic = 2
}
```

The XAML parser therefore allows multiple members separated by commas:

```
FontAttributes="Bold,Italic"
```

This demonstration of the mechanical nature of the XAML parser should be very good news. It means that you can include custom classes in XAML, and these classes can have properties of custom types, or the properties can be of standard types but allow additional values. All you need is to flag these types or properties with a C# `TypeConverter` attribute and provide a class that derives from `TypeConverter`.

Property-element syntax

Here is some C# that is similar to the **FramedText** code in Chapter 4. In one statement it instantiates a `Frame` and a `Label` and sets the `Label` to the `Content` property of the `Frame`:

```
new Frame
{
    OutlineColor = Color.Accent,
    HorizontalOptions = LayoutOptions.Center,
    VerticalOptions = LayoutOptions.Center,
    Content = new Label
    {
        Text = "Greetings, Xamarin.Forms!"
    }
};
```

But when you start to duplicate this in XAML, you might become a little stymied at the point where you set the `Content` attribute:

```
<Frame OutlineColor="Accent"
       HorizontalOptions="Center"
```

```
        VerticalOptions="Center"
        Content=" what goes here? " />
```

How can that `Content` attribute be set to an entire `Label` object?

The solution to this problem is the most fundamental feature of XAML syntax. The first step is to separate the `Frame` tag into start and end tags:

```
<Frame OutlineColor="Accent"
       HorizontalOptions="Center"
       VerticalOptions="Center">

</Frame>
```

Within those tags, add two more tags that consist of the element (`Frame`) and the property you want to set (`Content`) connected with a period:

```
<Frame OutlineColor="Accent"
       HorizontalOptions="Center"
       VerticalOptions="Center">
    <Frame.Content>

    </Frame.Content>
</Frame>
```

Now put the `Label` within those tags:

```
<Frame OutlineColor="Accent"
       HorizontalOptions="Center"
       VerticalOptions="Center">
    <Frame.Content>
        <Label Text="Greetings, Xamarin.Forms!" />
    </Frame.Content>
</Frame>
```

That syntax is how you set a `Label` to the `Content` property of the `Frame`.

You might wonder if this XAML feature violates XML syntax rules. It does not. The period has no special meaning in XML, so `Frame.Content` is a perfectly valid XML tag. However, XAML imposes its own rules about these tags: The `Frame.Content` tags must appear within `Frame` tags, and no attributes can be set in the `Frame.Content` tag. The object set to the `Content` property appears as the XML content of those tags.

Once this syntax is introduced, some terminology becomes necessary. In the final XAML snippet shown above:

- `Frame` and `Label` are C# objects expressed as XML elements. They are called *object elements*.

- `OutlineColor`, `HorizontalOptions`, `VerticalOptions`, and `Text` are C# properties expressed as XML attributes. They are called *property attributes*.

- `Frame.Content` is a C# property expressed as an XML element, and it is therefore called a *property element.*

Property elements are very common in real-life XAML. You'll see numerous examples in this chapter and future chapters, and you'll soon find property elements becoming second nature to your use of XAML. But watch out: Sometimes developers must remember so much that we forget the basics. Even after you've been using XAML for a while, you'll probably encounter a situation where it doesn't seem possible to set a particular object to a particular property. The solution is very often a property element.

You can also use property-element syntax for simpler properties, for example:

```
<Frame HorizontalOptions="Center">
    <Frame.VerticalOptions>
        Center
    </Frame.VerticalOptions>
    <Frame.OutlineColor>
        Accent
    </Frame.OutlineColor>
    <Frame.Content>
        <Label>
            <Label.Text>
                Greetings, Xamarin.Forms!
            </Label.Text>
        </Label>
    </Frame.Content>
</Frame>
```

Now the `VerticalOptions` and `OutlineColor` properties of `Frame` and the `Text` property of `Label` have all become property elements. The value of these attributes is the content of the property element without quotation marks.

Of course, it doesn't make much sense to define these properties as property elements. It's unnecessarily verbose. But it works as it should.

Let's go a little further: Instead of setting `HorizontalOptions` to "Center" (corresponding to the static property `LayoutOptions.Center`), you can express `HorizontalOptions` as a property element and set it to a `LayoutOptions` value with its individual properties set:

```
<Frame>
    <Frame.HorizontalOptions>
        <LayoutOptions Alignment="Center"
                       Expands="False" />
    </Frame.HorizontalOptions>
    <Frame.VerticalOptions>
        Center
    </Frame.VerticalOptions>
    <Frame.OutlineColor>
        Accent
    </Frame.OutlineColor>
    <Frame.Content>
        <Label>
```

```
            <Label.Text>
                Greetings, Xamarin.Forms!
            </Label.Text>
        </Label>
    </Frame.Content>
</Frame>
```

And you can express these properties of `LayoutOptions` as property elements:

```
<Frame>
    <Frame.HorizontalOptions>
        <LayoutOptions>
            <LayoutOptions.Alignment>
                Center
            </LayoutOptions.Alignment>
            <LayoutOptions.Expands>
                False
            </LayoutOptions.Expands>
        </LayoutOptions>
    </Frame.HorizontalOptions>
    ...
</Frame>
```

You can't set the same property as a property attribute and a property element. That's setting the property twice, and it's not allowed. And remember that nothing else can appear in the property-element tags. The value being set to the property is always the XML content of those tags.

Now you should know how to use a `StackLayout` in XAML. First express the `Children` property as the property element `StackLayout.Children`, and then include the children of the `StackLayout` as XML content of the property-element tags. Here's an example where each child of the first `StackLayout` is another `StackLayout` with a horizontal orientation:

```
<StackLayout>
    <StackLayout.Children>
        <StackLayout Orientation="Horizontal">
            <StackLayout.Children>
                <BoxView Color="Red" />
                <Label Text="Red"
                       VerticalOptions="Center" />
            </StackLayout.Children>
        </StackLayout>

        <StackLayout Orientation="Horizontal">
            <StackLayout.Children>
                <BoxView Color="Green" />
                <Label Text="Green"
                       VerticalOptions="Center" />
            </StackLayout.Children>
        </StackLayout>

        <StackLayout Orientation="Horizontal">
            <StackLayout.Children>
                <BoxView Color="Blue" />
```

```
            <Label Text="Blue"
                   VerticalOptions="Center" />
        </StackLayout.Children>
    </StackLayout>
  </StackLayout.Children>
</StackLayout>
```

Each horizontal `StackLayout` has a `BoxView` with a color and a `Label` with that color name.

Of course, the repetitive markup here looks rather scary! What if you wanted to display 16 colors? Or 140? You might succeed at first with a lot of copying and pasting, but if you then needed to refine the visuals a bit, you'd be in bad shape. In code you'd do this in a loop, but XAML has no such feature.

When markup threatens to be overly repetitious, you can always use code. Defining some of a user interface in XAML and the rest in code is perfectly reasonable. But there are other solutions, as you'll see in later chapters.

Adding a XAML page to your project

Now that you've seen some snippets of XAML, let's look at a whole XAML page in the context of a complete program. First, create a Xamarin.Forms solution named **CodePlusXaml** using the Portable Class Library solution template.

Now add a XAML `ContentPage` to the PCL. Here's how:

In Visual Studio, right click the **CodePlusXaml** project in the **Solution Explorer**. Select **Add > New Item** from the menu. In the **Add New Item** dialog, select **Visual C#** and **Code** at the left, and **Forms Xaml Page** from the central list. Name it CodePlusXamlPage.cs.

In Xamarin Studio, invoke the drop-down menu on the **CodePlusXaml** project in the **Solution** list, and select **Add > New File**. In the **New File** dialog, select **Forms** at the left and **Forms ContentPage Xaml** in the central list. (Watch out: There's also a **Forms ContentView Xaml** in the list. You want a content *page*.) Name it CodePlusXamlPage.

In either case, two files are created:

- CodePlusXamlPage.xaml, the XAML file; and

- CodePlusXamlPage.xaml.cs, a C# file (despite the odd double extension on the filename).

In the file list, the second file is indented underneath the first, indicating their close relationship. The C# file is often referred to as the *code-behind* of the XAML file. It contains code that supports the markup. These two files both contribute to a class named `CodePlusXamlPage` that derives from `ContentPage`.

Let's examine the code file first. Excluding the `using` directives, it looks like this:

```
namespace CodePlusXaml
{
```

```
public partial class CodePlusXamlPage : ContentPage
{
    public CodePlusXamlPage()
    {
        InitializeComponent();
    }
}
}
```

It is indeed a class named `CodePlusXamlPage` that derives from `ContentPage`, just as anticipated. However, the class definition includes a `partial` keyword, which usually indicates that this is only part of the `CodePlusXamlPage` class definition. Somewhere else there should be another partial class definition for `CodePlusXamlPage`. So if it exists, where is it? It's a mystery! (For now.)

Another mystery is the `InitializeComponent` method that the constructor calls. Judging solely from the syntax, it seems as though this method should be defined or inherited by `ContentPage`. Yet, you won't find `InitializeComponent` in the API documentation.

Let's set those two mysteries aside temporarily and look at the XAML file. The Visual Studio and Xamarin Studio templates generate two somewhat different XAML files. If you're using Visual Studio, delete the markup for the `Label` and replace it with `ContentPage.Content` property-element tags so that it looks like the version in Xamarin Studio:

```
<ContentPage xmlns="http://xamarin.com/schemas/2014/forms"
             xmlns:x="http://schemas.microsoft.com/winfx/2009/xaml"
             x:Class="CodePlusXaml.CodePlusXamlPage">
    <ContentPage.Content>
    </ContentPage.Content>
</ContentPage>
```

The root element is `ContentPage`, which is the class that `CodePlusXamlPage` derives from. That tag begins with two XML namespace declarations, both of which are URIs. But don't bother checking the web addresses! There's nothing there. These URIs simply indicate who owns the namespace and what function it serves.

The default namespace belongs to Xamarin. This is the XML namespace for elements in the file with no prefix, such as the `ContentPage` tag. The URL includes the year that this namespace came into being and the word `forms` as an abbreviation for Xamarin.Forms.

The second namespace is associated with a prefix of `x` by convention, and it belongs to Microsoft. This namespace refers to elements and attributes that are intrinsic to XAML and are found in every XAML implementation. The word `winfx` refers to a name once used for the .NET Framework 3.0, which introduced WPF and XAML. The year 2009 refers to a particular XAML specification, which also implies a particular collection of elements and attributes that build upon the original XAML specification, which is dated 2006. However, Xamarin.Forms implements only a subset of the elements and attributes in the 2009 specification.

The next line is one of the attributes that is intrinsic to XAML, called `Class`. Because the `x` prefix is almost universally used for this namespace, this attribute is commonly referred to as `x:Class` and pro-nounced "x class."

The `x:Class` attribute can appear only on the root element of a XAML file. It specifies the .NET namespace and name of a derived class. The base class of this derived class is the root element. In other words, this `x:Class` specification indicates that the `CodePlusXamlPage` class in the `CodePlusXaml` namespace derives from `ContentPage`. That's exactly the same information as the `CodePlusXamlPage` class definition in the CodePlusXamlPage.xaml.cs file.

Let's add some content, which means setting something to the `Content` property, which in the XAML file means putting something between `ContentPage.Content` property-element tags. Begin the content with a `StackLayout`, and then add a `Label` to the `Children` property:

```
<ContentPage xmlns="http://xamarin.com/schemas/2014/forms"
             xmlns:x="http://schemas.microsoft.com/winfx/2009/xaml"
             x:Class="CodePlusXaml.CodePlusXamlPage">
    <ContentPage.Content>
        <StackLayout>
            <StackLayout.Children>
                <Label Text="Hello from XAML!"
                       IsVisible="True"
                       Opacity="0.75"
                       XAlign="Center"
                       VerticalOptions="CenterAndExpand"
                       TextColor="Blue"
                       BackgroundColor="#FF8080"
                       FontSize="Large"
                       FontAttributes="Bold,Italic" />
            </StackLayout.Children>
        </StackLayout>
    </ContentPage.Content>
</ContentPage>
```

That's the XAML `Label` you saw at the beginning of this chapter.

You'll now need to change the `App` class to instantiate this page just like you do with a code-only derivative of `ContentPage`:

```
namespace CodePlusXaml
{
    public class App : Application
    {
        public App()
        {
            MainPage = new CodePlusXamlPage();
        }
        ...
    }
}
```

You can now build and deploy this program. After you do so, it's possible to clear up a couple of mysteries:

In Visual Studio, in the **Solution Explorer**, select the **CodePlusXaml** project, find the icon at the top with the tooltip **Show All Files**, and toggle that on.

In Xamarin Studio, in the **Solution** file list, invoke the drop-down menu for the whole solution, and select **Display Options > Show All Files**.

In the **CodePlusXaml** Portable Class Library project, find the **obj** folder and within that, the **Debug** folder. You'll see a file named CodePlusXamlPage.xaml.g.cs. Notice the *g* in the filename. That stands for *generated*. Here it is, complete with the comment that tells you that this file is generated by a tool:

```
//------------------------------------------------------------------------------
// <auto-generated>
//     This code was generated by a tool.
//     Runtime Version:4.0.30319.35317
//
//     Changes to this file may cause incorrect behavior and will be lost if
//     the code is regenerated.
// </auto-generated>
//------------------------------------------------------------------------------

namespace CodePlusXaml {
    using System;
    using Xamarin.Forms;
    using Xamarin.Forms.Xaml;


    public partial class CodePlusXamlPage : ContentPage {

        private void InitializeComponent() {
            this.LoadFromXaml(typeof(CodePlusXamlPage));
        }
    }
}
```

During the build process, the XAML file is parsed, and this code file is generated. Notice that it's a partial class definition of `CodePlusXamlPage`, which derives from `ContentPage`, and the class contains a method named `InitializeComponent`.

In other words, it's a perfect fit for the CodePlusXamlPage.xaml.cs code-behind file. After the CodePlusXamlPage.xaml.g.cs file is generated, the two files can be compiled together as if they were just normal C# partial class definitions. The XAML file has no further role in the build process, but the entire XAML file is bound into the executable as an embedded resource (just like the Edgar Allan Poe story in the **BlackCat** program in Chapter 4).

At run time, the `App` class instantiates the `CodePlusXamlPage` class. The `CodePlusXamlPage` constructor (defined in the code-behind file) calls `InitializeComponent` (defined in the generated file), and `InitializeComponent` calls `LoadFromXaml`. This is an extension method for `View` defined in the `Extensions` class in the **Xamarin.Forms.Xaml** assembly. `LoadFromXaml` loads the XAML file (which you'll recall is bound into the executable as an embedded resource) and parses it for a second time. Because this parsing occurs at run time, `LoadFromXaml` can instantiate and initialize all the elements in the XAML file except for the root element, which already exists. When the `InitializeComponent` method returns, the whole page is in place, just as though everything had been instantiated and initialized in code in the `CodePlusXamlPage` constructor.

It's possible to continue adding content to the page after the `InitializeComponent` call returns in the constructor of the code-behind file. Let's use this opportunity to create another `Label` by using some code from earlier in this chapter:

```
namespace CodePlusXaml
{
    public partial class CodePlusXamlPage : ContentPage
    {
        public CodePlusXamlPage()
        {
            InitializeComponent();

            Label label = new Label
            {
                Text = "Hello from Code!",
                IsVisible = true,
                Opacity = 0.75,
                XAlign = TextAlignment.Center,
                VerticalOptions = LayoutOptions.CenterAndExpand,
                TextColor = Color.Blue,
                BackgroundColor = Color.FromRgb(255, 128, 128),
                FontSize = Device.GetNamedSize(NamedSize.Large, typeof(Label)),
                FontAttributes = FontAttributes.Bold | FontAttributes.Italic
            };

            (Content as StackLayout).Children.Insert(0, label);
        }
    }
}
```

The constructor concludes by accessing the `StackLayout` that we know is set to the `Content` property of the page and inserting the `Label` at the top. (In the next chapter, you'll see a much better way to reference objects in the XAML file by using the `x:Name` attribute.) You can create the `Label` prior to the `InitializeComponent` call, but you can't add it to the `StackLayout` because `InitializeComponent` is what causes the `StackLayout` (and all the other XAML elements) to be instantiated. Here's the result:

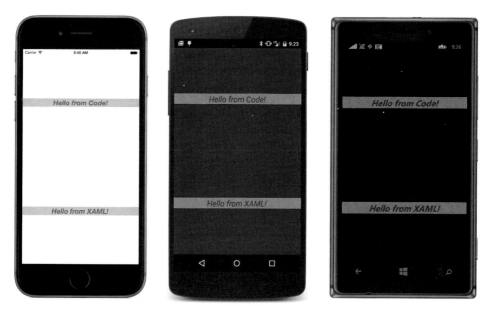

Aside from the text, the two buttons are identical.

You don't have to spend much time examining the generated code file that the XAML parser creates, but it's helpful to understand how the XAML file plays a role both in the build process and during run time. Also, sometimes an error in the XAML file raises a run-time exception at the `LoadFromXaml` call, so you will probably see the generated code file pop up frequently, and you should know what it is.

Platform specificity in the XAML file

Here is the XAML file for a program named **ScaryColorList** that's similar to a snippet of XAML that you saw earlier. But now the repetition is even scarier because each color item is surrounded by a `Frame`:

```
<ContentPage xmlns="http://xamarin.com/schemas/2014/forms"
             xmlns:x="http://schemas.microsoft.com/winfx/2009/xaml"
             x:Class="ScaryColorList.ScaryColorListPage">
    <ContentPage.Content>
        <StackLayout>
            <StackLayout.Children>
                <Frame OutlineColor="Accent">
                    <Frame.Content>
                        <StackLayout Orientation="Horizontal">
                            <StackLayout.Children>
                                <BoxView Color="Red" />
                                <Label Text="Red"
                                       VerticalOptions="Center" />
                            </StackLayout.Children>
```

```
                                </StackLayout>
                            </Frame.Content>
                        </Frame>

                        <Frame OutlineColor="Accent">
                            <Frame.Content>
                                <StackLayout Orientation="Horizontal">
                                    <StackLayout.Children>
                                        <BoxView Color="Green" />
                                            <Label Text="Green"
                                                   VerticalOptions="Center" />
                                    </StackLayout.Children>
                                </StackLayout>
                            </Frame.Content>
                        </Frame>

                        <Frame OutlineColor="Accent">
                            <Frame.Content>
                                <StackLayout Orientation="Horizontal">
                                    <StackLayout.Children>
                                        <BoxView Color="Blue" />
                                        <Label Text="Blue"
                                               VerticalOptions="Center" />
                                    </StackLayout.Children>
                                </StackLayout>
                            </Frame.Content>
                        </Frame>
                    </StackLayout.Children>
                </StackLayout>
        </ContentPage.Content>
</ContentPage>
```

The code-behind file contains only a call to `InitializeComponent`.

Aside from the repetitious markup, this program has a more practical problem: When it runs on iOS, the top item overlaps the status bar. This problem can be fixed with a call to `Device.OnPlatform` in the page's constructor (just as you saw in Chapter 2). Because `Device.OnPlatform` sets the `Padding` property on the page and doesn't require anything in the XAML file, it could go either before or after the `InitializeComponent` call. Here's one way to do it:

```
public partial class ScaryColorListPage : ContentPage
{
    public ScaryColorListPage()
    {
        Padding = Device.OnPlatform(new Thickness(0, 20, 0, 0),
                                    new Thickness(0),
                                    new Thickness(0));

        InitializeComponent();
    }
}
```

Or, you could set a uniform `Padding` value for all three platforms right in the root element of the

XAML file:

```
<ContentPage xmlns="http://xamarin.com/schemas/2014/forms"
             xmlns:x="http://schemas.microsoft.com/winfx/2009/xaml"
             x:Class="ScaryColorList.ScaryColorListPage"
             Padding="0, 20, 0, 0">
    <ContentPage.Content>
        …
    </ContentPage.Content>
</ContentPage>
```

That sets the `Padding` property for the page. The `ThicknessTypeConverter` class requires the values to be separated by commas, but you have the same flexibility as with the `Thickness` constructor. You can specify four values in the order left, top, right, and bottom; two values (the first for left and right, and the second for top and bottom); or one value.

However, you can also specify platform-specific values right in the XAML file by using the `OnPlatform` class, whose name suggests that it is similar in function to the `Device.OnPlatform` static method.

`OnPlatform` is a very interesting class, and it's worthwhile to get a sense of how it works. The class is generic, and it has three properties of type `T`, as well as an implicit conversion of itself to `T` that makes use of the `Device.OS` value:

```
public class OnPlatform<T>
{
    public T iOS { get; set; }

    public T Android { get; set; }

    public T WinPhone { get; set; }

    public static implicit operator T(OnPlatform<T> onPlatform)
    {
        // returns one of the three properties based on Device.OS
    }
}
```

In theory, you might use the `OnPlatform<T>` class like so in the constructor of a `ContentPage` derivative:

```
Padding = new OnPlatform<Thickness>
{
    iOS = new Thickness(0, 20, 0, 0),
    Android = new Thickness(0),
    WinPhone = new Thickness(0)
};
```

You can set an instance of this class directly to the `Padding` property because the `OnPlatform` class defines an implicit conversion of itself to the generic argument (in this case `Thickness`).

However, you shouldn't use `OnPlatform` in code. Use `Device.OnPlatform` instead. `OnPlatform` is designed for XAML, and the only really tricky part is figuring out how to specify the generic type argument.

Fortunately, the XAML 2009 specification includes an attribute designed specifically for generic classes, called `TypeArguments`. Because it's part of XAML itself, it's used with an `x` prefix, so it appears as `x:TypeArguments`. Here's how `OnPlatform` is used to select among three `Thickness` values:

```
<OnPlatform x:TypeArguments="Thickness"
            iOS="0, 20, 0, 0"
            Android="0"
            WinPhone="0" />
```

In this example (and in the previous code example), the `Android` and `WinPhone` settings aren't required because they are the defaults. Notice that the `Thickness` strings can be set directly to the properties because those properties are of type `Thickness`, and hence the XAML parser will use the `ThicknessTypeConverter` for converting those strings.

Now that we have the `OnPlatform` markup, how do we set it to the `Padding` property of the `Page`? By expressing `Padding` using property-element syntax, of course!

```
<ContentPage xmlns="http://xamarin.com/schemas/2014/forms"
             xmlns:x="http://schemas.microsoft.com/winfx/2009/xaml"
             x:Class="ScaryColorList.ScaryColorListPage">

    <ContentPage.Padding>
        <OnPlatform x:TypeArguments="Thickness"
                    iOS="0, 20, 0, 0" />
    </ContentPage.Padding>

    <ContentPage.Content>
        ...
    </ContentPage.Content>
</ContentPage>
```

This is how the **ScaryColorList** program appears in the collection of samples from this book and here's how it looks:

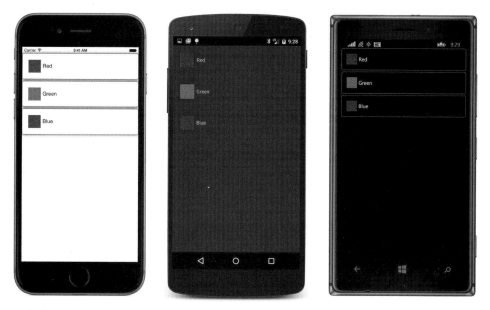

Similar to `OnDevice`, `OnIdiom` distinguishes between `Phone` and `Tablet`. For reasons that will become apparent in the next chapter, you should try to restrict the use of `OnDevice` and `OnIdiom` for small chunks of markup rather than large blocks. It shouldn't become a structural element in your XAML files.

The content property attribute

The XAML file in the **ScaryColorList** program is actually somewhat longer than it needs to be. You can delete the `ContentPage.Content` tags, all the `StackLayout.Children` tags, and all the `Frame.Content` tags, and the program will work the same:

```
<ContentPage xmlns="http://xamarin.com/schemas/2014/forms"
             xmlns:x="http://schemas.microsoft.com/winfx/2009/xaml"
             x:Class="ScaryColorList.ScaryColorListPage">

    <ContentPage.Padding>
        <OnPlatform x:TypeArguments="Thickness"
                    iOS="0, 20, 0, 0" />
    </ContentPage.Padding>

    <StackLayout>
        <Frame OutlineColor="Accent">
            <StackLayout Orientation="Horizontal">
                <BoxView Color="Red" />
                <Label Text="Red"
                       VerticalOptions="Center" />
            </StackLayout>
```

```
        </Frame>

        <Frame OutlineColor="Accent">
            <StackLayout Orientation="Horizontal">
                <BoxView Color="Green" />
                <Label Text="Green"
                    VerticalOptions="Center" />
            </StackLayout>
        </Frame>

        <Frame OutlineColor="Accent">
            <StackLayout Orientation="Horizontal">
                <BoxView Color="Blue" />
                <Label Text="Blue"
                    VerticalOptions="Center" />
            </StackLayout>
        </Frame>
    </StackLayout>
</ContentPage>
```

It looks a lot cleaner now. The only property element left is for the `Padding` property of `ContentPage`.

As with almost everything about XAML syntax, this elimination of some property elements is supported by the underlying classes. Every class used in XAML is allowed to define one property as a *content property* (sometimes also called the class's *default property*). For this content property, the property-element tags are not required, and any XML content within the start and end tags is automatically assigned to this property. Very conveniently, the content property of `ContentPage` is `Content`, the content property of `StackLayout` is `Children`, and the content property of `Frame` is `Content`.

These content properties are documented, but you need to know where to look. A class specifies its content property by using the `ContentPropertyAttribute`. If this attribute is attached to a class, it appears in the online Xamarin.Forms API documentation along with the class declaration. Here's how it appears in the documentation for `ContentPage`:

```
[Xamarin.Forms.ContentProperty("Content")]
public class ContentPage : Page
```

If you say it aloud, it sounds a bit redundant: The `Content` property is the content property of `ContentPage`.

The declaration for the `Frame` class is similar:

```
[Xamarin.Forms.ContentProperty("Content")]
public class Frame : ContentView
```

`StackLayout` doesn't have a `ContentProperty` attribute applied, but `StackLayout` derives from `Layout<View>`, and `Layout<T>` has a `ContentProperty` attribute:

```
[Xamarin.Forms.ContentProperty("Children")]
public abstract class Layout<T> : Layout, IViewContainer<T>
where T : Xamarin.Forms.View
```

The `ContentProperty` attribute is inherited by the classes that derive from `Layout<T>`, so `Children` is the content property of `StackLayout`.

Certainly, there's no problem if you include the property elements when they're not required, but in most cases they will no longer appear in the sample programs in this book.

Formatted text

Text displayed by a XAML file might involve just a word or two, but sometimes an entire paragraph is required, perhaps with some embedded character formatting. This is not always as obvious, or as easy, in XAML as might be suggested by our familiarity with HTML.

The **TextVariations** solution has a XAML file that contains seven `Label` views in a scrollable `StackLayout`:

```
<ContentPage xmlns="http://xamarin.com/schemas/2014/forms"
             xmlns:x="http://schemas.microsoft.com/winfx/2009/xaml"
             x:Class="TextVariations.TextVariationsPage">

    <ContentPage.Padding>
        <OnPlatform x:TypeArguments="Thickness"
                    iOS="0, 20, 0, 0" />
    </ContentPage.Padding>

    <ScrollView>
        <StackLayout>
            ...
        </StackLayout>
    </ScrollView>
</ContentPage>
```

Each of the seven `Label` views shows a somewhat different way of defining the displayed text. For reference purposes, here's the program running on all three platforms:

The simplest approach involves just setting a few words to the `Text` attribute of the `Label` element:

```
<Label VerticalOptions="CenterAndExpand"
       Text="Single lines of text are easy." />
```

You can also set the `Text` property by breaking it out as a property element:

```
<Label VerticalOptions="CenterAndExpand">
    <Label.Text>
        Text can also be content of the Text property.
    </Label.Text>
</Label>
```

`Text` is the content property of `Label`, so you don't need the `Label.Text` tags:

```
<Label VerticalOptions="CenterAndExpand">
    Text is the content property of Label.
</Label>
```

When you set text as the content of the `Label` (whether you use the `Label.Text` tags or not), the text is trimmed: all whitespace, including carriage returns, is removed from the beginning and end of the text. However, all embedded whitespace is retained, including end-of-line characters.

When you set the `Text` property as a property attribute, all whitespace within the quotation marks is retained but end-of-line characters are converted to spaces.

Displaying a whole paragraph of uniformly formatted text is somewhat problematic. The most fool-proof approach is setting `Text` as a property attribute. You can put the whole paragraph as a single line in the XAML file, but if you prefer to use multiple lines, you should left justify the whole paragraph in the XAML file surrounded by quotation marks, like so:

```
            <Label VerticalOptions="CenterAndExpand"
                    Text=
"Perhaps the best way to define a paragraph of
uniformly formatted text is by setting the Text
property as an attribute and left justifying
the block of text in the XAML file. End-of-line
characters are converted to a space character." />
```

The end-of-line characters are converted to space characters so the individual lines are properly con-catenated. But watch out: Don't leave any stray characters at the end or beginning of the individual lines. Those will show up as extraneous characters within the paragraph.

When multiple lines of text are specified as content of the Label, only whitespace at the beginning and end of the text is trimmed. All embedded whitespace is retained, including end-of-line characters:

```
            <Label VerticalOptions="CenterAndExpand">
Text as content has the curse
Of breaks at each line's close.
That's a format great for verse
But not the best for prose.
            </Label>
```

This text is rendered as four separate lines. If you're displaying lists or poetry in your Xamarin.Forms application, that's exactly what you want. Otherwise, probably not.

If your line or paragraph of text requires some nonuniform paragraph formatting, you'll want to use the FormattedText property of Label. As you might recall, you set this to a FormattedString ob-ject and then set multiple Span objects to the Spans collection of the FormattedString. In XAML, you need property-element tags for Label.FormattedString, but Spans is the content property of FormattedString:

```
            <Label VerticalOptions="CenterAndExpand">
                <Label.FormattedText>
                    <FormattedString>
                        <Span Text="A single line with " />
                        <Span Text="bold" FontAttributes="Bold" />
                        <Span Text=" and " />
                        <Span Text="italic" FontAttributes="Italic" />
                        <Span Text=" and " />
                        <Span Text="large" FontSize="Large" />
                        <Span Text=" text." />
                    </FormattedString>
                </Label.FormattedText>
            </Label>
```

Notice that the Text properties of the nonformatted items have spaces at the end or beginning of the text string, or both, so that the items don't run into each other.

In the general case, however, you might be working with an entire paragraph. You can set the Text attribute of Span to a long line, or you can wrap it on multiple lines. As with Label, keep the entire block left justified in the XAML file:

```
            <Label VerticalOptions="CenterAndExpand">
                <Label.FormattedText>
                    <FormattedString>
                        <Span Text=
"A paragraph of formatted text requires left justifying
it within the XAML file. But the text can include multiple
kinds of character formatting, including " />
                        <Span Text="bold" FontAttributes="Bold" />
                        <Span Text=" and " />
                        <Span Text="italic" FontAttributes="Italic" />
                        <Span Text=" and " />
                        <Span Text="large" FontSize="Large" />
                        <Span Text=
" and whatever combinations you might desire to adorn
your glorious prose." />
                    </FormattedString>
                </Label.FormattedText>
            </Label>
```

You'll notice in the screen shot that the text with the large font size is aligned with the regular text on the baseline, which is the typographically proper approach, and the line spacing is adjusted to accommodate the larger text.

In most Xamarin.Forms programs, neither XAML nor code exist in isolation but work together. Elements in XAML can trigger events handled in code, and code can modify elements in XAML. In the next chapter you'll see how this works.

Chapter 8
Code and XAML in harmony

A code file and a XAML file always exist as a pair. The two files complement each other. Despite being referred to as the "code-behind" file to the XAML, very often the code is prominent in taking on the more active and interactive parts of the application. This implies that the code-behind file must be able to refer to elements defined in XAML with as much ease as objects instantiated in code. Likewise, elements in XAML must be able to fire events that are handled in code-based event handlers. That's what this chapter is all about.

But first, let's explore a couple of unusual techniques for instantiating objects in a XAML file.

Passing arguments

As you've seen, the XAML parser instantiates elements by calling the parameterless constructor of the corresponding class or structure and then initializes the resultant object by setting properties from attribute values. This seems reasonable. However, developers using XAML sometimes have a need to instantiate objects with constructors that require arguments or by calling a static creation method. These needs usually don't involve the API itself, but instead involve external data classes referenced by the XAML file that interact with the API.

The 2009 XAML specification introduced an `x:Arguments` element and an `x:FactoryMethod` attribute for these cases, and Xamarin.Forms supports them. These techniques are not often used in ordinary circumstances, but you should see how they work in case the need arises.

Constructors with arguments

To pass arguments to a constructor of an element in XAML, the element must be separated into start and end tags. Follow the start tag of the element with `x:Arguments` start and end tags. Within those `x:Arguments` tags, include one or more constructor arguments.

But how do you specify multiple arguments of common types, such as `double` or `int`? Do you separate the arguments with commas?

No. Each argument must be delimited with start and end tags. Fortunately, the XAML 2009 specification defines XML elements for common basic types. You can use these tags to clarify the types of elements, to specify generic types in `OnPlatform`, or to delimit constructor arguments. Here's the complete set supported by Xamarin.Forms. Notice that they duplicate the .NET type names rather than the C# type names:

- `x:Object`

- `x:Boolean`

- `x:Byte`

- `x:Int16`

- `x:Int32`

- `x:Int64`

- `x:Single`

- `x:Double`

- `x:Decimal`

- `x:Char`

- `x:String`

- `x:TimeSpan`

- `x:Array`

- `x:DateTime` (supported by Xamarin.Forms but not the XAML 2009 specification)

You'll be hard-pressed to find a use for all of these, but you'll certainly discover uses for some of them.

The **ParameteredConstructorDemo** sample demonstrates the use of `x:Arguments` with arguments delimited by `x:Double` tags using three different constructors of the `Color` structure. The constructor with three parameters requires red, green, and blue values ranging from 0 to 1. The constructor with four parameters adds an alpha channel as the fourth parameter (which is set here to 0.5), and the constructor with a single parameter indicates a gray shade from 0 (black) to 1 (white):

```
<ContentPage xmlns="http://xamarin.com/schemas/2014/forms"
             xmlns:x="http://schemas.microsoft.com/winfx/2009/xaml"
             x:Class="ParameteredConstructorDemo.ParameteredConstructorDemoPage">

    <StackLayout>
        <BoxView WidthRequest="100"
                 HeightRequest="100"
                 HorizontalOptions="Center"
                 VerticalOptions="CenterAndExpand">
            <BoxView.Color>
                <Color>
                    <x:Arguments>
                        <x:Double>1</x:Double>
                        <x:Double>0</x:Double>
                        <x:Double>0</x:Double>
                    </x:Arguments>
                </Color>
            </BoxView.Color>
        </BoxView>
```

```
                    <BoxView WidthRequest="100"
                             HeightRequest="100"
                             HorizontalOptions="Center"
                             VerticalOptions="CenterAndExpand">
                        <BoxView.Color>
                            <Color>
                                <x:Arguments>
                                    <x:Double>0</x:Double>
                                    <x:Double>0</x:Double>
                                    <x:Double>1</x:Double>
                                    <x:Double>0.5</x:Double>
                                </x:Arguments>
                            </Color>
                        </BoxView.Color>
                    </BoxView>

                    <BoxView WidthRequest="100"
                             HeightRequest="100"
                             HorizontalOptions="Center"
                             VerticalOptions="CenterAndExpand">
                        <BoxView.Color>
                            <Color>
                                <x:Arguments>
                                    <x:Double>0.5</x:Double>
                                </x:Arguments>
                            </Color>
                        </BoxView.Color>
                    </BoxView>
                </StackLayout>
            </ContentPage>
```

The number of elements within the x:Arguments tags, and the types of these elements, must match one of the constructors of the class or structure. Here's the result:

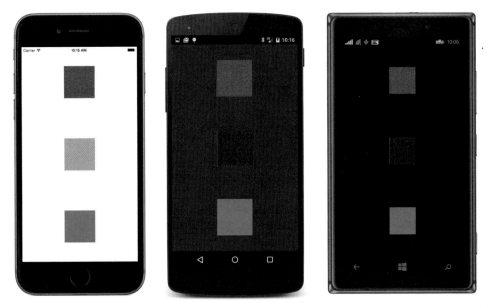

The blue `BoxView` is light against the light background and dark against the dark background because it's 50 percent transparent and lets the background show through.

Can I call methods from XAML?

At one time, the answer to this question was "Don't be ridiculous," but now it's a qualified "Yes." Don't get too excited, though. The only methods you can call in XAML are those that return objects (or values) of the same type as the class (or structure) that defines the method. These methods must be public and static. They are sometimes called *creation methods* or *factory methods*. You can instantiate an element in XAML through a call to one of these methods by specifying the method's name using the `x:FactoryMethod` attribute and its arguments using the `x:Arguments` element.

The `Color` structure defines seven static methods that return `Color` values, so these qualify. This XAML file makes use of three of them:

```
<ContentPage xmlns="http://xamarin.com/schemas/2014/forms"
             xmlns:x="http://schemas.microsoft.com/winfx/2009/xaml"
             x:Class="FactoryMethodDemo.FactoryMethodDemoPage">

    <StackLayout>
        <BoxView WidthRequest="100"
                 HeightRequest="100"
                 HorizontalOptions="Center"
                 VerticalOptions="CenterAndExpand">
            <BoxView.Color>
                <Color x:FactoryMethod="FromRgb">
                    <x:Arguments>
                        <x:Int32>255</x:Int32>
                        <x:Int32>0</x:Int32>
```

```
                            <x:Int32>0</x:Int32>
                        </x:Arguments>
                    </Color>
                </BoxView.Color>
            </BoxView>

            <BoxView WidthRequest="100"
                     HeightRequest="100"
                     HorizontalOptions="Center"
                     VerticalOptions="CenterAndExpand">
                <BoxView.Color>
                    <Color x:FactoryMethod="FromRgb">
                        <x:Arguments>
                            <x:Double>0</x:Double>
                            <x:Double>1.0</x:Double>
                            <x:Double>0</x:Double>
                        </x:Arguments>
                    </Color>
                </BoxView.Color>
            </BoxView>

            <BoxView WidthRequest="100"
                     HeightRequest="100"
                     HorizontalOptions="Center"
                     VerticalOptions="CenterAndExpand">
                <BoxView.Color>
                    <Color x:FactoryMethod="FromHsla">
                        <x:Arguments>
                            <x:Double>0.67</x:Double>
                            <x:Double>1.0</x:Double>
                            <x:Double>0.5</x:Double>
                            <x:Double>1.0</x:Double>
                        </x:Arguments>
                    </Color>
                </BoxView.Color>
            </BoxView>
        </StackLayout>
</ContentPage>
```

The first two static methods invoked here are both named `Color.FromRgb`, but the types of elements within the `x:Arguments` tags distinguish between `int` arguments that range from 0 to 255 and `double` arguments that range from 0 to 1. The third one is the `Color.FromHsla` method, which creates a `Color` value from hue, saturation, luminosity, and alpha components. Interestingly, this is the only way to define a `Color` value from HSL values in a XAML file by using the Xamarin.Forms API. Here's the result:

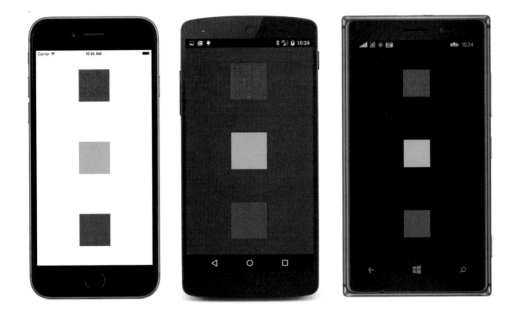

The x:Name attribute

In most real applications, the code-behind file needs to reference elements defined in the XAML file. You saw one way to do this in the **CodePlusXaml** program in the previous chapter: If the code-behind file has knowledge of the layout of the visual tree defined in the XAML file, it can start from the root element (the page itself) and locate specific elements within the tree. This process is called "walking the tree" and can be useful for locating particular elements on a page.

Generally, a better approach is to give elements in the XAML file a name similar to a variable name. To do this you use an attribute that is intrinsic to XAML, called `Name`. Because the prefix `x` is almost universally used for attributes intrinsic to XAML, this `Name` attribute is commonly referred to as `x:Name`.

The **XamlClock** project demonstrates the use of `x:Name`. Here is the XamlClockPage.xaml file containing two `Label` controls, named `timeLabel` and `dateLabel`:

```
<ContentPage xmlns="http://xamarin.com/schemas/2014/forms"
             xmlns:x="http://schemas.microsoft.com/winfx/2009/xaml"
             x:Class="XamlClock.XamlClockPage">
    <StackLayout>
        <Label x:Name="timeLabel"
               FontSize="Large"
               HorizontalOptions="Center"
               VerticalOptions="EndAndExpand" />

        <Label x:Name="dateLabel"
               HorizontalOptions="Center"
               VerticalOptions="StartAndExpand" />
```

```
    </StackLayout>
</ContentPage>
```

The rules for `x:Name` are the same as for C# variable names. (You'll see why shortly.) The name must begin with a letter or underscore and must contain only letters, underscores, and numbers.

Like the clock program in Chapter 5, **XamlClock** uses `Device.StartTimer` to fire a periodic event for updating the time and date. Here's the `XamlClockPage` code-behind file:

```
namespace XamlClock
{
    public partial class XamlClockPage
    {
        public XamlClockPage()
        {
            InitializeComponent();

            Device.StartTimer(TimeSpan.FromSeconds(1), OnTimerTick);
        }

        bool OnTimerTick()
        {
            DateTime dt = DateTime.Now;
            timeLabel.Text = dt.ToString("T");
            dateLabel.Text = dt.ToString("D");
            return true;
        }
    }
}
```

This timer callback method is called once per second. The method must return `true` to continue the timer. If it returns `false`, the timer stops and must be restarted with another call to `Device.Start-Timer`.

The callback method references `timeLabel` and `dateLabel` as though they were normal variables and sets the `Text` properties of each:

This is not a visually impressive clock, but it's definitely functional.

How is it that the code-behind file can reference the elements identified with x:Name? Is it magic? Of course not. The mechanism is very evident when you examine the XamlClockPage.xaml.g.cs file that the XAML parser generates from the XAML file as the project is being built:

```
//------------------------------------------------------------------------------
// <auto-generated>
//     This code was generated by a tool.
//     Runtime Version:4.0.30319.35317
//
//     Changes to this file may cause incorrect behavior and will be lost if
//     the code is regenerated.
// </auto-generated>
//------------------------------------------------------------------------------

namespace XamlClock {
    using System;
    using Xamarin.Forms;
    using Xamarin.Forms.Xaml;

    public partial class XamlClockPage : ContentPage {

        private Label timeLabel;

        private Label dateLabel;

        private void InitializeComponent() {
            this.LoadFromXaml(typeof(XamlClockPage));
            timeLabel = this.FindByName<Label>("timeLabel");
            dateLabel = this.FindByName<Label>("dateLabel");
```

```
            }
      }
}
```

As the build-time XAML parser chews through the XAML file, every `x:Name` attribute becomes a private field in this generated code file. This allows code in the code-behind file to reference these names as though they were normal fields—which they definitely are. However, the fields are initially `null`. Only when `InitializeComponent` is called at run time are the two fields set via the `FindByName` method, which is defined in the `NameScopeExtensions` class. If the constructor of your code-behind file tries to reference these two fields prior to the `InitializeComponent` call, they will have `null` values.

This generated code file also implies another rule for `x:Name` values that is now very obvious but rarely stated explicitly: the names cannot duplicate names of fields or properties defined in the code-behind file.

Because these are private fields, they can be accessed only from the code-behind file and not from other classes. If a `ContentPage` derivative needs to expose public fields or properties to other classes, you must define those yourself.

Obviously, `x:Name` values must be unique within a XAML page. This can sometimes be a problem if you're using `OnPlatform` for platform-specific elements in the XAML file. For example, here's a XAML file that expresses the `iOS`, `Android`, and `WinPhone` properties of `OnPlatform` as property elements to select one of three `Label` views:

```xml
<ContentPage xmlns="http://xamarin.com/schemas/2014/forms"
             xmlns:x="http://schemas.microsoft.com/winfx/2009/xaml"
             x:Class="PlatformSpecificLabels.PlatformSpecificLabelsPage">

    <OnPlatform x:TypeArguments="View">
        <OnPlatform.iOS>
            <Label Text="This is an iOS device"
                   HorizontalOptions="Center"
                   VerticalOptions="Center" />
        </OnPlatform.iOS>

        <OnPlatform.Android>
            <Label Text="This is an Android device"
                   HorizontalOptions="Center"
                   VerticalOptions="Center" />
        </OnPlatform.Android>

        <OnPlatform.WinPhone>
            <Label Text="This is an Windows Phone device"
                   HorizontalOptions="Center"
                   VerticalOptions="Center" />
        </OnPlatform.WinPhone>
    </OnPlatform>
</ContentPage>
```

The x:TypeArguments attribute of OnPlatform must match the type of the target property exactly. This OnPlatform element is implicitly being set to the Content property of ContentPage, and this Content property is of type View, so the x:TypeArguments attribute of OnPlatform must specify View. However, the properties of OnPlatform can be set to any class that derives from that type. The objects set to the iOS, Android, and WinPhone properties can in fact be different types just as long as they derive from View.

Although that XAML file works, it's not exactly optimum. All three Label views are instantiated and initialized, but only one is set to the Content property of the ContentPage. The problem with this approach arises if you need to refer to the Label from the code-behind file and you give each of them the same name, like so:

The following XAML file does not work!

```
<ContentPage xmlns="http://xamarin.com/schemas/2014/forms"
             xmlns:x="http://schemas.microsoft.com/winfx/2009/xaml"
             x:Class="PlatformSpecificLabels.PlatformSpecificLabelsPage">

    <OnPlatform x:TypeArguments="View">
        <OnPlatform.iOS>
            <Label x:Name="deviceLabel"
                   Text="This is an iOS device"
                   HorizontalOptions="Center"
                   VerticalOptions="Center" />
        </OnPlatform.iOS>

        <OnPlatform.Android>
            <Label x:Name="deviceLabel"
                   Text="This is an Android device"
                   HorizontalOptions="Center"
                   VerticalOptions="Center" />
        </OnPlatform.Android>

        <OnPlatform.WinPhone>
            <Label x:Name="deviceLabel"
                   Text="This is a Windows Phone device"
                   HorizontalOptions="Center"
                   VerticalOptions="Center" />
        </OnPlatform.WinPhone>
    </OnPlatform>
</ContentPage>
```

This will not work because multiple elements cannot have the same name.

You could give them different names and handle the three names in the code-behind file using Device.OnPlatform, but a better solution is to keep the platform specificities as small as possible. Here's the version of the **PlatformSpecificLabels** program that is included with the sample code for this chapter. It has a single Label, and everything is platform independent except for the Text property:

```
<ContentPage xmlns="http://xamarin.com/schemas/2014/forms"
```

```
         xmlns:x="http://schemas.microsoft.com/winfx/2009/xaml"
         x:Class="PlatformSpecificLabels.PlatformSpecificLabelsPage">

    <Label x:Name="deviceLabel"
         HorizontalOptions="Center"
         VerticalOptions="Center">
        <Label.Text>
            <OnPlatform x:TypeArguments="x:String"
                        iOS="This is an iOS device"
                        Android="This is an Android device"
                        WinPhone="This is a Windows Phone device" />
        </Label.Text>
    </Label>
</ContentPage>
```

Here's what it looks like:

The `Text` property is the content property for `Label`, so you don't need the `Label.Text` tags in the previous example. This works as well:

```
<ContentPage xmlns="http://xamarin.com/schemas/2014/forms"
         xmlns:x="http://schemas.microsoft.com/winfx/2009/xaml"
         x:Class="PlatformSpecificLabels.PlatformSpecificLabelsPage">

    <Label x:Name="deviceLabel"
         HorizontalOptions="Center"
         VerticalOptions="Center">
        <OnPlatform x:TypeArguments="x:String"
                    iOS="This is an iOS device"
                    Android="This is an Android device"
                    WinPhone="This is a Windows Phone device" />
```

```
    </Label>
</ContentPage>
```

Custom XAML-based views

The **ScaryColorList** program in the previous chapter listed a few colors in a `StackLayout` using `Frame`, `BoxView`, and `Label`. Even with just three colors, the repetitive markup was starting to look very ominous. Unfortunately there is no XAML markup that duplicates the C# `for` and `while` loops, so your choice is to use code for generating multiple similar items, or to find a better way to do it in markup.

In this book, you'll be seeing several ways to list colors in XAML, and eventually, a very clean and elegant way to do this job will become clear. But that requires a few more steps into learning Xamarin.Forms. Until then, we'll looking at some other approaches that you might find useful in similar circumstances.

One strategy is to create a custom view that has the sole purpose of displaying a color with a name and a colored box. And while we're at it, let's display the hexadecimal RGB values of the colors as well. You can then use that custom view in a XAML page file for the individual colors.

What might this look like in XAML?

Or the better question is: How would you *like* it to look?

If the markup looked something like this, the repetition is not bad at all, and not so much worse than explicitly defining an array of `Color` values in code:

```
<StackLayout>
    <MyColorView Color="Red" />
    <MyColorView Color="Green" />
    <MyColorView Color="Blue" />
    …
</StackLayout>
```

Well, actually it won't look exactly like that. `MyColorView` is obviously a custom class and not part of the Xamarin.Forms API. Therefore, it cannot appear in the XAML file without a namespace prefix that is defined in an XML namespace declaration.

With this XML prefix applied, there won't be any confusion about this custom view being part of the Xamarin.Forms API, so let's give it a more dignified name of `ColorView` rather than `MyColorView`.

This hypothetical `ColorView` class is an example of a fairly easy custom view because it consists solely of existing views—specifically `Label`, `Frame`, and `BoxView`—arranged in a particular way using `StackLayout`. Xamarin.Forms defines a view designed specifically for the purpose of parenting such an arrangement of views, and it's called `ContentView`. Like `ContentPage`, `ContentView` has a Con-

`tent` property that you can set to a visual tree of other views. You can define the contents of the `Con-tentView` in code, but it's more fun to do it in XAML.

Let's put together a solution named **ColorViewList**. This solution will have two sets of XAML and code-behind files, the first for a class named `ColorViewListPage`, which derives from `ContentPage` (as usual), and the second for a class named `ColorView`, which derives from `ContentView`.

To create the `ColorView` class in Visual Studio, use the same procedure as when adding a new XAML page to the **ColorViewList** project: Right-click the project name in the **Solution Explorer**, and select **Add > New Item** from the context menu. In the **Add New Item** dialog, select **Visual C# > Code** at the left and **Forms Xaml Page**. Enter the name ColorView.cs. But right away, before you forget, go into the ColorView.xaml file and change the `ContentPage` start and end tags to `ContentView`. In the ColorView.xaml.cs file, change the base class to `ContentView`.

The process is a little easier in Xamarin Studio. From the tool menu for the **ColorViewList** project, select **Add > New File**. In the **New File** dialog, select **Forms** at the left and **Forms ContentView Xaml** (not **Forms ContentPage Xaml**). Give it a name of ColorView.

You'll also need to create a XAML file and code-behind file for the `ColorViewListPage` class, as usual.

The ColorView.xaml file describes the layout of the individual color items but without any actual color values. Instead, the `BoxView` and two `Label` views are given names:

```
<ContentView xmlns="http://xamarin.com/schemas/2014/forms"
             xmlns:x="http://schemas.microsoft.com/winfx/2009/xaml"
             x:Class="ColorViewList.ColorView">

    <Frame OutlineColor="Accent">
        <StackLayout Orientation="Horizontal">
            <BoxView x:Name="boxView"
                     WidthRequest="70"
                     HeightRequest="70" />

            <StackLayout>
                <Label x:Name="colorNameLabel"
                       FontSize="Large"
                       VerticalOptions="CenterAndExpand" />

                <Label x:Name="colorValueLabel"
                       VerticalOptions="CenterAndExpand" />
            </StackLayout>
        </StackLayout>
    </Frame>
</ContentView>
```

In a real-life program, you'll have plenty of time later to fine-tune the visuals. Initially, you'll just want to get all the named views in there.

Besides the visuals, this `ColorView` class will need a new property to set the color. This property must be defined in the code-behind file. At first, it seems reasonable to give `ColorView` a property named `Color` of type `Color` (as the earlier XAML snippet with `MyColorView` seems to suggest). But if this property were of type `Color`, how would the code get the name of the color from that `Color` value? It can't.

Instead, it makes more sense to define a property named `ColorName` of type `string`. The code-behind file can then use reflection to obtain the static field of the `Color` class corresponding to that name.

But wait: Xamarin.Forms includes a public `ColorTypeConverter` class that the XAML parser uses to convert a text color name like "Red" or "Blue" into a `Color` value. Why not take advantage of that?

Here's the code-behind file for `ColorView`. It defines a `ColorName` property with a `set` accessor that sets the `Text` property of the `colorNameLabel` to the color name, and then uses `Color-TypeConverter` to convert the name to a `Color` value. This `Color` value is then used to set the `Color` property of `boxView` and the `Text` property of the `colorValueLabel` to the RGB values:

```
public partial class ColorView : ContentView
{
    string colorName;
    ColorTypeConverter colorTypeConv = new ColorTypeConverter();

    public ColorView()
    {
        InitializeComponent();
    }

    public string ColorName
    {
        set
        {
            // Set the name.
            colorName = value;
            colorNameLabel.Text = value;

            // Get the actual Color and set the other views.
            Color color = (Color)colorTypeConv.ConvertFrom(colorName);
            boxView.Color = color;
            colorValueLabel.Text = String.Format("{0:X2}-{1:X2}-{2:X2}",
                                        (int)(255 * color.R),
                                        (int)(255 * color.G),
                                        (int)(255 * color.B));
        }
        get
        {
            return colorName;
        }
    }
}
```

The `ColorView` class is finished. Now let's look at `ColorViewListPage`. The ColorView-

ListPage.xaml file must list multiple `ColorView` instances, so it needs a new XML namespace declaration with a new namespace prefix to reference the `ColorView` element.

The `ColorView` class is part of the same project as `ColorViewListPage`. Generally, programmers use an XML namespace prefix of `local` for such cases. The new namespace declaration appears in the root element of the XAML file (like the other two) with the following format:

```
xmlns:local="clr-namespace:ColorViewList;assembly=ColorViewList"
```

In the general case, a custom XML namespace declaration for XAML must specify a common language runtime (CLR) namespace—also known as the .NET namespace—and an assembly. The keywords to specify these are `clr-namespace` and `assembly`. Often the CLR namespace is the same as the assembly, as they are in this case, but they don't need to be. The two parts are connected by a semicolon.

Notice that a colon follows `clr-namespace`, but an equal sign follows `assembly`. This apparent inconsistency is deliberate: the format of the namespace declaration is intended to mimic a URI found in conventional namespace declarations, in which a colon follows the URI scheme name.

You use the same syntax for referencing objects in external portable class libraries. The only difference in those cases is that the project also needs a reference to that external PCL. (You'll see an example in Chapter 10, "XAML markup extensions.").

The `local` prefix is common for code in the same assembly, and in that case the assembly part is not required:

```
xmlns:local="clr-namespace:ColorViewList"
```

You can include it with you want but it's not necessary. Here's the XAML for the `ColorViewListPage` class. The code-behind file contains nothing beyond the `InitializeComponent` call:

```
<ContentPage xmlns="http://xamarin.com/schemas/2014/forms"
             xmlns:x="http://schemas.microsoft.com/winfx/2009/xaml"
             xmlns:local="clr-namespace:ColorViewList"
             x:Class="ColorViewList.ColorViewListPage">

    <ContentPage.Padding>
        <OnPlatform x:TypeArguments="Thickness"
                    iOS="0, 20, 0, 0" />
    </ContentPage.Padding>

    <ScrollView>
        <StackLayout Padding="6, 0">
            <local:ColorView ColorName="Aqua" />
            <local:ColorView ColorName="Black" />
            <local:ColorView ColorName="Blue" />
            <local:ColorView ColorName="Fuchsia" />
            <local:ColorView ColorName="Gray" />
            <local:ColorView ColorName="Green" />
            <local:ColorView ColorName="Lime" />
            <local:ColorView ColorName="Maroon" />
            <local:ColorView ColorName="Navy" />
```

```
                <local:ColorView ColorName="Olive" />
                <local:ColorView ColorName="Purple" />
                <local:ColorView ColorName="Pink" />
                <local:ColorView ColorName="Red" />
                <local:ColorView ColorName="Silver" />
                <local:ColorView ColorName="Teal" />
                <local:ColorView ColorName="White" />
                <local:ColorView ColorName="Yellow" />
            </StackLayout>
        </ScrollView>
</ContentPage>
```

This is not quite as odious as the earlier example seemed to suggest, and it demonstrates how you can encapsulate visuals in their own XAML-based classes. Notice that the `StackLayout` is the child of a `ScrollView`, so the list can be scrolled:

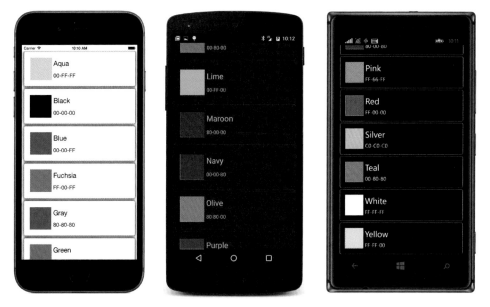

However, there is one aspect of the **ColorViewList** project that does not qualify as a "best practice." It is the definition of the `ColorName` property in `ColorView`. This should really be implemented as a `BindableProperty` object. Delving into bindable objects and bindable properties is a high priority and will be explored in Chapter 11, "The bindable infrastructure."

Events and handlers

When you tap a Xamarin.Forms `Button`, it fires a `Clicked` event. You can instantiate a `Button` in XAML, but the `Clicked` event handler itself must reside in the code-behind file. The `Button` is only one of a bunch of views that exist primarily to generate events, so the process of handling events is crucial to coordinating XAML and code files.

Attaching an event handler to an event in XAML is as simple as setting a property; it is, in fact, visually indistinguishable from a property setting. The **XamlKeypad** project is a XAML version of the **PersistentKeypad** project from Chapter 6. It illustrates setting event handlers in XAML and handling these events in the code-behind file. It also includes logic to save keypad entries when the program is terminated.

If you take a look back at the constructor code of the `SimplestKeypadPage` or `PersistentKeypadPage` classes, you'll see a couple of loops to create the buttons that make up the numeric part of the keypad. Of course, this is precisely the type of thing you can't do in XAML, but look at how much cleaner the markup in `XamlKeypadPage` is when compared with that code:

```
<ContentPage xmlns="http://xamarin.com/schemas/2014/forms"
             xmlns:x="http://schemas.microsoft.com/winfx/2009/xaml"
             x:Class="XamlKeypad.XamlKeypadPage">

    <StackLayout VerticalOptions="Center"
                 HorizontalOptions="Center">

        <Label x:Name="displayLabel"
               Font="Large"
               VerticalOptions="Center"
               XAlign="End" />

        <Button x:Name="backspaceButton"
                Text="&#x21E6;"
                Font="Large"
                IsEnabled="False"
                Clicked="OnBackspaceButtonClicked" />

        <StackLayout Orientation="Horizontal">
            <Button Text="7" StyleId="7" Font="Large"
                    Clicked="OnDigitButtonClicked" />
            <Button Text="8" StyleId="8" Font="Large"
                    Clicked="OnDigitButtonClicked" />
            <Button Text="9" StyleId="9" Font="Large"
                    Clicked="OnDigitButtonClicked" />
        </StackLayout>

        <StackLayout Orientation="Horizontal">
            <Button Text="4" StyleId="4" Font="Large"
                    Clicked="OnDigitButtonClicked" />
            <Button Text="5" StyleId="5" Font="Large"
                    Clicked="OnDigitButtonClicked" />
            <Button Text="6" StyleId="6" Font="Large"
                    Clicked="OnDigitButtonClicked" />
        </StackLayout>

        <StackLayout Orientation="Horizontal">
            <Button Text="1" StyleId="1" Font="Large"
                    Clicked="OnDigitButtonClicked" />
```

```
            <Button Text="2" StyleId="2" Font="Large"
                    Clicked="OnDigitButtonClicked" />
            <Button Text="3" StyleId="3" Font="Large"
                    Clicked="OnDigitButtonClicked" />
        </StackLayout>

        <Button Text="0" StyleId="0" Font="Large"
                Clicked="OnDigitButtonClicked" />

    </StackLayout>
</ContentPage>
```

The file is a lot shorter than it would have been had the three properties on each numeric `Button` been formatted into three lines, but packing these all together makes the uniformity of the markup very obvious and provides clarity rather than obscurity.

The big question is which would you rather maintain and modify: the code in the `SimplestKeypadPage` or `PersistentKeypadPage` constructors or the markup in the `XamlKeypadPage` XAML file?

Here's the screen shot. You'll see that these keys are now arranged in calculator order rather than telephone order:

The **Backspace** button has its `Clicked` event set to the `OnBackspaceButtonClicked` handler, while the digit buttons share the `OnDigitButtonClicked` handler. As you'll recall, the `StyleId` property is often used to distinguish views sharing the same event handler, which means that the two event handlers can be implemented in the code-behind file exactly the same as in the code-only program:

```
public partial class XamlKeypadPage
{
```

```
    App app = Application.Current as App;

    public XamlKeypadPage()
    {
        InitializeComponent();

        displayLabel.Text = app.DisplayLabelText;
        backspaceButton.IsEnabled = displayLabel.Text != null &&
                                    displayLabel.Text.Length > 0;
    }

    void OnDigitButtonClicked(object sender, EventArgs args)
    {
        Button button = (Button)sender;
        displayLabel.Text += (string)button.StyleId;
        backspaceButton.IsEnabled = true;

        app.DisplayLabelText = displayLabel.Text;
    }

    void OnBackspaceButtonClicked(object sender, EventArgs args)
    {
        string text = displayLabel.Text;
        displayLabel.Text = text.Substring(0, text.Length - 1);
        backspaceButton.IsEnabled = displayLabel.Text.Length > 0;

        app.DisplayLabelText = displayLabel.Text;
    }
}
```

Part of the job of the `LoadFromXaml` method called by `InitializeComponent` involves attaching these event handlers to the objects instantiated from the XAML file.

The **XamlKeypad** project includes the code that was added to the page and `App` classes in **PersistentKeypad** to save the keypad text when the program is terminated. The `App` class in **XamlKeypad** is basically the same as the one in **PersistentKeypad**.

Tap gestures

The Xamarin.Forms `Button` responds to finger taps, but you can actually get finger taps from any class that derives from `View`, including `Label`, `BoxView`, and `Frame`. These tap events are not built into the `View` class, but the `View` class defines a property named `GestureRecognizers`. Taps are enabled by adding an object to this `GestureRecognizers` collection. An instance of any class that derives from `GestureRecognizer` can be added to this collection, but so far there's only one: `TapGestureRecognizer`.

Here's how to add a `TapGestureRecognizer` to a `BoxView` in code:

```
BoxView boxView = new BoxView
```

```
{
    Color = Color.Blue
};
TapGestureRecognizer tapGesture = new TapGestureRecognizer();
tapGesture.Tapped += OnBoxViewTapped;
boxView.GestureRecognizers.Add(tapGesture);
```

`TapGestureRecognizer` also defines a `NumberOfTapsRequired` property with a default value of 1.

To generate `Tapped` events, the `View` object must have its `IsEnabled` property set to `true`, its `IsVisible` property set to `true` (or it won't be visible at all), and its `InputTransparent` property set to `false`. These are all default conditions.

The `Tapped` handler looks just like the `Clicked` handler for the `Button`:

```
void OnBoxViewTapped(object sender, EventArgs args)
{
    …
}
```

Normally, the `sender` argument of an event handler is the object that fires the event, which in this case would be the `TapGestureRecognizer` object. That would not be of much use. Instead, the `sender` argument to the `Tapped` handler is the view being tapped, in this case the `BoxView`. That's *much* more useful!

Like `Button`, `TapGestureRecognizer` also defines `Command` and `CommandParameter` properties; these are used when implementing the MVVM design pattern, and they are discussed in a later chapter.

`TapGestureRecognizer` also defines properties named `TappedCallback` and `TappedCallbackParameter` and a constructor that includes a `TappedCallback` argument. These are all deprecated and should not be used.

In XAML, you can attach a `TapGestureRecognizer` to a view by expressing the `GestureRecognizers` collection as a property element:

```
<BoxView Color="Blue">
    <BoxView.GestureRecognizers>
        <TapGestureRecognizer Tapped="OnBoxViewTapped" />
    </BoxView.GestureRecognizers>
</BoxView>
```

As usual, the XAML is a little shorter than the equivalent code.

Let's make a program that's inspired by one of the first standalone computer games.

The Xamarin.Forms version of this game is called **MonkeyTap** because it's an imitation game. It contains four `BoxView` elements, colored red, blue, yellow, green. When the game begins, one of the `BoxView` elements flashes, and you must then tap that `BoxView`. That `BoxView` flashes again followed by another one, and now you must tap both in sequence. Then those two flashes are followed by a third and so forth. (The original had sound as well, but **MonkeyTap** does not.) It's a rather cruel game because there is no way to win. The game just keeps on getting harder and harder until you lose.

The MonkeyTapPage.xaml file instantiates the four `BoxView` elements and a `Button` in the center labeled "Begin".

```xml
<ContentPage xmlns="http://xamarin.com/schemas/2014/forms"
             xmlns:x="http://schemas.microsoft.com/winfx/2009/xaml"
             x:Class="MonkeyTap.MonkeyTapPage">

    <ContentPage.Padding>
        <OnPlatform x:TypeArguments="Thickness"
                    iOS="0, 20, 0, 0" />
    </ContentPage.Padding>

    <StackLayout>
        <BoxView x:Name="boxview0"
                 VerticalOptions="FillAndExpand">
            <BoxView.GestureRecognizers>
                <TapGestureRecognizer Tapped="OnBoxViewTapped" />
            </BoxView.GestureRecognizers>
        </BoxView>

        <BoxView x:Name="boxview1"
                 VerticalOptions="FillAndExpand">
            <BoxView.GestureRecognizers>
                <TapGestureRecognizer Tapped="OnBoxViewTapped" />
            </BoxView.GestureRecognizers>
        </BoxView>

        <Button x:Name="startGameButton"
                Text="Begin"
                Font="Large"
                HorizontalOptions="Center"
                Clicked="OnStartGameButtonClicked" />

        <BoxView x:Name="boxview2"
                 VerticalOptions="FillAndExpand">
            <BoxView.GestureRecognizers>
                <TapGestureRecognizer Tapped="OnBoxViewTapped" />
            </BoxView.GestureRecognizers>
        </BoxView>

        <BoxView x:Name="boxview3"
                 VerticalOptions="FillAndExpand">
            <BoxView.GestureRecognizers>
                <TapGestureRecognizer Tapped="OnBoxViewTapped" />
            </BoxView.GestureRecognizers>
        </BoxView>
    </StackLayout>
</ContentPage>
```

All four `BoxView` elements here have a `TapGestureRecognizer` attached, but they aren't yet assigned colors. That's handled in the code-behind file because the colors won't stay constant. The colors need to be changed for the flashing effect.

The code-behind file begins with some constants and variable fields. (You'll notice that one of them is flagged as protected; in the next chapter, a class will derive from this one and require access to this field. Some methods are defined as protected as well.)

```
public partial class MonkeyTapPage
{
    const int sequenceTime = 750;        // in msec
    protected const int flashDuration = 250;

    const double offLuminosity = 0.4;    // somewhat dimmer
    const double onLuminosity = 0.75;    // much brighter

    BoxView[] boxViews;
    Color[] colors = { Color.Red, Color.Blue, Color.Yellow, Color.Green };
    List<int> sequence = new List<int>();
    int sequenceIndex;
    bool awaitingTaps;
    bool gameEnded;
    Random random = new Random();

    public MonkeyTapPage()
    {
        InitializeComponent();
        boxViews = new BoxView[] { boxview0, boxview1, boxview2, boxview3 };
        InitializeBoxViewColors();
    }

    void InitializeBoxViewColors()
    {
        for (int index = 0; index < 4; index++)
            boxViews[index].Color = colors[index].WithLuminosity(offLuminosity);
    }
    …
}
```

The constructor puts all four `BoxView` elements in an array; this allows them to be referenced by a simple index that has values of 0, 1, 2, and 3. The `InitializeBoxViewColors` method sets all the `Box-View` elements to their slightly dimmed nonflashed state.

The program is now waiting for the user to press the **Begin** button to start the first game. The same `Button` handles replays, so it includes a redundant initialization of the `BoxView` colors. The `Button` handler also prepares for building the sequence of flashed `BoxView` elements by clearing the `sequence` list and calling `StartSequence`:

```
public partial class MonkeyTapPage
{
    …
    protected void OnStartGameButtonClicked(object sender, EventArgs args)
```

```
    {
        gameEnded = false;
        startGameButton.IsVisible = false;
        InitializeBoxViewColors();
        sequence.Clear();
        StartSequence();
    }

    void StartSequence()
    {
        sequence.Add(random.Next(4));
        sequenceIndex = 0;
        Device.StartTimer(TimeSpan.FromMilliseconds(sequenceTime), OnTimerTick);
    }
    ...
}
```

StartSequence adds a new random integer to the sequence list, initializes sequenceIndex to 0, and starts the timer.

In the normal case, the timer tick handler is called for each index in the sequence list and causes the corresponding BoxView to flash with a call to FlashBoxView. The timer handler returns false when the sequence is at an end, also indicating by setting awaitingTaps that it's time for the user to imitate the sequence:

```
public partial class MonkeyTapPage
{
    ...
    bool OnTimerTick()
    {
        if (gameEnded)
            return false;

        FlashBoxView(sequence[sequenceIndex]);
        sequenceIndex++;
        awaitingTaps = sequenceIndex == sequence.Count;
        sequenceIndex = awaitingTaps ? 0 : sequenceIndex;
        return !awaitingTaps;
    }

    protected virtual void FlashBoxView(int index)
    {
        boxViews[index].Color = colors[index].WithLuminosity(onLuminosity);
        Device.StartTimer(TimeSpan.FromMilliseconds(flashDuration), () =>
            {
                if (gameEnded)
                    return false;

                boxViews[index].Color = colors[index].WithLuminosity(offLuminosity);
                return false;
            });
    }
    ...
```

```
}
```

The flash is just a quarter second in duration. The `FlashBoxView` method first sets the luminosity for a bright color and creates a "one-shot" timer, so called because the timer callback method (here expressed as a lambda function) returns `false` and shuts off the timer after restoring the color's luminosity.

The `Tapped` handler for the `BoxView` elements ignores the tap if the game is already ended (which only happens with a mistake by the user), and ends the game if the user taps prematurely without waiting for the program to go through the sequence. Otherwise, it just compares the tapped `BoxView` with the next one in the sequence, flashes that `BoxView` if correct, or ends the game if not:

```csharp
public partial class MonkeyTapPage
{
    …
    protected void OnBoxViewTapped(object sender, EventArgs args)
    {
        if (gameEnded)
            return;

        if (!awaitingTaps)
        {
            EndGame();
            return;
        }

        BoxView tappedBoxView = (BoxView)sender;
        int index = Array.IndexOf(boxViews, tappedBoxView);

        if (index != sequence[sequenceIndex])
        {
            EndGame();
            return;
        }

        FlashBoxView(index);

        sequenceIndex++;
        awaitingTaps = sequenceIndex < sequence.Count;

        if (!awaitingTaps)
            StartSequence();
    }

    protected virtual void EndGame()
    {
        gameEnded = true;

        for (int index = 0; index < 4; index++)
            boxViews[index].Color = Color.Gray;

        startGameButton.Text = "Try again?";
        startGameButton.IsVisible = true;
```

```
    }
}
```

If the user manages to "ape" the sequence all the way through, another call to `StartSequence` adds a new index to the sequence list and starts playing that new one. Eventually, though, there will be a call to `EndGame`, which colors all the boxes gray to emphasize the end, and reenables the `Button` for a chance to try it again.

Here's the program after the `Button` has been clicked and hidden:

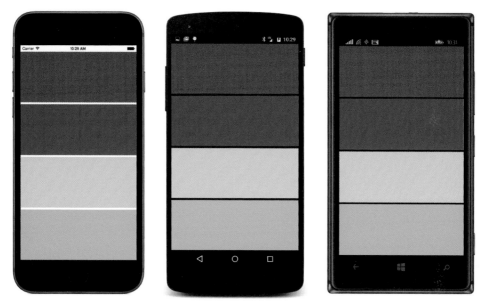

I know, I know. The game is a real drag without sound.

Let's take the opportunity in the next chapter to fix that.

Chapter 9
Platform-specific API calls

An emergency has arisen. Anyone playing with the **MonkeyTap** game from the previous chapter will quickly come to the conclusion that it desperately needs a very basic enhancement, and it simply cannot be allowed to exist without it.

MonkeyTap needs sound.

It doesn't need very sophisticated sound—just little beeps to accompany the flashes of the four `BoxView` elements. But the Xamarin.Forms API doesn't support sound, so sound is not something we can add to **MonkeyTap** with just a couple of API calls. Supporting sound requires going somewhat beyond Xamarin.Forms to make use of platform-specific sound-generation facilities. Figuring out how to make sounds in iOS, Android, and Windows Phone is hard enough. But how does a Xamarin.Forms program then make calls into the individual platforms?

Before tackling the complexities of sound, let's examine the different approaches to making platform-specific API calls with a much simpler example: The first three short programs shown below do the same thing: They all display two tiny items of information supplied by the underlying platform operating system that reveal the model of the device running the program and the operating system version.

Preprocessing in the Shared Asset Project

As you learned in Chapter 2, "Anatomy of an app," you can use either a Shared Asset Project (SAP) or a Portable Class Library (PCL) for the code that is common to all three platforms. An SAP contains code files that are shared among the platform projects, while a PCL encloses the common code in a library that is accessible only through public types.

Accessing platform APIs from a Shared Asset Project is a little more straightforward than from a Portable Class Library because it involves more traditional programming tools, so let's try that approach first. You can create a Xamarin.Forms solution with an SAP using the process described in Chapter 2. You can then add a XAML-based `ContentPage` class to the SAP the same way you add one to a PCL.

Here's the XAML file for a project named **DisplayPlatformInfoSap1**:

```
<ContentPage xmlns="http://xamarin.com/schemas/2014/forms"
             xmlns:x="http://schemas.microsoft.com/winfx/2009/xaml"
             x:Class="DisplayPlatformInfoSap1.DisplayPlatformInfoSap1Page">

    <StackLayout Padding="20">
```

```
            <StackLayout VerticalOptions="CenterAndExpand">
                <Label Text="Device Model:" />

                <ContentView Padding="50, 0, 0, 0">
                    <Label x:Name="modelLabel"
                           FontSize="Large"
                           FontAttributes="Bold" />
                </ContentView>
            </StackLayout>

            <StackLayout VerticalOptions="CenterAndExpand">
                <Label Text="Operating System Version:" />

                <ContentView Padding="50, 0, 0, 0">
                    <Label x:Name="versionLabel"
                           FontSize="Large"
                           FontAttributes="Bold" />
                </ContentView>
            </StackLayout>
        </StackLayout>
</ContentPage>
```

The code-behind file must set the `Text` properties for `modelLabel` and `versionLabel`.

Code files in a Shared Asset Project are extensions of the code in the individual platforms. This means that code in the SAP can make use of the C# preprocessor directives `#if`, `#elif`, `#else`, and `#endif` with conditional-compilation symbols defined for the three platforms, as demonstrated in Chapters 2 and 4. These symbols are `__IOS__` for iOS, `__ANDROID__` for Android, and `WIN-DOWS_PHONE` for Windows Phone.

The APIs involved in obtaining the model and version information are, of course, different for the three platforms:

- For iOS, use the `UIDevice` class in the `UIKit` namespace.

- For Android, use various properties of the `Build` class in the `Android.OS` namespace.

- For Windows Phone, use the `DeviceStatus` class in the `Microsoft.Phone.Info` namespace and the `Environment` class in the `System` namespace.

Here's the DisplayPlatformInfoSap1.xaml.cs code-behind file showing how `modelLabel` and `versionLabel` are set based on the conditional-compilation symbols:

```
using System;
using Xamarin.Forms;

#if __IOS__
using UIKit;

#elif __ANDROID__
using Android.OS;
```

```
#elif WINDOWS_PHONE
using Microsoft.Phone.Info;

#endif

namespace DisplayPlatformInfoSap1
{
    public partial class DisplayPlatformInfoSap1Page : ContentPage
    {
        public DisplayPlatformInfoSap1Page ()
        {
            InitializeComponent ();

#if __IOS__

            UIDevice device = new UIDevice();
            modelLabel.Text = device.Model.ToString();
            versionLabel.Text = String.Format("{0} {1}", device.SystemName,
                                                          device.SystemVersion);

#elif __ANDROID__

            modelLabel.Text = String.Format("{0} {1}", Build.Manufacturer,
                                                       Build.Model);
            versionLabel.Text = Build.VERSION.Release.ToString();

#elif WINDOWS_PHONE

            modelLabel.Text = String.Format("{0} {1}", DeviceStatus.DeviceManufacturer,
                                                       DeviceStatus.DeviceName);
            versionLabel.Text = Environment.OSVersion.ToString();

#endif

        }
    }
}
```

Notice that these preprocessor directives are used to select different `using` directives as well as to make calls to platform-specific APIs. In a program as simple as this, you could simply include the namespaces with the class names, but for longer blocks of code, you'll probably want those `using` directives.

And of course it works:

The advantage of this approach is that you have all the code for the three platforms in one place. But the code listing is—let's face it—quite ugly, and it harkens back to a much earlier era in programming. Using preprocessor directives might not seem so bad for short and less frequent calls such as this example, but in a larger program you'll need to juggle blocks of platform-specific code and shared code, and the multitude of preprocessor directives can easily become confusing. Preprocessor directives should be used for little fixes and generally not as structural elements in the application.

Let's try another approach.

Parallel classes and the Shared Asset Project

Although the Shared Asset Project is an extension of the platform projects, the relationship goes both ways: just as a platform project can make calls into code in a Shared Asset Project, the SAP can make calls into the individual platform projects.

This means that we can restrict the platform-specific API calls to classes in the individual platform projects. If the names and namespaces of these classes in the platform projects are the same, then code in the SAP can access these classes in a transparent platform-independent manner.

In the **DisplayPlatformInfoSap2** solution, each of the three platform projects has a class named PlatformInfo that contains two methods that return string objects named GetModel and GetVersion. Here's the version of this class in the iOS project:

```
using System;
using UIKit;
```

```
namespace DisplayPlatformInfoSap2
{
    public class PlatformInfo
    {
        UIDevice device = new UIDevice();

        public string GetModel()
        {
            return device.Model.ToString();
        }

        public string GetVersion()
        {
            return String.Format("{0} {1}", device.SystemName,
                                            device.SystemVersion);
        }
    }
}
```

Notice the namespace name. Although the other classes in this iOS project use the `DisplayPlat-`
`formInfoSap2.iOS` namespace, the namespace for this class is just `DisplayPlatformInfoSap2`.
This allows the SAP to access this class directly without any platform specifics.

Here's the parallel class in the Android project. Same namespace, same class name, and same
method names, but different implementations of these methods using Android API calls:

```
using System;
using Android.OS;

namespace DisplayPlatformInfoSap2
{
    public class PlatformInfo
    {
        public string GetModel()
        {
            return String.Format("{0} {1}", Build.Manufacturer,
                                            Build.Model);
        }

        public string GetVersion()
        {
            return Build.VERSION.Release.ToString();
        }
    }
}
```

And here's Windows Phone:

```
using System;
using Microsoft.Phone.Info;

namespace DisplayPlatformInfoSap2
{
    public class PlatformInfo
```

```
{
    public string GetModel()
    {
        return String.Format("{0} {1}", DeviceStatus.DeviceManufacturer,
                                        DeviceStatus.DeviceName);
    }

    public string GetVersion()
    {
        return Environment.OSVersion.ToString();
    }
    }
}
```

The XAML file in the **DisplayPlatformInfoSap2** project is basically the same as the one in **Display-PlatformInfoSap1** project. The code-behind file is considerably simpler:

```
using System;
using Xamarin.Forms;

namespace DisplayPlatformInfoSap2
{
    public partial class DisplayPlatformInfoSap2Page : ContentPage
    {
        public DisplayPlatformInfoSap2Page ()
        {
            InitializeComponent ();

            PlatformInfo platformInfo = new PlatformInfo();
            modelLabel.Text = platformInfo.GetModel();
            versionLabel.Text = platformInfo.GetVersion();
        }
    }
}
```

The particular version of `PlatformInfo` that is referenced by the class is the one in the compiled project. It's almost as if we've defined a little extension to Xamarin.Forms that resides in the individual platform projects.

DependencyService and the Portable Class Library

Can the technique illustrated in the **DisplayPlatformInfoSap2** program be implemented in a solution with a Portable Class Library? At first, it doesn't seem possible. Although application projects make calls to libraries all the time, libraries generally can't make calls to applications except in the context of events or callback functions. The PCL is bundled with a device-independent version of .NET and closed up tight—capable only of executing code within itself or other PCLs it might reference.

But wait: When a Xamarin.Forms application is running, it can use .NET reflection to get access to its own assembly and any other assemblies in the program. This means that code in the PCL can use re-flection to access classes that exist in the platform assembly from which the PCL is referenced. Those classes must be defined as public, of course, but that's just about the only requirement.

Before you start writing code that exploits this technique, you should know that this solution already exists in the form of a Xamarin.Forms class named `DependencyService`. This class uses .NET reflection to search through all the other assemblies in the application—including the particular platform assembly itself—and provide access to platform-specific code.

The use of `DependencyService` is illustrated in the **DisplayPlatformInfo** solution, which uses a Portable Class Library for the shared code. You begin the process of using `DependencyService` by defining an interface type in the PCL project that declares the signatures of the methods you want to implement in the platform projects. Here's `IPlatformInfo`:

```
namespace DisplayPlatformInfo
{
    public interface IPlatformInfo
    {
        string GetModel();

        string GetVersion();
    }
}
```

You've seen those two methods before. They're the same two methods implemented in the `PlatformInfo` classes in the platform projects in **DisplayPlatformInfoSap2**.

In a manner very similar to **DisplayPlatformInfoSap2**, all three platform projects in **DisplayPlatformInfo** must now have a class that implements the `IPlatformInfo` interface. Here's the class in the iOS project, named `PlatformInfo`:

```
using System;
using UIKit;
using Xamarin.Forms;

[assembly: Dependency(typeof(DisplayPlatformInfo.iOS.PlatformInfo))]

namespace DisplayPlatformInfo.iOS
{
    public class PlatformInfo : IPlatformInfo
    {
        UIDevice device = new UIDevice();

        public string GetModel()
        {
            return device.Model.ToString();
        }

        public string GetVersion()
        {
            return String.Format("{0} {1}", device.SystemName,
```

```
                                                 device.SystemVersion);
        }
    }
}
```

This class is not accessed directly by the PCL, so the namespace name can be anything you want. Here it's set to the same namespace as the other code in the iOS project. The class name can also be anything you want. Whatever you name it, however, the class must explicitly implement the `IPlatformInfo` interface defined in the PCL:

```
public class PlatformInfo : IPlatformInfo
```

Furthermore, this class must be referenced in a special attribute outside the namespace block. You'll see it near the top of the file following the `using` directives:

```
[assembly: Dependency(typeof(DisplayPlatformInfo.iOS.PlatformInfo))]
```

The `DependencyAttribute` class that defines this `Dependency` attribute is part of Xamarin.Forms and used specifically in connection with `DependencyService`. The argument is a `Type` object of a class in the platform project that is available for access by the PCL. In this case, it's this `PlatformInfo` class. This attribute is attached to the platform assembly itself, so code executing in the PCL doesn't have to search all over the library to find it.

Here's the Android version of `PlatformInfo`:

```
using System;
using Android.OS;
using Xamarin.Forms;

[assembly: Dependency(typeof(DisplayPlatformInfo.Droid.PlatformInfo))]

namespace DisplayPlatformInfo.Droid
{
    public class PlatformInfo : IPlatformInfo
    {
        public string GetModel()
        {
            return String.Format("{0} {1}", Build.Manufacturer,
                                            Build.Model);
        }

        public string GetVersion()
        {
            return Build.VERSION.Release.ToString();
        }
    }
}
```

And here's the one for Windows Phone:

```
using System;
using Microsoft.Phone.Info;
using Xamarin.Forms;
```

```
[assembly: Dependency(typeof(DisplayPlatformInfo.WinPhone.PlatformInfo))]

namespace DisplayPlatformInfo.WinPhone
{
    public class PlatformInfo : IPlatformInfo
    {
        public string GetModel()
        {
            return String.Format("{0} {1}", DeviceStatus.DeviceManufacturer,
                                            DeviceStatus.DeviceName);
        }

        public string GetVersion()
        {
            return Environment.OSVersion.ToString();
        }
    }
}
```

Code in the PCL can then get access to the particular platform's implementation of `IPlatformInfo` by using the `DependencyService` class. This is a static class with three public methods, the most important of which is named `Get`. `Get` is a generic method whose argument is the interface you've defined, in this case `IPlatformInfo`.

```
IPlatformInfo platformInfo = DependencyService.Get<IPlatformInfo>();
```

The `Get` method returns an instance of the platform-specific class that implements the `IPlatformInfo` interface. You can then use this object to make platform-specific calls. This is demonstrated in the code-behind file for the **DisplayPlatformInfo** project:

```
namespace DisplayPlatformInfo
{
    public partial class DisplayPlatformInfoPage : ContentPage
    {
        public DisplayPlatformInfoPage()
        {
            InitializeComponent();

            IPlatformInfo platformInfo = DependencyService.Get<IPlatformInfo>();
            modelLabel.Text = platformInfo.GetModel();
            versionLabel.Text = platformInfo.GetVersion();
        }
    }
}
```

`DependencyService` caches the instances of the objects that it obtains through the `Get` method. This speeds up subsequent uses of `Get` and also allows the platform implementations of the interface to maintain state: any fields and properties in the platform implementations will be preserved across multiple `Get` calls. These classes can also include events or implement callback methods.

`DependencyService` requires just a little more overhead than the approach shown in the **Display-PlatformInfoSap2** project and is somewhat more structured because the individual platform classes implement an interface defined in shared code.

`DependencyService` is not the only way to implement platform-specific calls in a PCL. Adventurous developers might want to use dependency-injection techniques to configure the PCL to make calls into the platform projects. But `DependencyService` is very easy to use, and it eliminates most reasons to use a Shared Asset Project in a Xamarin.Forms application.

Platform-specific sound rendering

Now for the real objective of this chapter: to give sound to **MonkeyTap**. All three platforms support APIs that allow a program to dynamically generate and play audio waveforms. This is the approach taken by the **MonkeyTapWithSound** program.

Commercial music files are often compressed in formats such as MP3. But when a program is algorithmically generating waveforms, an uncompressed format is much more convenient. The most basic technique—which is supported by all three platforms—is called pulse code modulation or PCM. Despite the fancy name, it's quite simple, and it's the technique used for storing sound on music CDs.

A PCM waveform is described by a series of samples at a constant rate, known as the sampling rate. Music CDs use a standard rate of 44,100 samples per second. Audio files generated by computer programs often use a sampling rate of half that (22,050) or one-quarter (11,025) if high audio quality is not required. The highest frequency that can be recorded and reproduced is one-half the sampling rate.

Each sample is a fixed size that defines the amplitude of the waveform at that point in time. The samples on a music CD are signed 16-bit values. Samples of 8 bits are common when sound quality doesn't matter as much. Some environments support floating-point values. Multiple samples can accommodate stereo or any number of channels. For simple sound effects on mobile devices, monaural sound is often fine.

The sound generation algorithm in **MonkeyTapWithSound** is hard-coded for 16-bit monaural samples, but the sampling rate is specified by a constant and can easily be changed.

Now that you know how `DependencyService` works, let's examine the code added to **MonkeyTap** to turn it into **MonkeyTapWithSound**, and let's look at it from the top down. To avoid reproducing a lot of code, the new project contains links to the MonkeyTap.xaml and MonkeyTap.xaml.cs files in the **MonkeyTap** project.

In Visual Studio, you can add items to projects as links to existing files by selecting **Add > Existing Item** from the project menu. Then use the **Add Existing Item** dialog to navigate to the file. Choose **Add as Link** from the drop-down on the **Add** button.

In Xamarin Studio, select **Add > Add File** from the project menu. After opening the file or files, an **Add File to Folder** alert box pops up. Choose **Add a link to the file**.

However, after taking these steps in Visual Studio, it was also necessary to manually edit the MonkeyTapWithSound.csproj file to change the MonkeyTapPage.xaml file to an **EmbeddedResource** and the **Generator** to **MSBuild:UpdateDesignTimeXaml**. Also, a **DependentUpon** tag was added to the MonkeyTapPage.xaml.cs file to reference the MonkeyTapPage.xaml file. This causes the code-behind file to be indented under the XAML file in the file list.

The `MonkeyTapWithSoundPage` class then derives from the `MonkeyTapPage` class. Although the `MonkeyTapPage` class is defined by a XAML file and a code-behind file, `MonkeyTapWithSoundPage` is code only. When a class is derived in this way, event handlers in the original code-behind file for events in the XAML file must be defined as `protected`, and this is the case.

The `MonkeyTap` class also defined a `flashDuration` constant as protected, and two methods were defined as `protected` and `virtual`. The `MonkeyTapWithSoundPage` overrides these two methods to call a static method named `SoundPlayer.PlaySound`:

```
namespace MonkeyTapWithSound
{
    class MonkeyTapWithSoundPage : MonkeyTap.MonkeyTapPage
    {
        const int errorDuration = 500;

        // Diminished 7th in 1st inversion: C, Eb, F#, A
        double[] frequencies = { 523.25, 622.25, 739.99, 880 };

        protected override void BlinkBoxView(int index)
        {
            SoundPlayer.PlaySound(frequencies[index], flashDuration);
            base.BlinkBoxView(index);
        }

        protected override void EndGame()
        {
            SoundPlayer.PlaySound(65.4, errorDuration);
            base.EndGame();
        }
    }
}
```

The `SoundPlayer.PlaySound` method accepts a frequency and a duration in milliseconds. Everything else—the volume, the harmonic makeup of the sound, and how the sound is generated—is the responsibility of the `PlaySound` method. However, this code makes an implicit assumption that `SoundPlayer.PlaySound` returns immediately and does not wait for the sound to complete playing. Fortunately, all three platforms support sound-generation APIs that behave in this way.

The `SoundPlayer` class with the `PlaySound` static method is part of the **MonkeyTapWithSound** PCL project. The responsibility of this method is to define an array of the PCM data for the sound. The size of this array is based on the sampling rate and the duration. The `for` loop calculates samples that define a triangle wave of the requested frequency:

```
namespace MonkeyTapWithSound
{
    class SoundPlayer
    {
        const int samplingRate = 22050;

        // Hard-coded for monaural, 16-bit-per-sample PCM
        public static void PlaySound(double frequency = 440, int duration = 250)
        {
            short[] shortBuffer = new short[samplingRate * duration / 1000];
            double angleIncrement = frequency / samplingRate;
            double angle = 0;    // normalized 0 to 1

            for (int i = 0; i < shortBuffer.Length; i++)
            {
                // Define triangle wave
                double sample;

                // 0 to 1
                if (angle < 0.25)
                    sample = 4 * angle;

                // 1 to -1
                else if (angle < 0.75)
                    sample = 4 * (0.5 - angle);

                // -1 to 0
                else
                    sample = 4 * (angle - 1);

                shortBuffer[i] = (short)(32767 * sample);
                angle += angleIncrement;

                while (angle > 1)
                    angle -= 1;
            }

            byte[] byteBuffer = new byte[2 * shortBuffer.Length];
            Buffer.BlockCopy(shortBuffer, 0, byteBuffer, 0, byteBuffer.Length);

            DependencyService.Get<IPlatformSoundPlayer>().PlaySound(samplingRate, byteBuffer);
        }
    }
}
```

Although the samples are 16-bit integers, two of the platforms want the data in the form of an array of bytes, so a conversion occurs near the end with `Buffer.BlockCopy`. The last line of the method uses `DependencyService` to pass this byte array with the sampling rate to the individual platforms.

The `DependencyService.Get` method references the `IPlatformSoundPlayer` interface that defines the signature of the `PlaySound` method:

```
namespace MonkeyTapWithSound
{
    public interface IPlatformSoundPlayer
    {
        void PlaySound(int samplingRate, byte[] pcmData);
    }
}
```

Now comes the hard part: writing this `PlaySound` method for the three platforms!

The iOS version uses `AVAudioPlayer`, which requires data that includes the header used in Waveform Audio File Format (.wav) files. The code here assembles that data in a `MemoryBuffer` and then converts that to an `NSData` object:

```
using System;
using System.IO;
using System.Text;
using Xamarin.Forms;
using AVFoundation;
using Foundation;

[assembly: Dependency(typeof(MonkeyTapWithSound.iOS.PlatformSoundPlayer))]

namespace MonkeyTapWithSound.iOS
{
    public class PlatformSoundPlayer : IPlatformSoundPlayer
    {
        const int numChannels = 1;
        const int bitsPerSample = 16;

        public void PlaySound(int samplingRate, byte[] pcmData)
        {
            int numSamples = pcmData.Length / (bitsPerSample / 8);

            MemoryStream memoryStream = new MemoryStream();
            BinaryWriter writer = new BinaryWriter(memoryStream, Encoding.ASCII);

            // Construct WAVE header.
            writer.Write(new char[] { 'R', 'I', 'F', 'F' });
            writer.Write(36 + sizeof(short) * numSamples);
            writer.Write(new char[] { 'W', 'A', 'V', 'E' });
            writer.Write(new char[] { 'f', 'm', 't', ' ' });             // format chunk
            writer.Write(16);                                            // PCM chunk size
            writer.Write((short)1);                                      // PCM format flag
            writer.Write((short)numChannels);
            writer.Write(samplingRate);
            writer.Write(samplingRate * numChannels * bitsPerSample / 8);  // byte rate
            writer.Write((short)(numChannels * bitsPerSample / 8));        // block align
            writer.Write((short)bitsPerSample);
            writer.Write(new char[] { 'd', 'a', 't', 'a' });             // data chunk
```

```
            writer.Write(numSamples * numChannels * bitsPerSample / 8);

            // Write data as well.
            writer.Write(pcmData, 0, pcmData.Length);

            memoryStream.Seek(0, SeekOrigin.Begin);
            NSData data = NSData.FromStream(memoryStream);
            AVAudioPlayer audioPlayer = AVAudioPlayer.FromData(data);
            audioPlayer.Play();
        }
    }
}
```

Notice the two essentials: PlatformSoundPlayer implements the IPlatformSoundPlayer interface, and the class is flagged with the Dependency attribute.

The Android version uses the AudioTrack class, and that turns out to be a little easier. However, AudioTrack objects can't overlap, so it's necessary to save the previous object and stop it playing before starting the next one:

```
using System;
using Android.Media;
using Xamarin.Forms;

[assembly: Dependency(typeof(MonkeyTapWithSound.Droid.PlatformSoundPlayer))]

namespace MonkeyTapWithSound.Droid
{
    public class PlatformSoundPlayer : IPlatformSoundPlayer
    {
        AudioTrack previousAudioTrack;

        public void PlaySound(int samplingRate, byte[] pcmData)
        {
            if (previousAudioTrack != null)
            {
                previousAudioTrack.Stop();
                previousAudioTrack.Release();
            }

            AudioTrack audioTrack = new AudioTrack(Stream.Music,
                                        samplingRate,
                                        ChannelOut.Mono,
                                        Android.Media.Encoding.Pcm16bit,
                                        pcmData.Length * sizeof(short),
                                        AudioTrackMode.Static);

            audioTrack.Write(pcmData, 0, pcmData.Length);
            audioTrack.Play();

            previousAudioTrack = audioTrack;
        }
    }
```

```
}
```

A Windows Phone program that uses the Silverlight API (as Xamarin.Forms programs do) has access to sound functions in XNA—a high-level managed-code interface to DirectX. The code to use `Dynamic-icSoundEffectInstance` is remarkably straightforward:

```
using System;
using Microsoft.Xna.Framework.Audio;
using Xamarin.Forms;

[assembly: Dependency(typeof(MonkeyTapWithSound.WinPhone.PlatformSoundPlayer))]

namespace MonkeyTapWithSound.WinPhone
{
    public class PlatformSoundPlayer : IPlatformSoundPlayer
    {
        public void PlaySound(int samplingRate, byte[] pcmData)
        {
            DynamicSoundEffectInstance playback =
                new DynamicSoundEffectInstance(samplingRate, AudioChannels.Mono);

            playback.SubmitBuffer(pcmData);
            playback.Play();
        }
    }
}
```

However, a little more is required. When using XNA to generate sound, a Windows Phone project requires another class that makes calls to `FrameworkDispatcher.Update` at a steady pace:

```
using System;
using System.Windows;
using System.Windows.Threading;
using Microsoft.Xna.Framework;

namespace MonkeyTapWithSound.WinPhone
{
    public class XnaFrameworkDispatcherService : IApplicationService
    {
        DispatcherTimer timer;

        public XnaFrameworkDispatcherService()
        {
            timer = new DispatcherTimer();
            timer.Interval = TimeSpan.FromTicks(333333);
            timer.Tick += OnTimerTick;
            FrameworkDispatcher.Update();
        }

        void OnTimerTick(object sender, EventArgs args)
        {
            FrameworkDispatcher.Update();
        }
```

```
        void IApplicationService.StartService(ApplicationServiceContext context)
        {
            timer.Start();
        }

        void IApplicationService.StopService()
        {
            timer.Stop();
        }
    }
}
```

An instance of this class must be started up by the application. A convenient place to do this is in the Windows Phone App.xaml file:

```
<Application
    x:Class="MonkeyTapWithSound.WinPhone.App"
    xmlns="http://schemas.microsoft.com/winfx/2006/xaml/presentation"
    xmlns:x="http://schemas.microsoft.com/winfx/2006/xaml"
    xmlns:phone="clr-namespace:Microsoft.Phone.Controls;assembly=Microsoft.Phone"
    xmlns:shell="clr-namespace:Microsoft.Phone.Shell;assembly=Microsoft.Phone"
    xmlns:local="clr-namespace:MonkeyTapWithSound.WinPhone">
    ...

    <Application.ApplicationLifetimeObjects>

        <!-- Required for playing music from a Silverlight app -->
        <local:XnaFrameworkDispatcherService />

        ...

    </Application.ApplicationLifetimeObjects>
</Application>
```

At this point, you should be able to read and comprehend a good chunk of this Windows Phone XAML file!

The use of `DependencyService` to perform platform-specific chores is very powerful, but this approach falls short when it comes to user-interface elements. If you need to expand the arsenal of views that adorn the pages of your Xamarin.Forms applications, that job involves creating platform-specific renderers, a process discussed in a later chapter.

Chapter 10
XAML markup extensions

In code, you can set a property in a variety of different ways from a variety of different sources:

```
triangle.Angle1 = 45;
triangle.Angle1 = 180 * radians / Math.PI;
triangle.Angle1 = angles[i];
triangle.Angle1 = animator.GetCurrentAngle();
```

If this `Angle1` property is a `double`, all that's required is that the source be a `double` or otherwise provide a numeric value that is convertible to a `double`.

In markup, however, a property of type `double` usually can be set only from a string that qualifies as a valid argument to `Double.Parse`. The only exception you've seen so far is when the target property is flagged with a `TypeConverter` attribute, such as the `FontSize` property.

It might be desirable if XAML were more flexible—if you could set a property from sources other than explicit text strings. For example, suppose you want to define another way to set a property of type `Color`, perhaps using the `Hue`, `Saturation`, and `Luminosity` values but without the hassle of the `x:FactoryMethod` element. Just offhand, it doesn't seem possible. The XAML parser expects that any value set to an attribute of type `Color` is a string acceptable to the `ColorTypeConverter` class.

The purpose of XAML *markup extensions* is to get around this apparent restriction. Rest assured that XAML markup extensions are *not* extensions to XML. XAML is always legal XML. XAML markup extensions are extensions only in the sense that they extend the possibilities of attribute settings in markup. A markup extension essentially *provides* a value of a particular type without necessarily being a text representation *of* a value.

The code infrastructure

Strictly speaking, a XAML markup extension is a class that implements `IMarkupExtension`, which is a public interface defined in the regular **Xamarin.Forms.Core** assembly but with the namespace `Xamarin.Forms.Xaml`:

```
public interface IMarkupExtension
{
    object ProvideValue(IServiceProvider serviceProvider);
}
```

As the name suggests, `ProvideValue` is the method that provides a value to a XAML attribute. `IServiceProvider` is part of the base class libraries of .NET and defined in the `System` namespace:

```
public interface IServiceProvider
{
    object GetService(Type type);
}
```

Obviously, this information doesn't provide much of a hint on writing custom markup extensions, and in truth, they can be tricky. (You'll see an example shortly and other examples later in this book.) Fortunately, Xamarin.Forms provides several valuable markup extensions for you. These fall into three categories:

- Markup extensions that are part of the XAML 2009 specification. These appear in XAML files with the customary `x` prefix and are:

  - `x:Static`

  - `x:Reference`

  - `x:Type`

  - `x:Null`

  - `x:Array`

  These are implemented in classes that consist of the name of the markup extension with the word `Extension` appended—for example, the `StaticExtension` and `ReferenceExtension` classes. These classes are defined in the **Xamarin.Forms.Xaml** assembly.

- The following markup extensions originated in the Windows Presentation Foundation (WPF) and, with the exception of `DynamicResource`, are supported by Microsoft's other implementations of XAML, including Silverlight, Windows Phone 7 and 8, and Windows 8 and 10:

  - `StaticResource`

  - `DynamicResource`

  - `Binding`

  The `DynamicResourceExtension` class is public; `StaticResourceExtension` and `BindingExtension` are not, but they are available for your use in XAML files because they are accessible by the XAML parser.

- There is only one markup extension that is unique to Xamarin.Forms: the `ConstraintExpression` class used in connection with `RelativeLayout`.

Although it's possible to play around with public markup-extension classes in code, they really only make sense in XAML.

Accessing static members

One of the simplest and most useful implementations of `IMarkupExtension` is encapsulated in the `StaticExtension` class. This is part of the original XAML specification, so it customarily appears in XAML with an `x` prefix. `StaticExtension` defines a single property named `Member` of type `string` that you set to a class and member name of a public constant, static property, static field, or enumeration member.

Let's see how this works. Here's a `Label` with six properties set as they would normally appear in XAML.

```
<Label Text="Just some text"
       BackgroundColor="Accent"
       TextColor="Black"
       FontAttributes="Italic"
       VerticalOptions="Center"
       XAlign="Center" />
```

Five of these attributes are set to text strings that eventually reference various static properties, fields, and enumeration members, but the conversion of those text strings occurs through type converters and the standard XAML parsing of enumeration types.

If you want to be more explicit in setting these attributes to those various static properties, fields, and enumeration members, you can use `x:StaticExtension` within property element tags:

```
<Label Text="Just some text">
    <Label.BackgroundColor>
        <x:StaticExtension Member="Color.Accent" />
    </Label.BackgroundColor>

    <Label.TextColor>
        <x:StaticExtension Member="Color.Black" />
    </Label.TextColor>

    <Label.FontAttributes>
        <x:StaticExtension Member="FontAttributes.Italic" />
    </Label.FontAttributes>

    <Label.VerticalOptions>
        <x:StaticExtension Member="LayoutOptions.Center" />
    </Label.VerticalOptions>

    <Label.XAlign>
        <x:StaticExtension Member="TextAlignment.Center" />
    </Label.XAlign>
</Label>
```

`Color.Accent` is a static property. `Color.Black` and `LayoutOptions.Center` are static fields. `FontAttributes.Italic` and `TextAlignment.Center` are enumeration members.

Considering the ease with which these attributes are set with text strings, the approach using `Stat-icExtension` initially seems ridiculous, but notice that it's a general-purpose mechanism. You can use *any* static property, field, or enumeration member in the `StaticExtension` tag if its type matches the type of the target property.

By convention, classes that implement `IMarkupExtension` incorporate the word `Extension` in their names, but you can leave that out in XAML, which is why this markup extension is usually called `x:Static` rather than `x:StaticExtension`. The following markup is marginally shorter than the previous block:

```
<Label Text="Just some text">
    <Label.BackgroundColor>
        <x:Static Member="Color.Accent" />
    </Label.BackgroundColor>

    <Label.TextColor>
        <x:Static Member="Color.Black" />
    </Label.TextColor>

    <Label.FontAttributes>
        <x:Static Member="FontAttributes.Italic" />
    </Label.FontAttributes>

    <Label.VerticalOptions>
        <x:Static Member="LayoutOptions.Center" />
    </Label.VerticalOptions>

    <Label.XAlign>
        <x:Static Member="TextAlignment.Center" />
    </Label.XAlign>
</Label>
```

And now for a really big syntax leap, a change in syntax that causes the property-element tags to disappear and the footprint to shrink considerably. XAML markup extensions almost always appear with the markup extension name and the arguments within a pair of curly braces:

```
<Label Text="Just some text"
       BackgroundColor="{x:Static Member=Color.Accent}"
       TextColor="{x:Static Member=Color.Black}"
       FontAttributes="{x:Static Member=FontAttributes.Italic}"
       VerticalOptions="{x:Static Member=LayoutOptions.Center}"
       XAlign="{x:Static Member=TextAlignment.Center}" />
```

This syntax with the curly braces is so ubiquitously used in connection with XAML markup extensions that many developers consider markup extensions to be synonymous with the curly-brace syntax. And that's nearly true: while curly braces always signal the presence of a XAML markup extension, in many cases a markup extension can appear in XAML without the curly braces (as demonstrated earlier) and it's sometimes convenient to use them in that way.

Notice there are no quotation marks within the curly braces. Within those braces, very different syntax rules apply. The `Member` property of the `StaticExtension` class is no longer an XML attribute. In terms of XML, the entire expression delimited by the curly braces is the value of the attribute, and the arguments within the curly braces appear without quotation marks.

Just like elements, markup extensions can have a `ContentProperty` attribute. Markup extensions that have only one property—such as the `StaticExtension` class with its single `Member` property— invariably mark that sole property as the content property. For markup extensions using the curly-brace syntax, this means that the `Member` property name and the equal sign can be removed:

```
<Label Text="Just some text"
       BackgroundColor="{x:Static Color.Accent}"
       TextColor="{x:Static Color.Black}"
       FontAttributes="{x:Static FontAttributes.Italic}"
       VerticalOptions="{x:Static LayoutOptions.Center}"
       XAlign="{x:Static TextAlignment.Center}" />
```

This is the common form of the `x:Static` markup extension.

Obviously, the use of `x:Static` for these particular properties is unnecessary, but you can define your own static members for implementing application-wide constants, and you can reference these in your XAML files. This is demonstrated in the **SharedStatics** project.

The **SharedStatics** project contains a class named `AppConstants` that defines some constants and static fields that might be of use for formatting text:

```
namespace SharedStatics
{
    static class AppConstants
    {
        public static Color LightBackground = Color.Yellow;
        public static Color DarkForeground = Color.Blue;

        public static double NormalFontSize = Device.OnPlatform(18, 18, 24);
        public static double TitleFontSize = 1.5 * NormalFontSize;
        public static double ParagraphSpacing =Device.OnPlatform(10, 10, 15);

        public const FontAttributes Emphasis = FontAttributes.Italic;
        public const FontAttributes TitleAttribute = FontAttributes.Bold;

        public const TextAlignment TitleAlignment = TextAlignment.Center;
    }
}
```

The XAML file then uses the `x:Static` markup extension to reference these items. Notice the XML namespace declaration that associates the `local` prefix with the namespace of the project:

```
<ContentPage xmlns="http://xamarin.com/schemas/2014/forms"
             xmlns:x="http://schemas.microsoft.com/winfx/2009/xaml"
             xmlns:local="clr-namespace:SharedStatics"
             x:Class="SharedStatics.SharedStaticsPage"
             BackgroundColor="{x:Static local:AppConstants.LightBackground}">
```

```
<ContentPage.Padding>
    <OnPlatform x:TypeArguments="Thickness"
                iOS="0, 20, 0, 0" />
</ContentPage.Padding>

<StackLayout Padding="10, 0"
             Spacing="{x:Static local:AppConstants.ParagraphSpacing}">

    <Label Text="The SharedStatics Program"
           TextColor="{x:Static local:AppConstants.DarkForeground}"
           FontSize="{x:Static local:AppConstants.TitleFontSize}"
           FontAttributes="{x:Static local:AppConstants.TitleAttribute}"
           XAlign="{x:Static local:AppConstants.TitleAlignment}" />

    <Label TextColor="{x:Static local:AppConstants.DarkForeground}"
           FontSize="{x:Static local:AppConstants.NormalFontSize}">
        <Label.FormattedText>
            <FormattedString>
                <Span Text="Through use of the " />
                <Span Text="x:Static"
                      FontSize="{x:Static local:AppConstants.NormalFontSize}"
                      FontAttributes="{x:Static local:AppConstants.Emphasis}" />
                <Span Text=
" XAML markup extension, an application can maintain a collection of
common property settings defined as constants, static properties or fields,
or enumeration members in a separate code file. These can then be
referenced within the XAML file." />
            </FormattedString>
        </Label.FormattedText>
    </Label>

    <Label TextColor="{x:Static local:AppConstants.DarkForeground}"
           FontSize="{x:Static local:AppConstants.NormalFontSize}">
        <Label.FormattedText>
            <FormattedString>
                <Span Text=
"However, this is not the only technique to share property settings.
You'll soon discover that you can store objects in a " />
                <Span Text="ResourceDictionary"
                      FontSize="{x:Static local:AppConstants.NormalFontSize}"
                      FontAttributes="{x:Static local:AppConstants.Emphasis}" />
                <Span Text=" and access them through the " />
                <Span Text="StaticResource"
                      FontSize="{x:Static local:AppConstants.NormalFontSize}"
                      FontAttributes="{x:Static local:AppConstants.Emphasis}" />
                <Span Text=
" markup extension, and even encapsultate multiple property settings in a " />
                <Span Text="Style"
                      FontSize="{x:Static local:AppConstants.NormalFontSize}"
                      FontAttributes="{x:Static local:AppConstants.Emphasis}" />
                <Span Text=" object." />
            </FormattedString>
        </Label.FormattedText>
```

```
        </Label>
      </StackLayout>
</ContentPage>
```

You might be curious why each of the `Span` objects with an `FontAttributes` setting repeats the `FontSize` setting that is set on the `Label` itself. Currently, `Span` objects do not properly inherit font-related settings from the `Label` when another font-related setting is applied.

And here it is:

This technique allows you to use these common property settings on multiple pages, and if you ever need to change the values, you need only change the `AppSettings` file.

It is also possible to use `x:Static` with static properties and fields defined in classes in external libraries. The following example, named **SystemStatics,** is rather contrived—it sets the `BorderWidth` of a `Button` equal to the `PI` static field defined in the `Math` class and uses the static `Environment.New-Line` property for line breaks in text. But it demonstrates the technique.

The `Math` and `Environment` classes are both defined in the .NET `System` namespace, so a new XML namespace declaration is required to define a prefix named (for example) `sys` for `System`. Notice that this namespace declaration specifies the CLR namespace as `System` but the assembly as `mscorlib`, which originally stood for Microsoft Common Object Runtime Library but now stands for Multilanguage Standard Common Object Runtime Library:

```
<ContentPage xmlns="http://xamarin.com/schemas/2014/forms"
             xmlns:x="http://schemas.microsoft.com/winfx/2009/xaml"
             xmlns:sys="clr-namespace:System;assembly=mscorlib"
             x:Class="SystemStatics.SystemStaticsPage">
    <StackLayout>
```

```
        <Button Text=" Button with &#x03C0; border width "
                BorderWidth="{x:Static sys:Math.PI}"
                HorizontalOptions="Center"
                VerticalOptions="CenterAndExpand">
            <Button.BackgroundColor>
                <OnPlatform x:TypeArguments="Color"
                            Android="#404040" />
            </Button.BackgroundColor>
            <Button.BorderColor>
                <OnPlatform x:TypeArguments="Color"
                            Android="White" />
            </Button.BorderColor>
        </Button>

        <Label VerticalOptions="CenterAndExpand"
               XAlign="Center"
               FontSize="Large">
            <Label.FormattedText>
                <FormattedString>
                    <Span Text="Three lines of text" />
                    <Span Text="{x:Static sys:Environment.NewLine}" />
                    <Span Text="separated by" />
                    <Span Text="{x:Static sys:Environment.NewLine}" />
                    <Span Text="Environment.NewLine"
                          FontSize="Large"
                          FontAttributes="Italic" />
                    <Span Text=" strings" />
                </FormattedString>
            </Label.FormattedText>
        </Label>
    </StackLayout>
</ContentPage>
```

The button border doesn't show up in Android unless the background color and border colors of the button are also set to nondefault values, so some additional markup takes care of that problem. On iOS platforms, a button border tends to crowd the button text, so the text is defined with spaces at the beginning and end.

Judging solely from the visuals, we really have to take it on trust that the button border width is about 3.14 units wide, but the line breaks definitely work:

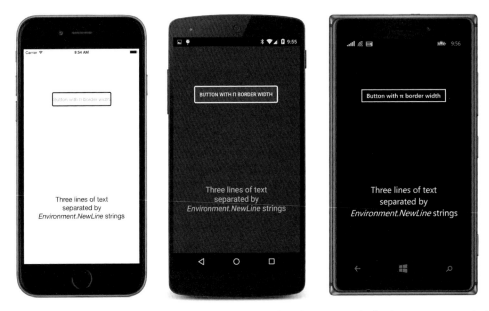

The use of curly braces for markup extensions implies that you can't display text surrounded by curly braces. The curly braces in this text will be mistaken for a markup extension:

```
<Label Text="{Text in curly braces}" />
```

That won't work. You can have curly braces elsewhere in the text string, but you can't begin with a left curly brace.

If you really need to, however, you can ensure that text is not mistaken for a XAML markup extension by beginning the text with an escape sequence that consists of a pair of left and right curly braces:

```
<Label Text="{}{Text in curly braces}" />
```

That will display the text you want.

Resource dictionaries

Xamarin.Forms also supports a second approach to sharing objects and values, and while this approach has a little more overhead than the `x:Static` markup extension, it is somewhat more versatile because everything—the shared objects and the visual elements that use them—can be expressed in XAML.

`VisualElement` defines a property named `Resources` that is of type `ResourceDictionary`—a dictionary with `string` keys and values of type `object`. Items can be added to this dictionary right in XAML, and they can be accessed in XAML with the `StaticResource` and `DynamicResource` markup extensions.

Although `x:Static` and `StaticResource` have somewhat similar names, they are quite different: `x:Static` references a constant, a static field, a static property, or an enumeration member, while `StaticResource` retrieves an object from a `ResourceDictionary`.

While the `x:Static` markup extension is intrinsic to XAML (and hence appears in XAML with an `x` prefix), the `StaticResource` and `DynamicResource` markup extensions are not. They were part of the original XAML implementation in the Windows Presentation Foundation, and `StaticResource` is also supported in Silverlight, Windows Phone 7 and 8, and Windows 8 and 10.

You'll use `StaticResource` for most purposes and reserve `DynamicResource` for some special applications, so let's begin with `StaticResource`.

StaticResource for most purposes

Suppose you've defined three buttons in a `StackLayout`:

```
<StackLayout>
    <Button Text=" Do this! "
            HorizontalOptions="Center"
            VerticalOptions="CenterAndExpand"
            BorderWidth="3"
            TextColor="Red"
            FontSize="Large" />

    <Button Text=" Do that! "
            HorizontalOptions="Center"
            VerticalOptions="CenterAndExpand"
            BorderWidth="3"
            TextColor="Red"
            FontSize="Large" />

    <Button Text=" Do the other thing! "
            HorizontalOptions="Center"
            VerticalOptions="CenterAndExpand"
            BorderWidth="3"
            TextColor="Red"
            FontSize="Large" />
</StackLayout>
```

Of course, this is somewhat unrealistic code. There are no `Clicked` events set for these buttons, and the `BorderWidth` has no effect on Android devices because the button background and border color have their default values. Here's what the buttons look like:

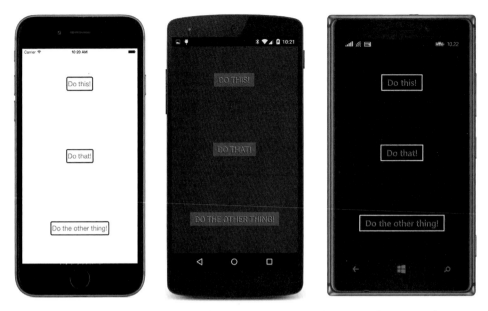

Aside from the text, all three buttons have the same properties set to the same values. Repetitious markup such as this tends to rub programmers the wrong way. It's an affront to the eye and difficult to maintain and change.

Eventually you'll see how to use styles to really cut down on the repetitious markup. For now, however, the goal is not to make the markup shorter but to consolidate the values in one place so that if you ever want to change the `TextColor` property from `Red` to `Blue`, you can do so with one edit rather than three.

Obviously, you can use `x:Static` for this job by defining the values in code. But let's do the whole thing in XAML by storing the values in a *resource dictionary*. Every class that derives from `VisualElement` has a `Resources` property of type `ResourceDictionary`. Resources that are used throughout a page are customarily stored in the `Resources` collection of the `ContentPage`.

The first step is to express the `Resources` property of `ContentPage` as a property element:

```
<ContentPage xmlns="http://xamarin.com/schemas/2014/forms"
             xmlns:x="http://schemas.microsoft.com/winfx/2009/xaml"
             x:Class="ResourceSharing.ResourceSharingPage">

    <ContentPage.Resources>

    </ContentPage.Resources>

    ...

</ContentPage>
```

If you're also defining a `Padding` property on the page by using property-element tags, the order doesn't matter.

For performance purposes, the `Resources` property is `null` by default, so you need to explicitly instantiate the `ResourceDictionary`:

```
<ContentPage xmlns="http://xamarin.com/schemas/2014/forms"
             xmlns:x="http://schemas.microsoft.com/winfx/2009/xaml"
             x:Class="ResourceSharing.ResourceSharingPage">

    <ContentPage.Resources>
        <ResourceDictionary>

        </ResourceDictionary>
    </ContentPage.Resources>

    ...

</ContentPage>
```

Between the `ResourceDictionary` tags, you define one or more objects or values. Each item in the dictionary must be identified with a dictionary key that you specify with the XAML `x:Key` attribute. For example, here's the syntax for including a `LayoutOptions` value in the dictionary with a descriptive key that indicates that this value is defined for setting horizontal options:

```
<LayoutOptions x:Key="horzOptions">Center</LayoutOptions>
```

Because this is a `LayoutOptions` value, the XAML parser accesses the `LayoutOptionsConverter` class (which is private to Xamarin.Forms) to convert the content of the tags, which is the text "Center".

A second way to store a `LayoutOptions` value in the dictionary is to let the XAML parser instantiate the structure and set `LayoutOptions` properties from attributes you specify:

```
<LayoutOptions x:Key="vertOptions"
               Alignment="Center"
               Expands="True" />
```

The `BorderWidth` property is of type `double`, so the `x:Double` datatype element defined in the XAML 2009 specification is ideal:

```
<x:Double x:Key="borderWidth">3</x:Double>
```

You can store a `Color` value in the resource dictionary with a text representation of the color as content. The XAML parser uses the normal `ColorTypeConverter` for the text conversion:

```
<Color x:Key="textColor">Red</Color>
```

You can't initialize a `Color` value by setting its R, G, and B properties because those are get-only. But you can invoke a `Color` constructor or one of the `Color` factory methods:

```
<Color x:Key="textColor"
       x:FactoryMethod="FromHsla">
    <x:Arguments>
        <x:Double>0</x:Double>
        <x:Double>1</x:Double>
        <x:Double>0.5</x:Double>
        <x:Double>1</x:Double>
    </x:Arguments>
</Color>
```

A dictionary item for the `FontSize` property is somewhat problematic. The `FontSize` property is of type `double`, so if you're storing an actual numeric value in the dictionary, that's no problem. But you can't store the word "Large" in the dictionary as if it were a `double`. Only when a "Large" string is set to a `FontSize` attribute does the XAML parser use the `FontSizeConverter`. For that reason, you'll need to store the `FontSize` item as a string:

```
<x:String x:Key="fontSize">Large</x:String>
```

Here's the complete dictionary at this point:

```
<ContentPage xmlns="http://xamarin.com/schemas/2014/forms"
             xmlns:x="http://schemas.microsoft.com/winfx/2009/xaml"
             x:Class="ResourceSharing.ResourceSharingPage">

    <ContentPage.Resources>
        <ResourceDictionary>
            <LayoutOptions x:Key="horzOptions">Center</LayoutOptions>

            <LayoutOptions x:Key="vertOptions"
                           Alignment="Center"
                           Expands="True" />

            <x:Double x:Key="borderWidth">3</x:Double>

            <Color x:Key="textColor">Red</Color>

            <x:String x:Key="fontSize">Large</x:String>
        </ResourceDictionary>
    </ContentPage.Resources>
    …

</ContentPage>
```

This is sometimes referred to as a *resources section* for the page. In real-life programming, almost every XAML file begins with a resources section.

You can reference items in the dictionary by using the `StaticResource` markup extension, which is supported by `StaticResourceExtension`, a class private to Xamarin.Forms. `StaticResourceExtension` defines a property named `Key` that you set to the dictionary key. You can use a `StaticResourceExtension` as an element within property-element tags, or you can use `StaticResourceExtension` or `StaticResource` in curly braces. If you're using the curly-brace syntax, you can leave out the `Key` and equal signs because `Key` is the content property of `StaticResourceExtension`.

The following complete XAML file illustrates three of these options. Do not put an `x` prefix on the `Key` property of `StaticResource`. The `x:Key` attribute is only for defining dictionary keys for items in the `ResourceDictionary`:

```
<ContentPage xmlns="http://xamarin.com/schemas/2014/forms"
             xmlns:x="http://schemas.microsoft.com/winfx/2009/xaml"
             x:Class="ResourceSharing.ResourceSharingPage">

    <ContentPage.Resources>
        <ResourceDictionary>
            <LayoutOptions x:Key="horzOptions">Center</LayoutOptions>

            <LayoutOptions x:Key="vertOptions"
                           Alignment="Center"
                           Expands="True" />

            <x:Double x:Key="borderWidth">3</x:Double>

            <Color x:Key="textColor">Red</Color>

            <x:String x:Key="fontSize">Large</x:String>
        </ResourceDictionary>
    </ContentPage.Resources>

    <StackLayout>
        <Button Text=" Do this! ">
            <Button.HorizontalOptions>
                <StaticResourceExtension Key="horzOptions" />
            </Button.HorizontalOptions>

            <Button.VerticalOptions>
                <StaticResourceExtension Key="vertOptions" />
            </Button.VerticalOptions>

            <Button.BorderWidth>
                <StaticResourceExtension Key="borderWidth" />
            </Button.BorderWidth>

            <Button.TextColor>
                <StaticResourceExtension Key="textColor" />
            </Button.TextColor>

            <Button.FontSize>
                <StaticResourceExtension Key="fontSize" />
            </Button.FontSize>
        </Button>

        <Button Text=" Do that! "
                HorizontalOptions="{StaticResource Key=horzOptions}"
                VerticalOptions="{StaticResource Key=vertOptions}"
                BorderWidth="{StaticResource Key=borderWidth}"
                TextColor="{StaticResource Key=textColor}"
```

```
                      FontSize="{StaticResource Key=fontSize}" />

        <Button Text=" Do the other thing! "
                HorizontalOptions="{StaticResource horzOptions}"
                VerticalOptions="{StaticResource vertOptions}"
                BorderWidth="{StaticResource borderWidth}"
                TextColor="{StaticResource textColor}"
                FontSize="{StaticResource fontSize}" />
    </StackLayout>
</ContentPage>
```

The simplest syntax in the third button is most common, and indeed, that syntax is so ubiquitous that many longtime XAML developers might be entirely unfamiliar with the other variations.

Objects and values in the dictionary are shared among all the `StaticResource` references. That's not so clear in the preceding example, but it's something to keep in mind. For example, suppose you store a `Button` object in the resource dictionary:

```
<ContentPage.Resources>
    <ResourceDictionary>
        <Button x:Key="button"
                Text="Shared Button?"
                HorizontalOptions="Center"
                VerticalOptions="CenterAndExpand"
                FontSize="Large" />
    </ResourceDictionary>
</ContentPage.Resources>
```

You can certainly use that `Button` object on your page by adding it to the `Children` collection of a `StackLayout` with the `StaticResourceExtension` element syntax:

```
<StackLayout>
    <StaticResourceExtension Key="button" />
</StackLayout>
```

However, you can't use that same dictionary item in hopes of putting another copy in the `StackLayout`:

```
<StackLayout>
    <StaticResourceExtension Key="button" />
    <StaticResourceExtension Key="button" />
</StackLayout>
```

That won't work. Both these elements reference the same `Button` object, and a particular visual element can be in only one particular location on the screen. It can't be in multiple locations.

For this reason, visual elements are not normally stored in a resource dictionary. If you need multiple elements on your page that have mostly the same properties, you'll want to use a `Style`, which is explored in Chapter 12.

A tree of dictionaries

The `ResourceDictionary` class imposes the same rules as other dictionaries: all the items in the dictionary must have keys, but duplicate keys are not allowed.

However, because every instance of `VisualElement` potentially has its own resource dictionary, your page can contain multiple dictionaries, and you can use the same keys in different dictionaries just as long as all the keys within each dictionary are unique. Conceivably, every visual element in the visual tree can have its own dictionary, but it really only makes sense for a resource dictionary to apply to multiple elements, so resource dictionaries are only commonly found defined on `Layout` or `Page` objects.

You can construct a tree of dictionaries with dictionary keys that effectively override the keys on other dictionaries. This is demonstrated in the **ResourceTrees** project. The XAML file for the ResourceTreesPage class shows a Resources dictionary for the `ContentPage` that defines resources with keys of `horzOptions`, `vertOptions`, and `textColor`. The `textColor` item incidentally demonstrates how to use `OnPlatform` in a `ResourceDictionary`.

A second `Resources` dictionary is attached to an inner `StackLayout` for resources named `textColor` and `FontSize`:

```
<ContentPage xmlns="http://xamarin.com/schemas/2014/forms"
             xmlns:x="http://schemas.microsoft.com/winfx/2009/xaml"
             x:Class="ResourceTrees.ResourceTreesPage">

    <ContentPage.Resources>
        <ResourceDictionary>
            <LayoutOptions x:Key="horzOptions">Center</LayoutOptions>

            <LayoutOptions x:Key="vertOptions"
                           Alignment="Center"
                           Expands="True" />

            <OnPlatform x:Key="textColor"
                        x:TypeArguments="Color"
                        iOS="Red"
                        Android="Pink"
                        WinPhone="Aqua" />
        </ResourceDictionary>
    </ContentPage.Resources>

    <StackLayout>
        <Button Text=" Do this! "
                HorizontalOptions="{StaticResource horzOptions}"
                VerticalOptions="{StaticResource vertOptions}"
                BorderWidth="{StaticResource borderWidth}"
                TextColor="{StaticResource textColor}"
                FontSize="{StaticResource fontSize}" />

        <StackLayout>
            <StackLayout.Resources>
```

```
                <ResourceDictionary>
                    <Color x:Key="textColor">Default</Color>
                    <x:String x:Key="fontSize">Default</x:String>
                </ResourceDictionary>
            </StackLayout.Resources>

            <Label Text="The first of two labels"
                   HorizontalOptions="{StaticResource horzOptions}"
                   TextColor="{StaticResource textColor}"
                   FontSize="{StaticResource fontSize}" />

            <Button Text=" Do that! "
                    HorizontalOptions="{StaticResource horzOptions}"
                    BorderWidth="{StaticResource borderWidth}"
                    TextColor="{StaticResource textColor}"
                    FontSize="{StaticResource fontSize}" />

            <Label Text="The second of two labels"
                   HorizontalOptions="{StaticResource horzOptions}"
                   TextColor="{StaticResource textColor}"
                   FontSize="{StaticResource fontSize}" />
        </StackLayout>

        <Button Text=" Do the other thing! "
                HorizontalOptions="{StaticResource horzOptions}"
                VerticalOptions="{StaticResource vertOptions}"
                BorderWidth="{StaticResource borderWidth}"
                TextColor="{StaticResource textColor}"
                FontSize="{StaticResource fontSize}" />
    </StackLayout>
</ContentPage>
```

The `Resources` dictionary on the inner `StackLayout` applies only to items within that `StackLay-out`, which are the items in the middle of this screen shot:

Here's how it works:

When the XAML parser encounters a `StaticResource` on an attribute of a visual element, it begins a search for that dictionary key. It first looks in the `ResourceDictionary` for that visual element, and if the key is not found, it looks for the key in the visual element's parent's `ResourceDictionary`, and up and up through the visual tree until it reaches the `ResourceDictionary` on the page.

But something's missing here! Where are the `borderWidth` and `fontSize` dictionary items? They don't seem to be defined in the page's resource dictionary!

Those items are elsewhere. The `Application` class also defines a `Resources` property of type `ResourceDictionary`. This is handy for defining resources that apply to the entire application and not just to a particular page or layout. When the XAML parser searches up the visual tree for a matching resource key, and that key is not found in the `ResourceDictionary` for the page, it finally checks the `ResourceDictionary` defined by the `Application` class. Only if it's not found there is a `XamlParseException` raised for the `StaticResource` key-not-found error.

The standard Xamarin.Forms solution template generates an `App` class that derives from `Application` and thus inherits the `Resources` property. You can add items to this dictionary in two ways:

One approach is to add the items in code in the `App` constructor. Make sure you do this before instantiating the main `ContentPage` class:

```
public class App : Application
{
    public App()
    {
        Resources = new ResourceDictionary();
```

```
        Resources.Add("borderWidth", 3.0);
        Resources.Add("fontSize", "Large");

        MainPage = new ResourceTreesPage();
    }
    ...
}
```

However, the `App` class can also have a XAML file of its own, and the application-wide resources can be defined in the `Resources` collection in that XAML file.

To do this, you'll want to delete the App.cs file created by the Xamarin.Forms solution template. There's no template item for an `App` class, so you'll need to fake it. Add a new XAML page class—**Forms Xaml Page** in Visual Studio or **Forms ContentPage Xaml** in Xamarin Studio—to the project. Name it `App`. And immediately—before you forget—go into the App.xaml file and change the root tags to `Application`, and go into the App.xaml.cs file and change the base class to `Application`.

Now you have an `App` class that derives from `Application` and has its own XAML file. In the App.xaml file you can then instantiate a `ResourceDictionary` within `Application.Resources` property-element tags and add items to it:

```
<Application xmlns="http://xamarin.com/schemas/2014/forms"
             xmlns:x="http://schemas.microsoft.com/winfx/2009/xaml"
             x:Class="ResourceTrees.App">
    <Application.Resources>
        <ResourceDictionary>
            <x:Double x:Key="borderWidth">3</x:Double>
            <x:String x:Key="fontSize">Large</x:String>
        </ResourceDictionary>
    </Application.Resources>
</Application>
```

The constructor in the code-behind file needs to call `InitializeComponent` to parse the App.xaml file at run time and add the items to the dictionary. This should be done prior to the normal job of instantiating the `ResourceTreesPage` class and setting it to the `MainPage` property:

```
public partial class App : Application
{
    public App()
    {
        InitializeComponent();

        MainPage = new ResourceTreesPage();
    }

    protected override void OnStart()
    {
        // Handle when your app starts
    }

    protected override void OnSleep()
    {
```

```
        // Handle when your app sleeps
    }

    protected override void OnResume()
    {
        // Handle when your app resumes
    }
}
```

Adding the lifecycle events is optional.

Be sure to call `InitializeComponent` before instantiating the page class. The constructor of the page class calls its own `InitializeComponent` to parse the XAML file for the page, and the `StaticResource` markup extensions need access to the `Resources` collection in the `App` class.

Every `Resources` dictionary has a particular scope: For the `Resources` dictionary on the `App` class, that scope is the entire application. A `Resources` dictionary on the `ContentPage` class applies to the whole page. A `Resources` dictionary on a `StackLayout` applies to all the children in the `StackLayout`. You should define and store your resources based on how you use them. Use the `Resources` dictionary in the `App` class for application-wide resources; use the `Resources` dictionary on the `ContentPage` for page-wide resources; but define additional `Resources` dictionaries deeper in the visual tree for resources required only in one part of the page.

As you'll see in Chapter 12, the most important items in a `Resources` dictionary are usually objects of type `Style`. In the general case, you'll have application-wide `Style` objects, `Style` objects for the page, and `Style` objects associated with smaller parts of the visual tree.

DynamicResource for special purposes

An alternative to `StaticResource` for referencing items from the `Resources` dictionary is `DynamicResource`, and if you just substitute `DynamicResource` for `StaticResource` in the example shown above, the program will seemingly run the same.

However, the two markup extensions are very different. `StaticResource` accesses the item in the dictionary only once while the XAML is being parsed and the page is being built. But `DynamicResource` maintains a link between the dictionary key and the property set from that dictionary item. If the item in the resource dictionary referenced by the key changes, `DynamicResource` will detect that change and set the new value to the property.

Skeptical? Let's try it out. The **DynamicVsStatic** project has a XAML file that defines a resource item of type `string` with a key of `currentDateTime`, even though the item in the dictionary is the string "Not actually a DateTime"!

This dictionary item is referenced four times in the XAML file, but one of the references is commented out. In the first two examples, the `Text` property of a `Label` is set using `StaticResource` and `DynamicResource`. In the second two examples, the `Text` property of a `Span` object is set similarly, but the use of `DynamicResource` on the `Span` object appears in comments:

```xml
<ContentPage xmlns="http://xamarin.com/schemas/2014/forms"
             xmlns:x="http://schemas.microsoft.com/winfx/2009/xaml"
             x:Class="DynamicVsStatic.DynamicVsStaticPage"
             Padding="5, 0">

    <ContentPage.Resources>
        <ResourceDictionary>
            <x:String x:Key="currentDateTime">Not actually a DateTime</x:String>
        </ResourceDictionary>
    </ContentPage.Resources>

    <StackLayout>
        <Label Text="StaticResource on Label.Text:"
               VerticalOptions="EndAndExpand"
               FontSize="Large" />

        <Label Text="{StaticResource currentDateTime}"
               VerticalOptions="StartAndExpand"
               XAlign="Center"
               FontSize="Large" />

        <Label Text="DynamicResource on Label.Text:"
               VerticalOptions="EndAndExpand"
               FontSize="Large" />

        <Label Text="{DynamicResource currentDateTime}"
               VerticalOptions="StartAndExpand"
               XAlign="Center"
               FontSize="Large" />

        <Label Text="StaticResource on Span.Text:"
               VerticalOptions="EndAndExpand"
               FontSize="Large" />

        <Label VerticalOptions="StartAndExpand"
               XAlign="Center"
               FontSize="Large">
            <Label.FormattedText>
                <FormattedString>
                    <Span Text="{StaticResource currentDateTime}" />
                </FormattedString>
            </Label.FormattedText>
        </Label>

        <!-- This raises a run-time exception! -->

        <!--<Label Text="DynamicResource on Span.Text:"
               VerticalOptions="EndAndExpand"
               FontSize="Large" />

        <Label VerticalOptions="StartAndExpand"
               XAlign="Center"
               FontSize="Large">
            <Label.FormattedText>
```

```
                <FormattedString>
                    <Span Text="{DynamicResource currentDateTime}" />
                </FormattedString>
            </Label.FormattedText>
        </Label>-->
    </StackLayout>
</ContentPage>
```

You'll probably expect all three of the references to the `currentDateTime` dictionary item to result in the display of the text "Not actually a DateTime". However, the code-behind file starts a timer going. Every second, the timer callback replaces that dictionary item with a new string representing an actual `DateTime` value:

```
public partial class DynamicVsStaticPage : ContentPage
{
    public DynamicVsStaticPage()
    {
        InitializeComponent();

        Device.StartTimer(TimeSpan.FromSeconds(1),
            () =>
            {
                Resources["currentDateTime"] = DateTime.Now.ToString();
                return true;
            });
    }
}
```

The result is that the `Text` properties set with `StaticResource` stay the same, while the one with `DynamicResource` changes every second to reflect the new item in the dictionary:

Here's another difference: if there is no item in the dictionary with the specified key name, `Stat-icResource` will raise a run-time exception, but `DynamicResource` will not.

You can try uncommenting the block of markup at the end of the **DynamicVsStatic** project, and you will indeed encounter a run-time exception to the effect that the `Text` property could not be found. Just offhand, that exception doesn't sound quite right, but it's referring to a very real difference.

The problem is that the `Text` properties in `Label` and `Span` are defined in significantly different ways, and that difference matters a lot for `DynamicResource`. This difference will be explored in the next chapter, "The bindable infrastructure."

Lesser-used markup extensions

Three markup extension are not used as much as the others. These are:

- `x:Null`

- `x:Type`

- `x:Array`

You use the `x:Null` extension to set a property to `null`. The syntax looks like this:

```
<SomeElement SomeProperty="{x:Null}" />
```

This doesn't make much sense unless `SomeProperty` has a default value that is not `null` when it's desirable to set the property to `null`. But as you'll see in Chapter 12, sometimes a property can acquire a non-`null` value from a style, and `x:Null` is pretty much the only way to override that.

The `x:Type` markup extension is used to set a property of type `Type`, the .NET class describing the type of a class or structure. Here's the syntax:

```
<AnotherElement TypeProperty="{x:Type Color}" />
```

You'll also use `x:Type` in connection with `x:Array`. The `x:Array` markup extension is always used with regular element syntax rather than curly-brace syntax. It has a required argument named `Type` that you set with the `x:Type` markup extension. This indicates the type of the elements in the array. Here's how an array might be defined in a resource dictionary:

```
<x:Array x:Key="array"
         Type="{x:Type x:String}">
    <x:String>One String</x:String>
    <x:String>Two String</x:String>
    <x:String>Red String</x:String>
    <x:String>Blue String</x:String>
</x:Array>
```

A custom markup extension

Let's create our own markup extension named `HslColorExtension`. This will allow us to set any property of type `Color` by specifying values of hue, saturation, and luminosity, but in a manner much simpler than the use of the `x:FactoryMethod` tag demonstrated in Chapter 8.

Moreover, let's put this class in a separate Portable Class Library so that you can use it from multiple applications. Such a library can be found with the other source code for this book. It's in a directory named **Libraries** that is parallel to the separate chapter directories. The name of this PCL (and the namespace of the classes within it) is **Xamarin.FormsBook.Toolkit**.

You can use this library yourself in your own applications by setting a reference to it or by including the project in your application solution. You can then add a new XML namespace declaration in your XAML files like so to specify this library:

```
xmlns:toolkit="clr-namespace:Xamarin.FormsBook.Toolkit;assembly=Xamarin.FormsBook.Toolkit"
```

With this `toolkit` prefix you can then reference the `HslColorExtension` class in the same way you use other XAML markup extensions:

```
<BoxView Color="{toolkit:HslColor H=0.67, S=1, L=0.5}" />
```

Unlike other XAML markup extensions shown so far, this one has multiple properties, and if you're setting them as arguments with the curly-brace syntax, they must be separated with commas.

Would something like that be useful? Let's first see how to create such a library for classes that you'd like to share among applications:

In Visual Studio, from the **File** menu, select **New** and **Project**. In the **New Project** dialog, select **Visual C#** and **Mobile Apps** at the left, and **Class Library (Xamarin.Forms Portable)** from the list. Find a location for the project and give it a name. For the PCL created for this example, the name is **Xamarin.FormsBook.Toolkit**. Click **OK**. Along with all the overhead for the project, the template creates a code file named Xamarin.FormsBook.Toolkit.cs containing a class named `Xamarin.FormsBook.Toolkit`. That's not a valid class name, so just delete that file.

In Xamarin Studio, from the **File** menu, select **New** and **Solution**. In the **New Solution** dialog, select **C#** and **Mobile Apps** at the left, and **Class Library (Xamarin.Forms Portable)** from the list. Find a location for it and give it a name (**Xamarin.FormsBook.Toolkit** for this example). Click **OK**. The solution template creates several files, including a file named MyPage.cs. Delete that file.

You can now add classes to this project in the normal way:

In Visual Studio, right-click the project name, select **Add** and **New Item**. In the **Add New Item** dialog, if you're just creating a code-only class, select **Visual C#** and **Code** at the left, and select **Class** from the list. Give it a name (HslColorExtension.cs for this example). Click the **Add** button.

In Xamarin Studio, in the tool menu for the project, select **Add** and **New File**. In the **New File** dialog, if you're just creating a code-only class, select **General** at the left and **Empty Class** in the list. Give it a name (HslColorExtension.cs for this example). Click the **New** button.

The HslColorExtension.cs file (including the required `using` directives) looks like this:

```
using System;
using Xamarin.Forms;
using Xamarin.Forms.Xaml;

namespace Xamarin.FormsBook.Toolkit
{
    public class HslColorExtension : IMarkupExtension
    {
        public HslColorExtension()
        {
            A = 1;
        }

        public double H { set; get; }

        public double S { set; get; }

        public double L { set; get; }

        public double A { set; get; }

        public object ProvideValue(IServiceProvider serviceProvider)
        {
            return Color.FromHsla(H, S, L, A);
        }
    }
}
```

Notice that the class is public, so it's visible from outside the library, and that it implements the `IMarkupExtension` interface, which means that it must include a `ProvideValue` method. However, the method doesn't make use of the `IServiceProvider` argument at all, mainly because it doesn't need to know about anything else external to itself. All it needs are the four properties to create a `Color` value, and if the `A` value isn't set, a default value of 1 (fully opaque) is used.

This is a solution with only a PCL project. The project can be built to generate a PCL assembly, but it cannot be run without an application that uses this assembly.

There are two ways to access this library from an application solution:

- In the common PCL project in the application solution, add a reference to the PCL assembly.

- Include a link to the library project in your application solution, and add a reference to that library project in the common PCL project.

The first option is necessary if you have only the PCL and not the project with source code. Perhaps you're licensing the library and don't have access to the source. But if you have access to the project, it's usually best to include a link to the library project in your solution so that you can easily make changes to the library code and rebuild the library project.

The final project in this chapter is **CustomExtensionDemo,** which makes use of the `HslColorExtension` class in the new library. The **CustomExtensionDemo** solution contains a link to the **Xamarin.FormsBook.Toolkit** PCL project, and the **References** section in the **CustomExtensionDemo** project lists the **Xamarin.FormsBook.Toolkit** assembly.

Now the application project is seemingly ready to access the library project to use the `HslColorExtension` class within the application's XAML file.

But first there's another step. Currently, a reference to the library from XAML is insufficient to ensure that the library is included with the application. The library needs to be accessed from actual code. You can add a simple statement in the `App` file to reference the `HslColorExtension` class:

```
namespace CustomExtensionDemo
{
    public class App : Application
    {
        public App()
        {
            new Xamarin.FormsBook.Toolkit.HslColorExtension();

            MainPage = new CustomExtensionDemoPage();
        }
        …
    }
}
```

The following XAML file shows the XML namespace declaration for the **Xamarin.FormsBook.Toolkit** library and three ways to access the custom XAML markup extension—by using an `HslColorExtension` element set with property-element syntax on the `Color` property and by using both `HslColorExtension` and `HslColor` with the more common curly-brace syntax. Again, notice the use of commas to separate the arguments within the curly braces:

```
<ContentPage xmlns="http://xamarin.com/schemas/2014/forms"
             xmlns:x="http://schemas.microsoft.com/winfx/2009/xaml"
             xmlns:toolkit=
                 "clr-namespace:Xamarin.FormsBook.Toolkit;assembly=Xamarin.FormsBook.Toolkit"
             x:Class="CustomExtensionDemo.CustomExtensionDemoPage">

    <StackLayout>
        <!-- Red -->
        <BoxView HorizontalOptions="Center"
                 VerticalOptions="CenterAndExpand">
            <BoxView.Color>
                <toolkit:HslColorExtension H="0" S="1" L="0.5" />
            </BoxView.Color>
        </BoxView>
```

```
    <!-- Green -->
    <BoxView HorizontalOptions="Center"
             VerticalOptions="CenterAndExpand">
        <BoxView.Color>
            <toolkit:HslColorExtension H="0.33" S="1" L="0.5" />
        </BoxView.Color>
    </BoxView>

    <!-- Blue -->
    <BoxView Color="{toolkit:HslColor H=0.67, S=1, L=0.5}"
             HorizontalOptions="Center"
             VerticalOptions="CenterAndExpand" />

    <!-- Gray -->
    <BoxView Color="{toolkit:HslColor H=0, S=0, L=0.5}"
             HorizontalOptions="Center"
             VerticalOptions="CenterAndExpand" />

    <!-- Semitransparent white -->
    <BoxView Color="{toolkit:HslColor H=0, S=0, L=1, A=0.5}"
             HorizontalOptions="Center"
             VerticalOptions="CenterAndExpand" />

    <!-- Semitransparent black -->
    <BoxView Color="{toolkit:HslColor H=0, S=0, L=0, A=0.5}"
             HorizontalOptions="Center"
             VerticalOptions="CenterAndExpand" />
    </StackLayout>
</ContentPage>
```

The last two examples set the A property for 50 percent transparency, so the boxes show up as a shade of gray (or not at all) depending on the background:

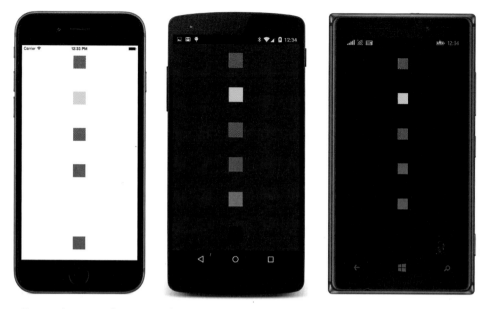

Two major uses of XAML markup extensions are yet to come. In Chapter 12, you'll see the `Style` class, which is without a doubt the most popular item for including in resource dictionaries, and in Chapter 16, you'll see the powerful markup extension named `Binding`.

Chapter 11
The bindable infrastructure

One of the most basic language constructs of C# is the class member known as the *property*. All of us very early on in our first encounters with C# learned the general routine of defining a property. The property is often backed by a private field and includes `set` and `get` accessors that reference the private field and do something with a new value:

```
public class MyClass
{
    …
    double quality;

    public double Quality
    {
        set
        {
            quality = value;
            // Do something with the new value
        }
        get
        {
            return quality;
        }
    }
    …
}
```

Properties are sometimes referred to as *smart fields*. Syntactically, code that accesses a property resembles code that accesses a field. Yet the property can execute some of its own code when the property is accessed.

Properties are also like methods. Indeed, C# code is compiled into intermediate language that implements a property such as `Quality` with a pair of methods named `set_Quality` and `get_Quality`. Yet despite the close functional resemblance between properties and a pair of *set* and *get* methods, the property syntax reveals itself to be much more suitable when moving from code to markup. It's hard to imagine XAML built on an underlying API that is missing properties.

So you may be surprised to learn that Xamarin.Forms implements an enhanced property definition that builds upon C# properties. Or maybe you won't be surprised. If you already have experience with Microsoft's XAML-based platforms, you'll encounter some familiar concepts in this chapter.

The property definition shown above is known as a *CLR property* because it's supported by the .NET common language runtime. The enhanced property definition in Xamarin.Forms builds upon the CLR property and is called a *bindable property,* encapsulated by the `BindableProperty` class and supported by the `BindableObject` class.

The Xamarin.Forms class hierarchy

Before exploring the details of the important `BindableObject` class, let's first discover how `BindableObject` fits into the overall Xamarin.Forms architecture by constructing a class hierarchy.

In an object-oriented programming framework such as Xamarin.Forms, a class hierarchy can often reveal important inner structures of the environment. The class hierarchy shows how various classes relate to one another and the properties, methods, and events that they share, including how bindable properties are supported.

You can construct such a class hierarchy by laboriously going through the online documentation and taking note of what classes derive from what other classes. Or you can write a Xamarin.Forms program to construct a class hierarchy and display it on the phone. Such a program makes use of .NET reflection to obtain all the public classes, structures, and enumerations in the **Xamarin.Forms.Core** and **Xamarin.Forms.Xaml** assemblies and arrange them in a tree. The **ClassHierarchy** application demonstrates this technique.

As usual, the **ClassHierarchy** project contains a class that derives from `ContentPage`, named `ClassHierarchyPage`, but it also contains two additional classes, named `TypeInformation` and `ClassAndSubclasses`.

The program creates one `TypeInformation` instance for every public class (and structure and enumeration) in the **Xamarin.Forms.Core** assembly, plus any .NET class that serves as a base class for any Xamarin.Forms class, with the exception of `Object`. (These .NET classes are `Attribute`, `Delegate`, `Enum`, `EventArgs`, `Exception`, `MulticastDelegate`, and `ValueType`.) The `TypeInformation` constructor requires a `Type` object identifying a type but also obtains some other information:

```
class TypeInformation
{
    bool isBaseGenericType;
    Type baseGenericTypeDef;

    public TypeInformation(Type type, bool isXamarinForms)
    {
        Type = type;
        IsXamarinForms = isXamarinForms;
        TypeInfo typeInfo = type.GetTypeInfo();
        BaseType = typeInfo.BaseType;

        if (BaseType != null)
        {
            TypeInfo baseTypeInfo = BaseType.GetTypeInfo();
            isBaseGenericType = baseTypeInfo.IsGenericType;

            if (isBaseGenericType)
            {
                baseGenericTypeDef = baseTypeInfo.GetGenericTypeDefinition();
            }
```

```
            }
    }

    public Type Type { private set; get; }
    public Type BaseType { private set; get; }
    public bool IsXamarinForms { private set; get; }

    public bool IsDerivedDirectlyFrom(Type parentType)
    {
        if (BaseType != null && isBaseGenericType)
        {
            if (baseGenericTypeDef == parentType)
            {
                return true;
            }
        }
        else if (BaseType == parentType)
        {
            return true;
        }
        return false;
    }
}
```

A very important part of this class is the `IsDerivedDirectlyFrom` method, which will return `true` if passed an argument that is this type's base type. This determination is complicated if generic classes are involved, and that issue largely accounts for the complexity of the class.

The `ClassAndSubclasses` class is considerably shorter:

```
class ClassAndSubclasses
{
    public ClassAndSubclasses(Type parent, bool isXamarinForms)
    {
        Type = parent;
        IsXamarinForms = isXamarinForms;
        Subclasses = new List<ClassAndSubclasses>();
    }

    public Type Type { private set; get; }
    public bool IsXamarinForms { private set; get; }
    public List<ClassAndSubclasses> Subclasses { private set; get; }
}
```

The program creates one instance of this class for every `Type` displayed in the class hierarchy, including `Object`, so the program creates one more `ClassAndSubclasses` instance than the number of `TypeInformation` instances. The `ClassAndSubclasses` instance associated with `Object` contains a collection of all the classes that derive directly from `Object`, and each of those `ClassAndSubclasses` instances contains a collection of all the classes that derive from that one, and so forth for the remainder of the hierarchy tree.

The `ClassHierarchyPage` class consists of a XAML file and a code-behind file, but the XAML file contains little more than a scrollable `StackLayout` ready for some `Label` elements:

```xml
<ContentPage xmlns="http://xamarin.com/schemas/2014/forms"
             xmlns:x="http://schemas.microsoft.com/winfx/2009/xaml"
             x:Class="ClassHierarchy.ClassHierarchyPage">

    <ContentPage.Padding>
        <OnPlatform x:TypeArguments="Thickness"
                    iOS="5, 20, 0, 0"
                    Android="5, 0, 0, 0"
                    WinPhone="5, 0, 0, 0" />
    </ContentPage.Padding>

    <ScrollView>
        <StackLayout x:Name="stackLayout"
                     Spacing="0" />
    </ScrollView>
</ContentPage>
```

The code-behind file obtains references to the two Xamarin.Forms `Assembly` objects and then ac-cumulates all the public classes, structures, and enumerations in the `classList` collection. It then checks for the necessity of including any base classes from the .NET assemblies, sorts the result, and then calls two recursive methods, `AddChildrenToParent` and `AddItemToStackLayout`:

```csharp
public partial class ClassHierarchyPage : ContentPage
{
    public ClassHierarchyPage()
    {
        InitializeComponent();

        List<TypeInformation> classList = new List<TypeInformation>();

        // Get types in Xamarin.Forms.Core assembly.
        GetPublicTypes(typeof(View).GetTypeInfo().Assembly, classList);

        // Get types in Xamarin.Forms.Xaml assembly.
        GetPublicTypes(typeof(Extensions).GetTypeInfo().Assembly, classList);

        // Ensure that all classes have a base type in the list.
        //   (i.e., add Attribute, ValueType, Enum, EventArgs, etc.)
        int index = 0;

        // Watch out! Loops through expanding classList!
        do
        {
            // Get a child type from the list.
            TypeInformation childType = classList[index];

            if (childType.Type != typeof(Object))
            {
                bool hasBaseType = false;

                // Loop through the list looking for a base type.
```

```
            foreach (TypeInformation parentType in classList)
            {
                if (childType.IsDerivedDirectlyFrom(parentType.Type))
                {
                    hasBaseType = true;
                }
            }

            // If there's no base type, add it.
            if (!hasBaseType && childType.BaseType != typeof(Object))
            {
                classList.Add(new TypeInformation(childType.BaseType, false));
            }
        }
        index++;
    }
    while (index < classList.Count);

    // Now sort the list.
    classList.Sort((t1, t2) =>
    {
        return String.Compare(t1.Type.Name, t2.Type.Name);
    });

    // Start the display with System.Object.
    ClassAndSubclasses rootClass = new ClassAndSubclasses(typeof(Object), false);

    // Recursive method to build the hierarchy tree.
    AddChildrenToParent(rootClass, classList);

    // Recursive method for adding items to StackLayout.
    AddItemToStackLayout(rootClass, 0);
}

void GetPublicTypes(Assembly assembly,
                    List<TypeInformation> classList)
{
    // Loop through all the types.
    foreach (Type type in assembly.ExportedTypes)
    {
        TypeInfo typeInfo = type.GetTypeInfo();

        // Public types only but exclude interfaces.
        if (typeInfo.IsPublic && !typeInfo.IsInterface)
        {
            // Add type to list.
            classList.Add(new TypeInformation(type, true));
        }
    }
}

void AddChildrenToParent(ClassAndSubclasses parentClass,
                         List<TypeInformation> classList)
{
```

```
        foreach (TypeInformation typeInformation in classList)
        {
            if (typeInformation.IsDerivedDirectlyFrom(parentClass.Type))
            {
                ClassAndSubclasses subClass =
                    new ClassAndSubclasses(typeInformation.Type,
                                           typeInformation.IsXamarinForms);
                parentClass.Subclasses.Add(subClass);
                AddChildrenToParent(subClass, classList);
            }
        }
    }

    void AddItemToStackLayout(ClassAndSubclasses parentClass, int level)
    {
        // If assembly is not Xamarin.Forms, display full name.
        string name = parentClass.IsXamarinForms ? parentClass.Type.Name :
                                                   parentClass.Type.FullName;

        TypeInfo typeInfo = parentClass.Type.GetTypeInfo();

        // If generic, display angle brackets and parameters.
        if (typeInfo.IsGenericType)
        {
            Type[] parameters = typeInfo.GenericTypeParameters;
            name = name.Substring(0, name.Length - 2);
            name += "<";

            for (int i = 0; i < parameters.Length; i++)
            {
                name += parameters[i].Name;
                if (i < parameters.Length - 1)
                {
                    name += ", ";
                }
            }
            name += ">";
        }

        // Create Label and add to StackLayout.
        Label label = new Label
        {
            Text = String.Format("{0}{1}", new string(' ', 4 * level), name),
            TextColor = parentClass.Type.GetTypeInfo().IsAbstract ?
                            Color.Accent : Color.Default
        };

        stackLayout.Children.Add(label);

        // Now display nested types.
        foreach (ClassAndSubclasses subclass in parentClass.Subclasses)
        {
            AddItemToStackLayout(subclass, level + 1);
        }
```

```
    }
}
```

The recursive `AddChildrenToParent` method assembles the linked list of `ClassAndSubclasses` instances from the flat `classList` collection. The `AddItemToStackLayout` method is also recursive because it is responsible for adding the `ClassesAndSubclasses` linked list to the `StackLayout` object by creating a `Label` view for each class, with a little blank space at the beginning for the proper indentation. The method displays the Xamarin.Forms types with just the class names, but the .NET types with the fully qualified name to distinguish them. The method uses the platform accent color for classes that are not instantiable because they are abstract or static:

Overall, you'll see that the Xamarin.Forms visual elements have the following general hierarchy:

```
System.Object
    BindableObject
        Element
            VisualElement
                View

                    ...
                    Layout

                        ...
                        Layout<T>

                            ...
                Page

                    ...
```

Aside from `Object`, all the classes in this abbreviated class hierarchy are implemented in the Xamarin.Forms.Core.dll assembly and associated with a namespace of `Xamarin.Forms`.

Let's examine some of these major classes in detail.

As the name of the `BindableObject` class implies, the primary function of this class is to support data binding—the linking of two properties of two objects so that they maintain the same value. But `BindableObject` also supports styles and the `DynamicResource` markup extension as well. It does this in two ways: through `BindableObject` property definitions in the form of `BindableProperty` objects and also by implementing the .NET `INotifyPropertyChanged` interface. All of this will be discussed in much more detail in this chapter and future chapters.

Let's continue down the hierarchy: as you've seen, user-interface objects in Xamarin.Forms are often arranged on the page in a parent-child hierarchy, and the `Element` class includes support for parent and child relationships.

`VisualElement` is an exceptionally important class in Xamarin.Forms. A visual element is anything in Xamarin.Forms that occupies an area on the screen. The `VisualElement` class defines 28 properties related to size, location, background color, and other visual and functional characteristics, such as `IsEnabled` and `IsVisible`.

In Xamarin.Forms the word *view* is often used to refer to individual visual objects such as buttons, sliders, and text-entry boxes, but you can see that the `View` class is the parent to the layout classes as well. Interestingly, `View` only adds a couple of public members to what it inherits from `VisualElement`. Those include `HorizontalOptions` and `VerticalOptions`—which make sense because these properties don't apply to pages—and `GestureRecognizers` to support touch input.

The descendants of `Layout` are capable of having children views. A child view appears on the screen visually within the boundaries of its parent. Classes that derive from `Layout` can have only one child of type `View`, but the generic `Layout<T>` class defines a `Children` property, which is a collection of multiple child views, including other layouts. You've already seen the `StackLayout`, which arranges its children in a horizontal or vertical stack. Although the `Layout` class derives from `View`, layouts are so important in Xamarin.Forms that they are often considered a category in themselves.

ClassHierarchy lists all the public classes, structures, and enumerations defined by Xamarin.Forms, but it does not list interfaces. Those are important as well, but you'll just have to explore them on your own. (Or enhance the program to list them.)

A peek into BindableObject and BindableProperty

The existence of classes named `BindableObject` and `BindableProperty` is likely to be a little confusing at first. Keep in mind that `BindableObject` is much like `Object` in that it serves as a base class to a large chunk of the Xamarin.Forms API, and particularly to `Element` and hence `VisualElement`.

BindableObject provides support for objects of type BindableProperty. A BindableProperty object extends a CLR property. The best insights into bindable properties come when you create a few of your own—as you'll be doing before the end of this chapter—but you can also glean some understanding by exploring the existing bindable properties.

Toward the beginning of Chapter 7, "XAML vs. code," two buttons were created with many of the same property settings, except that the properties of one button were set in code using the C# 3.0 object initialization syntax and the other button was instantiated and initialized in XAML.

Here's a similar code-only program named **PropertySettings** that also creates and initializes two buttons in two different ways. The properties of the first Label are set the old-fashioned way, while the properties of the second Label are set with a more verbose technique:

```
public class PropertySettingsPage : ContentPage
{
    public PropertySettingsPage()
    {
        Label label1 = new Label();
        label1.Text = "Text with CLR properties";
        label1.IsVisible = true;
        label1.Opacity = 0.75;
        label1.XAlign = TextAlignment.Center;
        label1.VerticalOptions = LayoutOptions.CenterAndExpand;
        label1.TextColor = Color.Blue;
        label1.BackgroundColor = Color.FromRgb(255, 128, 128);
        label1.FontSize = Device.GetNamedSize(NamedSize.Large, new Label());
        label1.FontAttributes = FontAttributes.Bold | FontAttributes.Italic;

        Label label2 = new Label();
        label2.SetValue(Label.TextProperty, "Text with bindable properties");
        label2.SetValue(Label.IsVisibleProperty, true);
        label2.SetValue(Label.OpacityProperty, 0.75);
        label2.SetValue(Label.XAlignProperty, TextAlignment.Center);
        label2.SetValue(Label.VerticalOptionsProperty, LayoutOptions.CenterAndExpand);
        label2.SetValue(Label.TextColorProperty, Color.Blue);
        label2.SetValue(Label.BackgroundColorProperty, Color.FromRgb(255, 128, 128));
        label2.SetValue(Label.FontSizeProperty,
                        Device.GetNamedSize(NamedSize.Large, new Label()));
        label2.SetValue(Label.FontAttributesProperty,
                        FontAttributes.Bold | FontAttributes.Italic);

        Content = new StackLayout
        {
            Children =
            {
                label1,
                label2
            }
        };
    }
}
```

These two ways to set properties are entirely consistent:

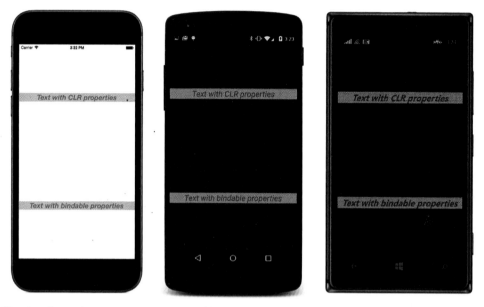

Yet the alternative syntax seems very odd. For example:

```
label2.SetValue(Label.TextProperty, "Text with bindable properties");
```

What is that `SetValue` method? `SetValue` is defined by `BindableObject`, from which every visual object derives. `BindableObject` also defines a `GetValue` method.

That first argument to `SetValue` has the name `Label.TextProperty`, which indicates that `TextProperty` is static, but despite its name, it's not a property at all. It's a static *field* of the `Label` class. `TextProperty` is also read-only, and it's defined in the `Label` class something like this:

```
public static readonly BindableProperty TextProperty;
```

That's an object of type `BindableProperty`. Of course, it may seem a little disturbing that a field is named `TextProperty`, but there it is. Because it's static, however, it exists independently of any `Label` objects that might or might not exist.

If you look in the documentation of the `Label` class, you'll see that it defines 10 properties, including `Text`, `TextColor`, `FontSize`, `FontAttributes`, and others. You'll also see 10 corresponding public static read-only fields of type `BindableProperty` with the names `TextProperty`, `TextColorProperty`, `FontSizeProperty`, `FontAttributesProperty`, and so forth.

These properties and fields are closely related. Indeed, internal to the `Label` class, the `Text` CLR property is defined like this to reference the corresponding `TextProperty` object:

```
public string Text
{
    set { SetValue(Label.TextProperty, value); }
    get { return (string)GetValue(Label.TextProperty); }
}
```

So you see why it is that your application calling `SetValue` on `Label.TextProperty` is exactly equiv-alent to setting the `Text` property directly, and perhaps just a tinier bit faster!

The internal definition of the `Text` property in `Label` isn't secret information. This is standard code. Although any class can define a `BindableProperty` object, only a class that derives from `BindableObject` can call the `SetValue` and `GetValue` methods that actually implement the property in the class. Casting is required for the `GetValue` method because it's defined as returning `object`.

All the real work involved with maintaining the `Text` property is going on in those `SetValue` and `GetValue` calls. The `BindableObject` and `BindableProperty` objects effectively extend the func-tionality of standard CLR properties to provide systematic ways to:

- Define properties

- Give properties default values

- Store their current values

- Provide mechanisms for validating property values

- Maintain consistency among related properties in a single class

- Respond to property changes

- Trigger notifications when a property is about to change and has changed

- Support data binding

- Support styles

- Support dynamic resources

The close relationship of a property named `Text` with a `BindableProperty` named `TextProperty` is reflected in the way that programmers speak about these properties: Sometimes a programmer says that the `Text` property is "backed by" a `BindableProperty` named `TextProperty` because `TextProperty` provides infrastructure support for `Text`. But a common shortcut is to say that `Text` is itself a "bindable property," and generally no one will be confused.

Not every Xamarin.Forms property is a bindable property. Neither the `Content` property of `ContentPage` nor the `Children` property of `Layout<T>` is a bindable property. Of the 28 properties defined by `VisualElement`, 26 are backed by bindable properties, but the `Bounds` property and the `Resources` properties are not.

The Span class used in connection with FormattedString does not derive from BindableOb-ject. Therefore, Span does not inherit SetValue and GetValue methods, and it cannot implement BindableProperty objects.

This means that the Text property of Label is backed by a bindable property, but the Text prop-erty of Span is not. Does it make a difference?

Of course it makes a difference! If you recall the **DynamicVsStatic** program in the previous chapter, you discovered that DynamicResource worked on the Text property of Label but not the Text property of Span. Can it be that DynamicResource works only with bindable properties?

This supposition is pretty much confirmed by the definition of the following public method defined by Element:

```
public void SetDynamicResource(BindableProperty property, string key);
```

This is how the dictionary key is attached to a particular property of an element when that property is the target of a DynamicResource markup extension.

The SetDynamicResource method also allows you to set a dynamic resource link on a property in code. Here's the page class from a code-only version of **DynamicVsStatic** called **DynamicVsStat-icCode**. It's somewhat simplified to exclude the use of a FormattedString and Span object, but oth-erwise it pretty accurately mimics how the previous XAML file is parsed and, in particular, how the Text properties of the Label elements are set by the XAML parser:

```
public class DynamicVsStaticCodePage : ContentPage
{
    public DynamicVsStaticCodePage()
    {
        Padding = new Thickness(5, 0);

        // Create resource dictionary and add item.
        Resources = new ResourceDictionary
        {
            { "currentDateTime", "Not actually a DateTime" }
        };

        Content = new StackLayout
        {
            Children =
            {
                new Label
                {
                    Text = "StaticResource on Label.Text:",
                    VerticalOptions = LayoutOptions.EndAndExpand,
                    FontSize = Device.GetNamedSize(NamedSize.Large, typeof(Label))
                },

                new Label
                {
                    Text = (string)Resources["currentDateTime"],
```

```
                            VerticalOptions = LayoutOptions.StartAndExpand,
                            XAlign = TextAlignment.Center,
                            FontSize = Device.GetNamedSize(NamedSize.Large, typeof(Label))
                        },

                        new Label
                        {
                            Text = "DynamicResource on Label.Text:",
                            VerticalOptions = LayoutOptions.EndAndExpand,
                            FontSize = Device.GetNamedSize(NamedSize.Large, typeof(Label))
                        }
                    }
            };

            // Create the final label with the dynamic resource.
            Label label = new Label
            {
                VerticalOptions = LayoutOptions.StartAndExpand,
                XAlign = TextAlignment.Center,
                FontSize = Device.GetNamedSize(NamedSize.Large, typeof(Label))
            };

            label.SetDynamicResource(Label.TextProperty, "currentDateTime");

            ((StackLayout)Content).Children.Add(label);

            // Start the timer going.
            Device.StartTimer(TimeSpan.FromSeconds(1),
                () =>
                {
                    Resources["currentDateTime"] = DateTime.Now.ToString();
                    return true;
                });
        }
    }
```

The Text property of the second Label is set directly from the dictionary entry and makes the use of the dictionary seem a little pointless in this context. But the Text property of the last Label is bound to the dictionary key through a call to SetDynamicResource, which allows the property to be updated when the dictionary contents change:

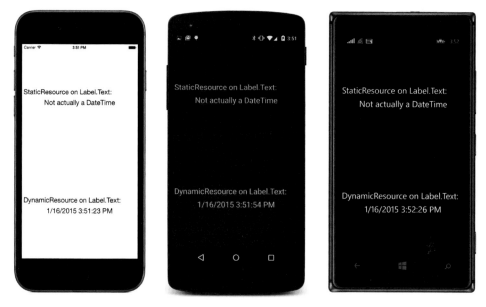

Consider this: What would the signature of this `SetDynamicResource` method be if it could not refer to a property using the `BindableProperty` object? It's easy to reference a property *value* in method calls, but not the property itself. There are a couple of ways, such as the `PropertyInfo` class in the `System.Reflection` namespace or the LINQ `Expression` object. But the `BindableProperty` object is designed specifically for this purpose, as well as the essential job of handling the underlying link between the property and the dictionary key.

Similarly, when we explore styles in the next chapter, you'll encounter a `Setter` class used in connection with styles. `Setter` defines a property named `Property` of type `BindableProperty`, which mandates that any property targeted by a style must be backed by a bindable property. This allows a style to be defined prior to the elements targeted by the style.

Likewise for data bindings. The `BindableObject` class defines a `SetBinding` method that is very similar to the `SetDynamicResource` method defined on `Element`:

```
public void SetBinding(BindableProperty targetProperty, BindingBase binding);
```

Again, notice the type of the first argument. Any property targeted by a data binding must be backed by a bindable property.

For these reasons, whenever you create a custom view and need to define public properties, your default inclination should be to define them as bindable properties. Only if after careful consideration you conclude that it is not necessary or appropriate for the property to be targeted by a style or a data binding should you retreat and define an ordinary CLR property instead.

So whenever you create a class that derives from `BindableObject`, one of the first pieces of code you should be typing in that class begins "public static readonly BindableProperty"—perhaps the most characteristic sequence of four words in all of Xamarin.Forms programming.

Defining bindable properties

Suppose you'd like an enhanced `Label` class that lets you specify font sizes in units of points. Let's call this class `AltLabel` for "alternative `Label`." It derives from `Label` and includes a new property named `PointSize`.

Should `PointSize` be backed by a bindable property? Of course! (Although the real advantages of doing so won't be demonstrated until upcoming chapters.)

The code-only `AltLabel` class is included in the **Xamarin.FormsBook.Toolkit** library, so it's accessible to multiple applications. The new `PointSize` property is implemented with a `BindableProperty` object named `PointSizeProperty` and a CLR property named `PointSize` that references `PointSizeProperty`:

```
public class AltLabel : Label
{
    public static readonly BindableProperty PointSizeProperty … ;
    …
    public double PointSize
    {
        set { SetValue(PointSizeProperty, value); }
        get { return (double)GetValue(PointSizeProperty); }
    }
    …
}
```

Both property definitions must be public.

Because `PointSizeProperty` is defined as `static` and `readonly`, it must be assigned either in a static constructor or right in the field definition, after which it cannot be changed. Generally, a `BindableProperty` object is assigned in the field definition using the static `BindableProperty.Create` method. Four arguments are required (shown here with the argument names):

- `propertyName`   The text name of the property (in this case "PointSize")

- `returnType`   The type of the property (a `double` in this example)

- `declaringType`   The type of the class defining the property (`AltLabel`)

- `defaultValue`   A default value (let's say 8 points)

The second and third arguments are generally defined with `typeof` expressions. Here's the assignment statement with these four arguments passed to `BindableProperty.Create`:

```
public class AltLabel : Label
{
    public static readonly BindableProperty PointSizeProperty =
        BindableProperty.Create("PointSize",          // propertyName
                                typeof(double),       // returnType
                                typeof(AltLabel),     // declaringType
                                8.0,                  // defaultValue
                                …);

    …
}
```

Notice that the default value is specified as 8.0 rather than just 8. Because `BindableProperty.Create` is designed to handle properties of any type, the `defaultValue` parameter is defined as `object`. When the C# compiler encounters just an 8 set as that argument, it will assume that the 8 is an `int` and pass an `int` to the method. The problem won't be revealed until run time, however, when the `BindableProperty.Create` method will be expecting the default value to be of type `double` and respond by raising a `TypeInitializationException`.

You must be explicit about the type of the value you're specifying as the default. Not doing so is a very common error in defining bindable properties.

`BindableProperty.Create` also has six optional arguments. Here they are with the argument names and their purpose:

- `defaultBindingMode`   Used in connection with data binding

- `validateValue`   A callback to check for a valid value

- `propertyChanged`   A callback to indicate when the property has changed

- `propertyChanging`   A callback to indicate when the property is about to change

- `coerceValue`   A callback to coerce a set value to another value (for example, to restrict the values to a range)

- `defaultValueCreator`   A callback to create a default value. This is generally used to instantiate a default object that can't be shared among all instances of the class; for example, a collection object such as `List` or `Dictionary`.

Do not perform any validation, coercion, or property-changed handling in the CLR property. The CLR property should be restricted to `SetValue` and `GetValue` calls. Everything else should be done in the callbacks provided by the bindable property infrastructure.

It is very rare that a particular call to `BindableProperty.Create` would need all of these optional arguments. For that reason, these optional arguments are commonly indicated with the named argument feature introduced in C# 4.0. To specify a particular optional argument, use the argument name followed by a colon. For example:

```
public class AltLabel : Label
{
    public static readonly BindableProperty PointSizeProperty =
        BindableProperty.Create("PointSize",              // propertyName
                                typeof(double),           // returnType
                                typeof(AltLabel),         // declaringType
                                8.0,                      // defaultValue
                                propertyChanged: OnPointSizeChanged);

    ...

}
```

Without a doubt, `propertyChanged` is the most important of the optional arguments because the class uses this callback to be notified when the property changes, either directly from a call to `Set-Value` or through the CLR property.

In this example, the property-changed handler is called `OnPointSizeChanged`. It will be called only when the property truly changes, and not when it's simply set to the same value. However, because `OnPointSizeChanged` is referenced from a static field, the method itself must also be static. Here's what it looks like:

```
public class AltLabel : Label
{
    ...
    static void OnPointSizeChanged(BindableObject bindable, object oldValue, object newValue)
    {
        ...
    }
    ...
}
```

This seems a little odd. We might have multiple `AltLabel` instances in a program, yet whenever the `PointSize` property changes in any one of these instances, this same static method is called. How does the method know exactly which `AltLabel` instance has changed?

The method knows because it's always the first argument. That first argument is actually of type `AltLabel` and indicates which `AltLabel` instance's property has changed. This means that you can safely cast the first argument to an `AltLabel` instance:

```
static void OnPointSizeChanged(BindableObject bindable, object oldValue, object newValue)
{
    AltLabel altLabel = (AltLabel)bindable;
    ...
}
```

You can then reference anything in the particular instance of `AltLabel` whose property has changed. The second and third arguments are actually of type `double` for this example and indicate the previous value and the new value.

Often it's convenient for this static method to call an instance method with the arguments converted to their actual types:

```
public class AltLabel : Label
{
    ...
    static void OnPointSizeChanged(BindableObject bindable, object oldValue, object newValue)
    {
        ((AltLabel)bindable).OnPointSizeChanged((double)oldValue, (double)newValue);
    }

    void OnPointSizeChanged(double oldValue, double newValue)
    {
        ...
    }
}
```

The instance method can then make use of any instance properties or methods of the underlying base class as it would normally.

For this class, this OnPointSizeChanged method needs to set the FontSize property based on the new point size and a device-dependent conversion factor. In addition, the constructor needs to initialize the FontSize property based on the default PointSize value. This is done through a simple SetLabelFontSize method. Here's the final complete class, which uses the platform-dependent resolutions discussed in Chapter 5, "Dealing with sizes":

```
public class AltLabel : Label
{
    public static readonly BindableProperty PointSizeProperty =
        BindableProperty.Create("PointSize",           // propertyName
                                typeof(double),          // returnType
                                typeof(AltLabel),        // declaringType
                                8.0,                     // defaultValue
                                propertyChanged: OnPointSizeChanged);

    public AltLabel()
    {
        SetLabelFontSize((double)PointSizeProperty.DefaultValue);
    }

    public double PointSize
    {
        set { SetValue(PointSizeProperty, value); }
        get { return (double)GetValue(PointSizeProperty); }
    }

    static void OnPointSizeChanged(BindableObject bindable, object oldValue, object newValue)
    {
        ((AltLabel)bindable).OnPointSizeChanged((double)oldValue, (double)newValue);
    }

    void OnPointSizeChanged(double oldValue, double newValue)
    {
        SetLabelFontSize(newValue);
    }
```

```
    void SetLabelFontSize(double pointSize)
    {
        FontSize = Device.OnPlatform(160, 160, 240) * pointSize / 72;
    }
}
```

It is also possible for the instance `OnPointSizeChanged` property to access the `PointSize` property directly rather than use `newValue`. By the time the property-changed handler is called, the underlying property value has already been changed. However, you don't have direct access to that underlying value, as you do when a private field backs a CLR property. That underlying value is private to `BindableObject` and accessible only through the `GetValue` call.

Of course, nothing prevents code that's using `AltLabel` from setting the `FontSize` property and overriding the `PointSize` setting, but let's hope such code is aware of that. Here's some code that is—a program called **PointSizedText,** which uses `AltLabel` to display point sizes from 4 through 12:

```
<ContentPage xmlns="http://xamarin.com/schemas/2014/forms"
             xmlns:x="http://schemas.microsoft.com/winfx/2009/xaml"
             xmlns:toolkit=
                 "clr-namespace:Xamarin.FormsBook.Toolkit;assembly=Xamarin.FormsBook.Toolkit"
             x:Class="PointSizedText.PointSizedTextPage">
    <ContentPage.Padding>
        <OnPlatform x:TypeArguments="Thickness"
                    iOS="5, 20, 0, 0"
                    Android="5, 0, 0, 0"
                    WinPhone="5, 0, 0, 0" />
    </ContentPage.Padding>

    <StackLayout x:Name="stackLayout">
        <toolkit:AltLabel Text="Text of 4 points" PointSize="4" />
        <toolkit:AltLabel Text="Text of 5 points" PointSize="5" />
        <toolkit:AltLabel Text="Text of 6 points" PointSize="6" />
        <toolkit:AltLabel Text="Text of 7 points" PointSize="7" />
        <toolkit:AltLabel Text="Text of 8 points" PointSize="8" />
        <toolkit:AltLabel Text="Text of 9 points" PointSize="9" />
        <toolkit:AltLabel Text="Text of 10 points" PointSize="10" />
        <toolkit:AltLabel Text="Text of 11 points" PointSize="11" />
        <toolkit:AltLabel Text="Text of 12 points" PointSize="12" />
    </StackLayout>
</ContentPage>
```

And here are the screen shots:

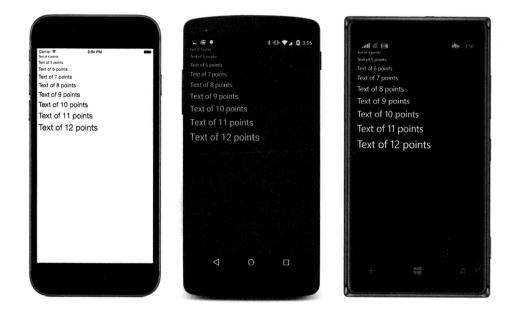

The generic Create method

Several problems can arise when defining a `BindableProperty` object. You might misspell the text rendition of the property name, or you might specify a default value that is not the same type as the property.

You can eliminate those two problems with an alternative generic form of the `BindableProperty.Create` method. The two generic arguments are the type of the class defining the property and the type of the property itself. With this information, the method can derive some of the standard properties and provide types for default value arguments and the callback methods. In addition, the first argument to this alternative generic method must be a LINQ `Expression` object referencing the CLR property. This allows the method to derive the text string of the property.

The following `AltLabelGeneric` class—also in the **Xamarin.FormsBook.Toolkit** library, but providing no additional functionality over `AltLabel`—demonstrates this technique and in addition uses a lambda function for the property-changed callback:

```
public class AltLabelGeneric : Label
{
    public static readonly BindableProperty PointSizeProperty =
        BindableProperty.Create<AltLabelGeneric, double>
            (label => label.PointSize,
            8,
            propertyChanged: (bindable, oldValue, newValue) =>
                {
                    ((AltLabelGeneric)bindable).SetLabelFontSize(newValue);
                });
```

```
    public AltLabelGeneric()
    {
        SetLabelFontSize((double)PointSizeProperty.DefaultValue);
    }

    public double PointSize
    {
        set { SetValue(PointSizeProperty, value); }
        get { return (double)GetValue(PointSizeProperty); }
    }

    void SetLabelFontSize(double pointSize)
    {
        FontSize = Device.OnPlatform(160, 160, 240) * pointSize / 72;
    }
}
```

The first argument to the generic form of the `BindableProperty.Create` method is an `Expression` object referencing the `PointSize` property:

```
label => label.PointSize
```

The object name can actually be very short:

```
l => l.PointSize
```

The `Create` method uses reflection on this `Expression` object to obtain the text name of the CLR property, which is "PointSize".

Notice that the default value is specified as 8 rather than 8.0. In the generic version of the `BindableProperty.Create` method, this argument is the same type as the second generic argument, so the simple 8 will be converted to a `double` during compilation. Also, the `oldValue` and `newValue` arguments to the property-changed handler are of type `double` and don't have to be converted.

This generic `BindableProperty.Create` method helps bulletproof your code, but it provides no additional functionality. Internal to Xamarin.Forms, it is converted into the standard `BindableProperty.Create` method.

The read-only bindable property

Suppose you're working with an application in which it's convenient to know the number of words in the text that is displayed by a `Label` element. Perhaps you'd like to build that facility right into a class that derives from `Label`. Let's call this new class `CountedLabel`.

By now, your first thought should be to define a `BindableProperty` object named `WordCountProperty` and a corresponding CLR property named `WordCount`.

But wait: It only makes sense for this `WordCount` property to be set from within the `CountedLabel` class. That means the `WordCount` CLR property should not have a public `set` accessor. It should be defined this way:

```
public int WordCount
{
    private set { SetValue(WordCountProperty, value); }
    get { return (double)GetValue(WordCountProperty); }
}
```

The `get` accessor is still public, but the `set` accessor is private. Is that sufficient?

Not exactly. Despite the private `set` accessor in the CLR property, code external to `CountedLabel` can still call `SetValue` with the `CountedLabel.WordCountProperty` bindable property object. That type of property setting should be prohibited as well. But how can that work if the `WordCountProp-erty` object is public?

The solution is to make a *read-only* bindable property using the `BindableProperty.CreateReadOnly` method. (Like `Create`, `CreateReadOnly` also exists in a generic form.) The Xamarin.Forms API itself defines several read-only bindable properties—for example, the `Width` and `Height` properties defined by `VisualElement`.

Here's how you can make one of your own:

The first step is to call `BindableProperty.CreateReadOnly` with the same arguments as for `BindableProperty.Create`. However, the `CreateReadOnly` method returns an object of `BindablePropertyKey` rather than `BindableProperty`. Define this object as `static` and `readonly`, as with the `BindableProperty`, but make it be private to the class:

```
public class CountedLabel : Label
{
    static readonly BindablePropertyKey WordCountKey =
        BindableProperty.CreateReadOnly("WordCount",          // propertyName
                                    typeof(int),              // returnType
                                    typeof(CountedLabel),     // declaringType
                                    0);                       // defaultValue
    ...
}
```

Don't think of this `BindablePropertyKey` object as an encryption key or anything like that. It's much simpler—really just an object that is private to the class.

The second step is to make a public `BindableProperty` object by using the `BindableProperty` property of the `BindablePropertyKey`:

```
public class CountedLabel : Label
{
    ...
    public static readonly BindableProperty WordCountProperty = WordCountKey.BindableProperty;
    ...
}
```

This `BindableProperty` object is public, but it's a special kind of `BindableProperty`: It cannot be used in a `SetValue` call. Attempting to do so will raise an `InvalidOperationException`.

However, there is an overload of the `SetValue` method that accepts a `BindablePropertyKey` object. The CLR `set` accessor can call `SetValue` using this object, but this `set` accessor must be private to prevent the property from being set outside the class:

```
public class CountedLabel : Label
{
    ...
    public int WordCount
    {
        private set { SetValue(WordCountKey, value); }
        get { return (int)GetValue(WordCountProperty); }
    }
    ...
}
```

The `WordCount` property can now be set from within the `CountedLabel` class, but when? This `CountedLabel` class derives from `Label`, but it needs to detect when the `Text` property has changed so that it can count up the words.

Does `Label` have a `TextChanged` event? No it does not. However, `BindableObject` implements the `INotifyPropertyChanged` interface. This is a very important .NET interface, particularly for applications that implement the Model-View-ViewModel architecture. Later in this book you'll see how to use it in your own data classes.

The `INotifyPropertyChanged` interface is defined in the `System.ComponentModel` namespace like so:

```
public interface INotifyPropertyChanged
{
    event PropertyChangedEventHandler PropertyChanged;
}
```

Every class that derives from `BindableObject` automatically fires this `PropertyChanged` event whenever any property backed by a `BindableProperty` changes. The `PropertyChangedEventArgs` object that accompanies this event includes a property named `PropertyName` of type `string` that identifies the property that has changed.

So all that's necessary is for `CountedLabel` to attach a handler for the `PropertyChanged` event and check for a property name of "Text". From there it can use whatever technique it wants for calculating a word count. The complete `CountedLabel` class uses a lambda function on the `Property-Changed` event. The handler calls `Split` to break the string into words and see how many pieces result. The `Split` method splits the text based on spaces, dashes, and em dashes (Unicode \u2014):

```
public class CountedLabel : Label
{
    static readonly BindablePropertyKey WordCountKey =
        BindableProperty.CreateReadOnly("WordCount",         // propertyName
                                 typeof(int),                // returnType
                                 typeof(CountedLabel),       // declaringType
                                 0);                         // defaultValue
```

```
    public static readonly BindableProperty WordCountProperty = WordCountKey.BindableProperty;

    public CountedLabel()
    {
        // Set the WordCount property when the Text property changes.
        PropertyChanged += (object sender, PropertyChangedEventArgs args) =>
            {
                if (args.PropertyName == "Text")
                {
                    if (String.IsNullOrEmpty(Text))
                    {
                        WordCount = 0;
                    }
                    else
                    {
                        WordCount = Text.Split(' ', '-', '\u2014').Length;
                    }
                }
            };
    }

    public int WordCount
    {
        private set { SetValue(WordCountKey, value); }
        get { return (int)GetValue(WordCountProperty); }
    }
}
```

The class includes a `using` directive for the `System.ComponentModel` namespace for the `Property-ChangedEventArgs` argument to the handler. Watch out: Xamarin.Forms defines a class named `PropertyChangingEventArgs` (present tense). That's not what you want for the `PropertyChanged` handler. You want `PropertyChangedEventArgs` (past tense).

Because this call of the `Split` method splits the text at blank characters, dashes, and em dashes, you might assume that `CountedLabel` will be demonstrated with text that contains some dashes and em dashes. This is true. The **BaskervillesCount** program is a variation of the **Baskervilles** program from Chapter 3, but here the paragraph of text is displayed with a `CountedLabel` and a regular `Label` is included to display the word count:

```
<ContentPage xmlns="http://xamarin.com/schemas/2014/forms"
             xmlns:x="http://schemas.microsoft.com/winfx/2009/xaml"
             xmlns:toolkit=
                 "clr-namespace:Xamarin.FormsBook.Toolkit;assembly=Xamarin.FormsBook.Toolkit"
             x:Class="BaskervillesCount.BaskervillesCountPage"
             Padding="5, 0">

    <StackLayout>
        <toolkit:CountedLabel x:Name="countedLabel"
                              VerticalOptions="CenterAndExpand"
                              Text=
"Mr. Sherlock Holmes, who was usually very late in
```

```
the mornings, save upon those not infrequent
occasions when he was up all night, was seated at
the breakfast table. I stood upon the hearth-rug
and picked up the stick which our visitor had left
behind him the night before. It was a fine, thick
piece of wood, bulbous-headed, of the sort which
is known as a &#x201C;Penang lawyer.&#x201D; Just
under the head was a broad silver band, nearly an
inch across, &#x201C;To James Mortimer, M.R.C.S.,
from his friends of the C.C.H.,&#x201D; was engraved
upon it, with the date &#x201C;1884.&#x201D; It was
just such a stick as the old-fashioned family
practitioner used to carry&#x2014;dignified, solid,
and reassuring." />

        <Label x:Name="wordCountLabel"
               Text="???"
               FontSize="Large"
               VerticalOptions="CenterAndExpand"
               HorizontalOptions="Center" />

    </StackLayout>
</ContentPage>
```

That regular `Label` is set in the code-behind file:

```
public partial class BaskervillesCountPage : ContentPage
{
    public BaskervillesCountPage()
    {
        InitializeComponent();

        int wordCount = countedLabel.WordCount;
        wordCountLabel.Text = wordCount + " words";
    }
}
```

The word count that it calculates is based on the assumption that all hyphens in the text separate two words and that "hearth-rug" and "bulbous-headed" should be counted as two words each. That's not always true, of course, but word counts are not quite as algorithmically simple as this code might imply:

How would the program be structured if the text changed dynamically while the program was running? In that case, it would be necessary to update the word count whenever the WordCount property of the CountedLabel object changed. You could attach a PropertyChanged handler on the CountedLabel object and check for the property named "WordCount".

However, exercise caution if you try to set such an event handler from XAML: That handler will fire when the Text property is set by the XAML parser, but the event handler in the code-behind file won't have access to a Label object to display a word count because that wordCountLabel field will still be set to null. This is an issue that will come up again in Chapter 15 when working with interactive controls, but it will be pretty much solved when we work with data binding in Chapter 16.

There is another variation of a bindable property coming up in Chapter 14: this is the *attached bindable property*, and it is very useful in implementing certain types of layouts.

Meanwhile, let's look at one of the most important applications of bindable properties: styles.

Chapter 12
Styles

Xamarin.Forms applications often contain multiple elements with identical property settings. For example, you might have several buttons with the same colors, font sizes, and layout options. In code, you can assign identical properties to multiple buttons in a loop, but loops aren't available in XAML. If you want to avoid a lot of repetitious markup, another solution is required.

The solution is the `Style` class, which is a collection of property settings consolidated in one convenient object. You can set a `Style` object to the `Style` property of any class that derives from `VisualElement`. Generally, you'll apply the same `Style` object to multiple elements, and the style is shared among these elements.

The `Style` is the primary tool for giving visual elements a consistent appearance in your Xamarin.Forms applications. Styles help reduce repetitious markup in XAML files and allow applications to be more easily changed and maintained.

Styles were designed primarily with XAML in mind, and they probably wouldn't have been invented in a code-only environment. However, you'll see in this chapter how to define and use styles in code and how to combine code and markup to change program styling dynamically at run time.

The basic Style

In Chapter 10, "XAML markup extensions," you saw a trio of buttons that contained a lot of identical markup. Here they are again:

```
<StackLayout>
    <Button Text=" Do this! "
            HorizontalOptions="Center"
            VerticalOptions="CenterAndExpand"
            BorderWidth="3"
            TextColor="Red"
            FontSize="Large" />

    <Button Text=" Do that! "
            HorizontalOptions="Center"
            VerticalOptions="CenterAndExpand"
            BorderWidth="3"
            TextColor="Red"
            FontSize="Large" />

    <Button Text=" Do the other thing! "
            HorizontalOptions="Center"
            VerticalOptions="CenterAndExpand"
```

```
                    BorderWidth="3"
                    TextColor="Red"
                    FontSize="Large" />
</StackLayout>
```

With the exception of the `Text` property, all three buttons have the same property settings.

One partial solution to this repetitious markup involves defining property values in a resource dictionary and referencing them with the `StaticResource` markup extension. As you saw in the
ResourceSharing project in Chapter 10, this technique doesn't reduce the markup bulk, but it does
consolidate the values in one place.

To reduce the markup bulk, you'll need a `Style`. A `Style` object is almost always defined in a
`ResourceDictionary`. Generally, you'll begin with a `Resources` section at the top of the page:

```
<ContentPage xmlns="http://xamarin.com/schemas/2014/forms"
             xmlns:x="http://schemas.microsoft.com/winfx/2009/xaml"
             x:Class="BasicStyle.BasicStylePage">

    <ContentPage.Resources>
        <ResourceDictionary>
            …
        </ResourceDictionary>
    </ContentPage.Resources>
    …
</ContentPage>
```

Instantiate a `Style` with separate start and end tags:

```
<ContentPage xmlns="http://xamarin.com/schemas/2014/forms"
             xmlns:x="http://schemas.microsoft.com/winfx/2009/xaml"
             x:Class="BasicStyle.BasicStylePage">

    <ContentPage.Resources>
        <ResourceDictionary>
            <Style x:Key="buttonStyle" TargetType="Button">
                …
            </Style>
        </ResourceDictionary>
    </ContentPage.Resources>
    …
</ContentPage>
```

Because the `Style` is an object in a `ResourceDictionary`, you'll need an `x:Key` attribute to give it a
descriptive dictionary key. You must also set the `TargetType` property. This is the type of the visual
element that the style is designed for, which in this case is `Button`.

As you'll see in the next section of this chapter, you can also define a `Style` in code. In code, the
`Style` constructor requires an object of type `Type` for the `TargetType` property. The `TargetType`
property does not have a public `set` accessor; hence the `TargetType` property cannot be changed
after the `Style` is created.

`Style` also defines another important get-only property named `Setters` of type `IList<Setter>`, which is a collection of `Setter` objects. Each `Setter` is responsible for defining a property setting in the style. The `Setter` class defines just two properties:

- `Property` of type `BindableProperty`

- `Value` of type `Object`

Properties set in the `Style` must be backed by bindable properties! But when you set the `Property` property in XAML, don't use the entire fully qualified bindable property name. Just specify the text name, which is the same as the name of the related CLR property. Here's an example:

```
<Setter Property="HorizontalOptions" Value="Center" />
```

The XAML parser uses the familiar `TypeConverter` classes when parsing the `Value` settings of these `Setter` instances, so you can use the same property settings that you use normally.

`Setters` is the content property of `Style`, so you don't need the `Style.Setters` tags to add `Setter` objects to the `Style`:

```
<ContentPage xmlns="http://xamarin.com/schemas/2014/forms"
             xmlns:x="http://schemas.microsoft.com/winfx/2009/xaml"
             x:Class="BasicStyle.BasicStylePage">

    <ContentPage.Resources>
        <ResourceDictionary>
            <Style x:Key="buttonStyle" TargetType="Button">
                <Setter Property="HorizontalOptions" Value="Center" />
                <Setter Property="VerticalOptions" Value="CenterAndExpand" />
                <Setter Property="BorderWidth" Value="3" />
                <Setter Property="TextColor" Value="Red" />
                <Setter Property="FontSize" Value="Large" />
            </Style>
        </ResourceDictionary>
    </ContentPage.Resources>
    ...
</ContentPage>
```

The final step is to set this `Style` object to the `Style` property of each `Button`. Use the familiar `StaticResource` markup extension to reference the dictionary key. Here is the complete XAML file in the **BasicStyle** project:

```
<ContentPage xmlns="http://xamarin.com/schemas/2014/forms"
             xmlns:x="http://schemas.microsoft.com/winfx/2009/xaml"
             x:Class="BasicStyle.BasicStylePage">

    <ContentPage.Resources>
        <ResourceDictionary>
            <Style x:Key="buttonStyle" TargetType="Button">
                <Setter Property="HorizontalOptions" Value="Center" />
                <Setter Property="VerticalOptions" Value="CenterAndExpand" />
                <Setter Property="BorderWidth" Value="3" />
```

```
                    <Setter Property="TextColor" Value="Red" />
                    <Setter Property="FontSize" Value="Large" />
                </Style>
            </ResourceDictionary>
        </ContentPage.Resources>

        <StackLayout>
            <Button Text=" Do this! "
                    Style="{StaticResource buttonStyle}" />

            <Button Text=" Do that! "
                    Style="{StaticResource buttonStyle}" />

            <Button Text=" Do the other thing! "
                    Style="{StaticResource buttonStyle}" />
        </StackLayout>
    </ContentPage>
```

Now all these property settings are in one `Style` object that is shared among multiple `Button` elements:

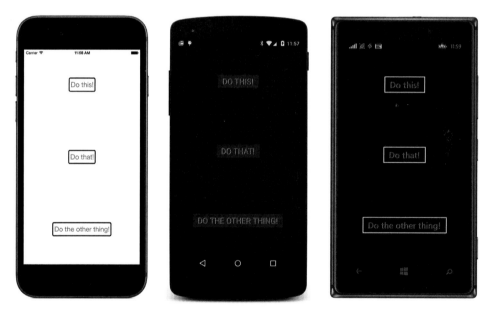

The visuals are the same as those in the **ResourceSharing** program in Chapter 10, but the markup is a lot more concise.

Suppose you'd like to define a `Setter` for the `TextColor` using the `Color.FromHsla` static method. You can define such a color by using the `x:FactoryMethod` attribute, but how can you possibly set such an unwieldy chunk of markup to the `Value` property of the `Setter` object?

You use property-element syntax, of course!

```
<ResourceDictionary>
    <Style x:Key="buttonStyle" TargetType="Button">
        ...
        <Setter Property="TextColor">
            <Setter.Value>
                <Color x:FactoryMethod="FromHsla">
                    <x:Arguments>
                        <x:Double>0.83</x:Double>
                        <x:Double>1</x:Double>
                        <x:Double>0.75</x:Double>
                        <x:Double>1</x:Double>
                    </x:Arguments>
                </Color>
            </Setter.Value>
        </Setter>
        ...
    </Style>
</ResourceDictionary>
```

Yes, you can express the `Value` property of `Setter` with property-element tags and then set the content to any object of type `Color`.

Here's another way to do it: Define the `Color` value as a separate item in the resource dictionary and then use `StaticResource` to set it to the `Value` property of the `Setter`:

```
<ResourceDictionary>
    <Color x:Key="btnTextColor"
           x:FactoryMethod="FromHsla">
        <x:Arguments>
            <x:Double>0.83</x:Double>
            <x:Double>1</x:Double>
            <x:Double>0.75</x:Double>
            <x:Double>1</x:Double>
        </x:Arguments>
    </Color>

    <Style x:Key="buttonStyle" TargetType="Button">
        ...
        <Setter Property="TextColor" Value="{StaticResource btnTextColor}" />
        ...
    </Style>
</ResourceDictionary>
```

This is a good technique if you're sharing the same `Color` value among multiple styles or multiple setters.

You can override a property setting from a `Style` by setting a property directly in the visual element. Notice that the second `Button` has its `TextColor` property set to `Maroon`:

```
<StackLayout>
    <Button Text=" Do this! "
            Style="{StaticResource buttonStyle}" />

    <Button Text=" Do that! "
            TextColor="Maroon"
            Style="{StaticResource buttonStyle}" />

    <Button Text=" Do the other thing! "
            Style="{StaticResource buttonStyle}" />
</StackLayout>
```

The center `Button` will have maroon text while the other two buttons get their `TextColor` settings from the `Style`. A property directly set on the visual element is sometimes called a *local setting* or a *manual setting*, and it always overrides the property setting from the `Style`.

The `Style` object in the **BasicStyle** program is shared among the three buttons. The sharing of styles has an important implication for the `Setter` objects. Any object set to the `Value` property of a `Setter` must be shareable. Don't try to do something like this:

```
<!-- Invalid XAML! -->
<Style x:Key="frameStyle" TargetType="Frame">
    <Setter Property="OutlineColor" Value="Accent" />
    <Setter Property="Content">
        <Setter.Value>
            <Label Text="Text in a Frame" />
        </Setter.Value>
    </Setter>
</Style>
```

This XAML doesn't work for two reasons: `Content` is not backed by a `BindableProperty` and therefore cannot be used in a `Setter`. But the obvious intent here is for every `Frame`—or at least every `Frame` on which this style is applied—to get that same `Label` object as content. A single `Label` object can't appear in multiple places on the page. A much better way to do something like this is to derive a class from `Frame` and set a `Label` as the `Content` property, or to derive a class from `ContentView` that includes a `Frame` and `Label`.

You might want to use a style to set an event handler for an event such as `Clicked`. That would be useful and convenient, but it is not supported. Event handlers must be set on the elements themselves. (However, the `Style` class does support objects called *triggers*, which can respond to events or property changes. Triggers are discussed in a future chapter.)

You cannot set the `GestureRecognizers` property in a style. That would be useful as well, but `GestureRecognizers` is not backed by a bindable property.

If a bindable property is a reference type, and if the default value is `null`, you can use a style to set the property to a non-`null` object. But you might also want to override that style setting with a local setting that sets the property back to `null`. You can set a property to `null` in XAML with the `{x:Null}` markup extension.

Styles in code

Although styles are mostly defined and used in XAML, you should know what they look like when defined and used in code. Here's the page class for the code-only **BasicStyleCode** project. The constructor of the `BasicStyleCodePage` class uses object-initialization syntax to mimic the XAML syntax in
defining the `Style` object and applying it to three buttons:

```csharp
public class BasicStyleCodePage : ContentPage
{
    public BasicStyleCodePage()
    {
        Resources = new ResourceDictionary
        {
            { "buttonStyle", new Style(typeof(Button))
                {
                    Setters =
                    {
                        new Setter
                        {
                            Property = View.HorizontalOptionsProperty,
                            Value = LayoutOptions.Center
                        },
                        new Setter
                        {
                            Property = View.VerticalOptionsProperty,
                            Value = LayoutOptions.CenterAndExpand
                        },
                        new Setter
                        {
                            Property = Button.BorderWidthProperty,
                            Value = 3
                        },
                        new Setter
                        {
                            Property = Button.TextColorProperty,
                            Value = Color.Red
                        },
                        new Setter
                        {
                            Property = Button.FontSizeProperty,
                            Value = Device.GetNamedSize(NamedSize.Large, typeof(Button))
                        }
                    }
                }
            }
        };

        Content = new StackLayout
        {
            Children =
            {
                new Button
```

```
            {
                Text = " Do this! ",
                Style = (Style)Resources["buttonStyle"]
            },
            new Button
            {
                Text = " Do that! ",
                Style = (Style)Resources["buttonStyle"]
            },
            new Button
            {
                Text = " Do the other thing! ",
                Style = (Style)Resources["buttonStyle"]
            }
        }
    };
    }
}
```

It's much more obvious in code than in XAML that the `Property` property of the `Setter` is of type `BindableProperty`.

The first two `Setter` objects in this example are initialized with the `BindableProperties` objects named `View.HorizontalOptionsProperty` and `View.VerticalOptionsProperty`. You could use `Button.HorizontalOptionsProperty` and `Button.VerticalOptionsProperty` instead because `Button` inherits these properties from `View`. Or you can change the class name to any other class that derives from `View`.

As usual, the use of a `ResourceDictionary` in code seems pointless. You could eliminate the dictionary and just assign the `Style` objects directly to the `Style` properties of the buttons. However, even in code, the `Style` is a convenient way to bundle all the property settings together into one compact package.

Style inheritance

The `TargetType` of the `Style` serves two different functions: One of these functions is described in the next section on implicit styles. The other function is for the benefit of the XAML parser. The XAML parser must be able to resolve the property names in the `Setter` objects and for that it needs a class name provided by the `TargetType`.

All the properties in the style must be defined by or inherited by the class specified in the `Target-Type` property. The type of the visual element on which the `Style` is set must be the same as the `TargetType` or a derived class of the `TargetType`.

If you need a `Style` only for properties defined by `View`, you can set the `TargetType` to `View` and still use the style on buttons or any other `View` derivative, as in this modified version of the **BasicStyle** program:

```
<ContentPage xmlns="http://xamarin.com/schemas/2014/forms"
             xmlns:x="http://schemas.microsoft.com/winfx/2009/xaml"
             x:Class="BasicStyle.BasicStylePage">

    <ContentPage.Resources>
        <ResourceDictionary>
            <Style x:Key="viewStyle" TargetType="View">
                <Setter Property="HorizontalOptions" Value="Center" />
                <Setter Property="VerticalOptions" Value="CenterAndExpand" />
                <Setter Property="BackgroundColor" Value="Pink" />
         </Style>
        </ResourceDictionary>
    </ContentPage.Resources>

    <StackLayout>
        <Button Text=" Do this! "
                Style="{StaticResource viewStyle}" />

        <Label Text ="A bit of text"
                Style="{StaticResource viewStyle}" />

        <Button Text=" Do that! "
                Style="{StaticResource viewStyle}" />

        <Label Text ="Another bit of text"
                Style="{StaticResource viewStyle}" />

        <Button Text=" Do the other thing! "
                Style="{StaticResource viewStyle}" />
    </StackLayout>
</ContentPage>
```

As you can see, the same style is applied to all the `Button` and `Label` children of the `StackLayout`:

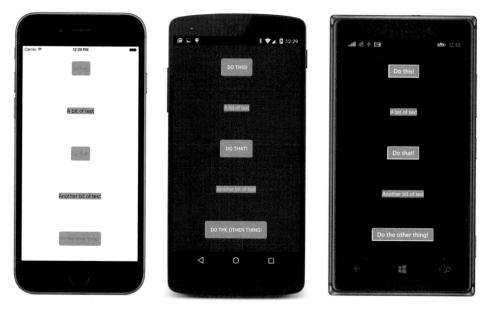

But suppose you now want to expand on this style, but differently for `Button` and `Label`. Is that possible?

Yes, it is. Styles can derive from other styles. The `Style` class includes a property named `BasedOn` of type `Style`. In code, you can set this `BasedOn` property directly to another `Style` object. In XAML you set the `BasedOn` attribute to a `StaticResource` markup extension that references a previously created `Style`. The new `Style` can include `Setter` objects for new properties or use them to override properties in the earlier `Style`. The `BasedOn` style must target the same class or an ancestor class of the new style's `TargetType`.

Here's the XAML file for a project named **StyleInheritance**. The application has a reference to the **Xamarin.FormsBook.Toolkit** assembly for two purposes: it uses the `HslColor` markup extension to demonstrate that markup extensions are legitimate value settings in `Setter` objects and to demonstrate that a style can be defined for a custom class, in this case `AltLabel`.

The `ResourceDictionary` contains four styles: The first has a dictionary key of "visualStyle". The `Style` with the dictionary key of "baseStyle" derives from "visualStyle". The styles with keys of "labelStyle" and "buttonStyle" derive from "baseStyle". The `Style` for the `Button` demonstrates how to set a `Value` property of a `Setter` to an `OnPlatform` object:

```
<ContentPage xmlns="http://xamarin.com/schemas/2014/forms"
             xmlns:x="http://schemas.microsoft.com/winfx/2009/xaml"
             xmlns:toolkit=
                 "clr-namespace:Xamarin.FormsBook.Toolkit;assembly=Xamarin.FormsBook.Toolkit"
             x:Class="StyleInheritance.StyleInheritancePage">

    <ContentPage.Resources>
        <ResourceDictionary>
```

```xml
            <Style x:Key="visualStyle" TargetType="VisualElement">
                <Setter Property="BackgroundColor"
                        Value="{toolkit:HslColor H=0, S=1, L=0.8}" />
            </Style>

            <Style x:Key="baseStyle" TargetType="View"
                    BasedOn="{StaticResource visualStyle}">
                <Setter Property="HorizontalOptions" Value="Center" />
                <Setter Property="VerticalOptions" Value="CenterAndExpand" />
            </Style>

            <Style x:Key="labelStyle" TargetType="toolkit:AltLabel"
                    BasedOn="{StaticResource baseStyle}">
                <Setter Property="TextColor" Value="Black" />
                <Setter Property="PointSize" Value="12" />
            </Style>

            <Style x:Key="buttonStyle" TargetType="Button"
                    BasedOn="{StaticResource baseStyle}">
                <Setter Property="TextColor" Value="Blue" />
                <Setter Property="FontSize" Value="Large" />
                <Setter Property="BorderColor" Value="Blue" />
                <Setter Property="BorderWidth">
                    <Setter.Value>
                        <OnPlatform x:TypeArguments="x:Double"
                                    iOS="1"
                                    Android="2"
                                    WinPhone="3" />
                    </Setter.Value>
                </Setter>
            </Style>
        </ResourceDictionary>
    </ContentPage.Resources>

    <ContentPage.Style>
        <StaticResourceExtension Key="visualStyle" />
    </ContentPage.Style>

    <StackLayout>
        <Button Text=" Do this! "
                Style="{StaticResource buttonStyle}" />

        <toolkit:AltLabel Text ="A bit of text"
                        Style="{StaticResource labelStyle}" />

        <Button Text=" Do that! "
                Style="{StaticResource buttonStyle}" />

        <toolkit:AltLabel Text ="Another bit of text"
                        Style="{StaticResource labelStyle}" />

        <Button Text=" Do the other thing! "
                Style="{StaticResource buttonStyle}" />
    </StackLayout>
```

```
</ContentPage>
```

Immediately after the `Resources` section is some markup that sets the `Style` property of the page itself to the "visualStyle" `Style`:

```
<ContentPage.Style>
    <StaticResourceExtension Key="visualStyle" />
</ContentPage.Style>
```

Because `Page` derives from `VisualElement` but not `View`, this is the only style in the resource dictionary that can be applied to the page. However, the style can't be applied to the page until after the `Resources` section, so using the element form of `StaticResource` is a good solution here. The entire background of the page is colored based on this style, and the style is also inherited by all the other styles:

If the `Style` for the `AltLabel` only included `Setter` objects for properties defined by `Label`, the `TargetType` could be `Label` instead of `AltLabel`. But the `Style` has a `Setter` for the `PointSize` property. That property is defined by `AltLabel` so the `TargetType` must be `tookit:AltLabel`.

A `Setter` can be defined for the `PointSize` property because `PointSize` is backed by a bindable property. If you change the accessibility of the `BindableProperty` object in `AltLabel` from `public` to `private`, the property will still work for many routine uses of `AltLabel`, but now `PointSize` cannot be set in a style `Setter`. The XAML parser will complain that it cannot find `PointSizeProperty`, which is the bindable property that backs the `PointSize` property.

You discovered in Chapter 10 how `StaticResource` works: When the XAML parser encounters a `StaticResource` markup extension, it searches up the visual tree for a matching dictionary key. This process has implications for styles. You can define a style in one `Resources` section and then override it with another style with the same dictionary key in a different `Resources` section lower in the visual tree. When you set the `BasedOn` property to a `StaticResource` markup extension, the style you're deriving from must be defined in the same `Resources` section (as demonstrated in the **StyleInheritance** program) or a `Resources` section higher in the visual tree.

This means that you can structure your styles in XAML in two hierarchical ways: you can use `BasedOn` to derive styles from other styles, and you can define styles at different levels in the visual tree that derive from styles higher in the visual tree or replace them entirely.

For larger applications with multiple pages and lots of markup, the recommendation for defining styles is very simple: define your styles as close as possible to the elements that use those styles.

Adhering to this recommendation aids in maintaining the program and becomes particularly important when working with *implicit styles*.

Implicit styles

Every entry in a `ResourceDictionary` requires a dictionary key. This is an indisputable fact. If you try to pass a `null` key to the `Add` method of a `ResourceDictionary` object, you'll raise an `Argument-NullException`.

However, there is one special case where a programmer is not required to supply this dictionary key and a dictionary key is instead generated automatically.

This special case is for a `Style` object added to a `ResourceDictionary` without an `x:Key` setting. The `ResourceDictionary` generates a key based on the `TargetType`, which is always required. (A little exploration will reveal that this special dictionary key is the fully qualified name associated with the `TargetType` of the `Style`. For a `TargetType` of `Button`, for example, the dictionary key is "Xamarin.Forms.Button". But you don't need to know that.)

You can also add a `Style` to a `ResourceDictionary` without a dictionary key in code: an overload of the `Add` method accepts an argument of type `Style` but doesn't require anything else.

A `Style` object in a `ResourceDictionary` that has one of these generated keys is known as an *implicit style*, and the generated dictionary key is very special. You can't refer to this key directly using `StaticResource`. However, if an element within the scope of the `ResourceDictionary` has the same type as the dictionary key, and if that element does not have its `Style` property explicitly set to another `Style` object, then this implicit style is automatically applied.

The following XAML from the **ImplicitStyle** project demonstrates this. It is the same as the **BasicStyle** XAML file except that the `Style` has no `x:Key` setting and the `Style` properties on the buttons aren't set using `StaticResource`:

```
<ContentPage xmlns="http://xamarin.com/schemas/2014/forms"
             xmlns:x="http://schemas.microsoft.com/winfx/2009/xaml"
```

```
            x:Class="ImplicitStyle.ImplicitStylePage">

    <ContentPage.Resources>
        <ResourceDictionary>
            <Style TargetType="Button">
                <Setter Property="HorizontalOptions" Value="Center" />
                <Setter Property="VerticalOptions" Value="CenterAndExpand" />
                <Setter Property="BorderWidth" Value="3" />
                <Setter Property="TextColor" Value="Red" />
                <Setter Property="FontSize" Value="Large" />
            </Style>
        </ResourceDictionary>
    </ContentPage.Resources>

    <StackLayout>
        <Button Text=" Do this! " />

        <Button Text=" Do that! " />

        <Button Text=" Do the other thing! " />
    </StackLayout>
</ContentPage>
```

Despite the absence of any explicit connection between the buttons and the style, the style is definitely applied:

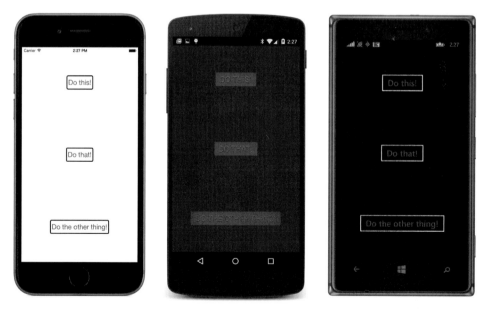

An implicit style is applied only when the class of the element matches the `TargetType` of the `Style` exactly. If you include an element that derives from `Button` in the `StackLayout`, it would not have the `Style` applied.

You can use local property settings to override properties set through the implicit style, just as you can override property settings in a style set with `StaticResource`.

You will find implicit styles to be very powerful and extremely useful. Whenever you have several views of the same type and you determine you want them all to have an identical property setting or two, it's very easy to quickly define an implicit style. You don't have to touch the elements themselves.

However, with great power comes at least *some* programmer responsibility. Because no style is referenced in the elements themselves, it can be confusing when simply examining the XAML to determine whether some elements are styled or not. Sometimes the appearance of a page indicates that an implicit style is applied to some elements, but it's not quite obvious where the implicit style is defined. If you then want to change that implicit style, you have to manually search for it up the visual tree.

For this reason, you should define implicit styles *as close as possible* to the elements they are applied to. If the views getting the implicit style are in a particular `StackLayout`, then define the implicit style in the `Resources` section on that `StackLayout`. A comment or two might help avoid confusion as well.

Interestingly, implicit styles have a built-in restriction that might persuade you to keep them close to the elements they are applied to. Here's the restriction: You can derive an implicit style from a `Style` with an explicit dictionary key, but you can't go the other way around. You can't use `BasedOn` to reference an implicit style.

If you define a chain of styles that use `BasedOn` to derive from one another, the implicit style (if any) is always at the end of the chain. No further derivations are possible.

This implies that you can structure your styles with three types of hierarchies:

- From styles defined on the `Application` and `Page` down to styles defined on layouts lower in the visual tree.

- From styles defined for base classes such as `VisualElement` and `View` to styles defined for specific classes.

- From styles with explicit dictionary keys to implicit styles.

This is demonstrated in the **StyleHierarchy** project, which uses a similar (but somewhat simplified) set of styles as you saw earlier in the **StyleInheritance** project. However, these styles are now spread out over three `Resources` sections.

Using a technique you saw in the **ResourceTrees** program in Chapter 10, the **StyleHierarchy** project was given a XAML-based `App` class. The App.xaml class has a `ResourceDictionary` containing a style with just one property setter:

```
<Application xmlns="http://xamarin.com/schemas/2014/forms"
             xmlns:x="http://schemas.microsoft.com/winfx/2009/xaml"
             x:Class="StyleHierarchy.App">
```

```
    <Application.Resources>
        <ResourceDictionary>
            <Style x:Key="visualStyle" TargetType="VisualElement">
                <Setter Property="BackgroundColor" Value="Pink" />
            </Style>
        </ResourceDictionary>
    </Application.Resources>
</Application>
```

In a multipage application, this style would be used throughout the application.

The code-behind file for the App class calls InitializeComponent to process the XAML file and sets the MainPage property:

```
public partial class App : Application
{
    public App()
    {
        InitializeComponent();
        MainPage = new StyleHierarchyPage();
    }
    …
}
```

The XAML file for the page class defines one Style for the whole page that derives from the style in the App class and then two implicit styles that derive from the Style for the page. Notice that the Style property of the page is set to the Style defined in the App class:

```
<ContentPage xmlns="http://xamarin.com/schemas/2014/forms"
             xmlns:x="http://schemas.microsoft.com/winfx/2009/xaml"
             x:Class="StyleHierarchy.StyleHierarchyPage"
             Style="{StaticResource visualStyle}">

    <ContentPage.Resources>
        <ResourceDictionary>
            <Style x:Key="baseStyle" TargetType="View"
                   BasedOn="{StaticResource visualStyle}">
                <Setter Property="HorizontalOptions" Value="Center" />
                <Setter Property="VerticalOptions" Value="CenterAndExpand" />
            </Style>
        </ResourceDictionary>
    </ContentPage.Resources>

    <StackLayout>
        <StackLayout.Resources>
            <ResourceDictionary>
                <Style TargetType="Label"
                       BasedOn="{StaticResource baseStyle}">
                    <Setter Property="TextColor" Value="Black" />
                    <Setter Property="FontSize" Value="Large" />
                </Style>

                <Style TargetType="Button"
                       BasedOn="{StaticResource baseStyle}">
```

```
                    <Setter Property="TextColor" Value="Blue" />
                    <Setter Property="FontSize" Value="Large" />
                    <Setter Property="BorderColor" Value="Blue" />
                    <Setter Property="BorderWidth" Value="2" />
                </Style>
            </ResourceDictionary>
        </StackLayout.Resources>

        <Button Text=" Do this! " />

        <Label Text ="A bit of text" />

        <Button Text=" Do that! " />

        <Label Text ="Another bit of text" />

        <Button Text=" Do the other thing! " />
    </StackLayout>
</ContentPage>
```

The implicit styles are defined as close to the target elements as possible.

Here's the result:

The incentive to separate `Style` objects into separate dictionaries doesn't make a lot of sense for very tiny programs like this one, but for larger programs, it becomes just as important to have a structured hierarchy of style definitions as it is to have a structured hierarchy of class definitions.

Sometimes you'll have a `Style` with an explicit dictionary key (for example "myButtonStyle"), but you'll want that same style to be implicit as well. Simply define a style based on that key with no key or setters of its own:

```
<Style TargetType="Button"
       BasedOn="{StaticResource myButtonStyle}" />
```

Dynamic styles

A `Style` is generally a static object that is created and initialized in XAML or code and then remains unchanged for the duration of the application. The `Style` class does not derive from `BindableObject` and does not internally respond to changes in its properties. For example, if you assign a `Style` object to an element and then modify one of the `Setter` objects by giving it a new value, the new value won't show up in the element. Similarly, the target element won't change if you add a `Setter` or remove a `Setter` from the `Setters` collection. For these new property setters to take effect, you need to use code to detach the style from the element by setting the `Style` property to `null` and then re-attach the style to the element.

However, your application can respond to style changes dynamically at run time through the use of `DynamicResource`. You'll recall that `DynamicResource` is similar to `StaticResource` in that it uses a dictionary key to fetch an object or a value from a resource dictionary. The difference is that `StaticResource` is a one-time dictionary lookup while `DynamicResource` maintains a link to the actual dictionary key. If the dictionary entry associated with that key is replaced with a new object, that change is propagated to the element.

This facility allows an application to implement a feature sometimes called *dynamic styles*. For example, you might include a facility in your program for stylistic themes (involving fonts and colors, perhaps), and you might make these themes selectable by the user. The application can switch between these themes because they are implemented with styles.

There's nothing in a style itself that indicates a dynamic style. A style becomes dynamic solely by being referenced using `DynamicResource` rather than `StaticResource`.

The **DynamicStyles** project demonstrates the mechanics of this process. Here is the XAML file for the `DynamicStylesPage` class:

```
<ContentPage xmlns="http://xamarin.com/schemas/2014/forms"
             xmlns:x="http://schemas.microsoft.com/winfx/2009/xaml"
             x:Class="DynamicStyles.DynamicStylesPage">

    <ContentPage.Padding>
        <OnPlatform x:TypeArguments="Thickness"
                    iOS="0, 20, 0, 0"
                    Android="0"
                    WinPhone="0" />
    </ContentPage.Padding>

    <ContentPage.Resources>
        <ResourceDictionary>
```

```
                    <Style x:Key="baseButtonStyle" TargetType="Button">
                        <Setter Property="FontSize" Value="Large" />
                    </Style>

                    <Style x:Key="buttonStyle1" TargetType="Button"
                            BasedOn="{StaticResource baseButtonStyle}">
                        <Setter Property="HorizontalOptions" Value="Center" />
                        <Setter Property="VerticalOptions" Value="CenterAndExpand" />
                        <Setter Property="TextColor" Value="Red" />
                    </Style>

                    <Style x:Key="buttonStyle2" TargetType="Button"
                            BasedOn="{StaticResource baseButtonStyle}">
                        <Setter Property="HorizontalOptions" Value="Start" />
                        <Setter Property="VerticalOptions" Value="EndAndExpand" />
                        <Setter Property="TextColor" Value="Green" />
                        <Setter Property="FontAttributes" Value="Italic" />
                    </Style>

                    <Style x:Key="buttonStyle3" TargetType="Button"
                            BasedOn="{StaticResource baseButtonStyle}">
                        <Setter Property="HorizontalOptions" Value="End" />
                        <Setter Property="VerticalOptions" Value="StartAndExpand" />
                        <Setter Property="TextColor" Value="Blue" />
                        <Setter Property="FontAttributes" Value="Bold" />
                    </Style>
                </ResourceDictionary>
        </ContentPage.Resources>

        <StackLayout>
            <Button Text=" Switch to Style #1 "
                    Style="{DynamicResource buttonStyle}"
                    Clicked="OnButton1Clicked" />

            <Button Text=" Switch to Style #2 "
                    Style="{DynamicResource buttonStyle}"
                    Clicked="OnButton2Clicked" />

            <Button Text=" Switch to Style #3 "
                    Style="{DynamicResource buttonStyle}"
                    Clicked="OnButton3Clicked" />

            <Button Text=" Reset "
                    Style="{DynamicResource buttonStyle}"
                    Clicked="OnResetButtonClicked" />
        </StackLayout>
</ContentPage>
```

The `Resources` section defines four styles: a simple style with the key "baseButtonStyle", and then three styles that derive from that style with the keys "buttonStyle1", "buttonStyle2", and "buttonStyle3".

However, the four `Button` elements toward the bottom of the XAML file all use `DynamicResource` to reference a style with the simpler key "buttonStyle". Where is the `Style` with that key? It does not exist. However, because the four button `Style` properties are set with `DynamicResource`, the missing dictionary key is not a problem. No exception is raised. But no `Style` is applied, which means that the buttons have a default appearance:

Each of the four `Button` elements has a `Clicked` handler attached, and in the code-behind file, the first three handlers set a dictionary entry with the key "buttonStyle" to one of the three numbered styles already defined in the dictionary:

```
public partial class DynamicStylesPage : ContentPage
{
    public DynamicStylesPage()
    {
        InitializeComponent();
    }

    void OnButton1Clicked(object sender, EventArgs args)
    {
        Resources["buttonStyle"] = Resources["buttonStyle1"];
    }

    void OnButton2Clicked(object sender, EventArgs args)
    {
        Resources["buttonStyle"] = Resources["buttonStyle2"];
    }

    void OnButton3Clicked(object sender, EventArgs args)
    {
        Resources["buttonStyle"] = Resources["buttonStyle3"];
    }
```

```
    void OnResetButtonClicked(object sender, EventArgs args)
    {
        Resources["buttonStyle"] = null;
    }
}
```

When you press one of the first three buttons, all four buttons get the selected style. Here's the program running on all three platforms showing the results (from left to right) when buttons 1, 2, and 3 are pressed:

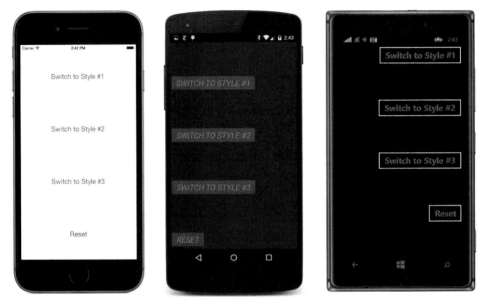

Pressing the fourth button returns everything to the initial conditions by setting the value associated with the "buttonStyle" key to null. (You might also consider calling Remove or Clear on the ResourceDictionary object to remove the key entirely, but that doesn't work in the version of Xamarin.Forms used for this chapter.)

Suppose you want to derive another Style from the Style with the key "buttonStyle". How do you do this in XAML, considering that the "buttonStyle" dictionary entry doesn't exist until one of the first three buttons is pressed?

You can't do it like this:

```
<!-- This won't work! -->
<Style x:Key="newButtonStyle" TargetType="Button"
       BasedOn="{StaticResource buttonStyle}">
    …
</Style>
```

StaticResource will raise an exception if the "buttonStyle" key does not exist, and even if the key does exist, the use of StaticResource won't allow changes in the dictionary entry to be reflected in this new style.

However, changing `StaticResource` to `DynamicResource` won't work either:

```
<!-- This won't work either! -->
<Style x:Key="newButtonStyle" TargetType="Button"
       BasedOn="{DynamicResource buttonStyle}">
   …
</Style>
```

`DynamicResource` works only with properties backed by bindable properties, and that is not the case here. `Style` doesn't derive from `BindableObject`, so it can't support bindable properties.

Instead, `Style` defines a property specifically for the purpose of inheriting dynamic styles. The property is `BaseResourceKey`, which is intended to be set directly to a dictionary key that might not yet exist or whose value might change dynamically, which is the case with the "buttonStyle" key:

```
<!-- This works!! -->
<Style x:Key="newButtonStyle" TargetType="Button"
       BaseResourceKey="buttonStyle">
   …
</Style>
```

The use of `BaseResourceKey` is demonstrated by the **DynamicStylesInheritance** project, which is very similar to the **DynamicStyles** project. Indeed, the code-behind processing is identical. Toward the bottom of the `Resources` section, a new `Style` is defined with a key of "newButtonStyle" that uses `BaseResourceKey` to reference the "buttonStyle" entry and add a couple of properties, including one that uses `OnPlatform`:

```
<ContentPage xmlns="http://xamarin.com/schemas/2014/forms"
             xmlns:x="http://schemas.microsoft.com/winfx/2009/xaml"
             x:Class="DynamicStylesInheritance.DynamicStylesInheritancePage">
    <ContentPage.Padding>
        <OnPlatform x:TypeArguments="Thickness"
                    iOS="0, 20, 0, 0"
                    Android="0"
                    WinPhone="0" />
    </ContentPage.Padding>

    <ContentPage.Resources>
        <ResourceDictionary>
            <Style x:Key="baseButtonStyle" TargetType="Button">
                <Setter Property="FontSize" Value="Large" />
            </Style>

            <Style x:Key="buttonStyle1" TargetType="Button"
                   BasedOn="{StaticResource baseButtonStyle}">
                <Setter Property="HorizontalOptions" Value="Center" />
                <Setter Property="VerticalOptions" Value="CenterAndExpand" />
                <Setter Property="TextColor" Value="Red" />
            </Style>
```

```xml
        <Style x:Key="buttonStyle2" TargetType="Button"
               BasedOn="{StaticResource baseButtonStyle}">
            <Setter Property="HorizontalOptions" Value="Start" />
            <Setter Property="VerticalOptions" Value="EndAndExpand" />
            <Setter Property="TextColor" Value="Green" />
            <Setter Property="FontAttributes" Value="Italic" />
        </Style>

        <Style x:Key="buttonStyle3" TargetType="Button"
               BasedOn="{StaticResource baseButtonStyle}">
            <Setter Property="HorizontalOptions" Value="End" />
            <Setter Property="VerticalOptions" Value="StartAndExpand" />
            <Setter Property="TextColor" Value="Blue" />
            <Setter Property="FontAttributes" Value="Bold" />
        </Style>

        <!-- New style definition. -->
        <Style x:Key="newButtonStyle" TargetType="Button"
               BaseResourceKey="buttonStyle">
            <Setter Property="BackgroundColor">
                <Setter.Value>
                    <OnPlatform x:TypeArguments="Color"
                                iOS="#C0C0C0"
                                Android="#404040"
                                WinPhone="Gray" />
                </Setter.Value>
            </Setter>
            <Setter Property="BorderColor" Value="Red" />
            <Setter Property="BorderWidth" Value="3" />
        </Style>
    </ResourceDictionary>
  </ContentPage.Resources>

  <StackLayout>
      <Button Text=" Switch to Style #1 "
              Style="{StaticResource newButtonStyle}"
              Clicked="OnButton1Clicked" />

      <Button Text=" Switch to Style #2 "
              Style="{StaticResource newButtonStyle}"
              Clicked="OnButton2Clicked" />

      <Button Text=" Switch to Style #3 "
              Style="{StaticResource newButtonStyle}"
              Clicked="OnButton3Clicked" />

      <Button Text=" Reset "
              Style="{DynamicResource buttonStyle}"
              Clicked="OnResetButtonClicked" />
  </StackLayout>
</ContentPage>
```

Notice that the first three `Button` elements reference the "newButtonStyle" dictionary entry with `StaticResource`. `DynamicResource` is not needed here because the `Style` object associated with the "newButtonStyle" will not itself change except for the `Style` that it derives from. The `Style` with the key "newButtonStyle" maintains a link with "buttonStyle" and internally alters itself when that underlying style changes. When the program begins to run, only the properties defined in the "newButtonStyle" are applied to those three buttons:

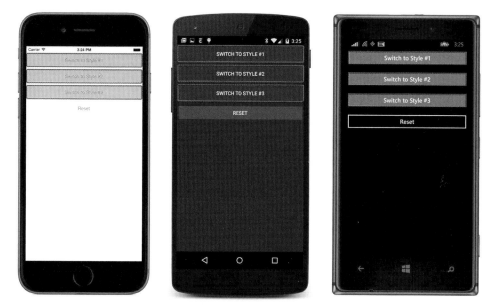

The **Reset** button continues to reference the "buttonStyle" entry.

As in the **DynamicStyles** program, the code-behind file sets that dictionary entry when you click one of the first three buttons, so all the buttons pick up the "buttonStyle" properties as well. Here are the results for (from left to right) clicks of buttons 3, 2, and 1:

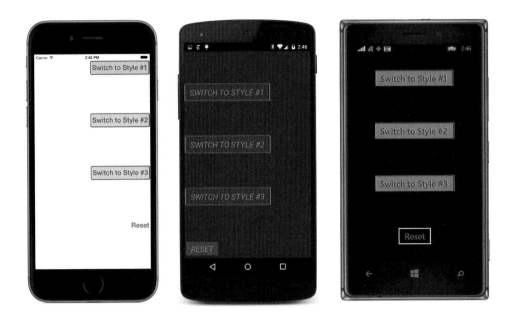

Device styles

Xamarin.Forms includes six built-in dynamic styles. These are known as *device styles*, and they are members of a nested class of `Device` named `Styles`. This `Styles` class defines 12 `static` and `readonly` fields that help reference these six styles in code:

- `BodyStyle` of type `Style`.

- `BodyStyleKey` of type `string` and equal to "BodyStyle."

- `TitleStyle` of type `Style`.

- `TitleStyleKey` of type `string` and equal to "TitleStyle."

- `SubtitleStyle` of type `Style`.

- `SubtitleStyleKey` of type `string` and equal to "SubtitleStyle."

- `CaptionStyle` of type `Style`.

- `CaptionStyleKey` of type `string` and equal to "CaptionStyle."

- `ListItemTextStyle` of type `Style`.

- `ListItemTextStyleKey` of type `string` and equal to "ListItemTextStyle."

- `ListItemDetailTextStyle` of type `Style`.

- `ListItemDetailTextStyleKey` of type `string` and equal to "ListItemDetailTextStyle."

All six styles have a `TargetType` of `Label` and are stored in a dictionary—but not a dictionary that application programs can access directly.

In code, you use the fields in this list for accessing the device styles. For example, you can set the `Device.Styles.BodyStyle` object directly to the `Style` property of a `Label` for text that might be appropriate for the body of a paragraph. If you're defining a style in code that derives from one of these device styles, set the `BaseResourceKey` to `Device.Styles.BodyStyleKey` or simply "BodyStyle" if you're not afraid of misspelling it.

In XAML, you'll simply use the text key "BodyStyle" with `DynamicResource` for setting this style to the `Style` property of a `Label` or to set `BaseResourceKey` when deriving a style from `Device.Styles.BodyStyle`.

The **DeviceStylesList** program demonstrates how to access these styles—and to define a new style that inherits from `SubtitleStyle`—both in XAML and in code. Here's the XAML file:

```
<ContentPage xmlns="http://xamarin.com/schemas/2014/forms"
             xmlns:x="http://schemas.microsoft.com/winfx/2009/xaml"
             x:Class="DeviceStylesList.DeviceStylesListPage">
    <ContentPage.Padding>
        <OnPlatform x:TypeArguments="Thickness"
                    iOS="10, 20, 10, 0"
                    Android="10, 0"
                    WinPhone="10, 0" />
    </ContentPage.Padding>

    <ContentPage.Resources>
        <ResourceDictionary>
            <Style x:Key="newSubtitleStyle" TargetType="Label"
                   BaseResourceKey="SubtitleStyle">
                <Setter Property="TextColor" Value="Accent" />
                <Setter Property="FontAttributes" Value="Italic" />
            </Style>
        </ResourceDictionary>
    </ContentPage.Resources>

    <ScrollView>
        <StackLayout Spacing="20">

            <!-- Device styles set with DynamicResource -->
            <StackLayout>
                <StackLayout HorizontalOptions="Start">
                    <Label Text="Device styles set with DynamicResource" />
                    <BoxView Color="Accent" HeightRequest="3" />
                </StackLayout>

                <Label Text="No Style whatsoever" />

                <Label Text="Body Style"
                       Style="{DynamicResource BodyStyle}" />
```

```
            <Label Text="Title Style"
                   Style="{DynamicResource TitleStyle}" />

            <Label Text="Subtitle Style"
                   Style="{DynamicResource SubtitleStyle}" />

            <!-- Uses style derived from device style. -->
            <Label Text="New Subtitle Style"
                   Style="{StaticResource newSubtitleStyle}" />

            <Label Text="Caption Style"
                   Style="{DynamicResource CaptionStyle}" />

            <Label Text="List Item Text Style"
                   Style="{DynamicResource ListItemTextStyle}" />

            <Label Text="List Item Detail Text Style"
                   Style="{DynamicResource ListItemDetailTextStyle}" />
        </StackLayout>

        <!-- Device styles set in code -->
        <StackLayout x:Name="codeLabelStack">
            <StackLayout HorizontalOptions="Start">
                <Label Text="Device styles set in code:" />
                <BoxView Color="Accent" HeightRequest="3" />
            </StackLayout>
        </StackLayout>
    </StackLayout>
  </ScrollView>
</ContentPage>
```

The `StackLayout` contains two `Label` and `BoxView` combinations (one at the top and one at the bottom) to display underlined headers. Following the first of these headers, `Label` elements reference the device styles with `DynamicResource`. The new subtitle style is defined in the `Resources` dictionary for the page.

The code-behind file accesses the device styles using the properties in the `Device.Styles` class and creates a new style by deriving from `SubtitleStyle`:

```
public partial class DeviceStylesListPage : ContentPage
{
    public DeviceStylesListPage()
    {
        InitializeComponent();

        var styleItems = new[]
        {
            new { style = (Style)null, name = "No style whatsoever" },
            new { style = Device.Styles.BodyStyle, name = "Body Style" },
            new { style = Device.Styles.TitleStyle, name = "Title Style" },
            new { style = Device.Styles.SubtitleStyle, name = "Subtitle Style" },
```

```
// Derived style
new { style = new Style(typeof(Label))
{
    BaseResourceKey = Device.Styles.SubtitleStyleKey,
    Setters =
    {
        new Setter
        {
            Property = Label.TextColorProperty,
            Value = Color.Accent
        },
        new Setter
        {
            Property = Label.FontAttributesProperty,
            Value = FontAttributes.Italic
        }
    }
}, name = "New Subtitle Style" },

new { style = Device.Styles.CaptionStyle, name = "Caption Style" },
new { style = Device.Styles.ListItemTextStyle, name = "List Item Text Style" },
new { style = Device.Styles.ListItemDetailTextStyle,
    name = "List Item Detail Text Style" },
};

foreach (var styleItem in styleItems)
{
    codeLabelStack.Children.Add(new Label
        {
            Text = styleItem.name,
            Style = styleItem.style
        });
}
}
}
}
```

The code and XAML result in identical styles, of course, but each platform implements these device styles in a different way:

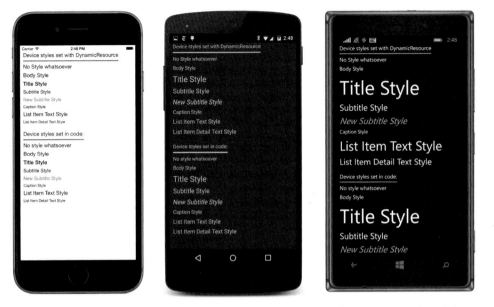

On iOS, the underlying code implements these styles mostly with static properties of the `UIFont` class. On Android, the implementation mostly involves `TextAppearance` properties of the `Resource.Attribute` class. On Windows Phone, they are application resources with keys beginning with "PhoneText."

The dynamic nature of these styles is most easily demonstrated on iOS: While the **DeviceStyles** program is running, tap the **Home** button and run **Settings**. Pick the **General** item, then **Accessibility**, and **Larger Text**. A slider is available to make text smaller or larger. Change that slider, double tap the **Home** button to show the current applications, and select **DeviceStyles** again. You'll see the text set from device styles (or the styles that derive from device styles) change size, but none of the unstyled text in the application changes size. New objects have replaced the device styles in the dictionary.

The dynamic nature of device styles is not quite as obvious on Android because changes to the **Font size** item of the **Display** section in **Settings** affect all font sizes in a Xamarin.Forms program. On Windows Phone, the **Text size** item in the **ease of access** section of **Settings** only plays a role in applications that use the Windows Runtime API. Xamarin.Forms currently uses the Silverlight API.

The next chapter includes a program that demonstrates how to make a little e-book reader that lets you read a chapter of *Alice in Wonderland*. This program uses device styles for controlling the formatting of all the text, including the book and chapter titles.

But what this little e-book reader also includes are illustrations, and that requires an exploration into the subject of bitmaps.

Chapter 13
Bitmaps

The visual elements of a graphical user interface can be roughly divided between elements used for presentation (such as text) and those capable of interaction with the user, such as buttons, sliders, and list boxes.

Text is essential for presentation, but pictures are often just as important as a way to supplement text and convey crucial information. The web, for example, would be inconceivable without pictures. These pictures are often in the form of rectangular arrays of picture elements (or pixels) known as *bitmaps*.

Just as a view named `Label` displays text, a view named `Image` displays bitmaps. The bitmap formats supported by iOS, Android, and Windows Phone are a little different, but if you stick to JPEG, PNG, GIF, and BMP in your Xamarin.Forms applications, you'll probably not experience any problems.

`Image` defines a `Source` property that you set to an object of type `ImageSource`, which references the bitmap displayed by `Image`. Bitmaps can come from a variety of sources, so the `ImageSource` class defines four static creation methods that return an `ImageSource` object:

- `ImageSource.FromUri` for accessing a bitmap over the web.

- `ImageSource.FromResource` for a bitmap stored as an embedded resource in the application PCL.

- `ImageSource.FromFile` for a bitmap stored as content in an individual platform project.

- `ImageSource.FromStream` for loading a bitmap by using a .NET `Stream` object.

`ImageSource` also has three descendant classes, named `UriImageSource`, `FileImageSource`, and `StreamImageSource`, that you can use instead of the first three static creation methods. Generally, the static methods are easier to use in code, but the descendant classes are sometimes required in XAML.

In general, you'll use the `ImageSource.FromUri` and `ImageSource.FromResource` methods to obtain platform-independent bitmaps for presentation purposes and `ImageSource.FromFile` to load platform-specific bitmaps for user-interface objects. Small bitmaps play a crucial role in `MenuItem` and `ToolbarItem` objects, and you can also add a bitmap to a `Button`.

This chapter begins with the use of platform-independent bitmaps obtained from the `ImageSource.FromUri` and `ImageSource.FromResource` methods. It then explores some uses of the `ImageSource.FromStream` method. The chapter concludes with the use of `ImageSource.FromFile` to obtain platform-specific bitmaps for toolbars and buttons.

Platform-independent bitmaps

Here's a code-only program named **WebBitmapCode** with a page class that uses `ImageSource.FromUri` to access a bitmap from the Xamarin website:

```
public class WebBitmapCodePage : ContentPage
{
    public WebBitmapCodePage()
    {
        string uri = "http://developer.xamarin.com/demo/IMG_1415.JPG";

        Content = new Image
        {
            Source = ImageSource.FromUri(new Uri(uri))
        };
    }
}
```

If the URI passed to `ImageSource.FromUri` does not point to a valid bitmap, no exception is raised.

Even this tiny program can be simplified. `ImageSource` defines an implicit conversion from `string` or `Uri` to an `ImageSource` object, so you can set the string with the URI directly to the `Source` property of `Image`:

```
public class WebBitmapCodePage : ContentPage
{
    public WebBitmapCodePage()
    {
        Content = new Image
        {
            Source = "http://developer.xamarin.com/demo/IMG_1415.JPG"
        };
    }
}
```

Or, to make it more verbose, you can set the `Source` property of `Image` to a `UriImageSource` object with its `Uri` property set to a `Uri` object:

```
public class WebBitmapCodePage : ContentPage
{
    public WebBitmapCodePage()
    {
        Content = new Image
        {
            Source = new UriImageSource
            {
                Uri = new Uri("http://developer.xamarin.com/demo/IMG_1415.JPG")
            }
        };
    }
}
```

The `UriImageSource` class might be preferred if you want to control the caching of web-based images. The class implements its own caching that uses the application's private storage area available on each platform. `UriImageSource` defines a `CachingEnabled` property that has a default value of `true` and a `CachingValidity` property of type `TimeSpan` that has a default value of one day. This means that if the image is reaccessed within a day, the cached image is used. You can disable caching entirely by setting `CachingEnabled` to `false`, or you can change the caching expiry time by setting the `CachingValidity` property to another `TimeSpan` value.

Regardless which way you do it, by default the bitmap displayed by the `Image` view is stretched to the size of its container—the `ContentPage` in this case—while respecting the bitmap's aspect ratio:

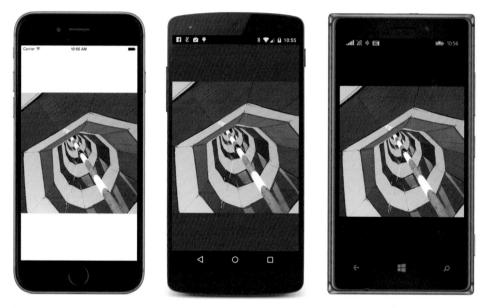

This bitmap is square, so blank areas appear above and below the image. As you turn your phone or emulator between portrait and landscape mode, a rendered bitmap can change size, and you'll see some blank space at the top and bottom or the left and right, where the bitmap doesn't reach. You can color that area by using the `BackgroundColor` property that `Image` inherits from `VisualElement`.

The bitmap referenced in the **WebBitmapCode** program is 4,096 pixels square, but a utility is installed on the Xamarin website that lets you download a much smaller bitmap file by specifying the URI like so:

```
Content = new Image
{
    Source = "http://developer.xamarin.com/demo/IMG_1415.JPG?width=25"
};
```

Now the downloaded bitmap is 25 pixels square, but it is again stretched to the size of its container. Each platform implements an interpolation algorithm in an attempt to smooth the pixels as the image is expanded to fit the page:

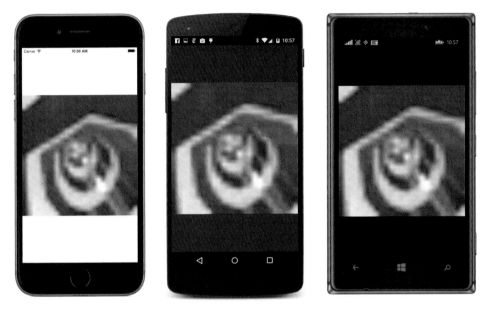

However, if you now set `HorizontalOptions` and `VerticalOptions` on the `Image` to `Center`— or put the `Image` element in a `StackLayout`—this 25-pixel bitmap collapses into a very tiny image. This phenomenon is discussed in more detail later in this chapter.

You can also instantiate an `Image` element in XAML and load a bitmap from a URI by setting the `Source` property directly to a web address. Here's the XAML file from the **WebBitmapXaml** program:

```
<ContentPage xmlns="http://xamarin.com/schemas/2014/forms"
             xmlns:x="http://schemas.microsoft.com/winfx/2009/xaml"
             x:Class="WebBitmapXaml.WebBitmapXamlPage">

  <Image Source="http://developer.xamarin.com/demo/IMG_3256.JPG" />

</ContentPage>
```

A more verbose approach involves explicitly instantiating a `UriImageSource` object and setting the `Uri` property:

```
<Image>
    <Image.Source>
        <UriImageSource Uri="http://developer.xamarin.com/demo/IMG_3256.JPG" />
    </Image.Source>
</Image>
```

Regardless, here's how it looks on the screen:

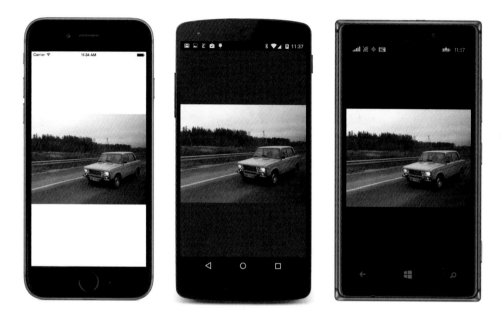

Fit and fill

If you set the `BackgroundColor` property of `Image` on any of the previous code and XAML examples, you'll see that `Image` actually occupies the entire rectangular area of the page. `Image` defines an `Aspect` property that controls how the bitmap is rendered within this rectangle. You set this property to a member of the `Aspect` enumeration:

- `AspectFit` — the default

- `Fill` — stretches without preserving the aspect ratio

- `AspectFill` — preserves the aspect ratio but crops the image

The default setting is the enumeration member `Aspect.AspectFit`, meaning that the bitmap fits into its container's boundaries while preserving the bitmap's aspect ratio. As you've already seen, the relationship between the bitmap's dimensions and the container's dimensions can result in background areas at the top and bottom or at the right and left.

Try this in the **WebBitmapXaml** project:

```
<Image Source="http://developer.xamarin.com/demo/IMG_3256.JPG"
       Aspect="Fill" />
```

Now the bitmap is expanded to the dimensions of the page. This results in the picture being stretched vertically, so the car appears rather short and stocky:

If you turn the phone sideways, the image is stretched horizontally, but the result isn't quite as extreme because the picture's aspect ratio is somewhat landscape to begin with.

The third option is `AspectFill`:

```
<Image Source="http://developer.xamarin.com/demo/IMG_3256.JPG"
       Aspect="AspectFill" />
```

With this option the bitmap completely fills the container, but the bitmap's aspect ratio is maintained at the same time. The only way this is possible is by cropping part of the image, and you'll see that the image is indeed cropped on either the top and bottom or the left and right, leaving only the central part of the bitmap:

Embedded resources

Accessing bitmaps over the Internet is convenient, but sometimes it's not optimum. The process re-quires an Internet connection, an assurance that the bitmaps haven't been moved, and some time for downloading. For fast and guaranteed access to bitmaps, they can be bound right into the application.

If you need access to images that are not platform specific, you can include bitmaps as embedded resources in the shared Portable Class Library project and access them with the `ImageSource.From-Resource` method. The **ResourceBitmapCode** solution demonstrates how to do it.

The **ResourceBitmapCode** PCL project within this solution has a folder named **Images** that con-tains two bitmaps, named ModernUserInterface.jpg (a very large bitmap) and ModernUserInter-face256.jpg (the same picture but with a 256-pixel width).

When adding any type of embedded resource to a PCL project, make sure to set the **Build Action** of the resource to **EmbeddedResource**. This is crucial.

In code, you set the `Source` property of an `Image` element to the `ImageSource` object returned from the static `ImageSource.FromResource` method. This method requires the resource ID. The re-source ID consists of the assembly name followed by a period, then the folder name followed by an-other period, and then the filename, which contains another period for the filename extension. For this example, the resource ID for accessing the smaller of the two bitmaps in the **ResourceBitmapCode** program is:

```
ResourceBitmapCode.Images.ModernUserInterface256.jpg
```

The code in this program references that smaller bitmap and also sets the `HorizontalOptions` and `VerticalOptions` on the `Image` element to `Center`:

```
public class ResourceBitmapCodePage : ContentPage
{
    public ResourceBitmapCodePage()
    {
        Content = new Image
        {
            Source = ImageSource.FromResource(
                        "ResourceBitmapCode.Images.ModernUserInterface256.jpg"),
            VerticalOptions = LayoutOptions.Center,
            HorizontalOptions = LayoutOptions.Center
        };
    }
}
```

As you can see, the bitmap in this instance is *not* stretched to fill the page:

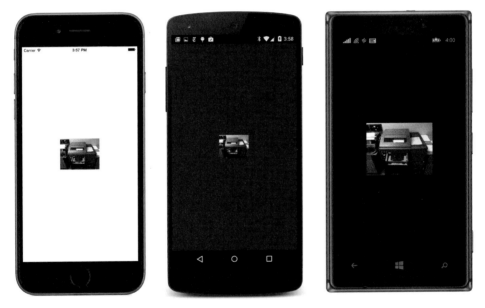

A bitmap is not stretched to fill its container if:

- it is smaller than the container, and

- the `VerticalOptions` and `HorizontalOptions` properties of the `Image` element are not set to `Fill`, or if `Image` is a child of a `StackLayout`.

If you comment out the `VerticalOptions` and `HorizontalOptions` settings, or if you reference the large bitmap (which does not have the "256" at the end of its filename), the image will again stretch to fill the container.

When a bitmap is not stretched to fit its container, it must be displayed in a particular size. What is that size?

On iOS and Android, the bitmap is displayed in its pixel size. In other words, the bitmap is rendered with a one-to-one mapping between the pixels of the bitmap and the pixels of the video display. The iPhone 6 used for these screen shots has a screen width of 750 pixels, and you can see that the 256-pixel width of the bitmap is about one-third that width. The Android phone here is a Nexus 5, which has a pixel width of 1080, and the bitmap is about one-quarter that width.

On Windows Phone, however, the bitmap is displayed in device-independent units—in this example, 256 device-independent units. The Nokia Lumia 925 used for these screen shots has a pixel width of 768, which is approximately the same as the iPhone 6. However, the screen width of this Windows Phone in device-independent units is 480, and you can see that the rendered bitmap width is a little more than half the screen width.

This discussion on sizing bitmaps continues in the next section.

How would you reference a bitmap stored as an embedded resource from XAML? Unfortunately, there is no `ResourceImageSource` class. If there were, you would probably try instantiating that class in XAML between `Image.Source` tags. But that's not an option.

You might consider using `x:FactoryMethod` to call `ImageSource.FromResource`, but that won't work. As currently implemented, the `ImageSource.FromResource` method requires that the bitmap resource be in the same assembly as the code that calls the method. When you use `x:FactoryMethod` to call `ImageSource.FromResource`, the call is made from the **Xamarin.Forms.Xaml** assembly.

What *will* work is a very simple XAML markup extension. Here's one in a project named **StackedBitmap**:

```
namespace StackedBitmap
{
    [ContentProperty ("Source")]
    public class ImageResourceExtension : IMarkupExtension
    {
        public string Source { get; set; }

        public object ProvideValue (IServiceProvider serviceProvider)
        {
            if (Source == null)
                return null;

            return ImageSource.FromResource(Source);
        }
    }
}
```

`ImageResourceExtension` has a single property named `Source` that you set to the resource ID. The `ProvideValue` method simply calls `ImageSource.FromResource` with the `Source` property. As is common for single-property markup extensions, `Source` is also the content property of the class. That means that you don't need to explicitly include "Source=" when you're using the curly-braces syntax for XAML markup extensions.

But watch out: You cannot move this `ImageResourceExtension` class to a toolkit library such as **Xamarin.FormsBook.Toolkit**. The class must be part of the same assembly that contains the embedded resources you want to load, which is generally the application's Portable Class Library.

Here's the XAML file from the **StackedBitmap** project. An `Image` element shares a `StackLayout` with two `Label` elements:

```
<ContentPage xmlns="http://xamarin.com/schemas/2014/forms"
             xmlns:x="http://schemas.microsoft.com/winfx/2009/xaml"
             xmlns:local="clr-namespace:StackedBitmap;assembly=StackedBitmap"
             x:Class="StackedBitmap.StackedBitmapPage">

    <StackLayout>
        <Label Text="400 x 300 Pixel Bitmap"
               FontSize="Large"
               VerticalOptions="CenterAndExpand"
               HorizontalOptions="Center" />

        <Image Source="{local:ImageResource StackedBitmap.Images.Sculpture_400x300.jpg}"
               BackgroundColor="Aqua"
               SizeChanged="OnImageSizeChanged" />

        <Label x:Name="label"
               FontSize="Large"
               VerticalOptions="CenterAndExpand"
               HorizontalOptions="Center" />
    </StackLayout>
</ContentPage>
```

The `local` prefix refers to the `StackedBitmap` namespace and **StackedBitmap** assembly. The `Source` property of the `Image` element is set to the `ImageResource` markup extension, which references a bitmap stored in the **Images** folder of the PCL project and flagged as an **EmbeddedResource**. The bitmap is 400 pixels wide and 300 pixels high. The `Image` also has its `BackgroundColor` property set; this will allow us to see the entire size of `Image` within the `StackLayout`.

The `Image` element has its `SizeChanged` event set to a handler in the code-behind file:

```
public partial class StackedBitmapPage : ContentPage
{
    public StackedBitmapPage()
    {
        InitializeComponent();
    }

    void OnImageSizeChanged(object sender, EventArgs args)
    {
        Image image = (Image)sender;
        label.Text = String.Format("Render size = {0:F0} x {1:F0}",
                                    image.Width, image.Height);
```

```
    }
}
```

The size of the `Image` element is constrained vertically by the `StackLayout`, so the bitmap is displayed in its pixel size (on iOS and Android) and in device-independent units on Windows Phone. The `Label` displays the size of the `Image` element in device-independent units, which differ on each platform:

The width of the `Image` element displayed by the bottom `Label` includes the aqua background and equals the width of the page in device-independent units. You can use `Aspect` settings of `Fill` or `AspectFill` to make the bitmap fill that entire aqua area.

If you prefer that the bottom `Label` displays only the width of the rendered bitmap, you can set the `HorizontalOptions` property of the `Image` to something other than the default value of `Fill`:

```
<Image Source="{local:ImageResource StackedBitmap.Images.Sculpture_400x300.jpg}"
       HorizontalOptions="Center"
       BackgroundColor="Aqua"
       SizeChanged="OnImageSizeChanged" />
```

Now the size of the `Image` element is the same size as the rendered bitmap in device-independent units. Settings of the `Aspect` property have no effect:

Let's refer to this rendered `Image` size as its *natural size* because it is based on the size of the bitmap being displayed.

The iPhone 6 has a pixel width of 750 pixels, but as you discovered when running the **WhatSize** program in Chapter 5, applications perceive a screen width of 375. There are two pixels to the device-independent unit, so this 400-pixel bitmap is displayed with a width of 200 DIUs.

The Nexus 5 has a pixel width of 1080, but applications perceive a width of 360, so there are three pixels to the device-independent unit, as the `Image` width of 133 DIUs confirms.

On both iOS and Android devices, when a bitmap is displayed in its natural size, there is a one-to-one mapping between the pixels of the bitmap and the pixels of the display. On Windows Phone, however, that's not the case. The Nokia Lumia 925 used for these screen shots has a pixel width of 768 with 1.6 pixels to the device-independent unit, so applications perceive a screen width of 480. But the 400 × 300 pixel bitmap is displayed in a size of 400 × 300 device-independent units.

This inconsistency between Windows Phone and the other two platforms is actually beneficial when you're accessing bitmaps from the individual platform projects. As you'll see, iOS and Android include a feature that lets you supply different sizes of bitmaps for different device resolutions. In effect, this allows you to specify bitmap sizes in device-independent units, which means that Windows Phone is consistent with those schemes.

But when using platform-independent bitmaps, you'll probably want to size the bitmaps consistently on all three platforms, and that requires a deeper plunge into the subject.

More on sizing

So far, you've seen two ways to size `Image` elements:

If the `Image` element is not constrained in any way, it will fill its container while maintaining the bitmap's aspect ratio, or fill the area entirely if you set the `Aspect` property to `Fill` or `AspectFill`.

If the bitmap is less than the size of its container and the `Image` is constrained horizontally or vertically by setting `HorizontalOptions` or `VerticalOptions` to something other than `Fill`, or if the `Image` is put in a `StackLayout`, the bitmap is displayed in its natural size. That's the pixel size on iOS and Android devices, but the size in device-independent units on Windows Phone.

You can also control size by setting `WidthRequest` or `HeightRequest` to an explicit dimension in device-independent units. However, there are some restrictions.

The following discussion is based on experimentation with the **StackedBitmap** sample. It pertains to `Image` elements that are vertically constrained by being a child of a vertical `StackLayout` or having the `VerticalOptions` property set to something other than `Fill`. The same principles apply to an `Image` element that is horizontally constrained.

If an `Image` element is vertically constrained, you can use `WidthRequest` to reduce the size of the bitmap from its natural size, but you cannot use it to increase the size. For example, try setting `WidthRequest` to 100:

```
<Image Source="{local:ImageResource StackedBitmap.Images.Sculpture_400x300.jpg}"
       WidthRequest="100"
       HorizontalOptions="Center"
       BackgroundColor="Aqua"
       SizeChanged="OnImageSizeChanged" />
```

The resultant height of the bitmap is governed by the specified width and the bitmap's aspect ratio, so now the `Image` is displayed with a size of 100 ×75 device-independent units on all three platforms:

The `HorizontalOptions` setting of `Center` does not affect the size of the rendered bitmap. If you remove that line, the `Image` element will be as wide as the screen (as the aqua background color will demonstrate), but the bitmap will remain the same size.

You cannot use `WidthRequest` to increase the size of the rendered bitmap beyond its natural size. For example, try setting `WidthRequest` to 1000:

```
<Image Source="{local:ImageResource StackedBitmap.Images.Sculpture_400x300.jpg}"
       WidthRequest="1000"
       HorizontalOptions="Center"
       BackgroundColor="Aqua"
       SizeChanged="OnImageSizeChanged" />
```

Even with `HorizontalOptions` set to `Center`, the resultant `Image` element is now wider than the rendered bitmap, as indicated by the background color:

But the bitmap itself is displayed in its natural size. The vertical `StackLayout` is effectively preventing the height of the rendered bitmap from exceeding its natural height.

To overcome that constraint of the vertical `StackLayout`, you need to set `HeightRequest`. However, you'll also want to leave `HorizontalOptions` at its default value of `Fill`. Otherwise, the `HorizontalOptions` setting will prevent the width of the rendered bitmap from exceeding its natural size.

Just as with `WidthRequest`, you can set `HeightRequest` to reduce the size of the rendered bitmap. The following code sets `HeightRequest` to 50 device-independent units:

```
<Image Source="{local:ImageResource StackedBitmap.Images.Sculpture_400x300.jpg}"
       HeightRequest="50"
       BackgroundColor="Aqua"
       SizeChanged="OnImageSizeChanged" />
```

The rendered bitmap is now 50 device-independent units high with a width governed by the aspect ratio. The `Image` itself stretches to the sides of the `StackLayout`:

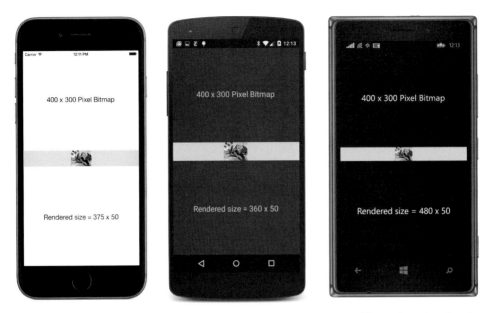

In this particular case, you can set `HorizontalOptions` to `Center` without changing the size of the rendered bitmap. The `Image` element will then be the size of the bitmap (67 × 50), and the aqua background will disappear.

It's important to leave `HorizontalOptions` at its default setting of `Fill` when setting the `HeightRequest` to a value greater than the bitmap's natural height, for example 250:

```
<Image Source="{local:ImageResource StackedBitmap.Images.Sculpture_400x300.jpg}"
       HeightRequest="250"
       BackgroundColor="Aqua"
       SizeChanged="OnImageSizeChanged" />
```

Now the rendered bitmap is larger than its natural size:

However, this technique has a built-in danger, which is revealed when you set the `HeightRequest` to 500:

```
<Image Source="{local:ImageResource StackedBitmap.Images.Sculpture_400x300.jpg}"
       HeightRequest="500"
       BackgroundColor="Aqua"
       SizeChanged="OnImageSizeChanged" />
```

Here's what happens: The `Image` element does indeed get a height of 500 device-independent units. But the width of the rendered bitmap in that `Image` element is limited by the width of the screen, which means that the height of the rendered bitmap is less than the height of the `Image` element:

In a real program you probably wouldn't have the `BackgroundColor` property set, and instead a wasteland of blank screen will occupy the area at the top and bottom of the rendered bitmap.

What this implies is that you should not use `HeightRequest` to control the size of bitmaps in a vertical `StackLayout` unless you write code that ensures that `HeightRequest` is limited to the width of the `StackLayout` times the ratio of the bitmap's height to width.

If you want to size bitmaps in a vertical `StackLayout` so that they look approximately the same size on a variety of devices, use `WidthRequest` instead. You've seen that `WidthRequest` in a vertical `StackLayout` can only decrease the size of bitmaps. This means that you should use bitmaps that are larger than the size at which they will be rendered. To obtain visual consistency among iOS, Android, and Windows Phone devices, you can size the bitmap by using a desired metrical size in inches together with the number of device-independent units to the inch for the particular device:

- iOS: 160 device-independent units to the inch

- Android: 160 device-independent units to the inch

- Windows Phone: 240 device-independent units to the inch

Here's a project very similar to **StackedBitmap** called **DeviceIndependentBitmapSize**. It's the same bitmap but now 1200 × 900 pixels, which is wider than the portrait-mode width of even high-resolution 1920 × 1080 displays. The platform-specific requested width of the bitmap corresponds to 1.5 inches:

```
<ContentPage xmlns="http://xamarin.com/schemas/2014/forms"
             xmlns:x="http://schemas.microsoft.com/winfx/2009/xaml"
             xmlns:local=
```

```
            "clr-namespace:DeviceIndependentBitmapSize;assembly=DeviceIndependentBitmapSize"
            x:Class="DeviceIndependentBitmapSize.DeviceIndependentBitmapSizePage">

    <StackLayout>
        <Label Text="1200 x 900 Pixel Bitmap"
               FontSize="Large"
               VerticalOptions="CenterAndExpand"
               HorizontalOptions="Center" />

        <Image Source=
            "{local:ImageResource DeviceIndependentBitmapSize.Images.Sculpture_1200x900.jpg}"
               HorizontalOptions="Center"
               SizeChanged="OnImageSizeChanged">
            <Image.WidthRequest>
                <!-- 1.5 inches -->
                <OnPlatform x:TypeArguments="x:Double"
                            iOS="240"
                            Android="240"
                            WinPhone="360" />
            </Image.WidthRequest>
        </Image>

        <Label x:Name="label"
               FontSize="Large"
               VerticalOptions="CenterAndExpand"
               HorizontalOptions="Center" />
    </StackLayout>
</ContentPage>
```

If the preceding analysis about sizing is correct and all goes well, this bitmap should look approximately the same size on all three platforms relative to the width of the screen:

With this knowledge about sizing bitmaps, it is now possible to make a little e-book reader with pictures, because what is the use of a book without pictures?

This e-book reader displays a scrollable `StackLayout` with the complete text of Chapter 7 of Lewis Carroll's *Alice's Adventures in Wonderland,* including three of John Tenniel's original illustrations. The text and illustrations were downloaded from the University of Adelaide's website. The illustrations are included as embedded resources in the **MadTeaParty** project. They have the same names and sizes as those on the website. The names refer to page numbers in the original book:

- image113.jpg — 709 × 553

- image122.jpg — 485 × 545

- image129.jpg — 670 × 596

Recall that the use of `WidthRequest` for `Image` elements in a `StackLayout` can only shrink the size of rendered bitmaps. These bitmaps are not wide enough to ensure that they will all shrink to a proper size on all three platforms, but it's worthwhile examining the results anyway because this is much closer to a real-life example.

The **MadTeaParty** program uses an implicit style for `Image` to set the `WidthRequest` property to a value corresponding to 1.5 inches. Just as in the previous example, this value is:

- 240 device-independent units for iOS

- 240 device-independent units for Android

- 360 device-independent units for Windows Phone

For the three devices used for these screen shots, this width corresponds to:

- 480 pixels on the iPhone 6

- 720 pixels on the Android Nexus 5

- 570 pixels on the Windows Phone Nokia Lumia 925

This means that all three images will shrink in size on the iPhone 6, and they will all have a rendered width of 240 device-independent units.

However, none of the three images will shrink in size on the Nexus 5 because they all have narrower pixel widths than the number of pixels in 1.5 inches. The three images will have a rendered width of (respectively) 236, 162, and 223 device-independent units on the Nexus 5. (That's the pixel width divided by 3.)

On the Windows Phone, the natural widths of the three images are (respectively) 709, 485, and 670 device-independent units. These widths are all wider than the Nokia Lumia 925 screen width of 480 units. Without a `WidthRequest` setting, these three images would all be displayed at the full width of the `StackLayout`. With a `WidthRequest` setting of 360, they will all be displayed with a width of 360 device-independent units.

Let's see if the predictions are correct. The XAML file includes a `BackgroundColor` setting on the root element that colors the entire page white, as is appropriate for a book. The `Style` definitions are confined to a `Resources` dictionary in the `StackLayout`. A style for the book title is based on the device `TitleStyle` but with black text and centered, and two implicit styles for `Label` and `Image` serve to style most of the `Label` elements and all three `Image` elements. Only the first and last paragraphs of the chapter's text are shown in this listing of the XAML file:

```
<ContentPage xmlns="http://xamarin.com/schemas/2014/forms"
             xmlns:x="http://schemas.microsoft.com/winfx/2009/xaml"
             xmlns:sys="clr-namespace:System;assembly=mscorlib"
             xmlns:local="clr-namespace:MadTeaParty;assembly=MadTeaParty"
             x:Class="MadTeaParty.MadTeaPartyPage"
             BackgroundColor="White">

    <ContentPage.Padding>
        <OnPlatform x:TypeArguments="Thickness"
                    iOS="5, 20, 5, 0"
                    Android="5, 0"
                    WinPhone="5, 0" />
    </ContentPage.Padding>

    <ScrollView>
        <StackLayout Spacing="10">
            <StackLayout.Resources>
                <ResourceDictionary>
                    <Style x:Key="titleLabel"
                           TargetType="Label"
                           BaseResourceKey="TitleStyle">
                        <Setter Property="TextColor" Value="Black" />
                        <Setter Property="XAlign" Value="Center" />
                    </Style>

                    <!-- Implicit styles -->
                    <Style TargetType="Label"
                           BaseResourceKey="BodyStyle">
                        <Setter Property="TextColor" Value="Black" />
                    </Style>

                    <Style TargetType="Image">
                        <Setter Property="WidthRequest">
                            <Setter.Value>
                                <!-- 1.5 inches -->
                                <OnPlatform x:TypeArguments="x:Double"
                                            iOS="240"
                                            Android="240"
                                            WinPhone="360" />
                            </Setter.Value>
                        </Setter>
                    </Style>
```

```xml
            ·   <!-- 1/4 inch indent for poetry -->
                <OnPlatform x:Key="poemIndent"
                            x:TypeArguments="Thickness"
                            iOS="40, 0, 0, 0"
                            Android="40, 0, 0, 0"
                            WinPhone="60, 0, 0, 0" />
            </ResourceDictionary>
        </StackLayout.Resources>

        <!-- Text and images from http://ebooks.adelaide.edu.au/c/carroll/lewis/alice/ -->
        <StackLayout Spacing="0">
            <Label Text="Alice's Adventures in Wonderland"
                   Style="{DynamicResource titleLabel}"
                   FontAttributes="Italic" />

            <Label Text="by Lewis Carroll"
                   Style="{DynamicResource titleLabel}" />
        </StackLayout>

        <Label Style="{DynamicResource SubtitleStyle}"
               TextColor="Black"
               XAlign="Center">
            <Label.FormattedText>
              <FormattedString>
                  <Span Text="Chapter VII" />
                  <Span Text="{x:Static sys:Environment.NewLine}" />
                  <Span Text="A Mad Tea-Party" />
              </FormattedString>
            </Label.FormattedText>
        </Label>

        <Label Text=
"There was a table set out under a tree in front of the
house, and the March Hare and the Hatter were having tea at
it: a Dormouse was sitting between them, fast asleep, and
the other two were using it as a cushion, resting their
elbows on it, and talking over its head. 'Very uncomfortable
for the Dormouse,' thought Alice; 'only, as it's asleep, I
suppose it doesn't mind.'" />

            ...

        <Label>
            <Label.FormattedText>
                <FormattedString>
                    <Span Text=
"Once more she found herself in the long hall, and close to
the little glass table. 'Now, I'll manage better this time,'
she said to herself, and began by taking the little golden
key, and unlocking the door that led into the garden. Then
she went to work nibbling at the mushroom (she had kept a
piece of it in her pocket) till she was about a foot high:
then she walked down the little passage: and " />
```

```
                    <Span Text="then" FontAttributes="Italic" />
                    <Span Text=
" – she found herself at last in the beautiful garden,
among the bright flower-beds and the cool fountains." />
                </FormattedString>
            </Label.FormattedText>
        </Label>
    </StackLayout>
  </ScrollView>
</ContentPage>
```

The three `Image` elements simply reference the three embedded resources and are given a setting of the `WidthRequest` property through the implicit style:

```
<Image Source="{local:ImageResource MadTeaParty.Images.image113.jpg}" />
...
<Image Source="{local:ImageResource MadTeaParty.Images.image122.jpg}" />
...
<Image Source="{local:ImageResource MadTeaParty.Images.image129.jpg}" />
```

Here's the first picture:

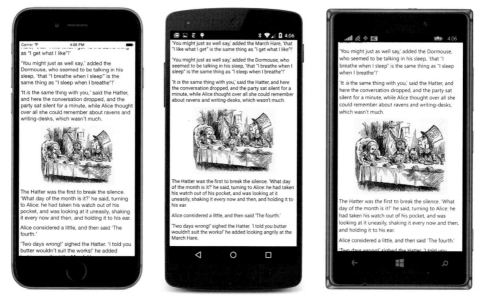

It's fairly consistent among the three platforms, even though it's displayed in its natural width of 709 pixels on the Nexus 5, but that's very close to the 720 pixels that a width of 240 device-independent units implies.

The difference is much greater with the second image:

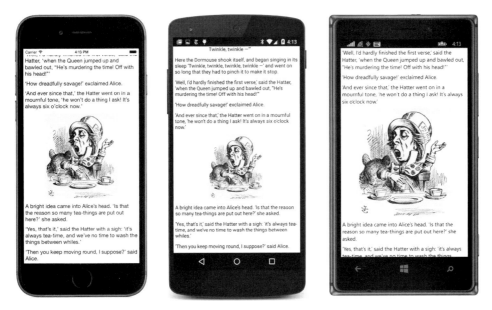

This is displayed in its pixel size on the Nexus 5, which corresponds to 162 device-independent units, but is displayed with a width of 240 units on the iPhone 6 and 360 units on the Nokia Lumia 925.

Although the pictures don't look bad on any of the platforms, getting them all about the same size would require starting out with larger bitmaps.

Browsing and waiting

Another feature of `Image` is demonstrated in the **ImageBrowser** program, which lets you browse the stock photos used for some of the samples in this book. As you can see in the following XAML file, an `Image` element shares the screen with a `Label` and two `Button` views. Notice that a `Property-Changed` handler is set on the `Image`. You learned in Chapter 11, "The bindable infrastructure," that the `PropertyChanged` handler is implemented by `BindableObject` and is fired whenever a bindable property changes value.

```
<ContentPage xmlns="http://xamarin.com/schemas/2014/forms"
             xmlns:x="http://schemas.microsoft.com/winfx/2009/xaml"
             x:Class="ImageBrowser.ImageBrowserPage">

    <ContentPage.Padding>
        <OnPlatform x:TypeArguments="Thickness"
                    iOS="0, 20, 0, 0" />
    </ContentPage.Padding>

    <StackLayout>
        <Image x:Name="image"
               VerticalOptions="CenterAndExpand"
               PropertyChanged="OnImagePropertyChanged" />
```

```
            <Label x:Name="filenameLabel"
                   HorizontalOptions="Center" />

            <ActivityIndicator x:Name="activityIndicator" />

            <StackLayout Orientation="Horizontal">
                <Button x:Name="prevButton"
                        Text="Previous"
                        IsEnabled="false"
                        HorizontalOptions="CenterAndExpand"
                        Clicked="OnPreviousButtonClicked" />

                <Button x:Name="nextButton"
                        Text="Next"
                        IsEnabled="false"
                        HorizontalOptions="CenterAndExpand"
                        Clicked="OnNextButtonClicked" />
            </StackLayout>
        </StackLayout>
</ContentPage>
```

Also on this page is an `ActivityIndicator`. You generally use this view when a program is waiting for a long operation to complete (such as downloading a bitmap) but can't provide any information about the progress of the operation. If your program knows what fraction of the operation has completed, you can use a `ProgressBar` instead. (`ProgressBar` is demonstrated in the next chapter.)

The `ActivityIndicator` has a Boolean property named `IsRunning`. Normally, that property is `false` and the `ActivityIndicator` is invisible. Set the property to `true` to make the `ActivityIndicator` visible. All three platforms implement an animated visual to indicate that the program is working, but it looks a little different on each platform. On iOS it's a spinning wheel, and on Android it's a spinning partial circle. On Windows Phone, a series of dots moves across the screen.

To provide browsing access to the stock images, the **ImageBrowser** needs to download a JSON file with a list of all the filenames. Over the years, various versions of .NET have introduced several classes capable of downloading objects over the web. However, not all of these are available in the version of .NET that is available in a Portable Class Library that has the profile compatible with Xamarin.Forms. A class that is available is `WebRequest` and its descendent class `HttpWebRequest`.

The `WebRequest.Create` method returns a `WebRequest` method based on a URI. (The return value is actually an `HttpWebRequest` object.) The `BeginGetResponse` method requires a callback function that is called when the `Stream` referencing the URI is available for access. The `Stream` is accessible from a call to `EndGetResponse` and `GetResponseStream`.

Once the program gets access to the `Stream` object in the following code, it uses the `DataContractJsonSerializer` class together with the embedded `ImageList` class defined near the top of the `ImageBrowserPage` class to convert the JSON file to an `ImageList` object:

```
public partial class ImageBrowserPage : ContentPage
{
    [DataContract]
```

```
class ImageList
{
    [DataMember(Name = "photos")]
    public List<string> Photos = null;
}

WebRequest request;
ImageList imageList;
int imageListIndex = 0;

public ImageBrowserPage()
{
    InitializeComponent();

    // Get list of stock photos.
    Uri uri = new Uri("http://docs.xamarin.com/demo/stock.json");
    request = WebRequest.Create(uri);
    request.BeginGetResponse(WebRequestCallback, null);
}

void WebRequestCallback(IAsyncResult result)
{
    Device.BeginInvokeOnMainThread(() =>
    {
        try
        {
            Stream stream = request.EndGetResponse(result).GetResponseStream();

            // Deserialize the JSON into imageList;
            var jsonSerializer = new DataContractJsonSerializer(typeof(ImageList));
            imageList = (ImageList)jsonSerializer.ReadObject(stream);

            if (imageList.Photos.Count > 0)
                FetchPhoto();
        }
        catch (Exception exc)
        {
            filenameLabel.Text = exc.Message;
        }
    });
}

void OnPreviousButtonClicked(object sender, EventArgs args)
{
    imageListIndex--;
    FetchPhoto();
}

void OnNextButtonClicked(object sender, EventArgs args)
{
    imageListIndex++;
    FetchPhoto();
}
```

```
void FetchPhoto()
{
    // Prepare for new image.
    image.Source = null;
    string url = imageList.Photos[imageListIndex];

    // Set the filename.
    filenameLabel.Text = url.Substring(url.LastIndexOf('/') + 1);

    // Create the UriImageSource.
    UriImageSource imageSource = new UriImageSource
    {
        Uri = new Uri(url + "?Width=1080"),
        CacheValidity = TimeSpan.FromDays(30)
    };

    // Set the Image source.
    image.Source = imageSource;

    // Enable or disable buttons.
    prevButton.IsEnabled = imageListIndex > 0;
    nextButton.IsEnabled = imageListIndex < imageList.Photos.Count - 1;
}

void OnImagePropertyChanged(object sender, PropertyChangedEventArgs args)
{
    if (args.PropertyName == "IsLoading")
    {
        activityIndicator.IsRunning = ((Image)sender).IsLoading;
    }
}
```

The entire body of the `WebRequestCallback` method is enclosed in a lambda function that is the argument to the `Device.BeginInvokeOnMainThread` method. `WebRequest` downloads the file referenced by the URI in a secondary thread of execution. This ensures that the operation doesn't block the program's main thread, which is handling the user interface. The callback method also executes in this secondary thread. However, user-interface objects in a Xamarin.Forms application can be accessed only from the main thread.

The purpose of the `Device.BeginInvokeOnMainThread` method is to get around this problem. The argument to this method is queued to run in the program's main thread and can safely access user-interface objects.

As you click the two buttons, calls to `FetchPhoto` use `UriImageSource` to download a new bitmap. This might take a second or so. The `Image` class defines a Boolean property named `IsLoading` that is `true` when `Image` is in the process of loading (or downloading) a bitmap. `IsLoading` is backed by the bindable property `IsLoadingProperty`. That also means that whenever `IsLoading` changes value, a `PropertyChanged` event is fired. The program uses the `PropertyChanged` event handler—

the `OnImagePropertyChanged` method at the very bottom of the class—to set the `IsRunning` property of the `ActivityIndicator` to the same value as the `IsLoading` property of `Image`.

You'll see in Chapter 16, "Data binding," how your applications can link properties like `IsLoading` and `IsRunning` so that they maintain the same value without any explicit event handlers.

Here's **ImageBrowser** in action:

Some of the images have an EXIF orientation flag set, and if the particular platform ignores that flag, the image is displayed sideways.

Streaming bitmaps

If the `ImageSource` class didn't have `FromUri` or `FromResource` methods, you would still be able to access bitmaps over the web or stored as resources in the PCL. You can do both of these jobs—as well as several others—with `ImageSource.FromStream` or the `StreamImageSource` class.

The `ImageSource.FromStream` method is somewhat easier to use than `StreamImageSource`, but both are a little odd. The argument to `ImageSource.FromStream` is not a `Stream` object but a `Func` object (a method with no arguments) that returns a `Stream` object. The `Stream` property of `StreamImageSource` is likewise not a `Stream` object but a `Func` object that has a `CancellationToken` argument and returns a `Task<Stream>` object.

This section is restricted to `ImageSource.FromStream`; the use of `StreamImageSource` is discussed later in a chapter on asynchronous operations.

Accessing the streams

The **BitmapStreams** program contains a XAML file with two `Image` elements waiting for bitmaps, each of which is set in the code-behind file by using `ImageSource.FromStream`:

```
<ContentPage xmlns="http://xamarin.com/schemas/2014/forms"
             xmlns:x="http://schemas.microsoft.com/winfx/2009/xaml"
             x:Class="BitmapStreams.BitmapStreamsPage">
    <StackLayout>
        <Image x:Name="image1"
               HorizontalOptions="Center"
               VerticalOptions="CenterAndExpand" />

        <Image x:Name="image2"
               HorizontalOptions="Center"
               VerticalOptions="CenterAndExpand" />
    </StackLayout>
</ContentPage>
```

The first `Image` is set from an embedded resource in the PCL; the second is set from a bitmap accessed over the web.

In the **BlackCat** program in Chapter 4, "Scrolling the stack," you saw how to obtain a `Stream` object for any resource stored with a **Build Action** of **EmbeddedResource** in the PCL. You can use this same technique for accessing a bitmap stored as an embedded resource:

```
public partial class BitmapStreamsPage : ContentPage
{
    public BitmapStreamsPage()
    {
        InitializeComponent();

        // Load embedded resource bitmap.
        string resourceID = "BitmapStreams.Images.IMG_0722_512.jpg";
        image1.Source = ImageSource.FromStream(() =>
            {
                Assembly assembly = GetType().GetTypeInfo().Assembly;
                Stream stream = assembly.GetManifestResourceStream(resourceID);
                return stream;
            });
        …
    }
}
```

The argument to `ImageSource.FromStream` is defined as a function that returns a `Stream` object, so that argument is here expressed as a lambda function. The call to the `GetType` method returns the type of the `BitmapStreamsPage` class, and `GetTypeInfo` provides more information about that type, including the `Assembly` object containing the type. That's the **BitmapStream** PCL assembly, which is the assembly with the embedded resource. `GetManifestResourceStream` returns a `Stream` object, which is the return value that `ImageSource.FromStream` wants.

Another method of the `Assembly` class helps in debugging embedded resources: the `GetMani-` `festResourceNames` returns an array of string objects with all the resource IDs in the PCL. If you can't figure out why your `GetManifestResourceStream` isn't working, first check to make sure your resources have a **Build Action** of **EmbeddedResource**, and then call `GetManifestResourceNames` to get all the resource IDs.

To download a bitmap over the web, you can use the same `WebRequest` method demonstrated earlier in the **ImageBrowser** program. In this program, the `BeginGetResponse` callback is a lambda function:

```
public partial class BitmapStreamsPage : ContentPage
{
    public BitmapStreamsPage()
    {
        …
        // Load web bitmap.
        Uri uri = new Uri("http://developer.xamarin.com/demo/IMG_0925.JPG?width=512");
        WebRequest request = WebRequest.Create (uri);
        request.BeginGetResponse((IAsyncResult arg) =>
            {
                Stream stream = request.EndGetResponse(arg).GetResponseStream();
                ImageSource imageSource = ImageSource.FromStream(() => stream);
                Device.BeginInvokeOnMainThread(() => image2.Source = imageSource);
            }, null);
    }
}
```

This `BeginGetResponse` callback also contains two more embedded lambda functions! The first line of the callback obtains the `Stream` object for the bitmap. The second line uses a short lambda function as the argument to `ImageSource.FromStream` to define a function that returns that stream. The last line of the `BeginGetResponse` callback is a call to `Device.BeginInvokeOnMainThread` to set the `ImageSource` object to the `Source` property of the `Image`.

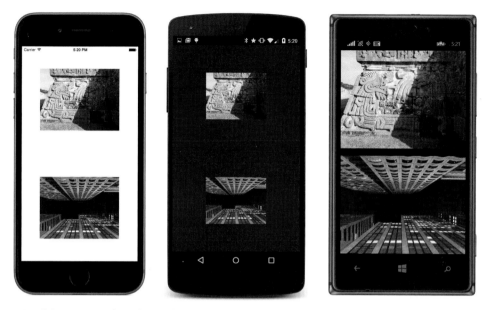

It might seem as though you have more control over the downloading of images by using `WebRequest` and `ImageSource.FromStream` than with `ImageSource.FromUri`, but the `ImageSource.FromUri` method has a big advantage: it caches the downloaded bitmaps in a storage area private to the application. As you've seen, you can turn off the caching, but if you're using `ImageSource.FromStream` instead of `ImageSource.FromUri`, you might find the need to cache the images, and that would be a much bigger job.

Generating bitmaps at run time

All three platforms support the BMP file format, which dates back to the very beginning of Microsoft Windows. Despite its ancient heritage, the file format is now fairly standardized with more extensive header information.

Although there are some BMP options that allow some rudimentary compression, most BMP files are uncompressed. This lack of compression is usually regarded as a disadvantage of the BMP file format, but in some cases it's not a disadvantage at all. For example, if you want to generate a bitmap algorithmically at run time, it's *much* easier to generate an uncompressed bitmap instead of one of the compressed file formats. (Indeed, even if you had a library function to create a JPEG or PNG file, you'd apply that function to the uncompressed pixel data.)

You can create a bitmap algorithmically at run time by filling a `MemoryStream` with the BMP file headers and pixel data and then passing that `MemoryStream` to the `ImageSource.FromStream` method. The `BmpMaker` class in the **Xamarin.FormsBook.Toolkit** library demonstrates this. It creates a BMP in memory using a 32-bit pixel format—8 bits each for red, green, blue, and alpha (opacity) channels. The `BmpMaker` class was coded with performance in mind, in hopes that it might be used for animation. Maybe someday it will be, but in this chapter the only demonstration is a simple color gradient.

The constructor creates a `byte` array named `buffer` that stores the entire BMP file beginning with the header information and followed by the pixel bits. The constructor then uses a `MemoryStream` for writing the header information to the beginning of this buffer:

```
public class BmpMaker
{
    const int headerSize = 54;
    readonly byte[] buffer;

    public BmpMaker(int width, int height)
    {
        Width = width;
        Height = height;

        int numPixels = Width * Height;
        int numPixelBytes = 4 * numPixels;
        int fileSize = headerSize + numPixelBytes;
        buffer = new byte[fileSize];

        // Write headers in MemoryStream and hence the buffer.
        using (MemoryStream memoryStream = new MemoryStream(buffer))
        {
            using (BinaryWriter writer = new BinaryWriter(memoryStream, Encoding.UTF8))
            {
                // Construct BMP header (14 bytes).
                writer.Write(new char[] { 'B', 'M' });  // Signature
                writer.Write(fileSize);                  // File size
                writer.Write((short)0);                  // Reserved
                writer.Write((short)0);                  // Reserved
                writer.Write(headerSize);                // Offset to pixels

                // Construct BitmapInfoHeader (40 bytes).
                writer.Write(40);                        // Header size
                writer.Write(Width);                     // Pixel width
                writer.Write(Height);                    // Pixel height
                writer.Write((short)1);                  // Planes
                writer.Write((short)32);                 // Bits per pixel
                writer.Write(0);                         // Compression
                writer.Write(numPixelBytes);             // Image size in bytes
                writer.Write(0);                         // X pixels per meter
                writer.Write(0);                         // Y pixels per meter
                writer.Write(0);                         // Number colors in color table
                writer.Write(0);                         // Important color count
            }
        }
    }

    public int Width
    {
```

```
        private set;
        get;
    }

    public int Height
    {
        private set;
        get;
    }

    public void SetPixel(int row, int col, Color color)
    {
        SetPixel(row, col, (int)(255 * color.R),
                           (int)(255 * color.G),
                           (int)(255 * color.B),
                           (int)(255 * color.A));
    }

    public void SetPixel(int row, int col, int r, int g, int b, int a = 255)
    {
        int index = (row * Width + col) * 4 + headerSize;
        buffer[index + 0] = (byte)b;
        buffer[index + 1] = (byte)g;
        buffer[index + 2] = (byte)r;
        buffer[index + 3] = (byte)a;
    }

    public ImageSource Generate()
    {
        // Create MemoryStream from buffer with bitmap.
        MemoryStream memoryStream = new MemoryStream(buffer);

        // Convert to StreamImageSource.
        ImageSource imageSource = ImageSource.FromStream(() =>
        {
            return memoryStream;
        });
        return imageSource;
    }
}
```

After creating a BmpMaker object, a program can then call one of the two SetPixel methods to set a color at a particular row and column. When making very many calls, the SetPixel call that uses a Color value is significantly slower than the one that accepts explicit red, green, and blue values.

The last step is to call the Generate method. This method instantiates another MemoryStream object based on the buffer array and uses it to create a FileImageSource object. You can call Generate multiple times after setting new pixel data. The method creates a new MemoryStream each time because ImageSource.FromStream closes the Stream object when it's finished with it.

The **DiyGradientBitmap** program—"DIY" stands for "Do It Yourself"—demonstrates how to use

`BmpMaker` to make a bitmap with a simple gradient and display it to fill the page. The XAML file includes the `Image` element:

```
<ContentPage xmlns="http://xamarin.com/schemas/2014/forms"
             xmlns:x="http://schemas.microsoft.com/winfx/2009/xaml"
             x:Class="DiyGradientBitmap.DiyGradientBitmapPage">
    <ContentPage.Padding>
        <OnPlatform x:TypeArguments="Thickness"
                    iOS="0, 20, 0, 0" />
    </ContentPage.Padding>

    <Image x:Name="image"
           Aspect="Fill" />

</ContentPage>
```

The code-behind file instantiates a `BmpMaker` and loops through the rows and columns of the bitmap to create a gradient that ranges from red at the top to blue at the bottom:

```
public partial class DiyGradientBitmapPage : ContentPage
{
    public DiyGradientBitmapPage()
    {
        InitializeComponent();

        int rows = 128;
        int cols = 64;
        BmpMaker bmpMaker = new BmpMaker(cols, rows);

        for (int row = 0; row < rows; row++)
            for (int col = 0; col < cols; col++)
            {
                bmpMaker.SetPixel(row, col, 2 * row, 0, 2 * (128 - row));
            }

        ImageSource imageSource = bmpMaker.Generate();
        image.Source = imageSource;
    }
}
```

Here's the result:

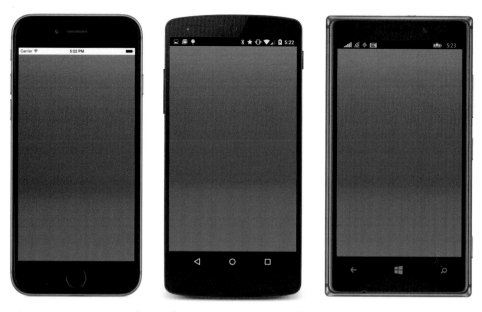

Now use your imagination and see what you can do with `BmpMaker`.

Platform-specific bitmaps

As you've seen, you can load bitmaps over the web or from the shared PCL project. You can also load bitmaps stored as resources in the individual platform projects. The tools for this job are the `Im-ageSource.FromFile` static method and the corresponding `FileImageSource` class.

You'll probably use this facility mostly for bitmaps connected with user-interface elements. The `Icon` property in `MenuItem` and `ToolBarItem` is of type `FileImageSource`. The `Image` property in `Button` is also of type `FileImageSource`.

Two other uses of `FileImageSource` won't be discussed in this chapter: the `Page` class defines an `Icon` property of type `FileImageSource` and a `BackgroundImage` property of type `string`, but which is assumed to be the name of a bitmap stored in the platform project.

The storage of bitmaps in the individual platform projects allows a high level of platform specificity. You might think you can get the same degree of platform specificity by storing bitmaps for each plat-form in the PCL project and using the `Device.OnPlatform` method or the `OnPlatform` class to select them. However, as you'll soon discover, both iOS and Android have provisions for storing bitmaps of different pixel resolutions and then automatically accessing the optimum one. You can take advantage of this valuable feature only if the individual platforms themselves load the bitmaps, and this is the case only when you use `ImageSource.FromFile` and `FileImageSource`.

The platform projects in a newly created Xamarin.Forms solution already contain several bitmaps. In the iOS project, you'll find these in the **Resources** folder. In the Android project, they're in subfolders of the **Resources** folder. In the Windows Phone project, they're in the **Assets** folder and subfolders. These bitmaps are application icons and splash screens, and you'll want to replace them when you prepare to bring an application to market.

Let's write a small project called **PlatformBitmaps** that accesses an application icon from each platform project and displays the rendered size of the `Image` element. If you're using `FileImageSource` to load the bitmap (as this program does), you need to set the `File` property to a `string` with the bitmap's filename. Almost always, you'll be using `Device.OnPlatform` in code or `OnPlatform` in XAML to specify the three filenames:

```
public class PlatformBitmapsPage : ContentPage
{
    public PlatformBitmapsPage()
    {
        Image image = new Image
        {
            Source = new FileImageSource
            {
                File = Device.OnPlatform(iOS: "Icon-Small-40.png",
                                         Android: "icon.png",
                                         WinPhone: "Assets/ApplicationIcon.png")
            },
            HorizontalOptions = LayoutOptions.Center,
            VerticalOptions = LayoutOptions.CenterAndExpand
        };

        Label label = new Label
        {
            FontSize = Device.GetNamedSize(NamedSize.Large, typeof(Label)),
            HorizontalOptions = LayoutOptions.Center,
            VerticalOptions = LayoutOptions.CenterAndExpand
        };

        image.SizeChanged += (sender, args) =>
            {
                label.Text = String.Format("Rendered size = {0} x {1}",
                                            image.Width, image.Height);
            };

        Content = new StackLayout
        {
            Children =
            {
                image,
                label
            }
        };
    }
}
```

When you access a bitmap stored in the **Resources** folder of the iOS project or the **Resources** folder (or subfolders) of the Android project, do not preface the filename with a folder name. These folders are the standard repositories for bitmaps on these platforms. But bitmaps can be anywhere in the Windows Phone project (including the project root), so the folder name (if any) is required.

In all three cases, the default icon is the famous hexagonal Xamarin logo (fondly known as the Xamagon), but each platform has different conventions for its icon size, so the rendered sizes are different:

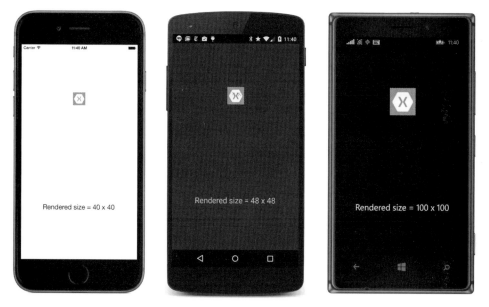

If you begin exploring the icon bitmaps in the iOS and Android projects, you might be a little confused: there seem to be multiple bitmaps with the same names (or similar names) in the iOS and Android projects.

It's time to dive deeper into the subject of bitmap resolution.

Bitmap resolutions

The iOS bitmap filename specified in **PlatformBitmaps** is Icon-Small-40.png, but if you look in the **Resources** folder of the iOS project, you'll see three files with variations of that name. They all have different sizes:

- Icon-Small-40.png — 40 pixels square

- Icon-Small-40@2x.png — 80 pixels square

- Icon-Small-40@3x.png — 120 pixels square

As you discovered earlier in this chapter, when an `Image` is a child of a `StackLayout`, iOS displays the bitmap in its pixel size with a one-to-one mapping between the pixels of the bitmap and the pixels of the screen. This is the optimum display of a bitmap.

However, on the iPhone 6 simulator used in the screen shot, the `Image` has a rendered size of 40 device-independent units. On the iPhone 6 there are two pixels per device-independent unit, which means that the actual bitmap being displayed in that screen shot is not Icon-Small-40.png but Icon-Small-40@2x.png, which is two times 40, or 80 pixels square.

If you instead run the program on the iPhone 6 Plus—which has a device-independent unit equal to three pixels—you'll again see a rendered size of 40 pixels, which means that the Icon-Small-40@3x.png bitmap is displayed. Now try it on the iPad 2 simulator. The iPad 2 has a screen size of just 768 × 1024, and device-independent units are the same as pixels. Now the Icon-Small-40.png bitmap is displayed, and the rendered size is still 40 pixels.

This is what you want. You want to be able to control the rendered size of bitmaps in device-independent units because that's how you can achieve perceptibly similar bitmap sizes on different devices and platforms. When you specify the Icon-Small-40.png bitmap, you want that bitmap to be rendered as 40 device-independent units—or about one-quarter inch—on all iOS devices. But if the program is running on an Apple Retina device, you don't want a 40-pixel-square bitmap stretched to be 40 device-independent units. For maximum visual detail, you want a higher resolution bitmap displayed, with a one-to-one mapping of bitmap pixels to screen pixels.

If you look in the Android **Resources** directory, you'll find four different versions of a bitmap named icon.png. These are stored in different subfolders of **Resources**:

- drawable/icon.png — 72 pixels square

- drawable-hdpi/icon.png — 72 pixels square

- drawable-xdpi/icon.png — 96 pixels square

- drawable-xxdpi/icon.png — 144 pixels square

Regardless of the Android device, the icon is rendered with a size of 48 device-independent units. On the Nexus 5 used in the screen shot, there are three pixels to the device-independent unit, which means that the bitmap actually displayed on that screen is the one in the **drawable-xxdpi** folder, which is 144 pixels square.

What's nice about both iOS and Android is that you only need to supply bitmaps of various sizes—and give them the correct names or store them in the correct folders—and the operating system chooses the optimum image for the particular resolution of the device.

The Silverlight platform of Windows Phone doesn't have such a system. The ApplicationIcon.png file is 100 pixels square, and it's rendered as 100 device-independent units.

Although the treatment of Windows Phone seems inconsistent with the other two platforms, it is not: in all three platforms you can control the size of bitmaps in device-independent units.

When creating your own platform-specific images, follow the guidelines in the next three sections.

Device-independent bitmaps for iOS

The iOS naming scheme for bitmaps involves a suffix on the filename. The operating system fetches a particular bitmap with the underlying filename based on the approximate pixel resolution of the device:

- No suffix for 160 DPI devices (1 pixel to the device-independent unit)

- @2x suffix for 320 DPI devices (2 pixels to the DIU)

- @3x suffix: 480 DPI devices (3 pixels to the DIU)

For example, suppose you want a bitmap named MyImage.jpg to show up as about one inch square on the screen. You should supply three versions of this bitmap:

- MyImage.jpg — 160 pixels square

- MyImage@2x.jpg — 320 pixels square

- MyImage@3x.jpg — 480 pixels square

The bitmap will render as 160 device-independent units. For rendered sizes smaller than one inch, decrease the pixels proportionally.

When creating these bitmaps, start with the largest one. Then you can use any bitmap-editing utility to reduce the pixel size. For some images, you might want to fine-tune or completely redraw the smaller versions.

As you might have noticed when examining the various icon files that the Xamarin.Forms template includes with the iOS project, not every bitmap comes in all three resolutions. If iOS can't find a bitmap with the particular suffix it wants, it will fall back and use one of the others, scaling the bitmap up or down in the process.

Device-independent bitmaps for Android

For Android, bitmaps are stored in various subfolders of **Resources** that correspond to a pixel resolution of the screen. Android defines six different directory names for six different levels of device resolution:

- **drawable-ldpi** (low DPI) for 120 DPI devices (0.75 pixels to the DIU)

- **drawable-mdpi** (medium) for 160 DPI devices (1 pixel to the DIU)

- **drawable-hdpi** (high) for 240 DPI devices (1.5 pixels to the DIU))

- **drawable-xhdpi** (extra high) for 320 DPI devices (2 pixels to the DIU)

- **drawable-xxhdpi** (extra extra high) for 480 DPI devices (3 pixels to the DIU)

- **drawable-xxxhdpi** (three extra highs) for 640 DPI devices (4 pixels to the DIU)

If you want a bitmap named MyImage.jpg to render as a one-inch square on the screen, you can supply up to six versions of this bitmap using the same name in all these directories. The size of this one-inch-square bitmap in pixels is equal to the DPI associated with that directory:

- drawable-ldpi/MyImage.jpg — 120 pixels square

- drawable-mdpi/MyImage.jpg — 160 pixels square

- drawable-hdpi/MyImage.jpg — 240 pixels square

- drawable-xhdpi/MyImage.jpg — 320 pixels square

- drawable-xxdpi/MyImage.jpg — 480 pixels square

- drawable-xxxhdpi/MyImage.jpg — 640 pixels square

The bitmap will render as 160 device-independent units.

You are not required to create bitmaps for all six resolutions. The Android project created by the Xamarin.Forms template includes only **drawable-hdpi**, **drawable-xhdpi**, and **drawable-xxdpi**, as well as an unnecessary **drawable** folder with no suffix. These encompass the most common devices. If the Android operating system does not find a bitmap of the desired resolution, it will fall back to a size that is available and scale it.

Device-independent bitmaps for Windows Phone

For a bitmap to be rendered as one inch square on Windows Phone, make it 240 pixels square.

Let's look at a program that actually does supply custom bitmaps of various sizes for the three platforms. These bitmaps are intended to be rendered about one inch square, which is approximately half the width of the phone's screen in portrait mode.

This **ImageTap** program creates a pair of rudimentary, tappable button-like objects that display not text but a bitmap. The two buttons that **ImageTap** creates might substitute for traditional **OK** and **Cancel** buttons, but perhaps you want to use faces from famous paintings for the buttons. Perhaps you want the **OK** button to display the face of Botticelli's Venus and the **Cancel** button to display the distressed man in Edvard Munch's *The Scream*.

In the sample code for this chapter is a directory named **Images** that contains such images, named Venus_xxx.jpg and Scream_xxx.jpg, where the xxx indicates the pixel size. Each image is in eight different sizes: 60, 80, 120, 160, 240, 320, 480, and 640 pixels square. In addition, some of the files have names of Venus_xxx_id.jpg and Scream_xxx_id.jpg. These versions have the actual pixel size displayed in the lower-right corner of the image so that we can see on the screen exactly what bitmap the operating system has selected.

To avoid confusion, the bitmaps with the original names were added to the project folders first, and then they were renamed within Visual Studio.

In the **Resources** folder of the iOS project, the following files were renamed:

- Venus_160_id.jpg became Venus.jpg

- Venus_320_id.jpg because Venus@2x.jpg

- Venus_480_id.jpg became Venus@3x.jpg

This was done similarly for the Scream.jpg bitmaps.

In the various subfolders of the Android project **Resources** folder, the following files were renamed:

- Venus_160_id.jpg became drawable-mdpi/Venus.jpg

- Venus_240_id.jpg became drawable-hdpi/Venus.jpg

- Venus_320_id.jpg became drawable-xhdpi/Venus.jpg

- Venus_480_id.jpg became drawable_xxhdpi/Venus.jpg

And similarly for the Scream.jpg bitmaps.

For the Windows Phone project, the Venus_240_id.jpg and Scream_240_id.jpg files were copied to the **Assets** folder and renamed Venus.jpg and Scream.jpg.

Each of the projects requires a different **Build Action** for these bitmaps. This should be set automatically when you add the files to the projects, but you definitely want to double-check to make sure the **Build Action** is set correctly:

- iOS: **BundleResource**

- Android: **AndroidResource**

- Windows Phone: **Content**

You don't have to memorize these. When in doubt, just check the **Build Action** for the bitmaps included by the Xamarin.Forms solution template in the platform projects.

The XAML file for the **ImageTap** program puts each of the two `Image` elements on a `ContentView` that is colored white from an implicit style. This white `ContentView` is entirely covered by the `Image`, but (as you'll see) it comes into play when the program flashes the picture to signal that it's been tapped.

```
<ContentPage xmlns="http://xamarin.com/schemas/2014/forms"
             xmlns:x="http://schemas.microsoft.com/winfx/2009/xaml"
             x:Class="ImageTap.ImageTapPage">

    <StackLayout>
        <StackLayout.Resources>
```

```
            <ResourceDictionary>
                <Style TargetType="ContentView">
                    <Setter Property="BackgroundColor" Value="White" />
                    <Setter Property="HorizontalOptions" Value="Center" />
                    <Setter Property="VerticalOptions" Value="CenterAndExpand" />
                </Style>
            </ResourceDictionary>
        </StackLayout.Resources>

        <ContentView>
            <Image>
                <Image.Source>
                    <OnPlatform x:TypeArguments="ImageSource"
                                iOS="Venus.jpg"
                                Android="Venus.jpg"
                                WinPhone="Assets/Venus.jpg" />
                </Image.Source>

                <Image.GestureRecognizers>
                    <TapGestureRecognizer Tapped="OnImageTapped" />
                </Image.GestureRecognizers>
            </Image>
        </ContentView>

        <ContentView>
            <Image>
                <Image.Source>
                    <OnPlatform x:TypeArguments="ImageSource"
                                iOS="Scream.jpg"
                                Android="Scream.jpg"
                                WinPhone="Assets/Scream.jpg" />
                </Image.Source>

                <Image.GestureRecognizers>
                    <TapGestureRecognizer Tapped="OnImageTapped" />
                </Image.GestureRecognizers>
            </Image>
        </ContentView>

        <Label x:Name="label"
                FontSize="Large"
                HorizontalOptions="Center"
                VerticalOptions="CenterAndExpand" />

    </StackLayout>
</ContentPage>
```

The XAML file uses `OnPlatform` to select the filenames of the platform resources. Notice that the `x:TypeArguments` attribute of `OnPlatform` is set to `ImageSource` because this type must exactly match the type of the target property, which is the `Source` property of `Image`. `ImageSource` defines an implicit conversion of `string` to itself, so specifying the filenames is sufficient. (The logic for this implicit conversion checks first whether the string has a URI prefix. If not, it assumes that the string is the name of an embedded file in the platform project.)

If you want to avoid using `OnPlatform` entirely in programs that use platform bitmaps, you can put the Windows Phone bitmaps in the root directory of the project rather than in the **Assets** folder.

Tapping one of these buttons does two things: The `Tapped` handler sets the `Opacity` property of the `Image` to 0.75, which results in partially revealing the white `ContentView` background and simulating a flash. A timer restores the `Opacity` to the default value of one tenth of a second later. The `Tapped` handler also displays the rendered size of the `Image` element:

```
public partial class ImageTapPage : ContentPage
{
    public ImageTapPage()
    {
        InitializeComponent();
    }

    void OnImageTapped(object sender, EventArgs args)
    {
        Image image = (Image)sender;
        image.Opacity = 0.75;

        Device.StartTimer(TimeSpan.FromMilliseconds(100), () =>
            {
                image.Opacity = 1;
                return false;
            });

        label.Text = String.Format("Rendered Image is {0} x {1}",
                                    image.Width, image.Height);

    }
}
```

That rendered size compared with the pixel sizes on the bitmaps confirms that iOS and Android have indeed selected the optimum bitmap:

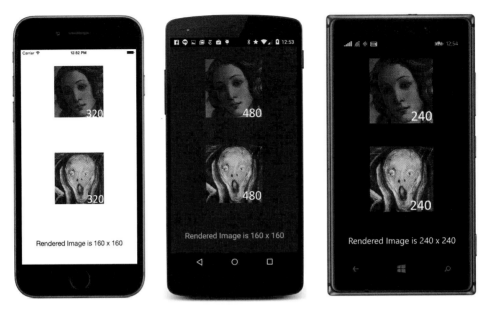

These buttons occupy roughly half the width of the screen on all three platforms. This sizing is based entirely on the size of the bitmaps themselves, without any additional sizing information in the code or markup.

Toolbars and their icons

One of the primary uses of bitmaps in the user interface is the Xamarin.Forms toolbar, which appears at the top of the page on iOS and Android devices and at the bottom of the page on Windows Phone devices. Toolbar items are tappable and fire `Clicked` events much like `Button`.

There is no class for toolbar itself. Instead, you add objects of type `ToolbarItem` to the `ToolbarItems` collection property defined by `Page`.

The `ToolbarItem` class does not derive from `View` like `Label` and `Button`. It instead derives from `Element` by way of `MenuItemBase` and `MenuItem`. (`MenuItem` is used only in connection with the `TableView` and won't be discussed until Chapter 19.) To define the characteristics of a toolbar item, use the following properties:

- `Text` — the text that might appear (depending on the platform and `Order`)

- `Icon` — a `FileImageSource` object referencing a bitmap from the platform project

- `Order` — a member of the `ToolbarItemOrder` enumeration: `Default`, `Primary`, or `Secondary`

There is also a `Name` property, but it just duplicates the `Text` property and should be considered obsolete.

```
            <ToolbarItem Text="search"
                         Order="Primary"
                         Clicked="OnToolbarItemClicked">
                <ToolbarItem.Icon>
                    <OnPlatform x:TypeArguments="FileImageSource"
                                iOS="search.png"
                                Android="ic_action_search.png"
                                WinPhone="Images/feature.search.png" />
                </ToolbarItem.Icon>
            </ToolbarItem>

            <ToolbarItem Text="refresh"
                         Order="Primary"
                         Clicked="OnToolbarItemClicked">
                <ToolbarItem.Icon>
                    <OnPlatform x:TypeArguments="FileImageSource"
                                iOS="reload.png"
                                Android="ic_action_refresh.png"
                                WinPhone="Images/refresh.png" />
                </ToolbarItem.Icon>
            </ToolbarItem>

            <ToolbarItem Text="explore"
                         Order="Secondary"
                         Clicked="OnToolbarItemClicked" />

            <ToolbarItem Text="discover"
                         Order="Secondary"
                         Clicked="OnToolbarItemClicked" />

            <ToolbarItem Text="evolve"
                         Order="Secondary"
                         Clicked="OnToolbarItemClicked" />
        </ContentPage.ToolbarItems>
</ContentPage>
```

All the `Clicked` events have the same handler assigned. You can use unique handlers for the items, of course. This handler just displays the text of the `ToolbarItem` using the centered `Label`:

```
public partial class ToolbarDemoPage : ContentPage
{
    public ToolbarDemoPage()
    {
        InitializeComponent();
    }

    void OnToolbarItemClicked(object sender, EventArgs args)
    {
        ToolbarItem toolbarItem = (ToolbarItem)sender;
        label.Text = "ToolbarItem '" + toolbarItem.Text + "' clicked";
    }
}
```

The screen shots show the icon toolbar items (and for iOS, the text items) and the centered `Label` with the most recently clicked item:

If you tap the ellipsis at the top of the Android screen or the ellipsis at the lower-right corner of the Windows Phone screen, the text items are displayed and, in addition, the text items associated with the icons are also displayed on Windows Phone:

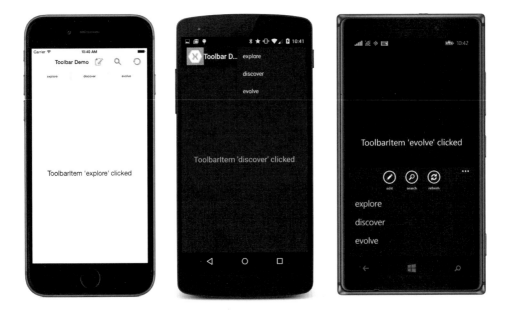

Regardless of the platform, the toolbar is the standard way to add common commands to a phone application.

Button images

`Button` defines an `Image` property of type `FileImageSource` that you can use to supply a small supplemental image that is displayed to the left of the button text. This feature is *not* intended for an image-only button; if that's what you want, the **ImageTap** program in this chapter is a good starting point.

You want the images to be about one-fifth inch in size. That means you want them to render at 32 device-independent units and to show up against the background of the `Button`. For iOS, that means a black image against a white or transparent background. For Android and Windows Phone, you'll want a white image against a transparent background. (Unfortunately, if the Windows Phone user switches to a light background scheme, the bitmap won't be visible.)

All the bitmaps in the **ButtonImage** project are from the **Action Bar** directory of the **Android Design Icons** collection and the **03_rating_good** and **03_rating_bad** subdirectories. These are "thumbs up" and "thumbs down" images.

The iOS images are from the **holo_light** directory (black images on transparent backgrounds) with the following filename conversions:

- drawable-mdpi/ic_action_good.png not renamed

- drawable-xhdpi/ic_action_good.png renamed to ic_action_good@2x.png

And similarly for ic_action_bad.png.

The Android images are from the **holo_dark** directory (white images on transparent backgrounds) and include all four sizes from the subdirectories **drawable-mdpi** (32 pixels square), **drawable-hdpi** (48 pixels), **drawable-xhdpi** (64 pixels), and **drawable-xxhdpi** (96 pixels square).

The Windows Phone images are also from the **holo_dark** directory but are only the 32-pixel bitmaps from the **drawable-mdpi** directories. (You might think that you should use 48-pixel bitmaps for Windows Phone, but the implementation of this feature in Xamarin.Forms limits the size, so it doesn't make a difference.)

Here's the XAML file that sets the `Icon` property for two `Button` elements:

```
<ContentPage xmlns="http://xamarin.com/schemas/2014/forms"
             xmlns:x="http://schemas.microsoft.com/winfx/2009/xaml"
             x:Class="ButtonImage.ButtonImagePage">

    <StackLayout VerticalOptions="Center"
                 Spacing="50">

        <StackLayout.Resources>
            <ResourceDictionary>
```

```
                    <Style TargetType="Button">
                        <Setter Property="HorizontalOptions">
                            <Setter.Value>
                                <OnPlatform x:TypeArguments="LayoutOptions"
                                            iOS="Fill"
                                            Android="Center"
                                            WinPhone="Center" />
                            </Setter.Value>
                        </Setter>
                    </Style>
                </ResourceDictionary>
            </StackLayout.Resources>

            <Button Text="Oh Yeah">
                <Button.Image>
                    <OnPlatform x:TypeArguments="FileImageSource"
                                iOS="ic_action_good.png"
                                Android="ic_action_good.png"
                                WinPhone="Assets/ic_action_good.png" />
                </Button.Image>
            </Button>

            <Button Text="No Way">
                <Button.Image>
                    <OnPlatform x:TypeArguments="FileImageSource"
                                iOS="ic_action_bad.png"
                                Android="ic_action_bad.png"
                                WinPhone="Assets/ic_action_bad.png" />
                </Button.Image>
            </Button>
        </StackLayout>
</ContentPage>
```

That implicit `Style` definition for `Button` requires an explanation: Originally, the buttons were given a `HorizontalOptions` of `Center` to prevent the button border from stretching to the sides of the screen on Android and Windows Phone. However, with that setting, the iOS button wasn't sizing itself correctly and truncated the button text. For that reason, this implicit `Style` gives the iOS button a `HorizontalOptions` setting of `Fill`. The iOS button doesn't have a border, so that setting doesn't change its appearance:

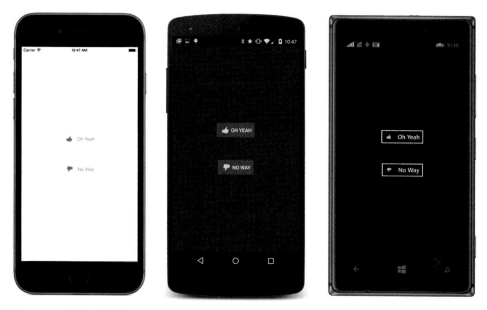

It's not much, but the bitmap adds a little panache to the normally text-only `Button`.

Another significant use for small bitmaps is the context menu available for items in the `TableView`. But a prerequisite for that is a deep exploration of the various views that contribute to the interactive interface of Xamarin.Forms. That's coming up in Chapter 15.

But first let's look at an alternative to `StackLayout` that lets you position child views in a completely flexible manner.

Chapter 14
Absolute layout

In Xamarin.Forms, the concept of layout encompasses all the ways that various views can be assembled on the screen. Here's the class hierarchy showing all the classes that derive from `Layout`:

```
System.Object
    BindableObject
        Element
            VisualElement
                View
                    Layout
                        ContentView
                            Frame
                        ScrollView
                        Layout<T>
                            AbsoluteLayout
                            Grid
                            RelativeLayout
                            StackLayout
```

You've already seen `ContentView`, `Frame`, and `ScrollView` (all of which have a `Content` property that you can set to one child), and you've seen `StackLayout`, which inherits a `Children` property from `Layout<T>` and displays its children in a vertical or horizontal stack. The `Grid` and `Relative-Layout` implement somewhat complex layout models and are explored in future chapters. `Absolute-Layout` is the subject of this chapter.

At first, the `AbsoluteLayout` class seems to implement a rather primitive layout model—one that harks back to the not-so-good old days of graphical user interfaces when programmers were required to individually size and position every element on the screen. Yet, you'll discover that `AbsoluteLay-out` also incorporates a proportional positioning and sizing feature that helps brings this ancient layout model into the modern age.

With `AbsoluteLayout`, many of the rules about layout that you've learned so far no longer apply: the `HorizontalOptions` and `VerticalOptions` properties that are so important when a `View` is the child of a `ContentPage` or `StackLayout` have absolutely no effect when a `View` is a child of an `Ab-soluteLayout`. A program must instead assign to each child of an `AbsoluteLayout` a specific location in device-independent coordinates. The child can also be assigned a specific size or allowed to size itself.

You can use `AbsoluteLayout` either in code or in XAML. For XAML, the class makes use of a feature supported by `BindableObject` and `BindableProperty`. This is the *attached bindable property*, which is a special type of bindable property that can be set on an instance of a class other than the class that defines the property.

AbsoluteLayout in code

You can add a child view to the `Children` collection of an `AbsoluteLayout` the same way as with `StackLayout`:

```
absoluteLayout.Children.Add(child);
```

However, you also have other options. The `AbsoluteLayout` redefines its `Children` property to be of type `AbsoluteLayout.IAbsoluteList<View>`, which includes two additional `Add` methods that allow you to specify the position of the child and (optionally) its size.

To specify both the position and size, you use a `Rectangle` value. `Rectangle` is a structure, and you can create a `Rectangle` value with a constructor that accepts `Point` and `Size` values:

```
Point point = new Point(x, y);
Size size = new Size(width, height);
Rectangle rect = new Rectangle(point, size);
```

Or you can pass the `x`, `y`, `width`, and `height` arguments directly to a `Rectangle` constructor:

```
Rectangle rect = new Rectangle(x, y, width, height);
```

You can then use an alternative `Add` method to add a view to the `Children` collection of the `AbsoluteLayout`:

```
absoluteLayout.Children.Add(child, rect);
```

The `x` and `y` values indicate the position of the upper-left corner of the child view relative to the upper-left corner of the `AbsoluteLayout` parent in device-independent coordinates. If you prefer the child to size itself, you can use just a `Point` value:

```
absoluteLayout.Children.Add(child, point);
```

Here's a little demo:

```
public class AbsoluteDemoPage : ContentPage
{
    public AbsoluteDemoPage()
    {
        AbsoluteLayout absoluteLayout = new AbsoluteLayout
        {
            Padding = new Thickness(50)
        };

        absoluteLayout.Children.Add(
```

```
    new BoxView
    {
        Color = Color.Accent
    },
    new Rectangle(0, 10, 200, 5));

absoluteLayout.Children.Add(
    new BoxView
    {
        Color = Color.Accent
    },
    new Rectangle(0, 20, 200, 5));

absoluteLayout.Children.Add(
    new BoxView
    {
        Color = Color.Accent
    },
    new Rectangle(10, 0, 5, 65));

absoluteLayout.Children.Add(
    new BoxView
    {
        Color = Color.Accent
    },
    new Rectangle(20, 0, 5, 65));

absoluteLayout.Children.Add(
    new Label
    {
        Text = "Stylish Header",
        FontSize = 24
    },
    new Point(30, 25));

absoluteLayout.Children.Add(
    new Label
    {
        FormattedText = new FormattedString
        {
            Spans =
            {
                new Span
                {
                    Text = "Although the "
                },
                new Span
                {
                    Text = "AbsoluteLayout",
                    FontAttributes = FontAttributes.Italic
                },
                new Span
                {
                    Text = " is usually employed for purposes other " +
```

```
                              "than the display of text using "
                },
                new Span
                {
                    Text = "Label",
                    FontAttributes = FontAttributes.Italic
                },
                new Span
                {
                    Text = ", obviously it can be used in that way. " +
                          "The text continues to wrap nicely " +
                          "within the bounds of the container " +
                          "and any padding that might be applied."
                }
            }
        }
    },
    new Point(0, 80));

    this.Content = absoluteLayout;
    }
}
```

Four `BoxView` elements form an overlapping crisscross pattern on the top to set off a header, and then a paragraph of text follows. The program positions and sizes all the `BoxView` elements, while it merely positions the two `Label` views because they size themselves:

A little trial and error was required to get the sizes of the four `BoxView` elements and the header text to be approximately the same size. But notice that the `BoxView` elements overlap: `AbsoluteLayout` allows you to overlap views in a very freeform way that's simply impossible with `StackLayout` (or without using transforms, which are covered in a later chapter).

The big drawback of `AbsoluteLayout` is that you need to come up with the positioning coordinates yourself or calculate them at run time. Anything not explicitly sized—such as the two `Label` views—will have a size that cannot be obtained until after the page is laid out. If you wanted to add another paragraph after the second `Label`, what coordinates would you use?

Actually, you can position multiple paragraphs of text by putting a `StackLayout` (or a `StackLayout` inside a `ScrollView`) in the `AbsoluteLayout` and then putting the `Label` views in that. Layouts can be nested.

As you can surmise, using `AbsoluteLayout` is more difficult than using `StackLayout`. In general it's much easier to let Xamarin.Forms and the other `Layout` classes handle much of the complexity of layout for you. But for some special uses, `AbsoluteLayout` is ideal.

Like all visual elements, `AbsoluteLayout` has its `HorizontalOptions` and `VerticalOptions` properties set to `Fill` by default, which means that `AbsoluteLayout` fills its container. With other settings, an `AbsoluteLayout` sizes itself to the size of its contents, but there are some exceptions: Try giving the `AbsoluteLayout` in the **AbsoluteDemo** program a `BackgroundColor` so that you can see exactly the space it occupies on the screen. It normally fills the whole page, but if you set the `HorizontalOptions` and `VerticalOptions` properties of the `AbsoluteLayout` to `Center`, you'll see that the size that the `AbsoluteLayout` computes for itself includes the contents and padding but only one line of the paragraph of text.

Figuring out sizes for visual elements in an `AbsoluteLayout` can be tricky. One simple approach is demonstrated by the **ChessboardFixed** program below. The program name has the suffix **Fixed** because the position and size of all the squares within the chessboard are set in the constructor. The constructor cannot anticipate the size of the screen, so it arbitrarily sets the size of each square to 35 units, as indicated by the `squareSize` constant at the top of the class. This value should be sufficiently small for the chessboard to fit on the screen of any device supported by Xamarin.Forms.

Notice that the `AbsoluteLayout` is centered so it will have a size that accommodates all its children. The board itself is given a color of buff, which is a pale yellow-brown, and then 32 dark-green `BoxView` elements are displayed in every other square position:

```
public class ChessboardFixedPage : ContentPage
{
    public ChessboardFixedPage()
    {
        const double squareSize = 35;

        AbsoluteLayout absoluteLayout = new AbsoluteLayout
        {
            BackgroundColor = Color.FromRgb(240, 220, 130),
            HorizontalOptions = LayoutOptions.Center,
            VerticalOptions = LayoutOptions.Center
        };
```

```
        for (int row = 0; row < 8; row++)
        {
            for (int col = 0; col < 8; col++)
            {
                // Skip every other square.
                if (((row ^ col) & 1) == 0)
                    continue;

                BoxView boxView = new BoxView
                    {
                        Color = Color.FromRgb(0, 64, 0)
                    };

                Rectangle rect = new Rectangle(col * squareSize,
                                               row * squareSize,
                                               squareSize, squareSize);

                absoluteLayout.Children.Add(boxView, rect);
            }
        }
        this.Content = absoluteLayout;
    }
}
```

The exclusive-or calculation on the `row` and `col` variables causes a `BoxView` to be created only when either the `row` or `col` variable is odd but both are not odd. Here's the result:

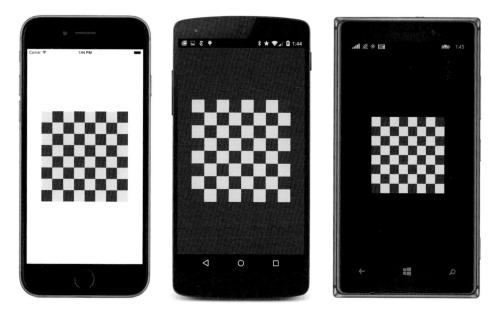

Attached bindable properties

If we wanted this chessboard to be as large as possible within the confines of the screen, we'd need to add the `BoxView` elements to the `AbsoluteLayout` during the `SizeChanged` handler for the page, or the `SizeChanged` handler would need to find some way to change the position and size of the `Box-View` elements already in the `Children` collection.

Both options are possible, but the second one is preferred because we can fill the `Children` collection of the `AbsoluteLayout` only once in the program's constructor and then adjust the sizes and position later.

At first encounter, the syntax to set the position and size of a child within an `AbsoluteLayout` might seem somewhat odd. If `view` is an object of type `View` and `rect` is a `Rectangle` value, here's the statement that gives `view` a location and size of `rect`:

```
AbsoluteLayout.SetLayoutBounds(view, rect);
```

That's not an instance of `AbsoluteLayout` on which you're making a `SetLayoutBounds` call. No. That's a static method of the `AbsoluteLayout` class. You can call `AbsoluteLayout.SetLayout-Bounds` either before or after you add the `view` child to the `AbsoluteLayout` children collection. Indeed, because it's a static method, you can call the method before the `AbsoluteLayout` has even been instantiated! A particular instance of `AbsoluteLayout` is not involved at all in this `SetLayout-Bounds` method.

Let's look at some code that makes use of this mysterious `AbsoluteLayout.SetLayoutBounds` method and then examine how it works.

The **ChessboardDynamic** program page constructor uses the simple `Add` method without positioning or sizing to add 32 `BoxView` elements to the `AbsoluteLayout` in one `for` loop. To provide a little margin around the chessboard, the `AbsoluteLayout` is a child of a `ContentView` and padding is set on the page. This `ContentView` has a `SizeChanged` handler to position and size the `AbsoluteLay-out` children based on the size of the container:

```
public class ChessboardDynamicPage : ContentPage
{
    AbsoluteLayout absoluteLayout;

    public ChessboardDynamicPage()
    {
        absoluteLayout = new AbsoluteLayout
        {
            BackgroundColor = Color.FromRgb(240, 220, 130),
            HorizontalOptions = LayoutOptions.Center,
            VerticalOptions = LayoutOptions.Center
        };

        for (int i = 0; i < 32; i++)
        {
```

```
                BoxView boxView = new BoxView
                   {
                        Color = Color.FromRgb(0, 64, 0)
                   };
                absoluteLayout.Children.Add(boxView);
        }

        ContentView contentView = new ContentView
        {
            Content = absoluteLayout
        };
        contentView.SizeChanged += OnContentViewSizeChanged;

        this.Padding = new Thickness(5, Device.OnPlatform(25, 5, 5), 5, 5);
        this.Content = contentView;
    }

    void OnContentViewSizeChanged(object sender, EventArgs args)
    {
        ContentView contentView = (ContentView)sender;
        double squareSize = Math.Min(contentView.Width, contentView.Height) / 8;
        int index = 0;

        for (int row = 0; row < 8; row++)
        {
            for (int col = 0; col < 8; col++)
            {
                // Skip every other square.
                if (((row ^ col) & 1) == 0)
                    continue;

                View view = absoluteLayout.Children[index];
                Rectangle rect = new Rectangle(col * squareSize,
                                               row * squareSize,
                                               squareSize, squareSize);

                AbsoluteLayout.SetLayoutBounds(view, rect);
                index++;
            }
        }
    }
}
```

The `SizeChanged` handler contains much the same logic as the constructor in **ChessboardFixed** except that the `BoxView` elements are already in the `Children` collection of the `AbsoluteLayout`. All that's necessary is to position and size each `BoxView` when the size of the container changes—for example, during phone orientation changes. The `for` loop concludes with a call to the static `Absolute-Layout.SetLayoutBounds` method for each `BoxView` with a calculated `Rectangle` value.

Now the chessboard is sized to fit the screen with a little margin:

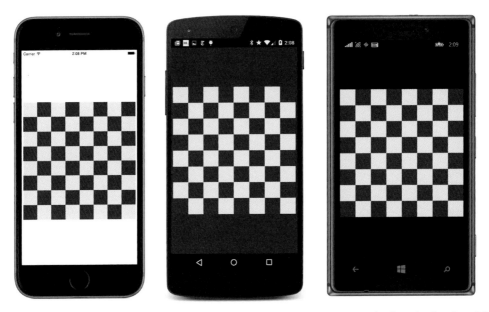

Obviously, the mysterious `AbsoluteLayout.SetLayoutBounds` method works, but how? What does it do? And how does it manage to do what it does without referencing a particular `Absolute-Layout` object?

The `AbsoluteLayout.SetLayoutBounds` call in the `SizeChanged` event handler in `Chess-boardDynamicPage` is this:

```
AbsoluteLayout.SetLayoutBounds(view, rect);
```

That method call is exactly equivalent to the following call on the child view:

```
view.SetValue(AbsoluteLayout.LayoutBoundsProperty, rect);
```

This is a `SetValue` call on the child view. These two method calls are exactly equivalent because the second one is how `AbsoluteLayout` internally defines the `SetLayoutBounds` static method. `Abso-luteLayout.SetLayoutBounds` is merely a shortcut method, and the similar static `AbsoluteLay-out.GetLayoutBounds` method is a shortcut for a `GetValue` call.

You'll recall that `SetValue` and `GetValue` are defined by `BindableObject` and used to imple-ment bindable properties. Judging solely from the name, `AbsoluteLayout.LayoutBoundsProperty` certainly appears to be a `BindableProperty` object, and that is so. However, it is a very special type of bindable property called an *attached bindable property*.

Normal bindable properties can be set only on instances of the class that defines the property or on instances of a derived class. Attached bindable properties can break that rule: Attached bindable prop-erties are defined by one class—in this case `AbsoluteLayout`—but set on another object, in this case a child of the `AbsoluteLayout`. The property is sometimes said to be *attached* to the child, hence the name.

The child of the `AbsoluteLayout` is ignorant of the purpose of the attached bindable property passed to its `SetValue` method, and the child makes no use of that value in its own internal logic. The `SetValue` method of the child simply saves the `Rectangle` value in a dictionary maintained by `BindableObject` within the child, in effect attaching this value to the child to be possibly used at some point by the parent—the `AbsoluteLayout` object.

When the `AbsoluteLayout` is laying out its children, it can interrogate the value of this property on each child by calling the `AbsoluteLayout.GetLayoutBounds` static method on the child, which in turn calls `GetValue` on the child with the `AbsoluteLayout.LayoutBoundsProperty` attached bindable property. The call to `GetValue` fetches the `Rectangle` value from the dictionary stored within the child.

You might wonder: Why is such a roundabout process required to set positioning and sizing information on a child of the `AbsoluteLayout`? Wouldn't it have been easier for `View` to define simple `X`, `Y`, `Width`, and `Height` properties that an application could set?

Maybe, but those properties would be suitable only for `AbsoluteLayout`. When using the `Grid`, an application needs to specify `Row` and `Column` values on the children of the `Grid`, and when using a layout class of your own devising, perhaps some other properties are required. Attached bindable properties can handle all these cases and more.

Attached bindable properties are a general-purpose mechanism that allows properties defined by one class to be stored in instances of another class. You can define your own attached bindable properties by using static creation methods of `BindableObject` named `CreateAttached` and `CreateAttachedReadOnly`. (You'll see an example later in this book.)

Attached properties are mostly used with layout classes. As you'll see, `Grid` defines attached bindable properties to specify the row and column of each child, and `RelativeLayout` also defines attached bindable properties.

Earlier you saw additional `Add` methods defined by the `Children` collection of `AbsoluteLayout`. These are actually implemented using these attached bindable properties. The call

```
absoluteLayout.Children.Add(view, rect);
```

is implemented like this:

```
AbsoluteLayout.SetLayoutBounds(view, rect);
absoluteLayout.Children.Add(view);
```

The `Add` call with only a `Point` argument merely sets the child's position and lets the child size itself:

```
absoluteLayout.Children.Add(view, new Point(x, y));
```

This is implemented with the same static `AbsoluteLayout.SetLayoutBounds` calls but using a special constant for the view's width and height:

```
AbsoluteLayout.SetLayoutBounds(view,
        new Rectangle(x, y, AbsoluteLayout.AutoSize, AbsoluteLayout.AutoSize));
```

```
absoluteLayout.Children.Add(view);
```

You can use that `AbsoluteLayout.AutoSize` constant in your own code.

Proportional sizing and positioning

As you saw, the **ChessboardDynamic** program repositions and resizes the `BoxView` children with calculations based on the size of the `AbsoluteLayout` itself. In other words, the size and position of each child are proportional to the size of the container. Interestingly, this is often the case with an `AbsoluteLayout`, and it might be nice if `AbsoluteLayout` accommodated such situations automatically.

It does!

`AbsoluteLayout` defines a second attached bindable property, named `LayoutFlagsProperty`, and two more static methods, named `SetLayoutFlags` and `GetLayoutFlags`. Setting this attached bindable property allows you to specify child position coordinates or sizes (or both) that are proportional to the size of the `AbsoluteLayout`. When laying out its children, `AbsoluteLayout` scales those coordinates and sizes appropriately.

You select how this feature works with a member of the `AbsoluteLayoutFlags` enumeration:

- `None` (equal to 0)
- `XProportional` (1)
- `YProportional` (2)
- `PositionProportional` (3)
- `WidthProportional` (4)
- `HeightProportional` (8)
- `SizeProportional` (12)
- `All` (\xFFFFFFFF)

You can set a proportional position and size on a child of `AbsoluteLayout` using the static methods:

```
AbsoluteLayout.SetLayoutBounds(view, rect);
AbsoluteLayout.SetLayoutFlags(view, AbsoluteLayoutFlags.All);
```

Or you can use a version of the `Add` method on the `Children` collection that accepts an `AbsoluteLayoutFlags` enumeration member:

```
absoluteLayout.Children.Add(view, rect, AbsoluteLayoutFlags.All);
```

For example, if you use the `SizeProportional` flag and set the width of the child to 0.25 and the height to 0.10, the child will be one-quarter of the width of the AbsoluteLayout and one-tenth the height. Easy enough.

The PositionProportional flag is similar, but it takes the size of the child into account: a position of (0, 0) puts the child in the upper-left corner, a position of (1, 1) puts the child in the lower-right corner, and a position of (0.5, 0.5) centers the child within the AbsoluteLayout. Taking the size of the child into account is great for some tasks—such as centering a child in an AbsoluteLayout or displaying it against the right or bottom edge—but a bit awkward for other tasks.

Here's **ChessboardProportional**. The bulk of the job of positioning and sizing has been moved back to the constructor. The SizeChanged handler now merely maintains the overall aspect ratio by setting the WidthRequest and HeightRequest properties of the AbsoluteLayout to the minimum of the width and height of the ContentView. Remove that SizeChanged handling and the chessboard expands to the size of the page less the padding.

```csharp
public class ChessboardProportionalPage : ContentPage
{
    AbsoluteLayout absoluteLayout;

    public ChessboardProportionalPage()
    {
        absoluteLayout = new AbsoluteLayout
        {
            BackgroundColor = Color.FromRgb(240, 220, 130),
            HorizontalOptions = LayoutOptions.Center,
            VerticalOptions = LayoutOptions.Center
        };

        for (int row = 0; row < 8; row++)
        {
            for (int col = 0; col < 8; col++)
            {
                // Skip every other square.
                if (((row ^ col) & 1) == 0)
                    continue;

                BoxView boxView = new BoxView
                {
                    Color = Color.FromRgb(0, 64, 0)
                };

                Rectangle rect = new Rectangle(col / 7.0,    // x
                                               row / 7.0,    // y
                                               1 / 8.0,      // width
                                               1 / 8.0);     // height

                absoluteLayout.Children.Add(boxView, rect, AbsoluteLayoutFlags.All);
            }
        }

        ContentView contentView = new ContentView
```

```
    {
        Content = absoluteLayout
    };
    contentView.SizeChanged += OnContentViewSizeChanged;

    this.Padding = new Thickness(5, Device.OnPlatform(25, 5, 5), 5, 5);
    this.Content = contentView;
}

void OnContentViewSizeChanged(object sender, EventArgs args)
{
    ContentView contentView = (ContentView)sender;
    double boardSize = Math.Min(contentView.Width, contentView.Height);
    absoluteLayout.WidthRequest = boardSize;
    absoluteLayout.HeightRequest = boardSize;
}
}
```

The screen looks the same as the **ChessboardDynamic** program.

Each `BoxView` is added to the `AbsoluteLayout` with the following code. All the denominators are floating-point values, so the results of the divisions are converted to `double`:

```
Rectangle rect = new Rectangle(col / 7.0,    // x
                               row / 7.0,    // y
                               1 / 8.0,      // width
                               1 / 8.0);     // height

absoluteLayout.Children.Add(boxView, rect, AbsoluteLayoutFlags.All);
```

The width and height are always equal to one-eighth the width and height of the `AbsoluteLayout`. That much is clear. But the `row` and `col` variables are divided by 7 (rather than 8) for the relative x and y coordinates. The `row` and `col` variables in the `for` loops range from 0 through 7. The `row` and `col` values of 0 correspond to left or top, but `row` and `col` values of 7 must map to x and y coordinates of 1 to position the child against the right or bottom edge.

If you think you might need some solid rules to derive proportional coordinates, read on.

Working with proportional coordinates

Working with proportional positioning in an `AbsoluteLayout` can be tricky. Sometimes you need to compensate for the internal calculation that takes the size into account. For example, you might prefer to specify coordinates so that an X value of 1 means that the left edge of the child is positioned at the right edge of the `AbsoluteLayout`, and you'll need to convert that to a coordinate that `Absolute-Layout` understands.

In the discussion that follows, a coordinate that does *not* take size into account—a coordinate in which 1 means that the child is positioned just outside the right or bottom edge of the `AbsoluteLay-out`—is referred to as a *fractional* coordinate. The goal of this section is to develop rules for converting a fractional coordinate to a proportional coordinate that you can use with `AbsoluteLayout`. This conversion requires that you know the size of the child view.

Suppose you're putting a view named `child` in an `AbsoluteLayout` named `absoluteLayout`, with a layout bounds rectangle for the child named `layoutBounds`. Let's restrict this analysis to horizontal coordinates and sizes. The process is the same for vertical coordinates and sizes.

This child must first get a width in some way. The child might calculate its own width, or a width in device-independent units might be assigned to it via the `LayoutBounds` attached property. But let's assume that the `AbsoluteLayoutFlags.WidthProportional` flag is set, which means that the width is calculated based on the `Width` field of the layout bounds and the width of the `AbsoluteLay-out`:

$$child.Width = layoutBounds.Width * absoluteLayout.Width$$

If the `AbsoluteLayoutFlags.XProportional` flag is also set, then internally the `AbsoluteLay-out` calculates a coordinate for the child relative to itself by taking the size of the child into account:

$$relativeChildCoordinate.X = (absoluteLayout.Width - child.Width) * layoutBounds.X$$

For example, if the `AbsoluteLayout` has a width of 400, and the child has a width of 100, and `lay-outBounds.X` is 0.5, then `relativeChildCoordinate.X` is calculated as 150. This means that the left edge of the child is 150 pixels from the left edge of the parent. That causes the child to be horizontally centered within the `AbsoluteLayout`.

It's also possible to calculate a fractional child coordinate:

$$fractionalChildCoordinate.X = \frac{relativeChildCoordinate.X}{absoluteLayout.Width}$$

This is not the same as the proportional coordinate because a fractional child coordinate of 1 means that the child's left edge is just outside the right edge of the `AbsoluteLayout`, and hence the child is outside the surface of the `AbsoluteLayout`. To continue the example, the fractional child coordinate is 150 divided by 400 or 0.375. The left of the child view is positioned at (0.375 * 400) or 150 units from the left edge of the `AbsoluteLayout`.

Let's rearrange the terms of the formula that calculates the relative child coordinate to solve for `layoutBounds.X`:

$$layoutBounds.X = \frac{relativeChildCoordinate.X}{(absoluteLayout.Width - child.Width)}$$

And let's divide both the top and bottom of that ratio by the width of the `AbsoluteLayout`:

$$layoutBounds.X = \frac{fractionalChildCoordinate.X}{\left(1 - \frac{child.Width}{absoluteLayout.Width}\right)}$$

If you're also using proportional width, then that ratio in the denominator is `layout-Bounds.Width`:

$$layoutBounds.X = \frac{fractionalChildCoordinate.X}{(1 - layoutBounds.Width)}$$

And that is often a very handy formula, for it allows you to convert from a fractional child coordinate to a proportional coordinate for use in the layout bounds rectangle.

In the **ChessboardProportional** example, when `col` equals 7, the `fractionalChildCoordinate.X` is 7 divided by the number of columns (8), or 7/8. The denominator is 1 minus 1/8 (the proportional width of the square), or 7/8 again. The ratio is 1.

Let's look at an example where the formula is applied in code to fractional coordinates. The **ProportionalCoordinateCalc** program attempts to reproduce this simple figure using eight blue `BoxView` elements on a pink `AbsoluteLayout`:

The whole figure has a 2:1 aspect. The pairs of horizontal blue rectangles at the top and bottom have a height of 0.1 fractional units (relative to the height of the `AbsoluteLayout`) and are spaced 0.1 units from the top and bottom and between each other. The vertical blue rectangles appear to be spaced and sized similarly, but because the aspect ratio is 2:1, the vertical rectangles have a width of 0.05 units and are spaced with 0.05 units from the left and right and between each other.

The `AbsoluteLayout` is defined and centered in a XAML file and colored pink:

```
<ContentPage xmlns="http://xamarin.com/schemas/2014/forms"
             xmlns:x="http://schemas.microsoft.com/winfx/2009/xaml"
             x:Class="ProportionalCoordinateCalc.ProportionalCoordinateCalcPage">
    <ContentPage.Padding>
        <OnPlatform x:TypeArguments="Thickness"
                    iOS="5, 25, 5, 5"
                    Android="5"
                    WinPhone="5" />
    </ContentPage.Padding>

    <ContentView SizeChanged="OnContentViewSizeChanged">
        <AbsoluteLayout x:Name="absoluteLayout"
                        BackgroundColor="Pink"
                        HorizontalOptions="Center"
                        VerticalOptions="Center" />
    </ContentView>
</ContentPage>
```

The code-behind file defines an array of Rectangle structures with the fractional coordinates for each of the eight BoxView elements. In a foreach loop, the program applies a slight variation of the final formula shown above. Rather than a denominator equal to 1 minus the value of layout-Bounds.Width (or layoutBounds.Height), it uses the Width (or Height) of the fractional bounds, which is the same value.

```
public partial class ProportionalCoordinateCalcPage : ContentPage
{
    public ProportionalCoordinateCalcPage()
    {
        InitializeComponent();

        Rectangle[] fractionalRects =
        {
            new Rectangle(0.05, 0.1, 0.90, 0.1),    // outer top
            new Rectangle(0.05, 0.8, 0.90, 0.1),    // outer bottom
            new Rectangle(0.05, 0.1, 0.05, 0.8),    // outer left
            new Rectangle(0.90, 0.1, 0.05, 0.8),    // outer right

            new Rectangle(0.15, 0.3, 0.70, 0.1),    // inner top
            new Rectangle(0.15, 0.6, 0.70, 0.1),    // inner bottom
            new Rectangle(0.15, 0.3, 0.05, 0.4),    // inner left
            new Rectangle(0.80, 0.3, 0.05, 0.4),    // inner right
        };

        foreach (Rectangle fractionalRect in fractionalRects)
        {
            Rectangle layoutBounds = new Rectangle
            {
                // Proportional coordinate calculations.
                X = fractionalRect.X / (1 - fractionalRect.Width),
                Y = fractionalRect.Y / (1 - fractionalRect.Height),

                Width = fractionalRect.Width,
                Height = fractionalRect.Height
            };

            absoluteLayout.Children.Add(
                new BoxView
                {
                    Color = Color.Blue
                },
                layoutBounds,
                AbsoluteLayoutFlags.All);
        }
    }

    void OnContentViewSizeChanged(object sender, EventArgs args)
    {
        ContentView contentView = (ContentView)sender;

        // Figure has an aspect ratio of 2:1.
        double height = Math.Min(contentView.Width / 2, contentView.Height);
```

```
        absoluteLayout.WidthRequest = 2 * height;
        absoluteLayout.HeightRequest = height;
    }
}
```

The `SizeChanged` handler simply fixes the aspect ratio.

Here's the result:

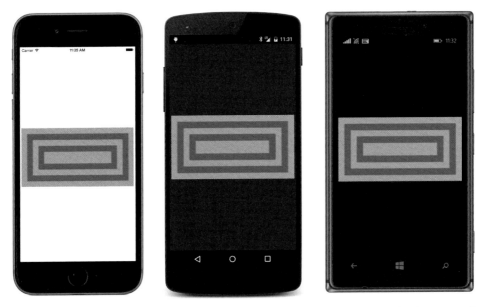

And, of course, you can turn the phone sideways and see a larger figure in landscape mode, which you'll have to view by turning this book sideways:

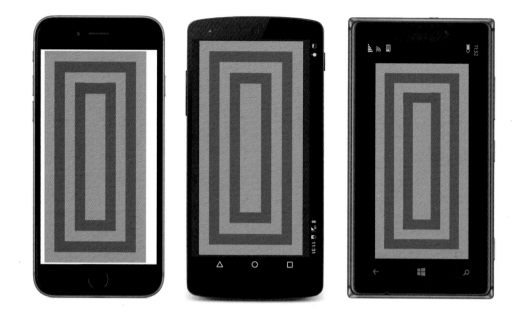

AbsoluteLayout and XAML

As you've seen, you can position and size a child of an `AbsoluteLayout` by using one of the `Add` methods available on the `Children` collection or by setting an attached property through a static method call.

But how on earth do you set the position and size of `AbsoluteLayout` children in XAML?

A very special syntax is involved. This syntax is illustrated by this XAML version of the earlier **AbsoluteDemo** program, called **AbsoluteXamlDemo**:

```
<ContentPage xmlns="http://xamarin.com/schemas/2014/forms"
             xmlns:x="http://schemas.microsoft.com/winfx/2009/xaml"
             x:Class="AbsoluteXamlDemo.AbsoluteXamlDemoPage">

    <AbsoluteLayout Padding="50">
        <BoxView Color="Accent"
                 AbsoluteLayout.LayoutBounds="0, 10, 200, 5" />

        <BoxView Color="Accent"
                 AbsoluteLayout.LayoutBounds="0, 20, 200, 5" />

        <BoxView Color="Accent"
                 AbsoluteLayout.LayoutBounds="10, 0, 5, 65" />

        <BoxView Color="Accent"
                 AbsoluteLayout.LayoutBounds="20, 0, 5, 65" />
```

```
        <Label Text="Stylish Header"
               FontSize="24"
               AbsoluteLayout.LayoutBounds="30, 25, AutoSize, AutoSize" />

        <Label AbsoluteLayout.LayoutBounds="0, 80, AutoSize, AutoSize">
            <Label.FormattedText>
                <FormattedString>
                    <Span Text="Although " />
                    <Span Text="AbsoluteLayout"
                          FontAttributes="Italic" />
                    <Span Text=
" is usually employed for purposes other
than the display of text using " />
                    <Span Text="Label"
                          FontAttributes="Italic" />
                    <Span Text=
", obviously it can be used in that way.
The text continues to wrap nicely
within the bounds of the container
and any padding that might be applied." />

                </FormattedString>
            </Label.FormattedText>
        </Label>
    </AbsoluteLayout>
</ContentPage>
```

The code-behind file contains only an `InitializeComponent` call.

Here's the first `BoxView`:

```
<BoxView Color="Accent"
         AbsoluteLayout.LayoutBounds="0, 10, 200, 5" />
```

In XAML, an attached bindable property is an attribute that consists of a class name (`AbsoluteLayout`) and a property name (`LayoutBounds`) separated by a period. Whenever you see such an attribute, it's an attached bindable property. That's the only application of this attribute syntax.

In summary, combinations of class names and property names only appear in XAML in three specific contexts: If they appear as elements, they are property elements. If they appear as attributes, they are attached bindable properties. And the only other context for a class name and property name is an argument to an `x:Static` markup extension.

In this case, the attribute is set to four numbers separated by commas. You can also express `AbsoluteLayout.LayoutBounds` as a property element:

```
<BoxView Color="Accent">
    <AbsoluteLayout.LayoutBounds>
        0, 10, 200, 5
    </AbsoluteLayout.LayoutBounds>
</BoxView>
```

Those four numbers are parsed by the `BoundsTypeConverter` and not the `RectangleTypeConverter` because the `BoundsTypeConverter` allows the use of `AutoSize` for the width and height parts. You can see the `AutoSize` arguments later in the XAML file:

```
<Label Text="Stylish Header"
       FontSize="24"
       AbsoluteLayout.LayoutBounds="30, 25, AutoSize, AutoSize" />
```

Or you can leave them out:

```
<Label Text="Stylish Header"
       FontSize="24"
       AbsoluteLayout.LayoutBounds="30, 25" />
```

The odd thing about attached bindable properties that you specify in XAML is that they don't really exist! There is no field, property, or method in `AbsoluteLayout` called `LayoutBounds`. There is certainly a public static read-only field of type `BindableProperty` named `LayoutBoundsProperty`, and there are public static methods named `SetLayoutBounds` and `GetLayoutBounds`, but there is nothing named `LayoutBounds`. The XAML parser recognizes the syntax as referring to an attached bindable property and then looks for `LayoutBoundsProperty` in the `AbsoluteLayout` class. From there it can call `SetValue` on the target view with that `BindableProperty` object together with the value from the `BoundsTypeConverter`.

The **Chessboard** series of programs seems an unlikely candidate for duplicating in XAML because the file would need 32 instances of `BoxView` without the benefit of loops. However, the **ChessboardXaml** program shows how to specify two properties of `BoxView` in an implicit style, including the `AbsoluteLayout.LayoutFlags` attached bindable property:

```
<ContentPage xmlns="http://xamarin.com/schemas/2014/forms"
             xmlns:x="http://schemas.microsoft.com/winfx/2009/xaml"
             x:Class="ChessboardXaml.ChessboardXamlPage">

    <ContentPage.Padding>
        <OnPlatform x:TypeArguments="Thickness"
                    iOS="5, 25, 5, 5"
                    Android="5"
                    WinPhone="5" />
    </ContentPage.Padding>

    <ContentPage.Resources>
        <ResourceDictionary>
            <Style TargetType="BoxView">
                <Setter Property="Color" Value="#004000" />
                <Setter Property="AbsoluteLayout.LayoutFlags" Value="All" />
            </Style>
        </ResourceDictionary>
    </ContentPage.Resources>

    <ContentView SizeChanged="OnContentViewSizeChanged">
        <AbsoluteLayout x:Name="absoluteLayout"
                        BackgroundColor="#F0DC82"
```

```
                         VerticalOptions="Center"
                         HorizontalOptions="Center">

        <BoxView AbsoluteLayout.LayoutBounds="0.00, 0.00, 0.125, 0.125" />
        <BoxView AbsoluteLayout.LayoutBounds="0.29, 0.00, 0.125, 0.125" />
        <BoxView AbsoluteLayout.LayoutBounds="0.57, 0.00, 0.125, 0.125" />
        <BoxView AbsoluteLayout.LayoutBounds="0.86, 0.00, 0.125, 0.125" />

        <BoxView AbsoluteLayout.LayoutBounds="0.14, 0.14, 0.125, 0.125" />
        <BoxView AbsoluteLayout.LayoutBounds="0.43, 0.14, 0.125, 0.125" />
        <BoxView AbsoluteLayout.LayoutBounds="0.71, 0.14, 0.125, 0.125" />
        <BoxView AbsoluteLayout.LayoutBounds="1.00, 0.14, 0.125, 0.125" />

        <BoxView AbsoluteLayout.LayoutBounds="0.00, 0.29, 0.125, 0.125" />
        <BoxView AbsoluteLayout.LayoutBounds="0.29, 0.29, 0.125, 0.125" />
        <BoxView AbsoluteLayout.LayoutBounds="0.57, 0.29, 0.125, 0.125" />
        <BoxView AbsoluteLayout.LayoutBounds="0.86, 0.29, 0.125, 0.125" />

        <BoxView AbsoluteLayout.LayoutBounds="0.14, 0.43, 0.125, 0.125" />
        <BoxView AbsoluteLayout.LayoutBounds="0.43, 0.43, 0.125, 0.125" />
        <BoxView AbsoluteLayout.LayoutBounds="0.71, 0.43, 0.125, 0.125" />
        <BoxView AbsoluteLayout.LayoutBounds="1.00, 0.43, 0.125, 0.125" />

        <BoxView AbsoluteLayout.LayoutBounds="0.00, 0.57, 0.125, 0.125" />
        <BoxView AbsoluteLayout.LayoutBounds="0.29, 0.57, 0.125, 0.125" />
        <BoxView AbsoluteLayout.LayoutBounds="0.57, 0.57, 0.125, 0.125" />
        <BoxView AbsoluteLayout.LayoutBounds="0.86, 0.57, 0.125, 0.125" />

        <BoxView AbsoluteLayout.LayoutBounds="0.14, 0.71, 0.125, 0.125" />
        <BoxView AbsoluteLayout.LayoutBounds="0.43, 0.71, 0.125, 0.125" />
        <BoxView AbsoluteLayout.LayoutBounds="0.71, 0.71, 0.125, 0.125" />
        <BoxView AbsoluteLayout.LayoutBounds="1.00, 0.71, 0.125, 0.125" />

        <BoxView AbsoluteLayout.LayoutBounds="0.00, 0.86, 0.125, 0.125" />
        <BoxView AbsoluteLayout.LayoutBounds="0.29, 0.86, 0.125, 0.125" />
        <BoxView AbsoluteLayout.LayoutBounds="0.57, 0.86, 0.125, 0.125" />
        <BoxView AbsoluteLayout.LayoutBounds="0.86, 0.86, 0.125, 0.125" />

        <BoxView AbsoluteLayout.LayoutBounds="0.14, 1.00, 0.125, 0.125" />
        <BoxView AbsoluteLayout.LayoutBounds="0.43, 1.00, 0.125, 0.125" />
        <BoxView AbsoluteLayout.LayoutBounds="0.71, 1.00, 0.125, 0.125" />
        <BoxView AbsoluteLayout.LayoutBounds="1.00, 1.00, 0.125, 0.125" />
    </AbsoluteLayout>
  </ContentView>
</ContentPage>
```

Yes, it's a lot of individual `BoxView` elements, but you can't argue with the cleanliness of the file. The code-behind file simply adjusts the aspect ratio:

```
public partial class ChessboardXamlPage : ContentPage
{
    public ChessboardXamlPage()
    {
        InitializeComponent();
```

```
    }

    void OnContentViewSizeChanged(object sender, EventArgs args)
    {
        ContentView contentView = (ContentView)sender;
        double boardSize = Math.Min(contentView.Width, contentView.Height);
        absoluteLayout.WidthRequest = boardSize;
        absoluteLayout.HeightRequest = boardSize;
    }
}
```

Overlays

The ability to overlap children in the `AbsoluteLayout` has some interesting and useful applications, among them being the ability to cover up your entire user interface with something sometimes called an *overlay*. Perhaps your page is carrying out a lengthy job and you don't want the user interacting with the page until the job is completed. You can place a semitransparent overlay over the page and perhaps display an `ActivityIndicator` or a `ProgressBar`.

Here's a program called **SimpleOverlay** that demonstrates this technique. The XAML file begins with an `AbsoluteLayout` covering the entire page. The first child of that `AbsoluteLayout` is a `StackLayout`, which you want to fill the page as well. However, the default `HorizontalOptions` and `VerticalOptions` settings of `Fill` on the `StackLayout` don't work for children of an `Absolute-Layout`. Instead, the `StackLayout` fills the `AbsoluteLayout` through the use of the `AbsoluteLay-out.LayoutBounds` and `AbsoluteLayout.LayoutFlags` attached bindable properties:

```
<ContentPage xmlns="http://xamarin.com/schemas/2014/forms"
             xmlns:x="http://schemas.microsoft.com/winfx/2009/xaml"
             x:Class="SimpleOverlay.SimpleOverlayPage">
    <AbsoluteLayout>
        <StackLayout AbsoluteLayout.LayoutBounds="0, 0, 1, 1"
                     AbsoluteLayout.LayoutFlags="All">
            <Label Text=
"This might be a page full of user-interface objects except
that the only functional user-interface object on the page
is a Button."
                   FontSize="Large"
                   VerticalOptions="CenterAndExpand"
                   XAlign="Center" />

            <Button Text="Run 5-Second Job"
                    FontSize="Large"
                    VerticalOptions="CenterAndExpand"
                    HorizontalOptions="Center"
                    Clicked="OnButtonClicked" />

            <Button Text="A Do-Nothing Button"
                    FontSize="Large"
                    VerticalOptions="CenterAndExpand"
```

```
                        HorizontalOptions="Center" />

            <Label Text=
"This continues the page full of user-interface objects except
that the only functional user-interface object on the page
is the Button."
                      FontSize="Large"
                      VerticalOptions="CenterAndExpand"
                      XAlign="Center" />
        </StackLayout>

        <!-- Overlay -->
        <ContentView x:Name="overlay"
                     AbsoluteLayout.LayoutBounds="0, 0, 1, 1"
                     AbsoluteLayout.LayoutFlags="All"
                     IsVisible="False"
                     BackgroundColor="#C0808080"
                     Padding="10, 0">

            <ProgressBar x:Name="progressBar"
                         VerticalOptions="Center" />

        </ContentView>
    </AbsoluteLayout>
</ContentPage>
```

The second child of the `AbsoluteLayout` is a `ContentView`, which also fills the `AbsoluteLayout` and basically sits on top of the `StackLayout`. However, notice that the `IsVisible` property is set to `False`, which means that this `ContentView` and its children do not participate in the layout. The `ContentView` is still a child of the `AbsoluteLayout`, but it's simply skipped when the layout system is sizing and rendering all the elements of the page.

This `ContentView` is the overlay. When `IsVisible` is set to `True`, it blocks user input to the views below it. The `BackgroundColor` is set to a semitransparent gray, and a `ProgressBar` is vertically centered within it.

A `ProgressBar` resembles a `Slider` without a thumb. A `ProgressBar` is always horizontally oriented. Do not set the `HorizontalOptions` property of a `ProgressBar` to `Start`, `Center`, or `End` unless you also set its `WidthRequest` property.

A program can indicate progress by setting the `Progress` property of the `ProgressBar` to a value between 0 and 1. This is demonstrated in the `Clicked` handler for the only functional `Button` in the application. This handler simulates a lengthy job being performed in code with a timer that determines when five seconds have elapsed:

```
public partial class SimpleOverlayPage : ContentPage
{
    public SimpleOverlayPage()
    {
        InitializeComponent();
    }
```

```
void OnButtonClicked(object sender, EventArgs args)
{
    // Show overlay with ProgressBar.
    overlay.IsVisible = true;

    TimeSpan duration = TimeSpan.FromSeconds(5);
    DateTime startTime = DateTime.Now;

    // Start timer.
    Device.StartTimer(TimeSpan.FromSeconds(0.1), () =>
        {
            double progress = (DateTime.Now - startTime).TotalMilliseconds /
                                duration.TotalMilliseconds;
            progressBar.Progress = progress;
            bool continueTimer = progress < 1;

            if (!continueTimer)
            {
                // Hide overlay.
                overlay.IsVisible = false;
            }
            return continueTimer;
        });
}
}
```

The `Clicked` handler begins by setting the `IsVisible` property of the overlay to `true`, which re-veals the overlay and its child `ProgressBar` and prevents further interaction with the user interface underneath. The timer is set for one-tenth second and calculates a new `Progress` property for the `ProgressBar` based on the elapsed time. When the five seconds are up, the overlay is again hidden and the timer callback returns `false`.

Here's what it looks like with the overlay covering the page and the lengthy job in progress:

An overlay need not be restricted to a `ProgressBar` or an `ActivityIndicator`. You can include a **Cancel** button or other views.

Some fun

As you can probably see by now, the `AbsoluteLayout` is often used for some special purposes that wouldn't be easy otherwise. Some of these might actually be classified as "fun."

DotMatrixClock displays the digits of the current time using a simulated 5 × 7 dot matrix display. Each dot is a `BoxView`, individually sized and positioned on the screen and colored either red or light-gray depending on whether the dot is on or off. Conceivably, the dots of this clock could be organized in nested `StackLayout` elements or a `Grid`, but each `BoxView` needs to be given a size anyway. The sheer quantity and regularity of these views suggests that the programmer knows better than a layout class how to arrange them on the screen, as the layout class needs to perform the location calculations in a more generalized manner. For that reason, this is an ideal job for `AbsoluteLayout`.

A XAML file sets a little padding on the page and prepares an `AbsoluteLayout` for filling by code:

```
<ContentPage xmlns="http://xamarin.com/schemas/2014/forms"
             xmlns:x="http://schemas.microsoft.com/winfx/2009/xaml"
             x:Class="DotMatrixClock.DotMatrixClockPage"
             Padding="10"
             SizeChanged="OnPageSizeChanged">

    <AbsoluteLayout x:Name="absoluteLayout"
                    VerticalOptions="Center" />
```

```
</ContentPage>
```

The code-behind file contains several fields, including two arrays, named `numberPatterns` and `colonPattern`, that define the dot matrix patterns for the 10 digits and a colon separator:

```
public partial class DotMatrixClockPage : ContentPage
{
    // Total dots horizontally and vertically.
    const int horzDots = 41;
    const int vertDots = 7;

    // 5 x 7 dot matrix patterns for 0 through 9.
    static readonly int[,,] numberPatterns = new int[10,7,5]
    {
        {
            { 0, 1, 1, 1, 0}, { 1, 0, 0, 0, 1}, { 1, 0, 0, 1, 1}, { 1, 0, 1, 0, 1},
            { 1, 1, 0, 0, 1}, { 1, 0, 0, 0, 1}, { 0, 1, 1, 1, 0}
        },
        {
            { 0, 0, 1, 0, 0}, { 0, 1, 1, 0, 0}, { 0, 0, 1, 0, 0}, { 0, 0, 1, 0, 0},
            { 0, 0, 1, 0, 0}, { 0, 0, 1, 0, 0}, { 0, 1, 1, 1, 0}
        },
        {
            { 0, 1, 1, 1, 0}, { 1, 0, 0, 0, 1}, { 0, 0, 0, 0, 1}, { 0, 0, 0, 1, 0},
            { 0, 0, 1, 0, 0}, { 0, 1, 0, 0, 0}, { 1, 1, 1, 1, 1}
        },
        {
            { 1, 1, 1, 1, 1}, { 0, 0, 0, 1, 0}, { 0, 0, 1, 0, 0}, { 0, 0, 0, 1, 0},
            { 0, 0, 0, 0, 1}, { 1, 0, 0, 0, 1}, { 0, 1, 1, 1, 0}
        },
        {
            { 0, 0, 0, 1, 0}, { 0, 0, 1, 1, 0}, { 0, 1, 0, 1, 0}, { 1, 0, 0, 1, 0},
            { 1, 1, 1, 1, 1}, { 0, 0, 0, 1, 0}, { 0, 0, 0, 1, 0}
        },
        {
            { 1, 1, 1, 1, 1}, { 1, 0, 0, 0, 0}, { 1, 1, 1, 1, 0}, { 0, 0, 0, 0, 1},
            { 0, 0, 0, 0, 1}, { 1, 0, 0, 0, 1}, { 0, 1, 1, 1, 0}
        },
        {
            { 0, 0, 1, 1, 0}, { 0, 1, 0, 0, 0}, { 1, 0, 0, 0, 0}, { 1, 1, 1, 1, 0},
            { 1, 0, 0, 0, 1}, { 1, 0, 0, 0, 1}, { 0, 1, 1, 1, 0}
        },
        {
            { 1, 1, 1, 1, 1}, { 0, 0, 0, 0, 1}, { 0, 0, 0, 1, 0}, { 0, 0, 1, 0, 0},
            { 0, 1, 0, 0, 0}, { 0, 1, 0, 0, 0}, { 0, 1, 0, 0, 0}
        },
        {
            { 0, 1, 1, 1, 0}, { 1, 0, 0, 0, 1}, { 1, 0, 0, 0, 1}, { 0, 1, 1, 1, 0},
            { 1, 0, 0, 0, 1}, { 1, 0, 0, 0, 1}, { 0, 1, 1, 1, 0}
        },
        {
            { 0, 1, 1, 1, 0}, { 1, 0, 0, 0, 1}, { 1, 0, 0, 0, 1}, { 0, 1, 1, 1, 1},
            { 0, 0, 0, 0, 1}, { 0, 0, 0, 1, 0}, { 0, 1, 1, 0, 0}
        },
```

```
    };

    // Dot matrix pattern for a colon.
    static readonly int[,] colonPattern = new int[7, 2]
    {
            { 0, 0 }, { 1, 1 }, { 1, 1 }, { 0, 0 }, { 1, 1 }, { 1, 1 }, { 0, 0 }
    };

    // BoxView colors for on and off.
    static readonly Color colorOn = Color.Red;
    static readonly Color colorOff = new Color(0.5, 0.5, 0.5, 0.25);

    // Box views for 6 digits, 7 rows, 5 columns.
    BoxView[,,] digitBoxViews = new BoxView[6, 7, 5];

    …

}
```

Fields are also defined for an array of `BoxView` objects for the six digits of the time—two digits each for hour, minutes, and seconds. The total number of dots horizontally (set as `horzDots`) includes five dots for each of the six digits, four dots for the colon between the hour and minutes, four for the colon between the minutes and seconds, and one dot width between the digits otherwise.

The program's constructor (shown below) creates a total of 238 `BoxView` objects and adds them to an `AbsoluteLayout`, but it also saves the `BoxView` objects for the digits in the `digitBoxViews` array. (In theory, the `BoxView` objects can be referenced later by indexing the `Children` collection of the `AbsoluteLayout`. But in that collection, they appear simply as a linear list. Storing them also in a multidimensional array allows them to be more easily identified and referenced.) All the positioning and sizing is proportional based on an `AbsoluteLayout` that is assumed to have an aspect ratio of 41 to 7, which encompasses the 41 `BoxView` widths and 7 `BoxView` heights.

```
public partial class DotMatrixClockPage : ContentPage
{

    …

    public DotMatrixClockPage()
    {
        InitializeComponent();

        // BoxView dot dimensions.
        double height = 0.85 / vertDots;
        double width = 0.85 / horzDots;

        // Create and assemble the BoxViews.
        double xIncrement = 1.0 / (horzDots - 1);
        double yIncrement = 1.0 / (vertDots - 1);
        double x = 0;

        for (int digit = 0; digit < 6; digit++)
        {
```

```
        for (int col = 0; col < 5; col++)
        {
            double y = 0;

            for (int row = 0; row < 7; row++)
            {
                // Create the digit BoxView and add to layout.
                BoxView boxView = new BoxView();
                digitBoxViews[digit, row, col] = boxView;
                absoluteLayout.Children.Add(boxView,
                                    new Rectangle(x, y, width, height),
                                    AbsoluteLayoutFlags.All);
                y += yIncrement;
            }
            x += xIncrement;
        }
        x += xIncrement;

        // Colons between the hour, minutes, and seconds.
        if (digit == 1 || digit == 3)
        {
            int colon = digit / 2;

            for (int col = 0; col < 2; col++)
            {
                double y = 0;

                for (int row = 0; row < 7; row++)
                {
                    // Create the BoxView and set the color.
                    BoxView boxView = new BoxView
                        {
                            Color = colonPattern[row, col] == 1 ?
                                        colorOn : colorOff
                        };
                    absoluteLayout.Children.Add(boxView,
                                        new Rectangle(x, y, width, height),
                                        AbsoluteLayoutFlags.All);
                    y += yIncrement;
                }
                x += xIncrement;
            }
            x += xIncrement;
        }
    }

    // Set the timer and initialize with a manual call.
    Device.StartTimer(TimeSpan.FromSeconds(1), OnTimer);
    OnTimer();
}

...

}
```

As you'll recall, the `horzDots` and `vertDots` constants are set to 41 and 7, respectively. To fill up the `AbsoluteLayout`, each `BoxView` needs to occupy a fraction of the width equal to 1 / `horzDots` and a fraction of the height equal to 1 / `vertDots`. The height and width set to each `BoxView` is 85 percent of that value to separate the dots enough so that they don't run into each other:

```
double height = 0.85 / vertDots;
double width = 0.85 / horzDots;
```

To position each `BoxView`, the constructor calculates proportional `xIncrement` and `yIncrement` values like so:

```
double xIncrement = 1.0 / (horzDots - 1);
double yIncrement = 1.0 / (vertDots - 1);
```

The denominators here are 40 and 6 so that the final X and Y positional coordinates are values of 1.

The `BoxView` objects for the time digits are not colored at all in the constructor, but those for the two colons are given a `Color` property based on the `colonPattern` array. The `DotMatrixClockPage` constructor concludes by a one-second timer.

The `SizeChanged` handler for the page is set from the XAML file. The `AbsoluteLayout` is automatically stretched horizontally to fill the width of the page (minus the padding), so the `HeightRequest` really just sets the aspect ratio:

```
public partial class DotMatrixClockPage : ContentPage
{
    ...

    void OnPageSizeChanged(object sender, EventArgs args)
    {
        // No chance a display will have an aspect ratio > 41:7
        absoluteLayout.HeightRequest = vertDots * Width / horzDots;
    }

    ...
}
```

It seems that the `Device.StartTimer` event handler should be rather complex because it is responsible for setting the `Color` property of each `BoxView` based on the digits of the current time. However, the similarity between the definitions of the `numberPatterns` array and the `digitBoxViews` array makes it surprisingly straightforward:

```
public partial class DotMatrixClockPage : ContentPage
{
    ...

    bool OnTimer()
    {
```

```
        DateTime dateTime = DateTime.Now;

        // Convert 24-hour clock to 12-hour clock.
        int hour = (dateTime.Hour + 11) % 12 + 1;

        // Set the dot colors for each digit separately.
        SetDotMatrix(0, hour / 10);
        SetDotMatrix(1, hour % 10);
        SetDotMatrix(2, dateTime.Minute / 10);
        SetDotMatrix(3, dateTime.Minute % 10);
        SetDotMatrix(4, dateTime.Second / 10);
        SetDotMatrix(5, dateTime.Second % 10);
        return true;
    }

    void SetDotMatrix(int index, int digit)
    {
        for (int row = 0; row < 7; row++)
            for (int col = 0; col < 5; col++)
            {
                bool isOn = numberPatterns[digit, row, col] == 1;
                Color color = isOn ? colorOn : colorOff;
                digitBoxViews[index, row, col].Color = color;
            }
    }
}
```

And here's the result:

Of course, bigger is better, so you'll probably want to turn the phone (or the book) sideways for something large enough to read from across the room:

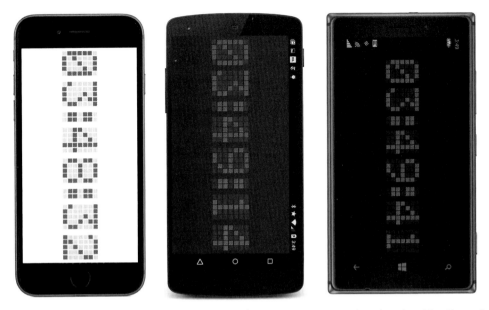

Another special type of application suitable for `AbsoluteLayout` is animation. The **BouncingText** program use its XAML file to instantiate two `Label` elements:

```
<ContentPage xmlns="http://xamarin.com/schemas/2014/forms"
             xmlns:x="http://schemas.microsoft.com/winfx/2009/xaml"
             x:Class="BouncingText.BouncingTextPage">

    <AbsoluteLayout>
        <Label x:Name="label1"
               Text="BOUNCE"
               FontSize="Large"
               AbsoluteLayout.LayoutFlags="PositionProportional" />

        <Label x:Name="label2"
               Text="BOUNCE"
               FontSize="Large"
               AbsoluteLayout.LayoutFlags="PositionProportional" />

    </AbsoluteLayout>
</ContentPage>
```

Notice that the `AbsoluteLayout.LayoutFlags` attributes are set to `PositionProportional`. The `Label` calculates its own size, but the positioning is proportional. Values between 0 and 1 can position the two `Label` elements anywhere within the page.

The code-behind file starts a timer going with a 15-millisecond duration. This is equivalent to approximately 60 ticks per second, which is generally the refresh rate of video displays. A 15-millisecond timer duration is ideal for performing animations:

```
public partial class BouncingTextPage : ContentPage
```

```
{
    const double period = 2000;                          // in milliseconds
    readonly DateTime startTime = DateTime.Now;

    public BouncingTextPage()
    {
        InitializeComponent();
        Device.StartTimer(TimeSpan.FromMilliseconds(15), OnTimerTick);
    }

    bool OnTimerTick()
    {
        TimeSpan elapsed = DateTime.Now - startTime;
        double t = (elapsed.TotalMilliseconds % period) / period;    // 0 to 1
        t = 2 * (t < 0.5 ? t : 1 - t);                               // 0 to 1 to 0

        AbsoluteLayout.SetLayoutBounds(label1,
            new Rectangle(t, 0.5, AbsoluteLayout.AutoSize, AbsoluteLayout.AutoSize));

        AbsoluteLayout.SetLayoutBounds(label2,
            new Rectangle(0.5, 1 - t, AbsoluteLayout.AutoSize, AbsoluteLayout.AutoSize));

        return true;
    }
}
```

The OnTimerTick handler computes an elapsed time since the program started and converts that to a value t (for time) that goes from 0 to 1 every two seconds. The second calculation of t makes it increase from 0 to 1 and then decrease back down to 0 every two seconds. This value is passed directly to the Rectangle constructor in the two AbsoluteLayout.SetLayoutBounds calls. The result is that the first Label moves horizontally across the center of the screen and seems to bounce off the left and right sides. The second Label moves vertically up and down the center of the screen and seems to bounce off the top and bottom:

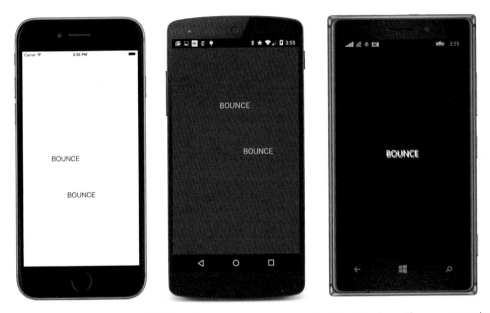

The two `Label` views meet briefly in the center every second, as the Windows Phone screen shot confirms.

From here on out, the pages of our Xamarin.Forms applications will become more active and animated and dynamic. In the next chapter, you'll see how the interactive views of Xamarin.Forms establish a means of communication between the user and the app.

Chapter 15
The interactive interface

Interactivity is the defining feature of modern computing. The many interactive views that Xamarin.Forms implements respond to touch gestures such as tapping and dragging, and a few even read keystrokes from the phone's virtual keyboard.

These interactive views incorporate paradigms that are familiar to users, and even have names that are familiar to programmers: users can trigger commands with `Button`, specify a number from a range of values with `Slider` and `Stepper`, enter text from the phone's keyboard using `Entry` and `Editor`, and select items from a collection with `Picker`, `ListView`, and `TableView`.

This chapter is devoted to demonstrating many of these interactive views.

View overview

Xamarin.Forms defines 19 instantiable classes that derive from `View` but not from `Layout`. You've already seen 6 of these classes in previous chapters: `Label`, `BoxView`, `Button`, `Image`, `ActivityIndicator`, and `ProgressBar`.

This chapter focuses on eight views that allow the user to select or interact with basic .NET data types:

Data type	Views
Double	Slider, Stepper
Boolean	Switch
String	Entry, Editor, SearchBar
DateTime	DatePicker, TimePicker

These views are often the visual representations of underlying data items. In the next chapter, you'll begin to explore data binding, which is a feature of Xamarin.Forms that links properties of views with properties of other classes so that these views and underlying data can be structured in correspondences.

The remaining five views are discussed in later chapters. In Chapter 16, "Data binding," you'll see:

- `WebView`, to display webpages or HTML.

Chapter 19, "Collection views" covers these three views:

- `Picker`, selectable strings for program options.

- `ListView`, a scrollable list of data items of the same type.

- `TableView`, a list of items separated into categories, which is flexible enough to be used for data, forms, menus, or settings.

Finally, this view is the subject of a chapter later in this book:

- `OpenGLView`, which allows a program to display 2-D and 3-D graphics by using the Open Graphics Library.

Slider and Stepper

Both `Slider` and `Stepper` let the user select a numeric value from a range. They have nearly identical programming interfaces but incorporate very different visual and interactive paradigms.

Slider basics

The Xamarin.Forms `Slider` is a horizontal bar that represents a range of values between a minimum at the left and a maximum at the right. (The Xamarin.Forms `Slider` does not support a vertical orientation.) The user selects a value on the `Slider` a little differently on the three platforms: On iOS devices, the user drags a round "thumb" along the horizontal bar. The Android and Windows Phone `Slider` views also have thumbs, but they are too small for a touch target, and the user can simply tap on the horizontal bar or drag his or her finger to a specific location.

The `Slider` defines three public properties of type double, named `Minimum`, `Maximum`, and `Value`. Whenever the `Value` property changes, the `Slider` fires a `ValueChanged` event indicating the new value.

When displaying a `Slider` you'll want a little padding at the left and right to prevent the `Slider` from extending to the edges of the screen. The XAML file in the **SliderDemo** program applies the `Padding` to the `StackLayout`, which is parent to both a `Slider` and a `Label` intended to display the current value of the `Slider`:

```
<ContentPage xmlns="http://xamarin.com/schemas/2014/forms"
             xmlns:x="http://schemas.microsoft.com/winfx/2009/xaml"
             x:Class="SliderDemo.SliderDemoPage">

    <StackLayout Padding="10, 0">
        <Slider VerticalOptions="CenterAndExpand"
                ValueChanged="OnSliderValueChanged" />

        <Label x:Name="label"
               FontSize="Large"
               HorizontalOptions="Center"
               VerticalOptions="CenterAndExpand" />
    </StackLayout>
</ContentPage>
```

When the program starts up, the `Label` displays nothing, and the `Slider` thumb is positioned at the far left:

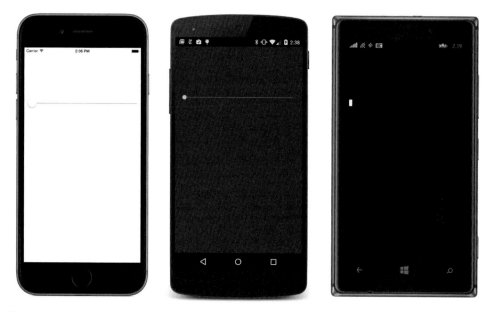

Do not set `HorizontalOptions` on the `Slider` to `Start`, `Center`, or `End` without also setting `WidthRequest` to an explicit value, or the `Slider` will collapse into a very small or even unusable width.

The `Slider` notifies code of changes to the `Value` property by firing the `ValueChanged` event. The event is fired if `Value` is changed programmatically or by user manipulation. Here's the **SliderDemo** code-behind file with the event handler:

```
public partial class SliderDemoPage : ContentPage
{
    public SliderDemoPage()
    {
        InitializeComponent();
    }

    void OnSliderValueChanged(object sender, ValueChangedEventArgs args)
    {
        label.Text = String.Format("Slider = {0}", args.NewValue);
    }
}
```

As usual, the first argument to the event handler is the object firing the event, in this case the `Slider`, and the second argument provides more information about this event. The handler for `ValueChanged` is of type `EventHandler<ValueChangedEventArgs>`, which means that the second argument to the handler is a `ValueChangedEventArgs` object. `ValueChangedEventArgs` defines two properties of type `double`—`OldValue` and `NewValue`. The handler simply uses `NewValue` in a string that it sets to the `Text` property of the `Label`:

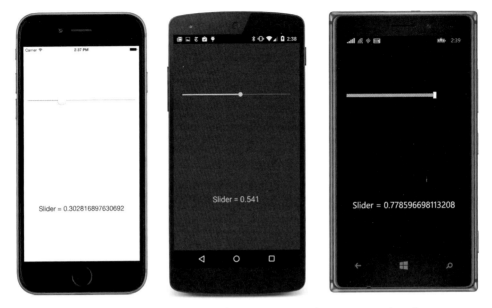

A little experimentation reveals that the default `Minimum` and `Maximum` settings for `Slider` are 0 and 1.

If you're not happy with the excessive precision of these displayed slider values, you can reduce the number of decimal places with a formatting specification in `String.Format`:

```
void OnSliderValueChanged(object sender, ValueChangedEventArgs args)
{
    label.Text = String.Format("Slider = {0:F2}", args.NewValue);
}
```

This is not the only way to write the `ValueChanged` handler. An alternative implementation involves casting the first argument to a `Slider` object and then accessing the `Value` property directly:

```
void OnSliderValueChanged(object sender, ValueChangedEventArgs args)
{
    Slider slider = (Slider)sender;
    label.Text = String.Format("Slider = {0}", slider.Value);
}
```

Using the `sender` argument is a good approach if you're sharing the event handler among multiple `Slider` views. By the time the `ValueChanged` event handler is called, the `Value` property already has its new value.

You can set the `Minimum` and `Maximum` properties of the `Slider` to any negative or positive value, with the stipulation that `Maximum` is always greater than `Minimum`. For example, try this:

```
<Slider ValueChanged="OnSliderValueChanged"
```

```
         Maximum="100"
         VerticalOptions="CenterAndExpand" />
```

Now the `Slider` value ranges from 0 to 100.

Common pitfalls

Suppose you want the `Slider` value to range from 1 to 100. You can set both `Minimum` and `Maximum` like this:

```
<Slider ValueChanged="OnSliderValueChanged"
        Minimum="1"
        Maximum="100"
        VerticalOptions="CenterAndExpand" />
```

However, when you run the new version of the program, an `ArgumentException` is raised with the text explanation "Value was an invalid value for Minimum." What does that mean?

When the XAML parser encounters the `Slider` tag, a `Slider` is instantiated, and then the properties and events are set in the order in which they appear in the `Slider` tag. But when the `Minimum` property is set to 1, the `Maximum` value now equals the `Minimum` value. That can't be. The `Maximum` property must be *greater* than the `Minimum`. The `Slider` signals this problem by raising an exception.

Internal to the `Slider` class, the `Minimum` and `Maximum` values are compared in a callback method set to the `validateValue` argument to the `BindableProperty.Create` method calls for the `Minimum` and `Maximum` bindable properties. The `validateValue` callback returns `true` if `Minimum` is less than `Maximum`, indicating that the values are valid. A return value of `false` from this callback triggers the exception. This is the standard way that bindable properties implement validity checks.

This isn't a problem specific to XAML. It also happens if you instantiate and initialize the `Slider` properties in this order in code. The solution is to reverse the order that `Minimum` and `Maximum` are set. First set the `Maximum` property to 100. That's legal because now the range is between 0 and 100. Then set the `Minimum` property to 1:

```
<Slider ValueChanged="OnSliderValueChanged"
        Maximum="100"
        Minimum="1"
        VerticalOptions="CenterAndExpand" />
```

However, this results in another run-time error. Now it's a `NullReferenceException` in the `ValueChanged` handler. Why is that?

The `Value` property of the `Slider` must be within the range of `Minimum` and `Maximum` values, so when the `Minimum` property is set to 1, the `Slider` automatically adjust its `Value` property to 1.

Internally, `Value` is adjusted in a callback method set to the `coerceValue` argument of the `BindableProperty.Create` method calls for the `Minimum`, `Maximum`, and `Value` properties. The callback method returns an adjusted value of the property being set after being subjected to this coercion. In this example, when `Minimum` is set to 1, the `coerceValue` method sets the slider's `Value` property to

1, and the `coerceValue` callback returns the new value of `Minimum`, which remains at the value 1.

However, as a result of the coercion, the `Value` property has changed, and this causes the `Value-Changed` event to fire. The `ValueChanged` handler in the code-behind file attempts to set the `Text` property of the `Label`, but the XAML parser has not yet instantiated the `Label` element. The `label` field is `null`.

There are a couple of solutions to this problem. The safest and most general solution is to check for a `null` value for `label` right in the event handler:

```
void OnSliderValueChanged(object sender, ValueChangedEventArgs args)
{
    if (label != null)
    {
        label.Text = String.Format("Slider = {0}", args.NewValue);
    }
}
```

However, you can also fix the problem by moving the assignment of the `ValueChanged` event in the tag to after the `Maximum` and `Minimum` properties have been set:

```
<Slider Maximum="100"
        Minimum="1"
        ValueChanged="OnSliderValueChanged"
        VerticalOptions="CenterAndExpand" />
```

The `Value` property is still coerced to 1 after the `Minimum` property is set, but the `ValueChanged` event handler has not yet been assigned, so no event is fired.

Let's assume that the `Slider` has the default range of 0 to 1. You might want the `Label` to display the initial value of the `Slider` when the program first starts up. You could initialize the `Text` property of the `Label` to "Slider = 0" in the XAML file, but if you ever wanted to change the text to something a little different, you'd need to change it in two places.

You might try giving the `Slider` a name of `slider` in the XAML file and then add some code to the constructor:

```
public SliderDemoPage()
{
    InitializeComponent();

    slider.Value = 0;
}
```

All the elements in the XAML file have been created and initialized when `InitializeComponent` returns, so if this code causes the `Slider` to fire a `ValueChanged` event, that shouldn't be a problem.

But it won't work. The value of the `Slider` is already 0, so setting it to 0 again does nothing. You could try this:

```
public SliderDemoPage()
```

```
{
    InitializeComponent();

    slider.Value = 1;
    slider.Value = 0;
}
```

That will work. But you might want to add a comment to the code so that another programmer doesn't later remove the statement that sets `Value` to 1 because it appears to be unnecessary.

Or you could simulate an event by calling the handler directly. The two arguments to the `Value-ChangedEventArgs` constructor are the old value and the new value (in that order), but the `On-SliderValueChanged` handler uses only the `NewValue` property, so it doesn't matter what the other argument is or whether they're equal:

```
public partial class SliderDemoPage : ContentPage
{
    public SliderDemoPage()
    {
        InitializeComponent();

        OnSliderValueChanged(null, new ValueChangedEventArgs(0, 0));
    }

    void OnSliderValueChanged(object sender, ValueChangedEventArgs args)
    {
        label.Text = String.Format("Slider = {0}", args.NewValue);
    }
}
```

That works as well. But remember to set the arguments to the call to `OnSliderValueChanged` so that they agree with what the handler expects. If you replaced the handler body with code that casts the `sender` argument to the `Slider` object, you then need a valid first argument in the `On-SliderValueChanged` call.

The problems involving the event handler disappear when you connect the `Label` with the `Slider` by using data bindings, which you'll learn about in the next chapter. You'll still need to set the properties of the `Slider` in the correct order, but you'll experience none of the problems with the event handler because the event handler will be gone.

Slider color selection

Here's a program named **RgbSliders** that contains three `Slider` elements for selecting red, green, and blue components of a `Color`. An implicit style for `Slider` sets the `Maximum` value to 255:

```
<ContentPage xmlns="http://xamarin.com/schemas/2014/forms"
             xmlns:x="http://schemas.microsoft.com/winfx/2009/xaml"
             x:Class="RgbSliders.RgbSlidersPage">
    <ContentPage.Padding>
        <OnPlatform x:TypeArguments="Thickness"
```

```
                    iOS="10, 20, 10, 10"
                    Android="10, 0, 10, 10"
                    WinPhone="10, 0, 10, 10" />
    </ContentPage.Padding>

    <StackLayout>
        <StackLayout.Resources>
            <ResourceDictionary>
                <Style TargetType="Slider">
                    <Setter Property="Maximum" Value="255" />
                </Style>

                <Style TargetType="Label">
                    <Setter Property="FontSize" Value="Large" />
                    <Setter Property="XAlign" Value="Center" />
                </Style>
            </ResourceDictionary>
        </StackLayout.Resources>

        <Slider x:Name="redSlider"
                ValueChanged="OnSliderValueChanged" />

        <Label x:Name="redLabel" />

        <Slider x:Name="greenSlider"
                ValueChanged="OnSliderValueChanged" />

        <Label x:Name="greenLabel" />

        <Slider x:Name="blueSlider"
                ValueChanged="OnSliderValueChanged" />

        <Label x:Name="blueLabel" />

        <BoxView x:Name="boxView"
                 VerticalOptions="FillAndExpand" />
    </StackLayout>
</ContentPage>
```

The Slider elements alternate with three Label elements to display their values, and the StackLayout concludes with a BoxView to show the resultant color.

The constructor of the code-behind file initializes the Slider settings to 128 for a medium gray. The shared ValueChanged handler checks to see which Slider has changed, and hence which Label needs to be updated, and then computes a new color for the BoxView:

```
public partial class RgbSlidersPage : ContentPage
{
    public RgbSlidersPage()
    {
        InitializeComponent();

        redSlider.Value = 128;
```

```
            greenSlider.Value = 128;
            blueSlider.Value = 128;
    }

    void OnSliderValueChanged(object sender, ValueChangedEventArgs args)
    {
        if (sender == redSlider)
        {
            redLabel.Text = String.Format("Red = {0:X2}", (int)redSlider.Value);
        }
        else if (sender == greenSlider)
        {
            greenLabel.Text = String.Format("Green = {0:X2}", (int)greenSlider.Value);
        }
        else if (sender == blueSlider)
        {
            blueLabel.Text = String.Format("Blue = {0:X2}", (int)blueSlider.Value);
        }

        boxView.Color = Color.FromRgb((int)redSlider.Value,
                                      (int)greenSlider.Value,
                                      (int)blueSlider.Value);
    }
}
```

Strictly speaking, the `if` and `else` statements here are not required. The code can simply set all three labels regardless of which slider is changing. The event hander accesses all three sliders anyway for setting a new color:

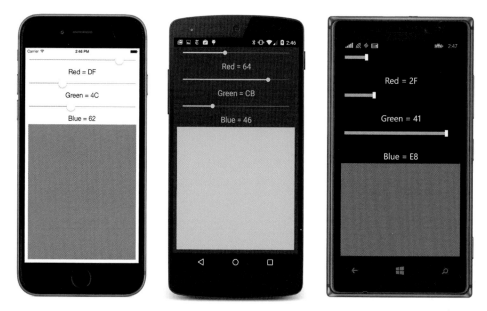

You can turn the phone sideways, but the `BoxView` becomes much shorter, particularly on the

Windows Phone, where the `Slider` seems to have a vertical height beyond what's required. Once the `Grid` is introduced in Chapter 18, you'll see how it becomes easier for applications to respond to orientation changes.

The following **TextFade** program uses a single `Slider` to control the `Opacity` and horizontal position of two `Label` elements in an `AbsoluteLayout`. In the initial layout, both `Label` elements are positioned at the left center of the `AbsoluteLayout,` but the second one has its `Opacity` set to 0:

```
<ContentPage xmlns="http://xamarin.com/schemas/2014/forms"
             xmlns:x="http://schemas.microsoft.com/winfx/2009/xaml"
             x:Class="TextFade.TextFadePage"
             Padding="10, 0, 10, 20">

    <StackLayout>
        <AbsoluteLayout VerticalOptions="CenterAndExpand">
            <Label x:Name="label1"
                   Text="TEXT"
                   FontSize="Large"
                   AbsoluteLayout.LayoutBounds="0, 0.5"
                   AbsoluteLayout.LayoutFlags="PositionProportional" />

            <Label x:Name="label2"
                   Text="FADE"
                   FontSize="Large"
                   Opacity="0"
                   AbsoluteLayout.LayoutBounds="0, 0.5"
                   AbsoluteLayout.LayoutFlags="PositionProportional" />
        </AbsoluteLayout>

        <Slider ValueChanged="OnSliderValueChanged" />

    </StackLayout>
</ContentPage>
```

The `Slider` event handler moves both `Label` elements from left to right across the screen. The proportional positioning helps a lot here because the `Slider` values range from 0 to 1, which results in the `Label` elements being positioned progressively from the far left to the far right of the screen:

```
public partial class TextFadePage : ContentPage
{
    public TextFadePage()
    {
        InitializeComponent();
    }

    void OnSliderValueChanged(object sender, ValueChangedEventArgs args)
    {
        AbsoluteLayout.SetLayoutBounds(label1,
            new Rectangle(args.NewValue, 0.5, AbsoluteLayout.AutoSize,
                                             AbsoluteLayout.AutoSize));
        AbsoluteLayout.SetLayoutBounds(label2,
            new Rectangle(args.NewValue, 0.5, AbsoluteLayout.AutoSize,
                                             AbsoluteLayout.AutoSize));
```

```
        label1.Opacity = 1 - args.NewValue;
        label2.Opacity = args.NewValue;
    }
}
```

At the same time, the `Opacity` values are set so that one `Label` seems to fade into the other as both labels move across the screen:

The Stepper difference

The `Stepper` view has very nearly the same programming interface as the `Slider`: It has `Minimum`, `Maximum`, and `Value` properties of type `double` and fires a `ValueChanged` event handler.

However, the `Maximum` property of `Stepper` has a default value of 100, and `Stepper` also adds an `Increment` property with a default value of 1. The `Stepper` visuals consist solely of two buttons labeled with minus and plus signs. Presses of those two buttons change the value incrementally between `Minimum` to `Maximum` based on the `Increment` property.

Although `Value` and other properties of `Stepper` are of type `double`, `Stepper` is often used for the selection of integral values. You probably don't want the value of (($Maximum - Minimum$) ÷ Increment) to be as high as 100 as the default values suggest. If you press and hold your finger on one of the buttons, you'll trigger a typematic repeat on iOS, but not on Android or Windows Phone. Unless your program provides another way for the user to change the `Stepper` value (perhaps with a text `Entry` view), you don't want to force the user to press a button 100 times to get from `Minimum` to `Maximum`.

The **StepperDemo** program sets the `Maximum` property of the `Stepper` to 10 and uses the `Stepper` as a rudimentary design aid in determining an optimum border width for a `Button` border. The `Button` at the top of the `StackLayout` is solely for display purposes and has the necessary property settings of `BackgroundColor` and `BorderColor` to enable the border display on Android.

The `Stepper` is the last child in the following `StackLayout`. Between the `Button` and `Stepper` are a pair of `Label` elements for displaying the current `Stepper` value:

```xml
<ContentPage xmlns="http://xamarin.com/schemas/2014/forms"
             xmlns:x="http://schemas.microsoft.com/winfx/2009/xaml"
             x:Class="StepperDemo.StepperDemoPage">

    <StackLayout>
        <Button x:Name="button"
                Text="  Sample Button  "
                FontSize="Large"
                HorizontalOptions="Center"
                VerticalOptions="CenterAndExpand">
            <Button.BackgroundColor>
                <OnPlatform x:TypeArguments="Color"
                            Android="#404040" />
            </Button.BackgroundColor>
            <Button.BorderColor>
                <OnPlatform x:TypeArguments="Color"
                            Android="#C0C0C0" />
            </Button.BorderColor>
        </Button>

        <StackLayout VerticalOptions="CenterAndExpand">

            <StackLayout Orientation="Horizontal"
                         HorizontalOptions="Center">
                <StackLayout.Resources>
                    <ResourceDictionary>
                        <Style TargetType="Label">
                            <Setter Property="FontSize" Value="Large" />
                        </Style>
                    </ResourceDictionary>
                </StackLayout.Resources>

                <Label Text="Button Border Width =" />
                <Label x:Name="label" />
            </StackLayout>

            <Stepper x:Name="stepper"
                     Maximum="10"
                     ValueChanged="OnStepperValueChanged"
                     HorizontalOptions="Center" />

        </StackLayout>
    </StackLayout>
</ContentPage>
```

The `Label` displaying the `Stepper` value is initialized from the constructor of the code-behind file. With each change in the `Value` property of the `Stepper`, the event handler displays the new value and sets the `Button` border width:

```
public partial class StepperDemoPage : ContentPage
{
    public StepperDemoPage()
    {
        InitializeComponent();

        // Initialize display.
        OnStepperValueChanged(stepper, null);
    }

    void OnStepperValueChanged(object sender, ValueChangedEventArgs args)
    {
        Stepper stepper = (Stepper)sender;
        button.BorderWidth = stepper.Value;
        label.Text = stepper.Value.ToString("F0");
    }
}
```

As you play with this program, keep in mind that the default value of `BorderWidth` is 0, which on Windows Phone results in the same border width as a setting of 3.

Switch and CheckBox

Application programs often need Boolean input from the user, which requires some way for the user to toggle a program option to On or Off, Yes or No, True or False, or however you want to think of it. In Xamarin.Forms, this is a view called the `Switch`.

Switch basics

`Switch` defines just one property on its own, named `IsToggled` of type `bool`, and it fires the `Toggled` event to indicate a change in this property. In code, you might be inclined to give a `Switch` a name of `switch`, but that's a C# keyword, so you'll want to pick something else. In XAML, however, you can set the `x:Name` attribute to `switch`, and the XAML parser will smartly create a field named `@switch`, which is how C# allows you to define a variable name using a C# keyword.

The **SwitchDemo** program creates two `Switch` elements with two identifying labels: "Italic" and "Boldface". Each `Switch` has its own event handler, which formats the larger `Label` at the bottom of the `StackLayout`:

```
<ContentPage xmlns="http://xamarin.com/schemas/2014/forms"
             xmlns:x="http://schemas.microsoft.com/winfx/2009/xaml"
             x:Class="SwitchDemo.SwitchDemoPage">

    <StackLayout Padding="10, 0">
        <StackLayout HorizontalOptions="Center"
                     VerticalOptions="CenterAndExpand">
            <StackLayout Orientation="Horizontal"
                         HorizontalOptions="End">
                <Label Text="Italic: "
                       VerticalOptions="Center" />
                <Switch Toggled="OnItalicSwitchToggled"
                        VerticalOptions="Center" />
            </StackLayout>

            <StackLayout Orientation="Horizontal"
                         HorizontalOptions="End">
                <Label Text="Boldface: "
                       VerticalOptions="Center" />
                <Switch Toggled="OnBoldSwitchToggled"
                        VerticalOptions="Center" />
            </StackLayout>
        </StackLayout>

        <Label x:Name="label"
               Text=
"Just a little passage of some sample text that can be formatted
 in italic or boldface by toggling the two Switch elements."
               FontSize="Large"
               XAlign="Center"
               VerticalOptions="CenterAndExpand" />
```

```
    </StackLayout>
</ContentPage>
```

The `Toggled` event handler has a second argument of `ToggledEventArgs`, which has a `Value` property of type `bool` that indicates the new state of the `IsToggled` property. The event handlers in **SwitchDemo** use this value to set or clear the particular `FontAttributes` flag in the `FontAttributes` property of the long `Label`:

```
public partial class SwitchDemoPage : ContentPage
{
    public SwitchDemoPage()
    {
        InitializeComponent();
    }

    void OnItalicSwitchToggled(object sender, ToggledEventArgs args)
    {
        if (args.Value)
        {
            label.FontAttributes |= FontAttributes.Italic;
        }
        else
        {
            label.FontAttributes &= ~FontAttributes.Italic;
        }
    }

    void OnBoldSwitchToggled(object sender, ToggledEventArgs args)
    {
        if (args.Value)
        {
            label.FontAttributes |= FontAttributes.Bold;
        }
        else
        {
            label.FontAttributes &= ~FontAttributes.Bold;
        }
    }
}
```

The `Switch` has a different appearance on the three platforms:

Notice that the program aligns the two `Switch` views, which gives it a more attractive look, but which also means that the text labels are necessarily somewhat misaligned. To accomplish this format-ting, the XAML file puts each of the pair of `Label` and `Switch` elements in a horizontal `StackLayout`. Each horizontal `StackLayout` has its `HorizontalOptions` set to `End`, which aligns each `StackLay-out` at the right, and a parent `StackLayout` centers the collection of labels and switches on the screen with a `HorizontalOptions` setting of `Center`. Within the horizontal `StackLayout`, both views have their `VerticalOptions` properties set to `Center`. If the `Switch` is taller than the `Label`, then the `La-bel` is vertically centered relative to the `Switch`. But if the `Label` is taller than the `Switch`, the `Switch` is also vertically centered relative to the `Label`.

A traditional CheckBox

In more traditional graphical environments, the user-interface object that allows users to choose a Boolean value is called a `CheckBox`, usually featuring some text with a box that can be empty or filled with an X or a check mark. One advantage of the `CheckBox` over the `Switch` is that the text identifier is part of the visual and doesn't need to be added with a separate `Label`.

One way to create custom views in Xamarin.Forms is by writing special classes called *renderers* that are specific to each platform and that reference views in each platform. That will be demonstrated in a later chapter.

However, it's also possible to create custom views right in Xamarin.Forms by assembling a view from other views. You first derive a class from `ContentView`, set its `Content` property to a `StackLayout` (for example), and then add one or more views on that. (You saw an example of this technique in the

`ColorView` class in Chapter 8.) You'll probably also need to define one or more properties, and possibly some events, but you'll want to take advantage of the bindable infrastructure established by the `BindableObject` and `BindableProperty` classes. That allows your properties to be styled and to be targets of data bindings.

A `CheckBox` consists of just two `Label` elements on a `ContentView`: one `Label` displays the text associated with the `CheckBox`, while the other displays a box. A `TapGestureRecognizer` detects when the `CheckBox` is tapped.

A `CheckBox` class has already been added to the **Xamarin.FormsBook.Toolkit** library that is included in the downloadable code for this book. Here's how you would do it on your own:

In Visual Studio, you can select **Forms Xaml Page** from the **Add New Item** dialog box. However, this creates a class that derives from `ContentPage` when you really want a class that derives from `ContentView`. Simply change the root element of the XAML file from `ContentPage` to `ContentView`, and change the base class in the code-behind file from `ContentPage` to `ContentView`.

In Xamarin Studio, however, you can simply choose **Forms ContentView Xaml** from the **New File** dialog.

Here's the CheckBox.xaml file:

```
<ContentView xmlns="http://xamarin.com/schemas/2014/forms"
             xmlns:x="http://schemas.microsoft.com/winfx/2009/xaml"
             x:Class="Xamarin.FormsBook.Toolkit.CheckBox">

    <StackLayout Orientation="Horizontal">
        <Label x:Name="boxLabel" Text="&#x2610;" />
        <Label x:Name="textLabel" />
    </StackLayout>

    <ContentView.GestureRecognizers>
        <TapGestureRecognizer Tapped="OnCheckBoxTapped" />
    </ContentView.GestureRecognizers>
</ContentView>
```

That Unicode character \u2610 is called the Ballot Box character, and it's just an empty square. Character \u2611 is a Ballot Box with Check, while \u2612 is a Ballot Box with X. To indicate a checked state, this `CheckBox` code-behind file sets the `Text` property of `boxLabel` to \u2611 (as you'll see shortly).

The code-behind file of `CheckBox` defines three properties:

- `Text`

- `FontSize`

- `IsChecked`

`CheckBox` also defines an event named `IsCheckedChanged`.

Should `CheckBox` also define `FontAttributes` and `FontFamily` properties like `Label` and `Button` do? Perhaps, but these additional properties are not quite as valuable for views devoted to user interaction.

All three of the properties that `CheckBox` defines are backed by bindable properties. The code-behind file creates all three `BindableProperty` objects with the generic form of the `BindableProperty.Create` method, and the property-changed handlers are defined as lambda functions within these methods.

Keep in mind that the property-changed handlers are static, so they need to cast the first argument to a `CheckBox` object to reference the instance properties and events in the class. The property-changed handler for `IsChecked` is responsible for changing the character representing the checked and unchecked state and firing the `IsCheckedChanged` event:

```
public partial class CheckBox : ContentView
{
    public static readonly BindableProperty TextProperty =
        BindableProperty.Create<CheckBox, string>(
            checkbox => checkbox.Text,
            null,
            propertyChanged: (bindable, oldValue, newValue) =>
            {
                ((CheckBox)bindable).textLabel.Text = (string)newValue;
            });

    public static readonly BindableProperty FontSizeProperty =
        BindableProperty.Create<CheckBox, double>(
            checkbox => checkbox.FontSize,
            Device.GetNamedSize(NamedSize.Default, typeof(Label)),
            propertyChanged: (bindable, oldValue, newValue) =>
            {
                CheckBox checkbox = (CheckBox)bindable;
                checkbox.boxLabel.FontSize = newValue;
                checkbox.textLabel.FontSize = newValue;
            });

    public static readonly BindableProperty IsCheckedProperty =
        BindableProperty.Create<CheckBox, bool>(
            checkbox => checkbox.IsChecked,
            false,
            propertyChanged: (bindable, oldValue, newValue) =>
            {
                // Set the graphic.
                CheckBox checkbox = (CheckBox)bindable;
                checkbox.boxLabel.Text = newValue ? "\u2611" : "\u2610";

                // Fire the event.
                EventHandler<bool> eventHandler = checkbox.CheckedChanged;
                if (eventHandler != null)
                {
                    eventHandler(checkbox, newValue);
                }
```

```
            });

    public event EventHandler<bool> CheckedChanged;

    public CheckBox()
    {
        InitializeComponent();
    }

    public string Text
    {
        set { SetValue(TextProperty, value); }
        get { return (string)GetValue(TextProperty); }
    }

    [TypeConverter(typeof(FontSizeConverter))]
    public double FontSize
    {
        set { SetValue(FontSizeProperty, value); }
        get { return (double)GetValue(FontSizeProperty); }
    }

    public bool IsChecked
    {
        set { SetValue(IsCheckedProperty, value); }
        get { return (bool)GetValue(IsCheckedProperty); }
    }

    // TapGestureRecognizer handler.
    void OnCheckBoxTapped(object sender, EventArgs args)
    {
        IsChecked = !IsChecked;
    }
}
```

Notice the `TypeConverter` on the `FontSize` property. That allows the property to be set in XAML with attribute values such as "Small" and "Large".

The `Tapped` handler for the `TapGestureRecognizer` is at the bottom of the class and simply toggles the `IsChecked` property by using the C# logical negation operator. An even shorter statement to toggle a Boolean variable uses the exclusive-OR assignment operator:

```
IsChecked ^= true;
```

The **CheckBoxDemo** program is very similar to the **SwitchDemo** program except that the markup is considerably simplified because the `CheckBox` includes its own `Text` property:

```
<ContentPage xmlns="http://xamarin.com/schemas/2014/forms"
             xmlns:x="http://schemas.microsoft.com/winfx/2009/xaml"
             xmlns:toolkit=
                 "clr-namespace:Xamarin.FormsBook.Toolkit;assembly=Xamarin.FormsBook.Toolkit"
             x:Class="CheckBoxDemo.CheckBoxDemoPage">
```

```
    <StackLayout Padding="10, 0">
        <StackLayout HorizontalOptions="Center"
                     VerticalOptions="CenterAndExpand">

            <toolkit:CheckBox Text="Italic"
                              FontSize="Large"
                              CheckedChanged="OnItalicCheckBoxChanged" />

            <toolkit:CheckBox Text="Boldface"
                              FontSize="Large"
                              CheckedChanged="OnBoldCheckBoxChanged" />
        </StackLayout>

        <Label x:Name="label"
               Text=
"Just a little passage of some sample text that can be formatted
in italic or boldface by toggling the two custom CheckBox views."
               FontSize="Large"
               XAlign="Center"
               VerticalOptions="CenterAndExpand" />
    </StackLayout>
</ContentPage>
```

The code-behind file is also very similar to the earlier program:

```
public partial class CheckBoxDemoPage : ContentPage
{
    public CheckBoxDemoPage()
    {
        // Ensure link to library.
        new Xamarin.FormsBook.Toolkit.CheckBox();

        InitializeComponent();
    }

    void OnItalicCheckBoxChanged(object sender, bool isChecked)
    {
        if (isChecked)
        {
            label.FontAttributes |= FontAttributes.Italic;
        }
        else
        {
            label.FontAttributes &= ~FontAttributes.Italic;
        }
    }

    void OnBoldCheckBoxChanged(object sender, bool isChecked)
    {
        if (isChecked)
        {
            label.FontAttributes |= FontAttributes.Bold;
        }
        else
```

```
        {
            label.FontAttributes &= ~FontAttributes.Bold;
        }
    }
}
```

Interestingly, the character for the checked box shows up in color on the Android and Windows Phone platforms:

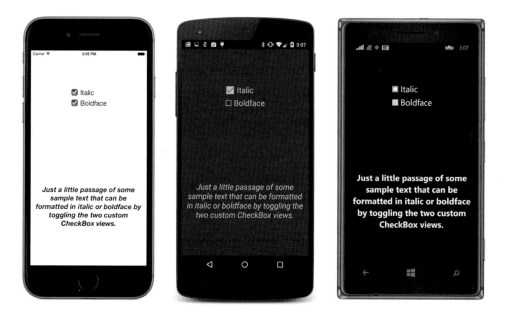

Typing text

Xamarin.Forms defines three views for obtaining text input from the user:

- `Entry` for a single line of text.

- `Editor` for multiple lines of text.

- `SearchBar` for a single line of text specifically for search operations.

Both `Entry` and `Editor` derive from `InputView`, which derives from `View`. `SearchBar` derives directly from `View`.

Both `Entry` and `SearchBar` implement horizontal scrolling if the entered text exceeds the width of the view. The `Editor` implements word wrapping and is capable of vertical scrolling for text that exceeds its height.

Keyboard and focus

`Entry`, `Editor`, and `SearchBar` are different from all the other views in that they make use of the phone's onscreen keyboard, sometimes called the *virtual keyboard*. From the user's perspective, tapping the `Entry`, `Editor`, or `SearchBar` view invokes the onscreen keyboard, which slides in from the bottom. Tapping anywhere else on the screen (except another `Entry`, `Editor`, or `SearchBar` view) often makes the keyboard go away, and sometimes the keyboard can be dismissed in other ways.

From the program's perspective, the presence of the keyboard is closely related to *input focus*, a concept that originated in desktop graphical user interface environments. On both desktop environments and mobile devices, input from the keyboard can be directed to only one user-interface object at a time, and that object must be clearly selectable and identifiable by the user. The object that receives keyboard input is known as the object with *keyboard input focus*, or more simply, just *input focus* or *focus*.

The `VisualElement` class defines several methods, properties, and events related to input focus:

- The `Focus` method attempts to set input focus to a visual element and returns `true` if successful.

- The `Unfocus` method removes input focus from a visual element.

- The `IsFocused` get-only property is `true` if a visual element currently has input focus.

- The `Focused` event is fired when a visual element acquires input focus.

- The `Unfocused` event is fired when a visual element loses input focus.

As you know, mobile environments make far less use of the keyboard than desktop environments do, and most mobile views (such as the `Slider`, `Stepper`, and `Switch` that you've already seen) don't make use of the keyboard at all. Although these five focus-related members of the `VisualElement` class appear to implement a generalized system for passing input focus between visual elements, they only pertain to `Entry`, `Editor`, and `SearchBar`.

On iOS, this rule is strongly enforced: The `Focus` method works only with `Entry`, `Editor`, and `SearchBar`. Consequently, the `Unfocus` method works only with these three views. The `IsFocused` property can only be `true` for these three views, and only these three views fire `Focused` and `Unfocused` events. Android is similar except that the `WebView` can also acquire input focus. On Windows Phone, other interactive views (such as `Button` and `Slider`) can acquire input focus. But only `Entry`, `Editor`, and `SearchBar` do anything with it.

The `Entry`, `Editor`, and `SearchBar` views signal that they have input focus with a flashing caret showing the text input point, and they trigger the keyboard to slide up. When the view loses input focus, the keyboard slides back down.

A view must have its `IsEnabled` property set to `true` (the default state) to acquire input focus, and of course the `IsVisible` property must also be `true` or the view won't be on the screen at all.

Choosing the keyboard

`Entry` and `Editor` are different from `SearchBar` in that they both derive from `InputView`. Interestingly, although `Entry` and `Editor` define similar properties and events, `InputView` defines just one property: `Keyboard`. This property allows a program to select the type of keyboard that is displayed. For example, a keyboard for typing a URL should be different from a keyboard for entering a phone number. All three platforms have various styles of virtual keyboards appropriate for different types of text input. A program cannot select the keyboard used for `SearchBar`.

This `Keyboard` property is of type `Keyboard`, a class that defines seven static read-only properties of type `Keyboard` appropriate for different keyboard uses:

- `Default`

- `Text`

- `Chat`

- `Url`

- `Email`

- `Telephone`

- `Numeric`

On all three platforms, the `Numeric` keyboard allows typing decimal points but does not allow typing a negative sign, so it's limited to positive numbers.

The following program creates seven `Entry` views that let you see how these keyboards are implemented in the three platforms. The particular keyboard attached to each `Entry` is identified by a property defined by `Entry` named `Placeholder`. This is the text that appears in the `Entry` prior to anything the user types as a hint for the nature of the text the program is expecting. Placeholder text is commonly a short phrase such as "First Name" or "Email Address":

```
<ContentPage xmlns="http://xamarin.com/schemas/2014/forms"
             xmlns:x="http://schemas.microsoft.com/winfx/2009/xaml"
             x:Class="EntryKeyboards.EntryKeyboardsPage">

    <ContentPage.Padding>
        <OnPlatform x:TypeArguments="Thickness"
                    iOS="10, 20, 10, 0"
                    Android="10, 0"
                    WinPhone="10, 0" />
    </ContentPage.Padding>

    <ScrollView>
        <StackLayout>
            <StackLayout.Resources>
                <ResourceDictionary>
                    <Style TargetType="Entry">
```

```
                    <Setter Property="VerticalOptions" Value="CenterAndExpand" />
                </Style>
            </ResourceDictionary>
        </StackLayout.Resources>

        <Entry Placeholder="Default"
               Keyboard="Default" />

        <Entry Placeholder="Text"
               Keyboard="Text" />

        <Entry Placeholder="Chat"
               Keyboard="Chat" />

        <Entry Placeholder="Url"
               Keyboard="Url" />

        <Entry Placeholder="Email"
               Keyboard="Email" />

        <Entry Placeholder="Telephone"
               Keyboard="Telephone" />

        <Entry Placeholder="Numeric"
               Keyboard="Numeric" />
    </StackLayout>
  </ScrollView>
</ContentPage>
```

The placeholders appear as gray text. Here's how the display looks when the program first begins to run:

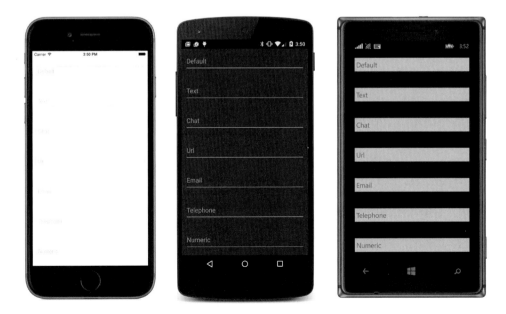

Just as with the `Slider`, you don't want to set `HorizontalOptions` on an `Entry` to `Left`, `Center`, or `Right` unless you also set the `WidthRequest` property. If you do so, the `Entry` collapses to a very small width. It can still be used—the `Entry` automatically provides horizontal scrolling for text longer than the `Entry` can display—but you should really try to provide an adequate size. In this program each `Entry` is as wide as the screen minus a 10-unit padding on the left and right.

You can estimate an adequate `WidthRequest` through experimentation with different text lengths. The next program in this chapter sets the `Entry` width to a value equivalent to one inch.

The **EntryKeyboards** program evenly spaces the seven `Entry` views vertically using a `VerticalOptions` value of `CenterAndExpand` set through an implicit style. Clearly there is enough vertical room for all seven `Entry` views, so you might be puzzled about the use of the `ScrollView` in the XAML file.

The `ScrollView` is specifically for iOS. If you tap an `Entry` close to the bottom of the Android or Windows Phone screen, the operating system will automatically move up the contents of the page when the keyboard pops up, so the `Entry` is still visible while you are typing. But iOS doesn't do that unless a `ScrollView` is provided.

Here's how each screen looks when text is being typed in one of the `Entry` views toward the bottom of the screen:

Entry properties and events

Besides inheriting the `Keyboard` property from `InputView`, `Entry` defines four more properties, only one of which you saw in the previous program:

- `Text` — the string that appears in the `Entry`

- `TextColor` — a `Color` value

- `IsPassword` — a Boolean that causes characters to be masked right after they're typed

- `Placeholder` — light-colored text that appears in the `Entry` but disappears as soon as the user begins typing (or, in Windows Phone, when the `Entry` gets input focus).

Generally, a program obtains what the user typed by accessing the `Text` property, but the program can also initialize the `Text` property. Perhaps the program wishes to suggest some text input.

The `Entry` also defines two events:

- `TextChanged`

- `Completed`

The `TextChanged` event is fired for every change in the `Text` property, which generally corresponds to every keystroke (except shift and some special keys). A program can monitor this event to perform validity checks. For example, you might check for valid numbers or valid email addresses to enable a **Calculate** or **Send** button.

The `Completed` event is fired when the user presses a particular key on the keyboard to indicate that the text is completed. This key is platform specific:

- iOS: The key is labeled **return**, which is not on the `Telephone` or `Numeric` keyboard.

- Android: The key is a green check mark in the lower-right corner of the keyboard.

- Windows Phone: The key is an enter (or return) symbol (↵) on most keyboards but is a go symbol (→) on the `Url` keyboard. Such a key is not present on the `Telephone` and `Numeric` keyboards.

On iOS and Android, the completed key dismisses the keyboard in addition to generating the `Completed` event. On Windows Phone it does not.

Android and Windows Phone users can also dismiss the keyboard by using the phone's **Back** button at the bottom left of the portrait screen. This causes the `Entry` to lose input focus but does not cause the `Completed` event to fire.

Let's write a program named **QuadraticEquations** that solves quadratic equations, which are equations of the form:

$$ax^2 + bx + c = 0$$

For any three constants *a*, *b*, and *c*, the program uses the quadratic equation to solve for *x*:

$$x = \frac{-b \pm \sqrt{b^2 - 4ac}}{2a}$$

You enter a, b, and c in three `Entry` views and then press a `Button` labeled **Solve for x**.

Here's the XAML file. Unfortunately, the `Numeric` keyboard is not suitable for this program because on all three platforms it does not allow entering negative numbers. For that reason, no particular keyboard is specified:

```
<ContentPage xmlns="http://xamarin.com/schemas/2014/forms"
             xmlns:x="http://schemas.microsoft.com/winfx/2009/xaml"
             x:Class="QuadaticEquations.QuadraticEquationsPage">

    <ContentPage.Resources>
        <ResourceDictionary>
            <Style TargetType="Label">
                <Setter Property="FontSize" Value="Large" />
                <Setter Property="VerticalOptions" Value="Center" />
            </Style>

            <Style TargetType="Entry">
                <Setter Property="WidthRequest">
                    <Setter.Value>
                        <OnPlatform x:TypeArguments="x:Double"
                                    iOS="180"
                                    Android="180"
                                    WinPhone="240" />
                    </Setter.Value>
                </Setter>
            </Style>
        </ResourceDictionary>
    </ContentPage.Resources>

    <StackLayout>
        <!-- Entry section -->
        <StackLayout Padding="20, 0, 0, 0"
                     VerticalOptions="CenterAndExpand"
                     HorizontalOptions="Center">

            <StackLayout Orientation="Horizontal">
                <Entry x:Name="entryA"
                       TextChanged="OnEntryTextChanged"
                       Completed="OnEntryCompleted" />
                <Label Text=" x&#178; +" />
            </StackLayout>

            <StackLayout Orientation="Horizontal">
                <Entry x:Name="entryB"
                       TextChanged="OnEntryTextChanged"
                       Completed="OnEntryCompleted" />
                <Label Text=" x +" />
            </StackLayout>

            <StackLayout Orientation="Horizontal">
                <Entry x:Name="entryC"
                       TextChanged="OnEntryTextChanged"
                       Completed="OnEntryCompleted" />
```

```
                        <Label Text=" = 0" />
                    </StackLayout>
                </StackLayout>

                <!-- Button -->
                <Button x:Name="solveButton"
                        Text="Solve for x"
                        FontSize="Large"
                        IsEnabled="False"
                        VerticalOptions="CenterAndExpand"
                        HorizontalOptions="Center"
                        Clicked="OnSolveButtonClicked" />

                <!-- Results section -->
                <StackLayout VerticalOptions="CenterAndExpand"
                             HorizontalOptions="Center">
                    <Label x:Name="solution1Label"
                           XAlign="Center" />

                    <Label x:Name="solution2Label"
                           XAlign="Center" />
                </StackLayout>
            </StackLayout>
        </ContentPage>
```

The `Label`, `Entry`, and `Button` views are divided into three sections: data input at the top, the `Button` in the middle, and the results at the bottom. Notice the platform-specific `WidthRequest` setting in the implicit `Style` for the `Entry`. This gives each `Entry` a one-inch width.

The program provides two ways to trigger a calculation: by pressing the completion key on the keyboard, or by pressing the `Button` in the middle of the page. Another option in a program such as this would be to perform the calculation for every keystroke (or to be more accurate, every `TextChanged` event). That would work here because the recalculation is very quick. However, in the present design the results are near the bottom of the screen and are covered when the virtual keyboard is active, so the page would have to be reorganized for such a scheme to make sense.

The **QuadraticEquations** program uses the `TextChanged` event but solely to determine the validity of the text typed into each `Entry`. The text is passed to `Double.TryParse`, and if the method returns `false`, the `Entry` text is displayed in red. (On Windows Phone, the red text coloring shows up only when the `Entry` loses input focus.) Also, the `Button` is enabled only if all three `Entry` views contain valid `double` values. Here's the first half of the code-behind file that shows all the program interaction:

```
public partial class QuadraticEquationsPage : ContentPage
{
    public QuadraticEquationsPage()
    {
        InitializeComponent();

        // Initialize Entry views.
        entryA.Text = "1";
        entryB.Text = "-1";
```

```
                entryC.Text = "-1";
        }

        void OnEntryTextChanged(object sender, TextChangedEventArgs args)
        {
            // Clear out solutions.
            solution1Label.Text = " ";
            solution2Label.Text = " ";

            // Color current entry text based on validity.
            Entry entry = (Entry)sender;
            double result;
            entry.TextColor = Double.TryParse(entry.Text, out result) ? Color.Default : Color.Red;

            // Enable the button based on validity.
            solveButton.IsEnabled = Double.TryParse(entryA.Text, out result) &&
                                    Double.TryParse(entryB.Text, out result) &&
                                    Double.TryParse(entryC.Text, out result);
        }

        void OnEntryCompleted(object sender, EventArgs args)
        {
            if (solveButton.IsEnabled)
            {
                Solve();
            }
        }

        void OnSolveButtonClicked(object sender, EventArgs args)
        {
            Solve();
        }
        ...
}
```

The `Completed` handler for the `Entry` calls the `Solve` method only when the `Button` is enabled, which (as you've seen) indicates that all three `Entry` views contain valid values. Therefore, the `Solve` method can safely assume that all three `Entry` views contain valid numbers that won't cause `Double.Parse` to raise an exception.

The `Solve` method is necessarily complicated because the quadratic equation might have one or two solutions, and each solution might have an imaginary part as well as a real part. The method initializes the real part of the second solution to `Double.NaN` ("not a number") and displays the second result only if that's no longer the case. The imaginary parts are displayed only if they're nonzero, and either a plus sign or an en dash (Unicode \u2013) connects the real and imaginary parts:

```
public partial class QuadraticEquationsPage : ContentPage
{
    ...
    void Solve()
    {
        double a = Double.Parse(entryA.Text);
```

```
        double b = Double.Parse(entryB.Text);
        double c = Double.Parse(entryC.Text);
        double solution1Real = 0;
        double solution1Imag = 0;
        double solution2Real = Double.NaN;
        double solution2Imag = 0;
        string str1 = " ";
        string str2 = " ";

        if (a == 0 && b == 0 && c == 0)
        {
            str1 = "x = anything";
        }
        else if (a == 0 && b == 0)
        {
            str1 = "x = nothing";
        }
        else
        {
            if (a == 0)
            {
                solution1Real = -c / b;
            }
            else
            {
                double discriminant = b * b - 4 * a * c;

                if (discriminant == 0)
                {
                    solution1Real = -b / (2 * a);
                }
                else if (discriminant > 0)
                {
                    solution1Real = (-b + Math.Sqrt(discriminant)) / (2 * a);
                    solution2Real = (-b - Math.Sqrt(discriminant)) / (2 * a);
                }
                else
                {
                    solution1Real = -b / (2 * a);
                    solution2Real = solution1Real;

                    solution1Imag = Math.Sqrt(-discriminant) / (2 * a);
                    solution2Imag = -solution1Imag;
                }
            }
            str1 = Format(solution1Real, solution1Imag);
            str2 = Format(solution2Real, solution2Imag);
        }
        solution1Label.Text = str1;
        solution2Label.Text = str2;
    }

    string Format(double real, double imag)
    {
```

```
        string str = " ";

        if (!Double.IsNaN(real))
        {
            str = String.Format("x = {0:F5}", real);

            if (imag != 0)
            {
                str += String.Format(" {0} {1:F5} i",
                                        Math.Sign(imag) == 1 ? "+" : "\u2013",
                                        Math.Abs(imag));
            }
        }
        return str;
    }
}
```

Here's a couple of solutions:

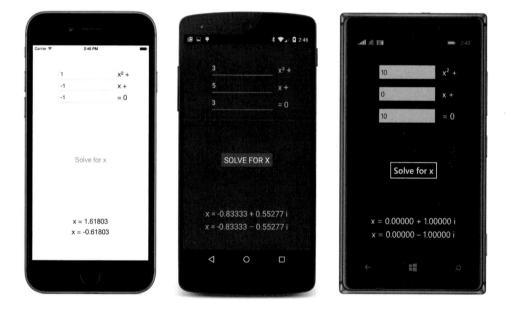

The Editor difference

You might assume that the `Editor` has a more extensive API than the `Entry` because it can handle multiple lines and even paragraphs of text. But in Xamarin.Forms, the API for `Editor` is actually some-what simpler. Besides inheriting the `Keyboard` property from `InputView`, `Editor` defines just one property on its own: the essential `Text` property. `Editor` also defines the same two events as `Entry`:

- `TextChanged`

- `Completed`

However, the `Completed` event is of necessity a little different. While a return or enter key can signal completion on an `Entry`, these same keys used with the `Editor` instead mark the end of a paragraph.

The `Completed` event for `Editor` works a little differently on the three platforms: For iOS, Xamarin.Forms displays a special **Done** button above the keyboard that dismisses the keyboard and causes a `Completed` event to fire. On Android and Windows Phone, the system **Back** button—the button at the lower-left corner of the phone in portrait mode—dismisses the keyboard and fires the `Completed` event. This **Back** button does *not* fire the `Completed` event for an `Entry` view, but it does dismiss the keyboard.

It is likely that what users type into an `Editor` is not telephone numbers and URLs but actual words, sentences, and paragraphs. In most cases, you'll want to use the `Text` keyboard for `Editor` because it provides spelling checks, suggestions, and automatic capitalization of the first word of sentences. If you don't want these features, the `Keyboard` class provides an alternative means of specifying a keyboard by using a static `Create` method and the following members of the `KeyboardFlags` enumeration:

- `CapitalizeSentence` (equal to 1)
- `Spellcheck` (2)
- `Suggestions` (4)
- `All` (\xFFFFFFFF)

The `Text` keyboard is equivalent to creating the keyboard with `KeyboardFlags.All`. The `Default` keyboard is equivalent to creating the keyboard with `(KeyboardFlags)0`.

You can't create a keyboard in XAML using these flags. It must be done in code. Some platforms restrict certain combinations: on Android, `Suggestions` enables `Spellcheck`, and on Windows Phone, `Suggestions` cannot be disabled if `CapitalizeSentence` and `Spellcheck` are enabled.

The **JustNotes** program is intended as a freeform note-taking program that automatically saves and restores the contents of an `Editor` view by using the `Properties` collection of the `Application` class. The page basically consists of a large `Editor`, but to give the user some clue about what the program does, the name of the program is displayed at the top. On iOS and Android, such text can be set by the `Title` property of the page, but to display that property, the `ContentPage` must be wrapped in an `ApplicationPage` (as you discovered with the **ToolbarDemo** program in Chapter 13). That's done in the constructor of the `App` class:

```
public class App : Application
{
    public App()
    {
        MainPage = new NavigationPage(new JustNotesPage());
    }

    protected override void OnStart()
    {
```

```
        // Handle when your app starts
    }

    protected override void OnSleep()
    {
        // Handle when your app sleeps
        ((JustNotesPage)(((NavigationPage)MainPage).CurrentPage)).OnSleep();
    }

    protected override void OnResume()
    {
        // Handle when your app resumes
    }
}
```

The `OnSleep` method in `App` calls a method also named `OnSleep` defined in the `JustNotesPage` code-behind file. This is how the contents of the `Editor` are saved in application memory.

The root element of the XAML page sets the `Title` property, but that's ignored on Windows Phone, so the page content begins with a display of a `Label` with the program name just for Windows Phone. The remainder of the page is occupied by an `AbsoluteLayout` filled with the `Editor`:

```xml
<ContentPage xmlns="http://xamarin.com/schemas/2014/forms"
             xmlns:x="http://schemas.microsoft.com/winfx/2009/xaml"
             x:Class="JustNotes.JustNotesPage"
             Title="Just Notes">

    <StackLayout>
        <ContentView>
            <OnPlatform x:TypeArguments="View">
                <OnPlatform.WinPhone>
                    <Label Text="Just Notes"
                           FontSize="Large"
                           HorizontalOptions="Center" />
                </OnPlatform.WinPhone>
            </OnPlatform>
        </ContentView>

        <AbsoluteLayout VerticalOptions="FillAndExpand">
            <Editor x:Name="editor"
                    Keyboard="Text"
                    AbsoluteLayout.LayoutBounds="0, 0, 1, 1"
                    AbsoluteLayout.LayoutFlags="All"
                    Focused="OnEditorFocused"
                    Unfocused="OnEditorUnfocused">
                <Editor.BackgroundColor>
                    <OnPlatform x:TypeArguments="Color"
                                WinPhone="#D0D0D0" />
                </Editor.BackgroundColor>
            </Editor>
        </AbsoluteLayout>
    </StackLayout>
</ContentPage>
```

Another item specific to Windows Phone in this XAML file is the `BackgroundColor` of the `Editor`.
When the `Editor` has input focus on Windows Phone, it displays a light background, but when it loses
input focus, the background becomes transparent and shows what's underneath, which is often the
black background of the page. Setting the `BackgroundColor` gives it a somewhat darker background
when it loses input focus than when it has focus, but you can still read the text.

But the big question is: Why the `AbsoluteLayout` for the `Editor`?

The **JustNotes** program is a work in progress. It doesn't quite work right for iOS. As you'll recall,
when an `Entry` view is positioned toward the bottom of the screen, you want to put it in a
`ScrollView` so that it scrolls up when the iOS virtual keyboard is displayed. However, because `Editor`
implements its own scrolling, you can't put it in a `ScrollView`.

For that reason, the code-behind file sets the height of the `Editor` to one-half the height of the
`AbsoluteLayout` when the `Editor` gets input focus so that the keyboard doesn't overlap it, and it
restores the `Editor` height when it loses input focus:

```
public partial class JustNotesPage : ContentPage
{
    public JustNotesPage()
    {
        InitializeComponent();

        // Retrieve last saved Editor text.
        IDictionary<string, object> properties = Application.Current.Properties;

        if (properties.ContainsKey("text"))
        {
            editor.Text = (string)properties["text"];
        }
    }

    void OnEditorFocused(object sender, FocusEventArgs args)
    {
        if (Device.OS == TargetPlatform.iOS)
        {
            AbsoluteLayout.SetLayoutBounds(editor, new Rectangle(0, 0, 1, 0.5));
        }
    }

    void OnEditorUnfocused(object sender, FocusEventArgs args)
    {
        if (Device.OS == TargetPlatform.iOS)
        {
            AbsoluteLayout.SetLayoutBounds(editor, new Rectangle(0, 0, 1, 1));
        }
    }

    public void OnSleep()
    {
        // Save Editor text.
```

```
        Application.Current.Properties["text"] = editor.Text;
    }
}
```

That adjustment is only approximate, of course. It varies by device, and it varies by portrait and landscape mode, but sufficient information is not currently available in Xamarin.Forms to do it more accurately. For now, you should probably restrict your use of `Editor` views to the top area of the page.

The code for saving and restoring the `Editor` contents is rather prosaic in comparison with the `Editor` manipulation. The `OnSleep` method (called from the `App` class) saves the text in the `Properties` dictionary with a key of "text" and the constructor restores it.

Here's the program running on all three platforms with the `Text` keyboard in view with word suggestions. On the Windows Phone screen, a word has been selected and might be copied to the clipboard for a later paste operation:

The SearchBar

The `SearchBar` doesn't derive from `InputView` like `Entry` and `Editor`, and it doesn't have a `Keyboard` property. The keyboard that `SearchBar` displays when it acquires input focus is platform specific and appropriate for a search command. The `SearchBar` itself is similar to an `Entry` view, but depending on the platform, it might be adorned with some other graphics and contain a button that erases the typed text.

`SearchBar` defines two events:

- `TextChanged`

- `SearchButtonPressed`

The `TextChanged` event allows your program to access a text entry in progress. Perhaps your program can actually begin a search or offer context-specific suggestions before the user completes typing. The `SearchButtonPressed` event is equivalent to the `Completed` event fired by `Entry`. It is triggered by a particular button on the keyboard in the same location as the completed button for `Entry` but possibly labeled differently.

`SearchBar` defines five properties:

- `Text` — the text entered by the user

- `Placeholder` — hint text displayed before the user begins typing

- `CancelButtonColor` — of type `Color`

- `SearchCommand` — for use with data binding

- `SearchCommandParameter` — for use with data binding

The **SearchBarDemo** program uses only `Text` and `Placeholder`, but the XAML file attaches handlers for both events:

```
<ContentPage xmlns="http://xamarin.com/schemas/2014/forms"
             xmlns:x="http://schemas.microsoft.com/winfx/2009/xaml"
             x:Class="SearchBarDemo.SearchBarDemoPage">
    <ContentPage.Padding>
        <OnPlatform x:TypeArguments="Thickness"
                    iOS="10, 20, 10, 0"
                    Android="10, 0"
                    WinPhone="10, 0" />
    </ContentPage.Padding>

    <StackLayout>
        <SearchBar x:Name="searchBar"
                   Placeholder="Search text"
                   TextChanged="OnSearchBarTextChanged"
                   SearchButtonPressed="OnSearchBarButtonPressed" />

        <ScrollView x:Name="resultsScroll"
                    VerticalOptions="FillAndExpand">
            <StackLayout x:Name="resultsStack" />
        </ScrollView>
    </StackLayout>
</ContentPage>
```

The program uses the scrollable `StackLayout` named `resultsStack` to display the results of the search.

Here's the `SearchBar` and keyboard for the three platforms. Notice the search icon and a delete button in the iOS and Android versions, as well as the special search keys on the iOS and Android keyboards:

You might guess from the entries in the three `SearchBar` views that the program allows searching through the text of Herman Melville's *Moby-Dick*. That is true! The entire novel is stored as an embedded resource in the **Texts** folder of the Portable Class Library project with the name MobyDick.txt. The file is a plain-text, one-line-per-paragraph format that originated with a file on the Gutenberg.net website.

The constructor of the code-behind file reads that whole file into a string field named `bookText`. The `TextChanged` handler clears the `resultsStack` of any previous search results so that there's no discrepancy between the text being typed into the `SearchBar` and this list. The `SearchButton-Pressed` event initiates the search:

```
public partial class SearchBarDemoPage : ContentPage
{
    const double MaxMatches = 100;
    string bookText;

    public SearchBarDemoPage()
    {
        InitializeComponent();

        // Load embedded resource bitmap.
        string resourceID = "SearchBarDemo.Texts.MobyDick.txt";
        Assembly assembly = GetType().GetTypeInfo().Assembly;

        using (Stream stream = assembly.GetManifestResourceStream(resourceID))
        {
            using (StreamReader reader = new StreamReader(stream))
            {
                bookText = reader.ReadToEnd();
```

```
            }
        }
    }

    void OnSearchBarTextChanged(object sender, TextChangedEventArgs args)
    {
        resultsStack.Children.Clear();
    }

    void OnSearchBarButtonPressed(object sender, EventArgs args)
    {
        // Detach resultsStack from layout.
        resultsScroll.Content = null;

        resultsStack.Children.Clear();
        SearchBookForText(searchBar.Text);

        // Reattach resultsStack to layout.
        resultsScroll.Content = resultsStack;
    }

    void SearchBookForText(string searchText)
    {
        int count = 0;
        bool isTruncated = false;

        using (StringReader reader = new StringReader(bookText))
        {
            int lineNumber = 0;
            string line;

            while (null != (line = reader.ReadLine()))
            {
                lineNumber++;
                int index = 0;

                while (-1 != (index = (line.IndexOf(searchText, index,
                                        StringComparison.OrdinalIgnoreCase))))
                {
                    if (count == MaxMatches)
                    {
                        isTruncated = true;
                        break;
                    }
                    index += 1;

                    // Add the information to the StackLayout.
                    resultsStack.Children.Add(
                        new Label
                        {
                            Text = String.Format("Found at line {0}, offset {1}",
                                        lineNumber, index)
                        });
```

```
                count++;
            }

            if (isTruncated)
            {
                break;
            }
        }
    }

    // Add final count to the StackLayout.
    resultsStack.Children.Add(
        new Label
        {
            Text = String.Format("{0} match{1} found{2}",
                                  count,
                                  count == 1 ? "" : "es",
                                  isTruncated ? " - stopped" : "")
        });
    }
}
```

The `SearchBookForText` method uses the search text with the `IndexOf` method applied to each line of the book for case-insensitive comparison and adds a `Label` to `resultsStack` for each match. However, this process has performance problems because each `Label` that is added to the `StackLayout` potentially triggers a new layout calculation. That's unnecessary. For this reason, before beginning the search, the program detaches the `StackLayout` from the visual tree by setting the `Content` property of its parent (the `ScrollView`) to `null`:

```
resultsScroll.Content = null;
```

After all the `Label` views have been added to the `StackLayout`, the `StackLayout` is added back to the visual tree:

```
resultsScroll.Content = resultsStack;
```

But even that's not a sufficient performance improvement for Android and Windows Phone, and that is why the program limits itself to the first 100 matches. (Notice the `MaxMatches` constant defined at the top of the class.) Here's the program showing the results of the searches you saw entered earlier:

You'll need to reference the actual file to see what those matches are.

Would running the search in a second thread of execution speed things up? No. The actual text search is very fast. The performance issues involve the user interface. If the `SearchBookForText` method were run in a secondary thread, then it would need to use `Device.BeginInvokeOnMain-Thread` to add each `Label` to the `StackLayout`. If that `StackLayout` is attached to the visual tree, this would make the program operate more dynamically—the individual items would appear on the screen following each item added to the list—but the switching back and forth between threads would slow down the overall operation.

Date and time selection

A Xamarin.Forms application that needs a date or time from the user can use the `DatePicker` or `TimePicker` view.

These are very similar: The two views simply display a date or time in a box similar to an `Entry` view. Tapping the view invokes the platform-specific date or time selector. The user then selects (or dials in) a new date or time and signals completion.

The Windows Phone implementations of `DatePicker` and `TimePicker` use some toolbar icons in the **Toolkit.Content** folder in the Windows Phone project. If the icons do not display correctly, go into that folder and give the PNG files you'll find there a **Build Action** of **Content**.

The DatePicker

DatePicker has three properties of type DateTime:

- MinimumDate, initialized to January 1, 1900

- MaximumDate, initialized to December 31, 2100

- Date, initialized to DateTime.Today

A program can set these properties to whatever it wants as long as MinimumDate is prior to MaximumDate. The Date property reflects the user's selection.

If you'd like to set those properties in XAML, you can do so using the x:DateTime element. Use a format that is acceptable to the DateTime.Parse method with a second argument of CultureInfo.InvariantCulture. Probably the easiest is the short-date format, which is a two-digit month, a two-digit day, and a two-digit year, separated by slashes:

```
<DatePicker … >
    <DatePicker.MinimumDate>
        03/01/2016
    </DatePicker.MinimumDate>

    <DatePicker.MaximumDate>
        10/31/2016
    </DatePicker.MaximumDate>

    <DatePicker.Date>
        07/14/2016
    </DatePicker.Date>
</DatePicker>
```

The DatePicker displays the selected date by using the normal ToString method, but you can set the Format property of the view to a custom .NET formatting string. The initial value is "d"—the short-date format.

Here's the XAML file from a program called **DaysBetweenDates** that lets you select two dates and then calculates the number of days between them. It contains two DatePicker views labeled **To** and **From**:

```
<ContentPage xmlns="http://xamarin.com/schemas/2014/forms"
             xmlns:x="http://schemas.microsoft.com/winfx/2009/xaml"
             x:Class="DaysBetweenDates.DaysBetweenDatesPage">

    <ContentPage.Padding>
        <OnPlatform x:TypeArguments="Thickness"
                    iOS="10, 30, 10, 0"
                    Android="10, 10, 10, 0"
                    WinPhone="10, 10, 10, 0" />
    </ContentPage.Padding>

    <StackLayout>
```

```xml
            <StackLayout.Resources>
                <ResourceDictionary>
                    <Style TargetType="DatePicker">
                        <Setter Property="Format" Value="D" />
                        <Setter Property="VerticalOptions" Value="Center" />
                        <Setter Property="HorizontalOptions" Value="FillAndExpand" />
                    </Style>
                </ResourceDictionary>
            </StackLayout.Resources>

            <!-- Underlined text header -->
            <StackLayout Grid.Row="0" Grid.Column="0" Grid.ColumnSpan="2"
                         VerticalOptions="CenterAndExpand"
                         HorizontalOptions="Center">
                <Label Text="Days between Dates"
                       FontSize="Large"
                       FontAttributes="Bold"
                       TextColor="Accent" />
                <BoxView Color="Accent"
                         HeightRequest="3" />
            </StackLayout>

            <StackLayout Orientation="Horizontal"
                         VerticalOptions="CenterAndExpand">
                <Label Text="From:"
                       VerticalOptions="Center" />

                <DatePicker x:Name="fromDatePicker"
                            DateSelected="OnDateSelected" />
            </StackLayout>

            <StackLayout Orientation="Horizontal"
                         VerticalOptions="CenterAndExpand">
                <Label Text="    To:"
                       VerticalOptions="Center" />

                <DatePicker x:Name="toDatePicker"
                            DateSelected="OnDateSelected" />
            </StackLayout>

            <Label x:Name="resultLabel"
                   FontSize="Large"
                   HorizontalOptions="Center"
                   VerticalOptions="CenterAndExpand" />
        </StackLayout>
</ContentPage>
```

An implicit style sets the `Format` property of the two `DatePicker` views to "D", which is the long-date format, to include the text day of the week and month name. The XAML file uses two horizontal `StackLayout` objects for displaying a `Label` and `DatePicker` side by side.

Watch out: If you use the long-date format, you'll want to avoid setting the `HorizontalOptions` property of the `DatePicker` to `Start`, `Center`, or `End`. If you put the `DatePicker` in a horizontal

StackLayout (as in this program), set the HorizontalOptions to FillAndExpand. Otherwise, if the user selects a date with a longer text string than the original date, the result is not formatted well. The **DaysBetweenDates** program uses an implicit style to give the DatePicker a HorizontalOptions value of FillAndExpand so that it occupies the entire width of the horizontal StackLayout except for what's occupied by the Label.

When you tap one of the DatePicker fields, a platform-specific panel comes up. On iOS, it occupies just the bottom part of the screen, but on Android and Windows Phone, it takes over the screen:

Notice the **Done** button on iOS, the **OK** button on Android, and the check-mark toolbar button on Windows Phone. All three of these buttons dismiss the date-picking panel and return to the program with a firing of the DateSelected event. The event handler in the **DaysBetweenDates** code-behind file accesses both DatePicker views and calculates the number of days between the two dates:

```
public partial class DaysBetweenDatesPage : ContentPage
{
    public DaysBetweenDatesPage()
    {
        InitializeComponent();

        // Initialize.
        OnDateSelected(null, null);
    }

    void OnDateSelected(object sender, DateChangedEventArgs args)
    {
        int days = (toDatePicker.Date - fromDatePicker.Date).Days;
        resultLabel.Text = String.Format("{0} day{1} between dates",
                                         days, days == 1 ? "" : "s");
```

```
    }
}
```

Here's the result:

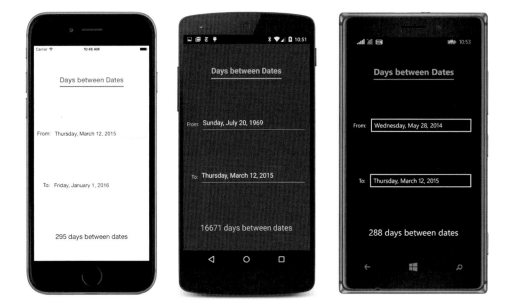

The TimePicker (or is it a TimeSpanPicker?)

The `TimePicker` is somewhat simpler than `DatePicker`. It defines only `Time` and `Format` properties, and it doesn't include an event to indicate a new selected `Time` value. If you need to be notified, you can install a handler for the `PropertyChanged` event.

Although `TimePicker` displays the selected time by using the `ToString` method of `DateTime`, the `Time` property is actually of type `TimeSpan`, indicating a duration of time since midnight.

The **SetTimer** program lets you select a time. The program assumes that this time is within the next 24 hours and then notifies you when that time has come. The XAML file puts a `TimePicker`, a `Switch`, and an `Entry` on the page.

```
<ContentPage xmlns="http://xamarin.com/schemas/2014/forms"
             xmlns:x="http://schemas.microsoft.com/winfx/2009/xaml"
             x:Class="SetTimer.SetTimerPage"
             Padding="50">

    <StackLayout Spacing="20"
                 VerticalOptions="Center">
        <TimePicker x:Name="timePicker"
                    PropertyChanged="OnTimePickerPropertyChanged" />

        <Switch x:Name="switch"
```

```
                    HorizontalOptions="End"
                    Toggled="OnSwitchToggled" />

        <Entry x:Name="entry"
               Text="Sample Timer"
               Placeholder="label" />
    </StackLayout>
</ContentPage>
```

The `TimePicker` has a `PropertyChanged` event handler attached. The `Entry` lets you remind your-self what the timer is supposed to remind you of.

When you tap the `TimePicker`, a platform-specific panel pops up. As with the `DatePicker`, the Android and Windows Phone panels obscure the whole program, but you can see the `SetTimer` user interface in the center of the iPhone screen:

In a real timer program—a timer program that is actually useful and not just a demonstration of the `TimePicker` view—the code-behind file would access the platform-specific notification interfaces so that the user would be notified even if the program were no longer active.

SetTimer doesn't do that. **SetTimer** instead uses a platform-specific alert box that a program can invoke by calling the `DisplayAlert` method defined by `Page` and inherited by `ContentPage`.

The `SetTriggerTime` method at the bottom of the code-behind file (shown below) calculates the timer time based on `DateTime.Today`—a property that returns a `DateTime` indicating the current date, but with a time of midnight—and the `TimeSpan` returned from the `TimePicker`. If that time has already passed today, then it's assumed to be tomorrow.

The timer, however, is set for one second. Every second the timer handler checks whether the

`Switch` is on and whether the current time is greater than or equal to the timer time:

```
public partial class SetTimerPage : ContentPage
{
    DateTime triggerTime;

    public SetTimerPage()
    {
        InitializeComponent();

        Device.StartTimer(TimeSpan.FromSeconds(1), OnTimerTick);
    }

    bool OnTimerTick()
    {
        if (@switch.IsToggled && DateTime.Now >= triggerTime)
        {
            @switch.IsToggled = false;
            DisplayAlert("Timer Alert",
                        "The '" + entry.Text + "' timer has elapsed",
                        "OK");
        }
        return true;
    }

    void OnTimePickerPropertyChanged(object obj, PropertyChangedEventArgs args)
    {
        if (args.PropertyName == "Time")
        {
            SetTriggerTime();
        }
    }

    void OnSwitchToggled(object obj, ToggledEventArgs args)
    {
        SetTriggerTime();
    }

    void SetTriggerTime()
    {
        if (@switch.IsToggled)
        {
            triggerTime = DateTime.Today + timePicker.Time;

            if (triggerTime < DateTime.Now)
            {
                triggerTime += TimeSpan.FromDays(1);
            }
        }
    }
}
```

When the timer time has come, the program uses `DisplayAlert` to signal a reminder to the user. Here's how this alert appears on the three platforms:

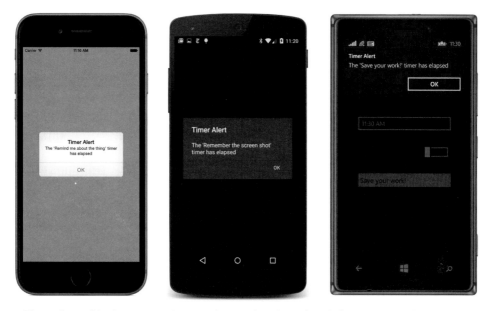

Throughout this chapter, you've seen interactive views that define events, and you've seen application programs that implement event handlers. Often these event handlers access a property of the view and set a property of another view.

In the next chapter, you'll see how these event handlers can be eliminated and how properties of different views can be linked, either in code or markup. This is the exciting feature of *data binding*.

Chapter 16
Data binding

Events and event handlers are a vital part of the interactive interface of Xamarin.Forms, but often event handlers perform very rudimentary jobs. They transfer values between properties of different objects and in some cases simply update a `Label` to show the new value of a view.

You can automate such connections between properties of two objects with a powerful feature of Xamarin.Forms called *data binding*. Under the covers, a data binding installs event handlers and handles the transfer of values from one property to another so that you don't have to. In most cases you define these data bindings in the XAML file, so there's no code (or very little code) involved. The use of data bindings helps reduce the number of "moving parts" in the application.

Data bindings also play a crucial role in the Model-View-ViewModel (MVVM) application architecture. As you'll see in a future chapter, data bindings provide the link between the View (the user interface often implemented in XAML) and the underlying data of the ViewModel and Model. This means that the connections between the user interface and underlying data can be represented in XAML along with the user interface.

Binding basics

Several properties, methods, and classes are involved in data bindings:

- The `Binding` class (which derives from `BindingBase`) defines many characteristics of a data binding.

- The `BindingContext` property is defined by the `BindableObject` class.

- The `SetBinding` method is also defined by the `BindableObject` class.

- The `BindableObjectExtensions` class defines two additional overloads of `SetBinding`.

Two classes support XAML markup extensions for bindings:

- The `BindingExtension` class, which is private to Xamarin.Forms, provides support for the `Binding` markup extension that you use to define a data binding in XAML.

- The `ReferenceExtension` class is also crucial to bindings.

Two interfaces also get involved in data binding. These are:

- `INotifyPropertyChanged` (defined in the `System.ComponentModel` namespace) is the standard interface that classes use when notifying external classes that a property has changed.

This interface plays a major role in MVVM.

- `IValueConverter` (defined in the `Xamarin.Forms` namespace) is used to define small classes that aid data binding by converting values from one type to another.

The most fundamental concept of data bindings is this: Data bindings always have a *source* and a *target*. The source is a property of an object, usually one that changes dynamically at run time. When that property changes, the data binding automatically updates the target, which is a property of another object.

Target ← Source

But as you'll see, sometimes the data flow between the source and target isn't in a constant direction. Even in those cases, however, the distinction between source and target is important because of one basic fact:

The target of a data binding must be backed by a `BindableProperty` *object.*

As you know, the `VisualElement` class derives from `BindableObject` by way of `Element`, and all the visual elements in Xamarin.Forms define most of their properties as bindable properties. For this reason, data-binding targets are almost always visual elements or—as you'll see in a future chapter on collection views—objects called *cells* that are translated to visual elements.

Although the target of a data binding must be backed by a `BindableProperty` object, there is no such requirement for a data-binding source. The source can be a plain old C# property. However, in all but the most trivial data bindings, a change in the source property causes a corresponding change in the target property. This means that the source object must implement some kind of notification mechanism to signal when the property changes. This notification mechanism is the `INotifyPropertyChanged` interface, which is a standard .NET interface involved in data bindings and used extensively for implementing the MVVM architecture.

The rule for a nontrivial data-binding source—that is, a data-binding source that can dynamically change value—is therefore:

The source of a nontrivial data binding must implement `INotifyPropertyChanged`.

Despite its importance, the `INotifyPropertyChanged` interface has the virtue of being very simple: it consists solely of one event, called `PropertyChanged`, that a class fires when a property has changed.

Very conveniently for our purposes, `BindableObject` implements `INotifyPropertyChanged`. Any property that is backed by a bindable property automatically fires a `PropertyChanged` event when that property changes. This automatic firing of the event extends to bindable properties you might define in your own classes.

This means that you can define data bindings between properties of visual objects. In the grand scheme of things, most data bindings probably link visual objects with underlying data, but for purposes of learning about data bindings and experimenting with them, it's nice to simply link properties of two views without defining data classes.

For the first few examples in this chapter, you'll see data bindings in which the source is the `Value` property of a `Slider` and target is the `Opacity` property of a `Label`. As you manipulate the `Slider`, the `Label` changes from transparent to opaque. Both properties are of type `double` and range from 0 to 1, so they are a perfect match.

You already know how to do this little job with a simple event handler. Let's see how to do it with a data binding.

Code and XAML

Although most data bindings are defined in XAML, you should know how to do one in code. Here's one way (but not the only way) to set a data binding in code:

- Set the `BindingContext` property on the target object to the source object.

- Call `SetBinding` on the target object to specify the target property and the source property.

The `BindingContext` property is defined by `BindableObject`. (It's the *only* property defined by `BindableObject`.) The `SetBinding` method is also defined by `BindableObject`, but there are two additional overloads of the `SetBinding` method in the `BindableObjectExtensions` class. The target property is specified as a `BindableProperty`; the source property is often specified as a string.

The **OpacityBindingCode** program creates two elements, a `Label` and a `Slider`, and defines a data binding that targets the `Opacity` property of the `Label` from the `Value` property of the `Slider`:

```
public class OpacityBindingCodePage : ContentPage
{
    public OpacityBindingCodePage()
    {
        Label label = new Label
        {
            Text = "Opacity Binding Demo",
            FontSize = Device.GetNamedSize(NamedSize.Large, typeof(Label)),
            VerticalOptions = LayoutOptions.CenterAndExpand,
            HorizontalOptions = LayoutOptions.Center
        };

        Slider slider = new Slider
        {
            VerticalOptions = LayoutOptions.CenterAndExpand
        };

        // Set the binding context: target is Label; source is Slider.
        label.BindingContext = slider;

        // Bind the properties: target is Opacity; source is Value.
        label.SetBinding(Label.OpacityProperty, "Value");
```

```
        // Construct the page.
        Padding = new Thickness(10, 0);
        Content = new StackLayout
        {
            Children = { label, slider }
        };
    }
}
```

Here's the property setting that connects the two objects:

```
label.BindingContext = slider;
```

The `label` object is the target and the `slider` object is the source. Here's the method call that links the two properties:

```
label.SetBinding(Label.OpacityProperty, "Value");
```

The first argument to `SetBinding` is of type `BindableProperty`, and that's the requirement for the target property. But the source property is merely specified as a string. It can be anything.

The screen shot demonstrates that you don't need to set an event handler to use the `Slider` for controlling other elements on the page:

Of course, *somebody* is setting an event handler. Under the covers, when the binding initializes it-self, it also performs initialization on the target by setting the `Opacity` property of the `Label` from the `Value` property of the `Slider`. (As you discovered in the previous chapter, when you set an event handler yourself, this initialization doesn't happen automatically.) Then the internal binding code checks whether the source object (in this case the `Slider`) implements the `INotifyProperty-Changed` interface. If so, a `PropertyChanged` handler is set on the `Slider`. Whenever the `Value` property changes, the binding sets the new value to the `Opacity` property of the `Label`.

Reproducing the binding in XAML involves two markup extensions that you haven't seen yet:

- `x:Refererence`, which is part of the XAML 2009 specification.

- `Binding`, which is part of Microsoft's XAML-based user interfaces.

The `x:Reference` binding extension is very simple, but the `Binding` markup extension is the most extensive and complex markup extension in all of Xamarin.Forms. It will be introduced incrementally over the course of this chapter.

Here's how you set the data binding in XAML:

- Set the `BindingContext` property of the target element (the `Label`) to an `x:Reference` markup extension that references the source element (the `Slider`).

- Set the target property (the `Opacity` property of the `Label`) to a `Binding` markup extension that references the source property (the `Value` property of the `Slider`).

The **OpacityBindingXaml** project shows the complete markup:

```
<ContentPage xmlns="http://xamarin.com/schemas/2014/forms"
             xmlns:x="http://schemas.microsoft.com/winfx/2009/xaml"
             x:Class="OpacityBindingXaml.OpacityBindingXamlPage"
             Padding="10, 0">
    <StackLayout>
        <Label Text="Opacity Binding Demo"
               FontSize="Large"
               VerticalOptions="CenterAndExpand"
               HorizontalOptions="Center"
               BindingContext="{x:Reference Name=slider}"
               Opacity="{Binding Path=Value}" />

        <Slider x:Name="slider"
                VerticalOptions="CenterAndExpand" />
    </StackLayout>
</ContentPage>
```

The two markup extensions for the binding are the last two attribute settings in the `Label`. The code-behind file contains nothing except the standard call to `InitializeComponent`.

When setting the `BindingContext` in markup, it is very easy to forget the `x:Reference` markup extension and simply specify the source name, but that doesn't work.

The `Path` argument of the `Binding` markup expression specifies the source property. Why is this argument called `Path` rather than `Property`? You'll see why later in this chapter.

You can make the markup a little shorter. The content property of `ReferenceExtension` (a public class that provides support for the `Reference` markup extension) is `Name`, and the content property of `BindingExtension` (which is not a public class) is `Path`, so you don't need those arguments and equal signs:

```
<Label Text="Opacity Binding Demo"
       FontSize="Large"
       VerticalOptions="CenterAndExpand"
       HorizontalOptions="Center"
       BindingContext="{x:Reference slider}"
       Opacity="{Binding Value}" />
```

Or if you'd like to make the markup longer, you can break out the `BindingContext` and `Opacity` properties as property elements and set them by using regular element syntax for `x:Reference` and `Binding`:

```
<Label Text="Opacity Binding Demo"
       FontSize="Large"
       VerticalOptions="CenterAndExpand"
       HorizontalOptions="Center">

    <Label.BindingContext>
        <x:Reference Name="slider" />
    </Label.BindingContext>

    <Label.Opacity>
        <Binding Path="Value" />
    </Label.Opacity>
</Label>
```

As you'll see, the use of property elements for bindings is sometimes convenient when other objects need to be instantiated in connection with the data binding.

Source and BindingContext

The `BindingContext` property is actually one of two ways to link the source and target objects. You can alternatively dispense with `BindingContext` and include a reference to the source object within the binding expression itself.

The **BindingSourceCode** project has a page class that is identical to the one in **OpacityBinding-Code** except that the binding is defined in two statements that don't involve the `BindingContext` property:

```
public class BindingSourceCodePage : ContentPage
{
    public BindingSourceCodePage()
    {
        Label label = new Label
        {
            Text = "Opacity Binding Demo",
```

```
            FontSize = Device.GetNamedSize(NamedSize.Large, typeof(Label)),
            VerticalOptions = LayoutOptions.CenterAndExpand,
            HorizontalOptions = LayoutOptions.Center
        };

        Slider slider = new Slider
        {
            VerticalOptions = LayoutOptions.CenterAndExpand
        };

        // Define Binding object with source object and property.
        Binding binding = new Binding
        {
            Source = slider,
            Path = "Value"
        };

        // Bind the Opacity property of the Label to the source.
        label.SetBinding(Label.OpacityProperty, binding);

        // Construct the page.
        Padding = new Thickness(10, 0);
        Content = new StackLayout
        {
            Children = { label, slider }
        };
    }
}
```

The target object and property are still specified in the call to the `SetBinding` method:

```
label.SetBinding(Label.OpacityProperty, binding);
```

However, the second argument references a `Binding` object that specifies the source object and property:

```
Binding binding = new Binding
{
    Source = slider,
    Path = "Value"
};
```

That is not the only way to instantiate and initialize a `Binding` object. An extensive `Binding` constructor allows for specifying many `Binding` properties. Here's how it could be used in the **BindingSourceCode** program:

```
Binding binding = new Binding("Value", BindingMode.Default, null, null, null, slider);
```

Or you can use a named argument to reference the `slider` object:

```
Binding binding = new Binding("Value", source: slider);
```

`Binding` also has a generic `Create` method that lets you specify the `Path` property as a `Func` object rather than as a string so that it's more immune from misspellings or changes in the property name. However, this `Create` method doesn't include an argument for the `Source` property, so you need to set it separately:

```
Binding binding = Binding.Create<Slider>(src => src.Value);
binding.Source = slider;
```

The `BindableObjectExtensions` class defines two overloads of `SetBinding` that allow you to avoid explicitly instantiating a `Binding` object. However, neither of these overloads includes the `Source` property, so they are restricted to cases where you're using the `BindingContext`.

The **BindingSourceXaml** program demonstrates how both the source object and source property can be specified in the `Binding` markup extension:

```
<ContentPage xmlns="http://xamarin.com/schemas/2014/forms"
             xmlns:x="http://schemas.microsoft.com/winfx/2009/xaml"
             x:Class="BindingSourceXaml.BindingSourceXamlPage"
             Padding="10, 0">
    <StackLayout>
        <Label Text="Binding Source Demo"
               FontSize="Large"
               VerticalOptions="CenterAndExpand"
               HorizontalOptions="Center"
               Opacity="{Binding Source={x:Reference Name=slider},
                                 Path=Value}" />

        <Slider x:Name="slider"
                VerticalOptions="CenterAndExpand" />
    </StackLayout>
</ContentPage>
```

The `Binding` markup extension now has two arguments, one of which is another markup extension for `x:Reference`, so a pair of curly braces are nested within the main curly braces:

```
Opacity="{Binding Source={x:Reference Name=slider},
                  Path=Value}" />
```

For clarity, the two `Binding` arguments are visually aligned within the markup extension, but that's not required. Arguments must be separated by a comma (here at the end of the first line) and no quotation marks must appear within the curly braces. You're not dealing with XML attributes within the markup extension. These are markup extension arguments.

You can simplify the nested markup extension by eliminating the `Name` argument name and equals sign in `x:Reference` because `Name` is the content property of the `ReferenceExtension` class:

```
Opacity="{Binding Source={x:Reference slider},
                  Path=Value}" />
```

However, you *cannot* similarly remove the `Path` argument name and equals sign. Even though `BindingExtension` defines `Path` as its content property, the argument name can only be eliminated when that argument is the first among multiple arguments. You need to switch around the arguments like so:

```
Opacity="{Binding Path=Value,
                   Source={x:Reference slider}}" />
```

And then you can eliminate the `Path` argument name, and perhaps move everything to one line:

```
Opacity="{Binding Value, Source={x:Reference slider}}" />
```

However, because the first argument is missing an argument name and the second argument has an argument name, the whole expression looks a bit peculiar, and it might be difficult to grasp the `Binding` arguments at first sight. Also, it makes sense for the `Source` to be specified *before* the `Path` because the particular property specified by the `Path` makes sense only for a particular type of object, and that's specified by the `Source`.

In this book, whenever the `Binding` markup extension includes a `Source` argument, it will be first, followed by the `Path`. Otherwise, the `Path` will be the first argument, and often the `Path` argument name will be eliminated.

You can avoid the issue entirely by expressing `Binding` in element form:

```
<Label Text="Binding Source Demo"
       FontSize="Large"
       VerticalOptions="CenterAndExpand"
       HorizontalOptions="Center">
    <Label.Opacity>
        <Binding Source="{x:Reference slider}"
                 Path="Value" />
    </Label.Opacity>
</Label>
```

The `x:Reference` markup extension still exists, but you can also express that in element form as well:

```
<Label Text="Binding Source Demo"
       FontSize="Large"
       VerticalOptions="CenterAndExpand"
       HorizontalOptions="Center">
    <Label.Opacity>
        <Binding Path="Value">
            <Binding.Source>
                <x:Reference Name="slider" />
            </Binding.Source>
        </Binding>
    </Label.Opacity>
</Label>
```

You have now seen two ways to specify the link between the source object with the target object:

- Use the `BindingContext` to reference the source object.

- Use the `Source` property of the `Binding` class or the `Binding` markup extension.

If you specify both, the `Source` property takes precedence over the `BindingContext`.

In the examples you've seen so far, these two techniques have been pretty much interchangeable.

However, they have some significant differences. For example, suppose you have one object with two properties that are targets of two different data bindings involving two different source objects—for example, a `Label` with the `Opacity` property bound to a `Slider` and the `IsVisible` property bound to a `Switch`. You can't use `BindingContext` for both bindings because `BindingContext` applies to the whole target object and can only specify a single source. You must use the `Source` property of `Binding` for at least one of these bindings.

`BindingContext` is itself backed by a bindable property. This means that `BindingContext` can be set from a `Binding` markup extension. (In contrast, you can't set the `Source` property of `Binding` to another `Binding` because `Binding` does not derive from `BindableObject`, which means `Source` is not backed by a bindable property and hence can't be the target of a data binding.)

In this variation of the **BindingSourceXaml** markup, the `BindingContext` property of the `Label` is set to a `Binding` markup extension that includes a `Source` and `Path`.

```
<Label Text="Binding Source Demo"
       FontSize="Large"
       VerticalOptions="CenterAndExpand"
       HorizontalOptions="Center"
       BindingContext="{Binding Source={x:Reference Name=slider},
                                Path=Value}"
       Opacity="{Binding}" />
```

This means that the `BindingContext` for this `Label` is not the `slider` object as in previous examples but the `double` that is the `Value` property of the `Slider`. To bind the `Opacity` property to this `double`, all that's required is an empty `Binding` markup extension that basically says "use the `BindingContext` for the entire data-binding source."

Perhaps the most important difference between `BindingContext` and `Source` is a very special characteristic that makes `BindingContext` unlike any other property in all of Xamarin.Forms:

The binding context is propagated through the visual tree.

In other words, if you set `BindingContext` on a `StackLayout`, it applies to all the children of that `StackLayout` and their children as well. The data bindings within that `StackLayout` don't have to specify `BindingContext` or the `Source` argument to `Binding`. They inherit `BindingContext` from the `StackLayout`. Or the children of the `StackLayout` can override that inherited `BindingContext` with `BindingContext` settings of their own or with a `Source` setting in their bindings.

This feature turns out to be exceptionally useful. Suppose a `StackLayout` contains a bunch of visuals with data bindings set to various properties of a particular class. These individual data bindings don't require either a `Source` specification or a `BindingContext` setting. You could then set the `BindingContext` of the `StackLayout` to different instances of that class to display the properties for each instance.

You'll see examples of this technique and other data-binding marvels in the chapters ahead, and particularly in the chapter on collection views.

Meanwhile, let's look at a much simpler example of `BindingContext` propagation through the visual tree.

The `WebView` is intended to embed a web browser inside your application. Alternatively, you can use `WebView` in conjunction with the `HtmlWebViewSource` class to display a chunk of HTML, perhaps saved as an embedded resource in the PCL.

For displaying webpages, you use `WebView` with the `UrlWebViewSource` class to specify an initial URL. However, `UrlWebViewSource` and `HtmlWebViewSource` both derive from the abstract class `WebViewSource`, and that class defines an implicit conversion of `string` and `Uri` to itself, so all you really need to do is set a string with a web address to the `Source` property of `WebView` to direct `WebView` to present that webpage.

`WebView` also defines two methods, named `GoBack` and `GoForward`, that internally implement the **Back** and **Forward** buttons typically found on web browsers. Your program needs to know when it can enable these buttons, so `WebView` also defines two get-only Boolean properties, named `CanGoBack` and `CanGoForward`. These two properties are backed by bindable properties, which means that any changes to these properties result in `PropertyChanged` events being fired, which further means that they can be used as data binding sources to enable and disable two buttons.

Here's the XAML file for **WebViewDemo**. Notice that the nested `StackLayout` containing the two `Button` elements has its `BindingContext` property set to the `WebView`. The two `Button` children in that `StackLayout` inherit the `BindingContext`, so the buttons can have very simple `Binding` expressions on their `IsEnabled` properties that reference only the `CanGoBack` and `CanGoForward` properties:

```
<ContentPage xmlns="http://xamarin.com/schemas/2014/forms"
             xmlns:x="http://schemas.microsoft.com/winfx/2009/xaml"
             x:Class="WebViewDemo.WebViewDemoPage">
    <ContentPage.Padding>
        <OnPlatform x:TypeArguments="Thickness"
                    iOS="10, 20, 10, 0"
                    Android="10, 0"
                    WinPhone="10, 0" />
    </ContentPage.Padding>

    <StackLayout>
        <Entry Keyboard="Url"
               Placeholder="web address"
               Completed="OnEntryCompleted" />

        <StackLayout Orientation="Horizontal"
                     BindingContext="{x:Reference webView}">

            <Button Text="&#x21D0;"
                    FontSize="Large"
                    HorizontalOptions="FillAndExpand"
                    IsEnabled="{Binding CanGoBack}"
                    Clicked="OnGoBackClicked" />
```

```
            <Button Text="&#x21D2;"
                    FontSize="Large"
                    HorizontalOptions="FillAndExpand"
                    IsEnabled="{Binding CanGoForward}"
                    Clicked="OnGoForwardClicked" />
        </StackLayout>

        <WebView x:Name="webView"
                 VerticalOptions="FillAndExpand"
                 Source="http://xamarin.com" />
    </StackLayout>
</ContentPage>
```

The code-behind file needs to handle the `Clicked` events for the **Back** and **Forward** buttons as well as the `Completed` event for the `Entry` that lets you enter a web address of your own:

```
public partial class WebViewDemoPage : ContentPage
{
    public WebViewDemoPage()
    {
        InitializeComponent();
    }

    void OnEntryCompleted(object sender, EventArgs args)
    {
        webView.Source = ((Entry)sender).Text;
    }

    void OnGoBackClicked(object sender, EventArgs args)
    {
        webView.GoBack();
    }

    void OnGoForwardClicked(object sender, EventArgs args)
    {
        webView.GoForward();
    }
}
```

You don't need to enter a web address when the program starts up because the XAML file is hard-coded to go to your favorite website, and you can navigate around from there:

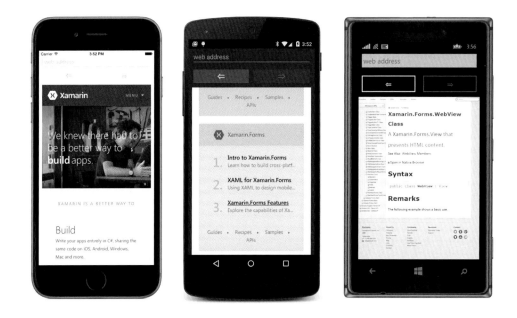

The binding mode

Here is a `BoxView` whose `WidthRequest` property is bound to the `Value` property of a `Slider`:

```
<BoxView WidthRequest="{Binding Source={x:Reference slider},
                                Path=Value}" />
<Slider x:Name="slider" />
```

That should work.

But here's a `BoxView` and `Slider` with the binding reversed. Instead of the `WidthRequest` property of the `BoxView` being the target, now that's the source of the data binding, and the target is the `Value` property of the `Slider`:

```
<BoxView x:Name="boxView1" />
<Slider Value="{Binding Source={x:Reference boxView1},
                        Path=WidthRequest}" />
```

That doesn't seem to make any sense.

Let's try them to see what happens. Here's a program called **BoxViewSizers** that contains those two snippets of markup as well as similar markup for two `Stepper` elements and two more `BoxView` elements. Implicit styles are defined for all three of these element types:

```
<ContentPage xmlns="http://xamarin.com/schemas/2014/forms"
             xmlns:x="http://schemas.microsoft.com/winfx/2009/xaml"
             x:Class="BoxViewSizers.BoxViewSizersPage"
             Padding="10, 0">
```

```xml
    <ContentPage.Resources>
        <ResourceDictionary>
            <Style TargetType="BoxView">
                <Setter Property="Color" Value="Accent" />
                <Setter Property="HorizontalOptions" Value="Center" />
            </Style>

            <Style TargetType="Slider">
                <Setter Property="Maximum" Value="300" />
            </Style>

            <Style TargetType="Stepper">
                <Setter Property="Maximum" Value="300" />
                <Setter Property="Increment" Value="10" />
            </Style>
        </ResourceDictionary>
    </ContentPage.Resources>

    <StackLayout>
        <StackLayout VerticalOptions="CenterAndExpand">
            <BoxView WidthRequest="{Binding Source={x:Reference slider},
                                    Path=Value}" />
            <Slider x:Name="slider" />
        </StackLayout>

        <StackLayout VerticalOptions="CenterAndExpand">
            <BoxView x:Name="boxView1" />
            <Slider Value="{Binding Source={x:Reference boxView1},
                            Path=WidthRequest}" />
        </StackLayout>

        <StackLayout VerticalOptions="CenterAndExpand">
            <BoxView WidthRequest="{Binding Source={x:Reference stepper},
                                    Path=Value}" />
            <Stepper x:Name="stepper" />
        </StackLayout>

        <StackLayout VerticalOptions="CenterAndExpand">
            <BoxView x:Name="boxView2" />
            <Stepper Value="{Binding Source={x:Reference boxView2},
                             Path=WidthRequest}" />
        </StackLayout>
    </StackLayout>
</ContentPage>
```

In particular, the implicit styles for the `Slider` and `Stepper` allow values to go up to 300, and the `Increment` property for the `Stepper` is set to 10 so that you don't have to push the button very many times to make the `BoxView` grow.

As expected, the binding that targets the `Value` property of the `Slider` from the `WidthRequest` property of the `BoxView` doesn't work, and that `BoxView` remains at its default width of 40:

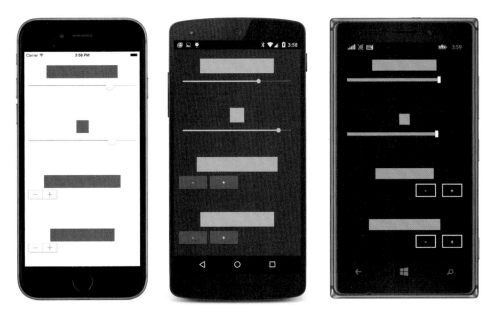

But wait:

The similar markup for the `Stepper` *does* work! It's the last one of the four groups and looks like this:

```
<BoxView x:Name="boxView2" />
<Stepper Value="{Binding Source={x:Reference boxView2},
                         Path=WidthRequest}" />
```

How can that be? And if that `Binding` works to change the `BoxView` width from the `Stepper` value, then why doesn't the similar markup with `Slider` work?

```
<BoxView x:Name="boxView1" />
<Slider Value="{Binding Source={x:Reference boxView1},
                        Path=WidthRequest}" />
```

The answer is that a `Slider` and a `Stepper` are a little different internally, and the difference involves the *binding mode.*

A data binding sets a target property from the value of a source property, but sometimes the data flow is not so clear cut. The relationship between target and source is defined by members of the `BindingMode` enumeration:

- `Default`

- `OneWay` — changes in the source affect the target (normal).

- `OneWayToSource` — changes in the target affect the source.

- `TwoWay` — changes in the source and target affect each other.

This `BindingMode` enumeration plays a role in two different classes:

When you create a `BindableProperty` object by using one of the static `Create` or `CreateReadOnly` static methods, you can specify a default `BindingMode` value to use when that property is the target of a data binding.

If you don't specify anything, the default binding mode is `OneWay` for bindable properties that are readable and writeable, and `OneWayToSource` for read-only bindable properties. If you specify `BindingMode.Default` when creating a bindable property, the default binding mode for the property is set to `OneWay`. (In other words, the `BindingMode.Default` member is not intended for defining bindable properties.)

You can override that default binding mode for the target property when you define a binding either in code or XAML. You override the default binding mode by setting the `Mode` property of `Binding` to one of the members of the `BindingMode` enumeration. The `Default` member means that you want to use the default binding mode defined for the target property.

When you set the `Mode` property to `OneWayToSource` you are *not* switching the target and the source. The target is still the object on which you've set the `BindingContext` and the property on which you've called `SetBinding` or applied the `Binding` markup extension. But the data flows in a different direction—from target to source.

Most bindable properties have a default binding mode of `OneWay`. However, there are some exceptions. Of the views you've encountered so far in this book, the following properties have a default mode of `TwoWay`:

Class	Property that is TwoWay
Stepper	Value
Switch	IsToggled
Entry	Text
Editor	Text
SearchBar	Text
DatePicker	Date
TimePicker	Time

Notice that the `Value` property of the `Stepper` is `TwoWay`, but the `Value` property of `Slider` is not listed here. That property is `OneWay`. This is why the seemingly backward binding on the `Stepper` works but it doesn't work on the `Slider`.

Of course, you can experiment with binding modes in the **BoxViewSizers** program. For example, try setting the `Mode` attribute in the `Binding` extension of the second `Slider` to `TwoWay`:

```
<BoxView x:Name="boxView1" />
<Slider Value="{Binding Source={x:Reference boxView1},
                        Path=WidthRequest,
                        Mode=TwoWay}" />
```

Now the `Slider` alters the `BoxView` width. The `OneWayToSource` mode also works here.

Similarly, you can prevent the last Stepper from changing the width of the BoxView by setting the binding mode to OneWay:

```
<BoxView x:Name="boxView2" />
<Stepper Value="{Binding Source={x:Reference boxView2},
                         Path=WidthRequest,
                         Mode=OneWay}" />
```

The properties that have a default binding mode of TwoWay are those most likely to be used with underlying data models in an MVVM scenario. With MVVM, the binding targets are visual objects and the binding sources are data objects. In general, you want the data to flow both ways. You want the visual objects to display the underlying data values (from source to target), and interactive visual objects should cause changes in the underlying data (target to source).

In the future chapter on MVVM, you'll see a Slider used with MVVM. The data bindings target the Value property of the Slider, and the binding mode must be set to TwoWay for the Slider to work right.

Here's a program called **ReverseBinding** that provides a little sneak preview. The program is very similar to the first binding examples you saw in this chapter, except the Slider is the binding target rather than the source and it has a Mode setting of TwoWay:

```
<ContentPage xmlns="http://xamarin.com/schemas/2014/forms"
             xmlns:x="http://schemas.microsoft.com/winfx/2009/xaml"
             x:Class="ReverseBinding.ReverseBindingPage"
             Padding="10, 0">
    <StackLayout>
        <Label x:Name="label"
               Text="Reverse Binding Demo"
               FontSize="Large"
               VerticalOptions="CenterAndExpand"
               HorizontalOptions="Center" />

        <Slider VerticalOptions="CenterAndExpand"
                Value="{Binding Source={x:Reference label},
                        Mode=TwoWay,
                        Path=Opacity}" />
    </StackLayout>
</ContentPage>
```

Despite the seemingly odd configuration, this program has a distinct advantage over the programs shown earlier in this chapter. As the binding is initialized, the value of the Opacity property of the Label is accessed and used to set the Value property of the Slider. When the program starts up, the Label is fully visible and the Slider is set to its far right position:

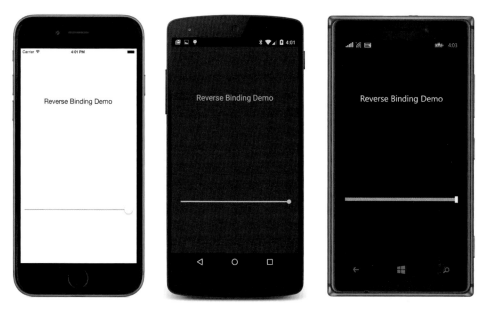

This is exactly the type of initialization you want to see when a `Slider` is bound to some data. For that reason, an argument could be made that this particular configuration of the `Slider` is *superior* to the ones shown earlier in this chapter.

Of course, you can change the earlier programs in this chapter for an initial display like this by explicitly setting the `Value` property of the `Slider` to 1. But it's very nice to see the `Slider` pick up the initial value automatically.

String formatting

Some of the sample programs in the previous chapter used event handlers to display the current values of the `Slider` and `Stepper` views. If you try defining a data binding that targets the `Text` property of a `Label` from the `Value` property of a `Slider`, you'll discover that it works, but you don't have much control over it. In general, you'll want to control any type conversion or value conversion required in data bindings.

String formatting is special. The `Binding` class has a `StringFormat` property that allows you to include an entire .NET formatting string. Almost always the target of such a binding is the `Text` property of a `Label`, but the binding source can be of any type.

The .NET formatting string that you supply to `StringFormat` must be suitable for a call to the `String.Format` static method, which means that it should contain a placeholder of "{0}" with or without a formatting specification suitable for the source data type—for example "{0:F3}" to display a `double` with three decimal places.

In XAML, this placeholder is a bit of a problem because the curly braces can be mistaken for the curly braces used to delimit markup extensions. The easiest solution is to put the entire formatting string in single quotation marks.

The **ShowViewValues** program contains four examples that display the current values of a `Slider`, `Entry`, `Stepper`, and `Switch`. The hexadecimal codes in the formatting string used for displaying the `Entry` contents are "smart quotes":

```xml
<ContentPage xmlns="http://xamarin.com/schemas/2014/forms"
             xmlns:x="http://schemas.microsoft.com/winfx/2009/xaml"
             x:Class="ShowViewValues.ShowViewValuesPage"
             Padding="10, 0">

    <StackLayout>
        <StackLayout VerticalOptions="CenterAndExpand">
            <Label Text="{Binding Source={x:Reference slider},
                                  Path=Value,
                                  StringFormat='The Slider value is {0:F3}'}" />
            <Slider x:Name="slider" />
        </StackLayout>

        <StackLayout VerticalOptions="CenterAndExpand">
            <Label Text="{Binding Source={x:Reference entry},
                                  Path=Text,
                                  StringFormat='The Entry text is &#x201C;{0}&#x201D;'}" />
            <Entry x:Name="entry" />
        </StackLayout>

        <StackLayout VerticalOptions="CenterAndExpand">
            <Label Text="{Binding Source={x:Reference stepper},
                                  Path=Value,
                                  StringFormat='The Stepper value is {0}'}" />
            <Stepper x:Name="stepper" />
        </StackLayout>

        <StackLayout VerticalOptions="CenterAndExpand">
            <Label Text="{Binding Source={x:Reference switch},
                                  Path=IsToggled,
                                  StringFormat='The Switch value is {0}'}" />
            <Switch x:Name="switch" />
        </StackLayout>
    </StackLayout>
</ContentPage>
```

When using `StringFormat` you need to pay particular attention to the placement of commas, single quotation marks, and curly braces.

Here's the result:

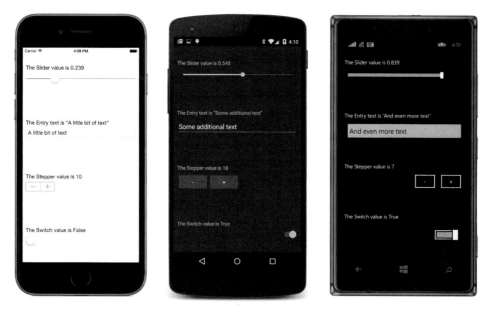

You might recall the **WhatSize** program from Chapter 5, "Dealing with sizes." That program used a `SizeChanged` event handler on the page to display the current width and height of the screen in device-independent units.

The **WhatSizeBindings** program does the whole job in XAML. First it adds an `x:Name` attribute to the root tag to give the `WhatSizeBindingsPage` object a name of `page`. Three `Label` views share a horizontal `StackLayout` in the center of the page, and two of them have bindings to the `Width` and `Height` properties. These properties are get-only, but they are backed by bindable properties, so they fire `PropertyChanged` events when they change:

```
<ContentPage xmlns="http://xamarin.com/schemas/2014/forms"
             xmlns:x="http://schemas.microsoft.com/winfx/2009/xaml"
             x:Class="WhatSizeBindings.WhatSizeBindingsPage"
             x:Name="page">

    <StackLayout Orientation="Horizontal"
                 Spacing="0"
                 HorizontalOptions="Center"
                 VerticalOptions="Center">

        <StackLayout.Resources>
            <ResourceDictionary>
                <Style TargetType="Label">
                    <Setter Property="FontSize" Value="Large" />
                </Style>
            </ResourceDictionary>
        </StackLayout.Resources>

        <Label Text="{Binding Source={x:Reference page},
                      Path=Width,
```

```
                                    StringFormat='{0:F0}'}" />

        <!-- Multiplication sign. -->
        <Label Text=" &#x00D7; " />

        <Label Text="{Binding Source={x:Reference page},
                              Path=Height,
                              StringFormat='{0:F0}'}" />
    </StackLayout>
</ContentPage>
```

Here's the result for the devices used for this book:

The displays changes as you turn the phone between portrait and landscape modes.

Alternatively, the `BindingContext` on the `StackLayout` could be set to an `x:Reference` markup extension referencing the `page` object, and the `Source` settings on the bindings wouldn't be necessary.

Why is it called "Path"?

The `Binding` class defines a property named `Path` that you use to set the source property name. But why is it called `Path`? Why isn't it called `Property`?

The `Path` property is called what it's called because it doesn't need to be one property. It can be a stack of properties, subproperties, and even indexers connected with periods.

Using `Path` in this way can be tricky, so here's a program called **BindingPathDemos** that has four

`Binding` markup extensions, each of which sets the `Path` argument to a string of property names and indexers:

```
<ContentPage xmlns="http://xamarin.com/schemas/2014/forms"
             xmlns:x="http://schemas.microsoft.com/winfx/2009/xaml"
             xmlns:globe="clr-namespace:System.Globalization;assembly=mscorlib"
             x:Class="BindingPathDemos.BindingPathDemosPage"
             x:Name="page">
    <ContentPage.Padding>
        <OnPlatform x:TypeArguments="Thickness"
                    iOS="10, 20, 10, 0"
                    Android="10, 0"
                    WinPhone="10, 0" />
    </ContentPage.Padding>

    <ContentPage.Resources>
        <ResourceDictionary>
            <Style x:Key="baseStyle" TargetType="View">
                <Setter Property="VerticalOptions" Value="CenterAndExpand" />
            </Style>

            <Style TargetType="Label" BasedOn="{StaticResource baseStyle}">
                <Setter Property="FontSize" Value="Large" />
                <Setter Property="XAlign" Value="Center" />
            </Style>

            <Style TargetType="Slider" BasedOn="{StaticResource baseStyle}" />
        </ResourceDictionary>
    </ContentPage.Resources>

    <StackLayout BindingContext="{x:Reference page}">
        <Label Text="{Binding Path=Padding.Top,
                             StringFormat='The top padding is {0}'}" />

        <Label Text="{Binding Path=Content.Children[4].Value,
                             StringFormat='The Slider value is {0:F2}'}" />

        <Label Text="{Binding Source={x:Static globe:CultureInfo.CurrentCulture},
                             Path=DateTimeFormat.DayNames[3],
                             StringFormat='The middle day of the week is {0}'}" />

        <Label Text="{Binding Path=Content.Children[2].Text.Length,
                             StringFormat='The preceding Label has {0} characters'}" />
        <Slider />
    </StackLayout>
</ContentPage>
```

Only one element here has an `x:Name`, and that's the page itself. The `BindingContext` of the `StackLayout` is that page, so all the bindings within the `StackLayout` are relative to the page (except for the binding that has an explicit `Source` property set).

The first `Binding` looks like this:

```
<Label Text="{Binding Path=Padding.Top,
                      StringFormat='The top padding is {0}'}" />
```

The `Path` begins with the `Padding` property of the page. That property is of type `Thickness`, so it's possible to access a property of the `Thickness` structure with a property name such as `Top`. Of course, `Thickness` is a structure and therefore does not derive from `BindableObject` so `Top` can't be a `BindableProperty`. The binding infrastructure can't set a `PropertyChanged` handler on that property, but it will set a `PropertyChanged` handler on the `Padding` property of the page, and if that changes, the binding will update the target.

The second `Binding` references the `Content` property of the page, which is the `StackLayout`. That `StackLayout` has a `Children` property, which is a collection, so it can be indexed:

```
<Label Text="{Binding Path=Content.Children[4].Value,
                      StringFormat='The Slider value is {0:F2}'}" />
```

The view at index 4 of the `Children` collection is a `Slider` (down at the bottom of the markup, with no attributes set), which has a `Value` property, and that's what's displayed here.

The third `Binding` overrides the `BindingContext` that it inherits by setting the `Source` argument to a static property using `x:Static`. The `globe` prefix is defined in the root tag to refer to the .NET `System.Globalization` namespace, and the `Source` is set to the `CultureInfo` object that encapsulates the culture of the user's phone:

```
<Label Text="{Binding Source={x:Static globe:CultureInfo.CurrentCulture},
                      Path=DateTimeFormat.DayNames[3],
                      StringFormat='The middle day of the week is {0}'}" />
```

One of the properties of `CultureInfo` is `DateTimeFormat`, which is a `DateTimeFormatInfo` object that contains information about date and time formatting, including a property named `DayNames` that is an array of the seven days of the week. The index 3 picks out the middle one.

None of the classes in the `System.Globalization` namespace implement `INotifyPropertyChanged`, but that's okay because the values of these properties don't change at run time.

The final `Binding` references the child of the `StackLayout` with a child index of 2. That's the previous `Label`. It has a `Text` property, which is of type `string`, and `string` has a `Length` property:

```
<Label Text="{Binding Path=Content.Children[2].Text.Length,
                      StringFormat='The preceding Label has {0} characters'}" />
```

The binding system installs a property-changed handler for the `Text` property of the `Label`, so if it changes, the binding will get the new length.

For the following screen shots, the Android phone was switched to German and the Windows Phone was switched to French. This affects the formatting of the `Slider` value—notice the comma rather than a period for the decimal divider—and the name of the middle day of the week:

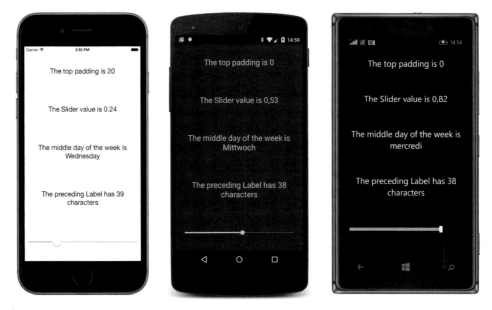

These `Path` specifications can be hard to configure and debug. Keep in mind that class names do not appear in the `Path` specifications—only property names and indexers. Also keep in mind that you can build up a `Path` specification incrementally, testing each new piece with a placeholder of "{0}" in `StringFormat`. This will often display the fully qualified class name of the type of the value set to the last property in the `Path` specification, and that can be very useful information.

You'll also want to keep an eye on the **Output** window in Visual Studio or Xamarin Studio when running your program under the debugger. You'll see messages there relating to run-time errors encountered by the binding infrastructure.

Binding value converters

You now know how to convert any binding source object to a string by using `StringFormat`. But what about other data conversions? Perhaps you're using a `Slider` for a binding source but the target is expecting an integer rather than a double. Or maybe you want to display the value of a `Switch` as text but you want "Yes" and "No" rather than "True" and "False".

The tool for this job is a class—often a very tiny class—informally called a *value converter* or (sometimes) a *binding converter*. More formally, such a class implements the `IValueConverter` interface. This interface is defined in the `Xamarin.Forms` namespace, but it is similar to an interface available in Microsoft's XAML-based environments.

An example: Sometimes applications need to enable or disable a `Button` based on the presence of text in an `Entry`. Perhaps the `Button` is labeled **Save** and the `Entry` is a filename. Or the `Button` is labeled **Send** and the `Entry` contains a mail recipient. The `Button` shouldn't be enabled unless the `Entry` contains at least one character of text.

There are a couple of ways to do this job. In a later chapter, you'll see how a data trigger can do it (and can also perform validity checks of the text in the `Entry`). But for this chapter, let's do it with a value converter.

The data-binding target is the `IsEnabled` property of the `Button`. That property is of type `bool`. The binding source is the `Text` property of an `Entry`, or rather the `Length` property of that `Text` property. That `Length` property is of type `int`. The value converter needs to convert an `int` equal to 0 to a `bool` of `false` and a positive `int` to a `bool` of `true`. The code is trivial. We just need to wrap it in a class that implements `IValueConverter`.

Here is that class in the **Xamarin.FormsBook.Toolkit** library, complete with `using` directives. The `IValueConverter` interface consists of two methods, named `Convert` and `ConvertBack`, with identical parameters. You can make the class as generalized or as specialized as you want:

```
using System;
using System.Globalization;
using Xamarin.Forms;

namespace Xamarin.FormsBook.Toolkit
{
    public class IntToBoolConverter : IValueConverter
    {
        public object Convert(object value, Type targetType,
                              object parameter, CultureInfo culture)
        {
            return (int)value != 0;
        }

        public object ConvertBack(object value, Type targetType,
                                  object parameter, CultureInfo culture)
        {
            return (bool)value ? 1 : 0;
        }
    }
}
```

When you include this class in a data binding—and you'll see how to do that shortly—the `Convert` method is called whenever a value passes from the source to the target.

The `value` argument to `Convert` is the value from the data binding source to be converted. You can use `GetType` to determine its type, or you can assume that it's always a particular type. In this example, the `value` argument is assumed to be of type `int`, so casting to an `int` won't raise an exception. More sophisticated value converters can perform more validity checks.

The `targetType` is the type of the data-binding target property. Versatile value converters can use this argument to tailor the conversion for different target types. The `Convert` method should return an object or value that matches this `targetType`. This particular `Convert` method assumes that target-Type is `bool`.

The `parameter` argument is an optional conversion parameter that you can specify as a property to the `Binding` class. (You'll see an example in the chapter on MVVM.)

Finally, if you need to perform a culture-specific conversion, the last argument is the `CultureInfo` object that you should use.

The body of this particular `Convert` method assumes that `value` is an `int`, and the method returns a `bool` that is `true` if that integer is nonzero.

The `ConvertBack` method is called only for `TwoWay` or `OneWayToSource` bindings. For the `ConvertBack` method, the `value` argument is the value from the target and the `targetType` argument is actually the type of the source property. If you know that the `ConvertBack` method will never be called, you can simply ignore all the arguments and return `null` or 0 from it. With some value converters, implementing a `ConvertBack` body is virtually impossible, but sometimes it's fairly simple (as in this case).

When you use a value converter in code, you set an instance of the converter to the `Converter` property of `Binding`. You can optionally pass an argument to the value converter by setting the `ConverterParameter` property of `Binding`.

If the binding also has a `StringFormat`, the value that is returned by the value converter is the value that is formatted as a string.

Generally, in a XAML file you'll want to instantiate the value converter in a `Resources` dictionary and then reference it in the `Binding` expression by using `StaticResource`. The value converter shouldn't maintain state and can thus be shared among multiple bindings.

Here's the **ButtonEnabler** program that uses the value converter:

```
<ContentPage xmlns="http://xamarin.com/schemas/2014/forms"
             xmlns:x="http://schemas.microsoft.com/winfx/2009/xaml"
             xmlns:toolkit=
                 "clr-namespace:Xamarin.FormsBook.Toolkit;assembly=Xamarin.FormsBook.Toolkit"
             x:Class="ButtonEnabler.ButtonEnablerPage"
             Padding="10, 50, 10, 0">

    <ContentPage.Resources>
        <ResourceDictionary>
            <toolkit:IntToBoolConverter x:Key="intToBool" />
        </ResourceDictionary>
    </ContentPage.Resources>

    <StackLayout Spacing="20">
        <Entry x:Name="entry"
               Text=""
               Placeholder="text to enable button" />
```

```
        <Button Text="Save or Send (or something)"
                FontSize="Large"
                HorizontalOptions="Center"
                IsEnabled="{Binding Source={x:Reference entry},
                                    Path=Text.Length,
                                    Converter={StaticResource intToBool}}" />
    </StackLayout>
</ContentPage>
```

The `IntToBoolConverter` is instantiated in the `Resources` dictionary and referenced in the `Binding` set on the `IsEnabled` property of the `Button` as a nested markup extension.

Notice that the `Text` property is explicitly initialized in the `Entry` tag to an empty string. By default, the `Text` property is `null`, which means that the binding `Path` setting of `Text.Length` doesn't result in a valid value.

You might remember from previous chapters that a class in the **Xamarin.FormsBook.Toolkit** library that is referenced only in XAML is not sufficient to establish a link from the application to the library. For that reason, the code-behind file in **ButtonEnabler** instantiates a class in the library:

```
public partial class ButtonEnablerPage : ContentPage
{
    public ButtonEnablerPage()
    {
        // Ensure that Toolkit library is linked.
        new Xamarin.FormsBook.Toolkit.IntToBoolConverter();

        InitializeComponent();
    }
}
```

Similar code appears in all the programs in this chapter that use the **Xamarin.FormsBook.Toolkit** library.

The screen shots confirm that the `Button` is not enabled unless the `Entry` contains some text:

If you're using only one instance of a value converter, you don't need to store it in the `Resources` dictionary. You can instantiate it right in the `Binding` tag with the use of property-element tags for the target property and for the `Converter` property of `Binding`:

```
<Button Text="Save or Send (or something)"
        FontSize="Large"
        HorizontalOptions="Center">
    <Button.IsEnabled>
        <Binding Source="{x:Reference entry}"
                 Path="Text.Length">
            <Binding.Converter>
                <toolkit:IntToBoolConverter />
            </Binding.Converter>
        </Binding>
    </Button.IsEnabled>
</Button>
```

Sometimes it's convenient for a value converter to define a couple of simple properties. For example, suppose you want to display some text for the two settings of a `Switch` but you don't want to use "True" and "False", and you don't want to hard-code alternatives into the value converter. Here's a `BoolToStringConverter` with a pair of public properties for two text strings:

```
namespace Xamarin.FormsBook.Toolkit
{
    public class BoolToStringConverter : IValueConverter
    {
        public string TrueText { set; get; }

        public string FalseText { set; get; }
```

```
        public object Convert(object value, Type targetType,
                              object parameter, CultureInfo culture)
        {
            return (bool)value ? TrueText : FalseText;
        }

        public object ConvertBack(object value, Type targetType,
                                  object parameter, CultureInfo culture)
        {
            return false;
        }
    }
}
```

The body of the `Convert` method is trivial: it just selects between the two strings based on the Boolean `value` argument.

A similar value converter converts a Boolean to one of two colors:

```
namespace Xamarin.FormsBook.Toolkit
{
    public class BoolToColorConverter : IValueConverter
    {
        public Color TrueColor { set; get; }

        public Color FalseColor { set; get; }

        public object Convert(object value, Type targetType,
                              object parameter, CultureInfo culture)
        {
            return (bool)value ? TrueColor : FalseColor;
        }

        public object ConvertBack(object value, Type targetType,
                                  object parameter, CultureInfo culture)
        {
            return false;
        }
    }
}
```

The **SwitchText** program instantiates the `BoolToStringConverter` converter twice for two different pairs of strings: once in the `Resources` dictionary, and then within `Binding.Converter` property-element tags. Two properties of the final `Label` are subjected to the `BoolToStringConverter` and the `BoolToColorConverter` based on the same `IsToggled` property from the `Switch`:

```
<ContentPage xmlns="http://xamarin.com/schemas/2014/forms"
             xmlns:x="http://schemas.microsoft.com/winfx/2009/xaml"
             xmlns:toolkit=
                 "clr-namespace:Xamarin.FormsBook.Toolkit;assembly=Xamarin.FormsBook.Toolkit"
             x:Class="SwitchText.SwitchTextPage"
             Padding="10, 0">
```

```xml
<ContentPage.Resources>
    <ResourceDictionary>
        <toolkit:BoolToStringConverter x:Key="boolToString"
                                       TrueText="Let's do it"
                                       FalseText="Not now" />

        <Style TargetType="Label">
            <Setter Property="FontSize" Value="Large" />
            <Setter Property="VerticalOptions" Value="Center" />
        </Style>
    </ResourceDictionary>
</ContentPage.Resources>

<StackLayout>
    <!-- First Switch with text. -->
    <StackLayout Orientation="Horizontal"
                 VerticalOptions="CenterAndExpand">
        <Label Text="Learn more?" />

        <Switch x:Name="switch1"
                VerticalOptions="Center" />

        <Label Text="{Binding Source={x:Reference switch1},
                              Path=IsToggled,
                              Converter={StaticResource boolToString}}"
               HorizontalOptions="FillAndExpand" />
    </StackLayout>

    <!-- Second Switch with text. -->
    <StackLayout Orientation="Horizontal"
                 VerticalOptions="CenterAndExpand">
        <Label Text="Subscribe?" />

        <Switch x:Name="switch2"
                VerticalOptions="Center" />

        <Label Text="{Binding Source={x:Reference switch2},
                              Path=IsToggled,
                              Converter={StaticResource boolToString}}"
               HorizontalOptions="FillAndExpand" />
    </StackLayout>

    <!-- Third Switch with text and color. -->
    <StackLayout Orientation="Horizontal"
                 VerticalOptions="CenterAndExpand">
        <Label Text="Leave page?" />

        <Switch x:Name="switch3"
                VerticalOptions="Center" />

        <Label HorizontalOptions="FillAndExpand">
            <Label.Text>
                <Binding Source="{x:Reference switch3}"
                         Path="IsToggled">
```

```
                                <Binding.Converter>
                                    <toolkit:BoolToStringConverter TrueText="Yes"
                                                                   FalseText="No" />
                                </Binding.Converter>
                            </Binding>
                        </Label.Text>

                        <Label.TextColor>
                            <Binding Source="{x:Reference switch3}"
                                     Path="IsToggled">
                                <Binding.Converter>
                                    <toolkit:BoolToColorConverter TrueColor="Green"
                                                                  FalseColor="Red" />
                                </Binding.Converter>
                            </Binding>
                        </Label.TextColor>
                    </Label>
                </StackLayout>
            </StackLayout>
    </ContentPage>
```

With the two fairly trivial binding converters, the `Switch` can now display whatever text you want
for the two states and can color that text with custom colors:

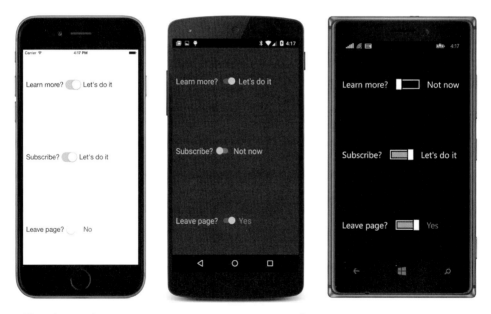

Now that you've seen a `BoolToStringConverter` and a `BoolToColorConverter`, can you gen-
eralize the technique to objects of any type? Here is a generic `BoolToObjectConverter` also in the
Xamarin.FormsBook.Toolkit library:

```
public class BoolToObjectConverter<T> : IValueConverter
{
    public T TrueObject { set; get; }
```

```
    public T FalseObject { set; get; }

    public object Convert(object value, Type targetType,
                          object parameter, CultureInfo culture)
    {
        return (bool)value ? this.TrueObject : this.FalseObject;
    }

    public object ConvertBack(object value, Type targetType,
                              object parameter, CultureInfo culture)
    {
        return ((T)value).Equals(this.TrueObject);
    }
}
}
```

The next sample uses this class.

Bindings and custom views

In Chapter 15, "The interactive interface," you saw a custom view named CheckBox. This view defines a Text property for setting the text of the CheckBox as well as a FontSize property. It could also have defined all the other text-related properties—TextColor, FontAttributes, and FontFamily—but it did not, mostly because of the work involved. Each property requires a BindableProperty definition, a CLR property definition, and a property-changed handler that transfers the new setting of the property to the Label views that comprise the visuals of the CheckBox.

Data bindings can help simplify this process for some properties by eliminating the property-changed handlers. Here's the code-behind file for a new version of CheckBox called NewCheckBox. Like the earlier class, it's part of the **Xamarin.FormsBook.Toolkit** library. The file has been reorganized a bit so that each BindableProperty definition is paired with its corresponding CLR property definition. You might prefer this type of organization of the properties, or perhaps not.

```
public partial class NewCheckBox : ContentView
{
    public event EventHandler<bool> CheckedChanged;

    public NewCheckBox()
    {
        InitializeComponent();
    }

    // Text property.
    public static readonly BindableProperty TextProperty =
        BindableProperty.Create<NewCheckBox, string>(
            checkbox => checkbox.Text,
            null);

    public string Text
```

```
{
    set { SetValue(TextProperty, value); }
    get { return (string)GetValue(TextProperty); }
}

// TextColor property.
public static readonly BindableProperty TextColorProperty =
    BindableProperty.Create<NewCheckBox, Color>(
        checkbox => checkbox.TextColor,
        Color.Default);

public Color TextColor
{
    set { SetValue(TextColorProperty, value); }
    get { return (Color)GetValue(TextColorProperty); }
}

// FontSize property.
public static readonly BindableProperty FontSizeProperty =
    BindableProperty.Create<NewCheckBox, double>(
        checkbox => checkbox.FontSize,
        Device.GetNamedSize(NamedSize.Default, typeof(Label)));

[TypeConverter(typeof(FontSizeConverter))]
public double FontSize
{
    set { SetValue(FontSizeProperty, value); }
    get { return (double)GetValue(FontSizeProperty); }
}

// FontAttributes property.
public static readonly BindableProperty FontAttributesProperty =
    BindableProperty.Create<NewCheckBox, FontAttributes>(
        checkbox => checkbox.FontAttributes,
        FontAttributes.None);

public FontAttributes FontAttributes
{
    set { SetValue(FontAttributesProperty, value); }
    get { return (FontAttributes)GetValue(FontAttributesProperty); }
}

// IsChecked property.
public static readonly BindableProperty IsCheckedProperty =
    BindableProperty.Create<NewCheckBox, bool>(
        checkbox => checkbox.IsChecked,
        false,
        propertyChanged: (bindable, oldValue, newValue) =>
        {
            // Fire the event.
            NewCheckBox checkbox = (NewCheckBox)bindable;
            EventHandler<bool> eventHandler = checkbox.CheckedChanged;
            if (eventHandler != null)
            {
```

```
                                eventHandler(checkbox, newValue);
                    }
            });

    public bool IsChecked
    {
        set { SetValue(IsCheckedProperty, value); }
        get { return (bool)GetValue(IsCheckedProperty); }
    }

    // TapGestureRecognizer handler.
    void OnCheckBoxTapped(object sender, EventArgs args)
    {
        IsChecked = !IsChecked;
    }
}
```

Besides the earlier `Text` and `FontSize` properties, this code file now also defines `TextColor` and `FontAttributes` properties. However, the only property-changed handler is for the `IsChecked` handler to fire the `CheckedChanged` event. Everything else is handled by data bindings in the XAML file:

```
<ContentView xmlns="http://xamarin.com/schemas/2014/forms"
             xmlns:x="http://schemas.microsoft.com/winfx/2009/xaml"
             xmlns:toolkit="clr-namespace:Xamarin.FormsBook.Toolkit"
             x:Class="Xamarin.FormsBook.Toolkit.NewCheckBox"
             x:Name="checkbox">

    <StackLayout Orientation="Horizontal"
                 BindingContext="{x:Reference checkbox}">

        <Label x:Name="boxLabel" Text="&#x2610;"
                                 TextColor="{Binding TextColor}"
                                 FontSize="{Binding FontSize}">
            <Label.Text>
                <Binding Path="IsChecked">
                    <Binding.Converter>
                        <toolkit:BoolToStringConverter TrueText="&#x2611;"
                                                       FalseText="&#x2610;" />
                    </Binding.Converter>
                </Binding>
            </Label.Text>
        </Label>

        <Label x:Name="textLabel" Text="{Binding Path=Text}"
                                  TextColor="{Binding TextColor}"
                                  FontSize="{Binding FontSize}"
                                  FontAttributes="{Binding FontAttributes}" />
    </StackLayout>

    <ContentView.GestureRecognizers>
        <TapGestureRecognizer Tapped="OnCheckBoxTapped" />
    </ContentView.GestureRecognizers>
</ContentView>
```

The root element is given a name of `checkbox`, and the `StackLayout` sets that as its `Bind-ingContext`. All the data bindings within that `StackLayout` can then refer to properties defined by the code-behind file. The first `Label` that displays the box has its `TextColor` and `FontSize` properties bound to the values of the underlying properties, while the `Text` property is targeted by a binding that uses a `BoolToStringConverter` to display an empty box or a checked box based on the `Is-Checked` property. The second `Label` is more straightforward: the `Text`, `TextColor`, `FontSize`, and `FontAttributes` properties are all bound to the corresponding properties defined in the code-behind file.

If you'll be creating several custom views that include `Text` elements and require definitions of all the text-related properties, you'll probably want to first create a code-only class (named `CustomView-Base`, for example) that derives from `ContentView` and includes only those text-based property definitions. You can then derive other classes from `CustomViewBase` and have `Text` and all the text-related properties readily available.

Let's write a little program called **NewCheckBoxDemo** that demonstrates the `NewCheckBox` view. Like the earlier **CheckBoxDemo** program, these check boxes control the bold and italic formatting of a paragraph of text. But to demonstrate the new properties, these check boxes are given colors and font attributes, and to demonstrate the `BoolToObjectConverter`, one of the check boxes controls the horizontal alignment of that paragraph:

```
<ContentPage xmlns="http://xamarin.com/schemas/2014/forms"
             xmlns:x="http://schemas.microsoft.com/winfx/2009/xaml"
             xmlns:toolkit=
                "clr-namespace:Xamarin.FormsBook.Toolkit;assembly=Xamarin.FormsBook.Toolkit"
             x:Class="NewCheckBoxDemo.NewCheckBoxDemoPage">

    <StackLayout Padding="10, 0">
        <StackLayout HorizontalOptions="Center"
                     VerticalOptions="CenterAndExpand">

            <StackLayout.Resources>
                <ResourceDictionary>
                    <Style TargetType="toolkit:NewCheckBox">
                        <Setter Property="FontSize" Value="Large" />
                    </Style>
                </ResourceDictionary>
            </StackLayout.Resources>

            <toolkit:NewCheckBox Text="Italic"
                                 TextColor="Aqua"
                                 FontSize="Large"
                                 FontAttributes="Italic"
                                 CheckedChanged="OnItalicCheckBoxChanged" />

            <toolkit:NewCheckBox Text="Boldface"
                                 FontSize="Large"
                                 TextColor="Green"
                                 FontAttributes="Bold"
                                 CheckedChanged="OnBoldCheckBoxChanged" />
```

```
                    <toolkit:NewCheckBox x:Name="centerCheckBox"
                                         Text="Center Text" />
        </StackLayout>

        <Label x:Name="label"
               Text=
"Just a little passage of some sample text that can be formatted
in italic or boldface by toggling the two custom CheckBox views."
               FontSize="Large"
               VerticalOptions="CenterAndExpand">
            <Label.XAlign>
                <Binding Source="{x:Reference centerCheckBox}"
                         Path="IsChecked">
                    <Binding.Converter>
                        <toolkit:BoolToObjectConverter x:TypeArguments="TextAlignment"
                                                       TrueObject="Center"
                                                       FalseObject="Start" />
                    </Binding.Converter>
                </Binding>
            </Label.XAlign>
        </Label>
    </StackLayout>
</ContentPage>
```

Notice the `BoolToObjectConverter` between the `Binding.Converter` tags. Because it's a generic class, it requires an `x:TypeArguments` attribute that indicates the type of the `TrueObject` and `FalseObject` properties and the type of the return value of the `Convert` method. Both `TrueObject` and `FalseObject` are set to members of the `TextAlignment` enumeration, and the converter selects one to be set to the `XAlign` property of the `Label`, as the following screen shots demonstrate:

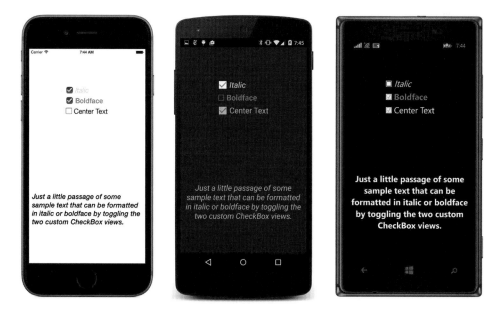

However, this program still needs a code-behind file to manage applying the italic and boldface attributes to the block of text. These methods are identical to those in the early **CheckBoxDemo** program:

```
public partial class NewCheckBoxDemoPage : ContentPage
{
    public NewCheckBoxDemoPage()
    {
        // Ensure link to Toolkit library.
        new Xamarin.FormsBook.Toolkit.NewCheckBox();

        InitializeComponent();
    }

    void OnItalicCheckBoxChanged(object sender, bool isChecked)
    {
        if (isChecked)
        {
            label.FontAttributes |= FontAttributes.Italic;
        }
        else
        {
            label.FontAttributes &= ~FontAttributes.Italic;
        }
    }

    void OnBoldCheckBoxChanged(object sender, bool isChecked)
    {
        if (isChecked)
        {
            label.FontAttributes |= FontAttributes.Bold;
        }
        else
        {
            label.FontAttributes &= ~FontAttributes.Bold;
        }
    }
}
```

Xamarin.Forms does not support a "multi-binding" that might allow multiple binding sources to be combined to change a single binding target. Bindings can do a lot, but without some additional code support, they can't do everything.

There's still a role for code.